Direct Investment in Economies in Transition

NEW HORIZONS IN INTERNATIONAL BUSINESS

General Editor: Peter J. Buckley
Centre for International Business,
University of Leeds (CIBUL), UK

This series is aimed at the frontiers of international business research. The study of international business is important not least because it gives researchers the opportunity to innovate in theory, technique, empirical investigation and interpretation. The area is fruitful for interdisciplinary and comparative research. This series is established as a central forum for the presentation of new ideas in international business.

Titles in the series include:

90 0361413 1

Direct Investment in Economies in Transition

Klaus Meyer
Associate Professor
Center for East European Studies
Copenhagen Business School
Denmark

NEW HORIZONS IN INTERNATIONAL BUSINESS

Edward Elgar
Cheltenham, UK • Northampton, MA, USA

Published by
Edward Elgar Publishing Limited
8 Lansdown Place
Cheltenham
Glos GL50 2HU
UK

Edward Elgar Publishing, Inc.
6 Market Street
Northampton
Massachusetts 01060
USA

A catalogue record for this book
is available from the British Library

Library of Congress Cataloguing in Publication Data

Meyer, Klaus, 1964–
    Direct investment in economies in transition / Klaus Meyer.
        (New horizons in international business)
    Includes bibliographical references and index.
        1. Investments, Foreign—Europe, Eastern. I. Title. II. Series.
    HG5430.7.A3M39 1998
    332.67'3'0947—dc21   98–13453
                                                  CIP

ISBN 1 85898 736 9

Printed and bound in Great Britain by MPG Books Ltd, Bodmin, Cornwall

Contents

List of Figures

List of Tables

Acknowledgements

Engaging in a major research project, is like embarking on a long journey. At the start, ambitions are welcomed by the fresh wind of the sea. Yet somewhere along the way, one wonders why we came here. Exploring a new territory can be so rewarding. Yet getting there, getting the right tools at the right place, and understanding this strange country of data can be a very exhausting and lonely experience. Looking back on this journey I see many light and dark days, as optimism and pessimism were sometimes just a few regressions apart.

I remember friends, colleagues and advisors who have helped this expedition to succeed. I would like to thank all of you for your encouragement and advice. Just a few names can be mentioned here in these acknowledgements. First and foremost, this is to my supervisor at London Business School, Saul Estrin, who was constantly available for so many questions, and helped to focus this research. From him, I learned to get the essentials out of sometimes rather confusing data sets. His never-ending energy and optimism have been of great encouragement throughout.

I also would like to thank my co-supervisor David, now Lord, Currie for many insights, even when my travels took me into waters other than those envisaged. Peter Rühmann (Göttingen) and Stephen Hall advised me in the early stages of my journey. Alessandro Lomi, Mario Nuti and Jim Short gave valuable advice when I was steering through stormy waves. Mark Casson (Reading) made some very thoughtful comments on the project which led to substantial focussing of the arguments in Chapters 4 and 7. Lord Meghnad Desai (LSE) ensured the project's smooth arrival and acceptance as a PhD thesis with the University of London.

The journey was made enjoyable by a number of colleagues in London, as well as my new colleagues at Copenhagen Business School. Often helpful advice came over a coffee after lunch, or an office chat. *Inter alia* and alphabetically, I wish to mention Adam Rosevear, Anne Ku, Chris Walters, Irwin Jao, Jonathan Levie, Ken Charman, Sarah Todd and Zoltan Antal. Kathryn Vagneur calmed premature optimism, and Wenyi Chu took care of pessimistic hours. In Copenhagen, Niels Mygind and Snejina Michailova provided a very encouraging research environment at the Center for East European Studies that greatly facilitated the preparation of this book version of the study.

Furthermore, I would like to thank all respondents to my questionnaire in the UK and in Germany without whom the survey would not have been possible. Dieter Bös at the University of Bonn has kindly helped with the German survey. Sabine Küster has checked the translation of the questionnaire to German. Martin Jepsen and Sheela Maini made a major contribution to communicate the research project in this book, and Sheela also took care of the tedious details of formatting, checking the references and compiling the index.

Last but not least, I would like to thank my parents and other members of our family for their encouragement on this academic journey, and for giving me the moral support and financial security to sail through unknown waters, on sunny and on stormy days.

PART ONE

Overview and Research Issues

1. Introduction

After the fall of the Iron Curtain in 1989, most countries of the former Soviet bloc moved successfully from centrally planned economies and one-party governments towards market economies with multiparty parliamentary democracy. This systemic change now appears irreversible as many institutions in both the economic and political spheres have been established that will tend to resist any reversal of this change. However, the progress of transition varies within the region. The Visegrad countries (the Czech and Slovak Republics, Hungary and Poland) have to a great extent transformed their political systems, while progress has been slower in South-Eastern Europe. In Russia and other states of the former Soviet Union, the political changes have been more erratic and are still subject to a high degree of political uncertainty. These differences in political reform are reflected in the progress of economic reform and systemic transformation.

In the transition process, Central and Eastern Europe (CEE) opened to Western business in 1989. For fifty years, the region followed a policy of economic autarky. International business occurred mainly in the form of barter trade. Direct foreign investment (DFI) was impossible or tightly regulated, except for Yugoslavia. Within a short time, the policy environment changed radically, creating new conditions for international investment. Many multinational enterprises (MNEs) moved into the CEE region, but at different rates and with different types of local operations and business activity.

Of the various forms of international business, DFI creates the greatest expectations of policy makers in the region. DFI is the transfer of multiple resources to a host economy and requires a high degree of commitment to operating in the country. From the perspective of politicians and economists in CEE,[1] DFI is often seen as a potential source of knowledge transfer. It is expected to introduce new management and marketing know-how and the latest production technology. Western DFI is hoped to provide urgently needed capital for countries with limited access to international capital markets; to generate cash revenues via privatization for empty government budgets; and to contribute to the restructuring of industries and upgrading of the ageing capital stock in the region.[2] The entry of Western firms is also expected to foster change in the economic system, create competition and promote the development of the private sector. Furthermore, investors facilitate exports to Western markets through knowledge of the relevant markets, as well as access to brand names and distribution networks.

For the business community in Western Europe, the fall of the Iron Curtain brought threats to established business operations, but also potential opportunities for expansion or reorganization. The region offered major business opportunities for West-East business because of its untapped 'virgin' markets and low labour costs. Consumers in the region were eager to assume the Western lifestyle and purchase consumer goods that they knew of from years of watching Western television, while being denied access by the rule of the Iron Curtain. Businesses concerned with their competitiveness in the high-wage countries of Western Europe saw new opportunities to compete with East-Asian manufacturers. The opening of CEE provided unique opportunities for expansion at a time of slow growth of West European economies. On the other hand, Western labour unions became concerned about the relocation of production and the loss of jobs of relatively less skilled blue collar workers.

The outcomes of these diverse expectations are explored, using the evidence in this first major analytical firm-level study on determinants of DFI in CEE. It investigates DFI in the first years of systemic transformation from 1989 to 1994. This was the period of most radical economic and political change in the region, when new political systems were emerging, radical policies for economic stabilization were implemented and the economies took many big steps towards systemic transformation.

ISSUES IN ECONOMICS OF TRANSITION

The focus of this research is on the microeconomic determinants of investment during the early, volatile years of transition. Its starting points are research questions arising from the analysis of the economic transition in Eastern Europe. Direct Foreign Investment (DFI) interacts with many aspects of the transition process. The transition affects incoming DFI and *vice versa*. Direct investment influences the transition in several ways: through its direct impact on macro-economic variables such as the balance of payments and employment, through the transfer of knowledge and through the role of investors as new owners of formerly state-owned enterprises. The latter brings a contribution of DFI to the host economy that is specific to the transition economies. Foreign investors are in a superior position to induce corporate restructuring because they can provide managerial and financial resources, they can create immediately effective corporate governance, and they contribute crucially needed managerial know-how [Meyer 1997].

To understand this interaction between foreign investors and the local economy, it is first of all necessary to understand the foreign investors as such.

What are they doing in the region, why are they doing it and which factors influence what they are doing? These questions have motivated this study because transition economists need to understand the motives, strategies and determinants of DFI before engaging in impact analysis. Without understanding investors, impact analysis is build on sand. Some studies modeling impact have made very simplified, in my view inappropriate, assumptions about DFI and as a result reached peculiar conclusions.[3] However, better models can only build on a better understanding of international business.

When this study was conceptualized in 1993/94, little systematic analysis of DFI in transition economies was available. Several authors expressed expectations of how DFI may contribute to the transition economies. Others discussed the often confusing statistical evidence, for example for the Soviet Union [Gutman 1992, World Bank 1992] and Hungary [Marton 1993, Csáki 1993]. The evidence from different countries has been brought together in comparative surveys in Meyer [1995] and EBRD [1995]. The motives of DFI in the region have been analysed by survey studies, for example Pfohl et al. [1992], Gatling [1993] and Genco, Taurelli and Viezzoli [1993]. This work has been advanced in the contemporary research reviewed in Chapter 2. Recently, the discussion on the impact of DFI has been advanced in conceptual papers, in particular with Bruce Kogut's [1996] contribution.

This study directly addresses three issues of concern to transition economists. Firstly, the actual flows of DFI have been disappointing in the first years of transition, but increased remarkably by 1995. Although Hungary already received substantial DFI, South-Eastern Europe and the former Soviet Union received only minimal amounts. The research attempts not only to understand why certain firms choose to invest in the region, but also why many others did not invest. Therefore, the empirical part of the study covers firms with and without direct investment in the region.

The second issue is the interaction of the specific transition environment with the strategies of Western enterprises. This analysis compares activity in CEE (Chapter 2) with the patterns posited by the international business literature (Chapters 3 and 4). In addition, the variation of MNE activity within the region is explored. The third theme is the comparison of enterprises from two countries that have shown quite different patterns of activity in the region. Firms from neighbouring countries, especially Germany, have been quickest to react to the new opportunities. Conversely, British firms have been surprisingly inactive.

The survey confirms that German firms are more active in the region not only in terms of DFI volume, but also by various criteria describing the extent of their business (Chapter 5). Patterns of business are generally similar to British firms active in CEE, except that they show more interest in utilizing the East-West factor cost differential. A surprising result is that by the number of projects, DFI varies far less among the Visegrad countries than official statistics on DFI capital would suggest. The main differences are between Central Europe on the one hand, and Russia and Romania on the other. This can be explained by the slower progress of economic reform and greater distance to the countries of origin. Furthermore, the data show that most investors follow market-seeking motives. At best, labour costs appear as a complementary motive.

The empirical analysis finds most propositions on determinants of international business to be confirmed (Part three). By and large, business with CEE thus follows the same motivations as business among other countries. However, the study finds some exceptions that are discussed below.

ISSUES IN INTERNATIONAL BUSINESS

The reseach uses concepts, theories and methods developed in the international business literature to analyse DFI as one aspect of economic transition (Figure 1.1). The results are hoped to advance knowledge in both fields of study. The theoretical foundation of this study is the Ownership-Location-Internalization paradigm (OLI) developed by John Dunning [1977, 1993]. Within this broad paradigm, two lines of inquiry are refined and applied: internalization theory and the developmental model of DFI.

Ultimately, the internalization literature draws on the work by Ronald Coase [1937]. Richard Caves [1971], Peter Buckley and Mark Casson [1976] and others have advanced its application to multinational enterprises in the 1970s. Recent work has broadened the concepts of internalization incentives, considering for instance the transfer of tacit knowledge [Kogut and Zander 1993], information economics and trust [Casson 1995]. In this study, a comprehensive model of transaction cost economics is presented for the international context by means of a synthesis of recent contributions in the field. It focuses on the trade-off between internal and external transaction costs. Postulated determinants of transaction costs relate to characteristics of the products, asset specificity and information content, as well as environmental characteristics of contract uncertainty and the likelihood of opportunism.

The empirical part of this study tests aspects of the internalization theory. It builds on the literature on choices between investment and licensing [for instance Davidson and McFetridge 1985] and between joint ventures (JVs) and full ownership [for instance Gatignon and Anderson 1988, Hennart 1991a]. Moreover, the analysis considers entry mode decisions regarding the choice between greenfield and acquisition entry. This follows lines of inquiry by Kogut and Singh [1988] and Hennart and Park [1993].

The results emphasize the nature of firms' capabilities as determinants of international business, their impact on internalization of business and on entry modes. Economists have modelled the functioning of markets as a determinant

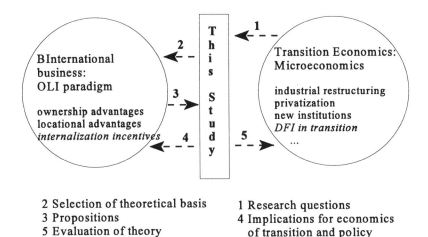

2 Selection of theoretical basis
3 Propositions
5 Evaluation of theory

1 Research questions
4 Implications for economics
of transition and policy

Figure 1.1 Analytical approach

of the expansion of multinational business and foreign investment. The theoretical work of this study suggests that characteristics of the firm should be an equally important component of the model. The empirical analysis confirms this view.

Complementing this work is a developmental model based on research on DFI in East Asia, for example Ozawa [1992] and Markusen [1991]. The model also incorporates aspects of the development cycle [Dunning 1986, Narula 1995]. It explains DFI as a function of environmental characteristics in the home and host economy, subject to barriers to relocation. If push-factors of structural change in an advanced economy combine with pull-factors from attractive locations in less advanced economies, then the model posits factor-cost oriented DFI. The model describes a special case within the OLI paradigm.

The empirical evidence for the application of this approach to CEE is however weak. The study detects slow growth as an incentive for DFI in CEE as predicted by this model, but in contrast to the growth theory of the firm. Yet market orientation dominates over investment-seeking factor costs which contrasts with patterns frequently reported for DFI within East Asia.

STRUCTURE AND METHODS OF ANALYSIS

The structure of this study is as follows: Part one gives an overview of the issues and outlines the research questions. Part two develops the theoretical basis for the empirical analysis in Part three. Part four concludes. The methods of inquiry change for each stage of the analysis.

Since this research covers a new and under-researched area, the basic facts on the local environment and on recent trends in DFI are summarized first. Chapter 2 provides a synopsis of the CEE business environment, DFI trends and contemporary research. The region offers unique business opportunities for West European business due to untapped markets and lower costs of production. The evidence has initially been clouded by the poor quality of available statistical data. Yet it is possible to outline the main trends of DFI since 1989 for host and home countries as well as investment characteristics. Recent studies have shed light on a variety of aspects of DFI, from the perspective of both the investors and the hosts. However, this research has only recently moved towards comprehensive studies and a systematic analysis of the phenomenon.

The second part of the study develops the theoretical foundations for the empirical analysis. The multitude of analytical and empirical approaches by economists on determinants of DFI are reviewed in Chapter 3, with a special appendix for the developmental model. The transaction costs (TC) approach has been selected as the analytical framework. In Chapter 4, an eclectic model is presented which focuses on the trade-off between internal and external TC. This is a middle-range theory which guides the empirical inquiry on the research questions of this study. The application in the empirical investigation provides insights that are hoped to advance the underlying theory.

Part three contains an empirical analysis of the determinants of international business in CEE (Figure 1.2). Prior and contemporary research on DFI in CEE has concentrated on actual investment projects and neglected firms which are not involved. However, decisions concerning involvement or non-involvement in a country are part of the decision process. Therefore, a broad base population has been selected for this analysis. The database for this study was developed with a questionnaire survey of a stratified random sample of German and British manufacturing enterprises. It contains information on the nature of the business relationships of 269 participating firms with CEE as well as company-specific data. Chapter 5 outlines the methodology of the survey and provides some summary results.

The empirical analysis consists of three tests related by one decision tree model. Firstly, a firm decides whether to engage in business with the region, then whether to invest directly, and finally the details of their investment project. In Dunning's OLI terminology, ownership and locational advantages are decisive during the first stage, while internalization incentives apply at the second stage and aspects of the third stage.

In Chapter 6, the differences between active and inactive firms are analysed. Hypotheses are tested on the determinants of the propensity of firms to be active in one or several countries of the region, using Probit and ordered Probit

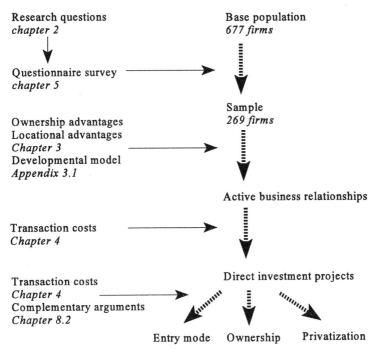

Figure 1.2   Structure of the empirical analysis

regression analysis. The incidence of business activity and the number of countries with whom business relationships exist, are explored. Firms with ownership advantages that can profitably be combined with the locational advantages in CEE are predicted to be more active. Evidence is found in favour of all four groups of proposed variables: intangible assets, common governance, barriers to growth and proximity. Common governance variables receive the strongest support: large, internationally experienced and undiversified firms are most active. Interestingly, slow-growing firms and German companies are more active, particularly in the Visegrad countries.

In Chapter 7, the active firms are investigated further to distinguish investors from firms with trade or contractual relationships. Ordered and multinomial Logit models are regressed and compared as alternatives in order to assess the notion that contracts are an intermediate form between trade and DFI. Internalization incentives are predicted to increase the preference for DFI relative to trade and contractual arrangements. Hypotheses are derived from the transaction cost model. The empirical results show that economies of common governance are the prime determinants of a firm's propensity to invest. This effect dominates over variables derived from traditional transaction cost proxies. Furthermore, the ordered model is rejected in favour of the multinomial, suggesting that contracts are a distinct mode of business. They are used even by high technology firms which are presumably most sensitive to market failure.

In Chapter 8, DFI projects are analysed with respect to equity ownership and mode of entry. Logit models are applied to analyse the preference for full versus joint ownership, and the choice of entry mode between greenfield, acquisition and JV, and JV-acquisition. As in Chapters 6 and 7, most hypotheses derived from general theories of DFI receive empirical support. Firms sensitive to market failure prefer full ownership while institutional constraints lead to a higher proportion of JVs in Russia and Romania. The nature of core capabilities explains preferences for greenfield entry by technology-intensive and non-food consumer good manufacturers. Surprisingly, acquisitions and JVs are not preferred in industries where the strategic motive of speedy entry is presumed to be important. Here, the weakness of local firms and the privatization process lead to unusual patterns. The effects of international experience and proximity are shown to be theoretically ambiguous. The empirical evidence suggests that the dominant effect is that inexperienced and distant investors prefer JVs as a mode of learning and risk-sharing.

An additional test finds that, by and large, the same firms participate in the privatization process and enter by acquisition or JV-acquisition. Two differences in the pattern emerge: German firms with international experience are more likely to acquire privatized firms while technology-intensive firms abstain.

The fourth and final part of this thesis is the concluding chapter. It presents an interpretation of the research findings and their limitations. Policy implications and suggestions for further research are discussed for both Transition Economics and the International Business literature.

NOTES

1. CEE refers to all countries of the former socialist bloc, including Albania, Bulgaria, Czech Republic, Hungary, Poland, Romania, Slovakia, and the former Yugoslavia, Estonia, Latvia and Lithuania, Russia, Ukraine, Belarus, Moldova, as well as the Central Asian and Caucasian states of the former Soviet Union. The 'Visegrad countries' refers to Poland, Hungary, the Czech Republic and Slovakia.

2. Such expectations were expressed by the joint study of the international financial institutions [IMF et al. 1991] as well as a number of research papers, for example Dunning [1991], Scott [1992], Csáki [1993], McMillan [1993].

3. See for instance Sinn and Weichenrieder [1997], or Devreux and Roberts [1997].

2. Direct Foreign Investment in Central and Eastern Europe: The Issues

This chapter describes how the transition environment affects foreign firms wishing to engage in business in the region, and how East-West business has developed since 1989. This first section gives a brief synopsis of the tasks of economic reform, macroeconomic developments and research in the new field of economics of transition. The following section summarizes the microeconomic structures of the transition economies that influence strategies of potential foreign investors. The fourth section discusses recent trends in DFI in the region. Some groundwork is laid by assessing the quality of data on the subject, and subsequently the main trends of DFI are discussed by destination and source countries, and by sectoral pattern. Section five summarizes research analysing various aspects of DFI in CEE, mostly contemporary with this study. The final section sets the directions for this research project.

ECONOMICS OF TRANSITION

The new field of 'Economics of Transition' developed with the transition process. Its antecedents lie in the field of comparative economic systems. Scholars in this field could offer an understanding of the old economic systems, but no blueprints for systemic transformation. The new field of study started with the analysis of the initial conditions in CEE and the discussion on the necessary steps of transformation, for instance in IMF et al. [1991], Corbo, Corricelli and Bossak [1991] and Clague and Rausser [1992]. By 1997, the first experiences of the transition have been described and analysed in the literature. Several large studies attempt a comprehensive assessment of the transition experiences across the region [World Bank 1996, Zecchini 1997, Desai 1997]. Scholars critical to the policies in the early transition process emphasize for instance the need to focus on microeconomic transformation and an active, but not controlling, government role [Eatwell et al. 1996]. Furthermore, the systemic transformation requires fundamental changes in all spheres of society, not only the economic system [Mygind 1994, Csaba 1995]. This study focuses on economic aspects of transition, as they are most relevant for DFI.

Table 2.1 Selected indicators of CEE business environments in 1994

	Czech R.	Hungary	Poland	Russia	Romania
Demand Indicators					
GDP *per capita* in US$	3,500	4,070	2,750	1,930	1,324
GDP growth 1994	2.6%	2.9%	5.2%	-12.6%	3.9%
GDP growth 1996	4.1%	0.5%	6.0%	-6.0%	4.3%
Population, million	10.3	10.3	38.6	148.2	22.7
Labour Costs					
Gross monthly wages, (in US$)	240	317	241	96	n.a.
Unit labour costs (change of 1994 over 1991)	61%	27%	30%	n.a.	-29%
Technological Capacities					
Secondary school	88.5%	81.4%	82.0%	71.7%	75.5%
Industry share in GDP	39.3%	25.9%	37.8%	n.a.	41.0%
Progress in Transition					
Legal reform	++++	++++	++++	++	++
Banking reform	+++	+++	+++	++	+++
private sector in GDP 1989	11.2	29.0	28.6	5.3	12.8
private sector in GDP 1994	56.3	55.6[(1993)]	56.0	25.0	35.0
Main mode of privatization	voucher	direct sale	mixed	voucher	delayed
International Trade					
Association Agreements with the EU	1992	1992	1992	none	1993
Intra-regional trade 1987[a]	54.1%	50.0%	47.0%	n.a.	28.4%
Intra-regional trade 1994[a]	32.9%	23.1%	15.6%	n.a.	18.6%
Risk Indicators					
Inflation	10.0%	21.2%	29.5%	203%	61.7%
Euromoney ranking[b]	39	46	73	136	77

Source: EBRD [1995, 1997] except where shown. Data refer to 1994 unless otherwise shown.
Notes: [a] Share of exports to CMEA/transition economies in total exports [source UNECE 1996a],
[b] country ranking based on the credit rating assigned to the countries in September 1994 (1 = lowest risk).

The early discussion emphasized macroeconomic issues of stabilization and price liberalization as core ingredients of reform, plus the need to privatize industry. In 1990, the CEE region required economic reform on an unprecedented scale. Since the economies had deteriorated during the last years of the central-planning regime, not only the introduction of free markets but also economic stabilization and industrial restructuring became imperative. The discussion on economic reform involved three central issues: stabilization, liberalization and privatization [Fischer and Gelb 1991]. The initial economic conditions varied across the region, especially with respect to macroeconomic stability, the degree of state control over the economy and the political conditions for reform.

Macroeconomic imbalances have been a major problem in most countries with the notable exception of Czechoslovakia and Romania. The combination of a large monetary overhang and external debt required a radical stabilization program at the beginning of transition. These were mostly successful, such that by 1994 the Visegrad countries had achieved reasonably low inflation rates, though still above OECD standards (see Table 2.1). On the other hand, the former Soviet Union went through a period of hyperinflation, which was only brought under control after the break-up of the rouble zone and the conduct of more responsible monetary policy by the new successor states.

Price liberalization was a cornerstone of transition because prices determined by the interplay of supply and demand are the essence of a market economy. However, liberating prices led to a jump in inflation. In some countries, this was a one-off adjustment while it undermined the stabilization policy elsewhere, especially in the former Soviet Union. Also, a lack of competition and market institutions inhibited the functioning of the price mechanism, especially in labour, housing and capital markets. Nevertheless, price liberalization has generally been considered as a success and has improved allocation, primarily for consumer goods [Portes 1994].

Despite successful stabilization and liberalization policies, the region experienced an unprecedented drop in industrial output. The causes of the output drop have been widely debated. Arguments range from an overly tight stabilization policy and credit crunch [Calvo and Corricelli 1993], a fall in aggregate demand, an elimination of negative value added, measurement errors, the abrupt opening to Western competition, lack of microeconomic reform and slow restructuring of production [Murrell 1992, Nuti and Portes 1993, Mygind 1994]. International trade collapsed after the break-up of the mutual trade regime of the socialist countries, the CMEA. This contributed to the output drop because these countries were highly interdependent. Some countries, especially the Visegrad countries, have been very successful in reorienting their trade towards the West.

Recent research focused more on the details of microeconomic restructuring and institution building which is far more complex than the basic notion of private ownership suggests. The starting point of microeconomic transition was the transfer of ownership from the state to individual private owners [Estrin 1994, Brada 1996]. However, this is part of a much wider task, as the economic transition requires changes at the level of industries, of firms, of organizational structures within firms, and of individual behavioural patterns. Although these microeconomic and institutional aspects of a market economy are not fully implemented, the dynamics of the process of change are moving towards a Western-style economic system.

Poland was the first country to return to positive economic growth, followed by most Central European countries, and some countries further East (Figure 2.1). Yet growth rates are moderate compared to other emerging economies and subject to severe recessions in some slowly reforming countries, notably Bulgaria in 1996. In the former Soviet Union, performance ranges from successful recovery in Estonia to continued decline in Ukraine. However, the medium-term macroeconomic perspective is generally viewed positively. The Economist Intelligence Unit [1996] predicts economic growth for the region, including Russia, to be on average 4.6 per cent for the years 1995 to 2000. Growth is expected to be even higher in several Central European countries, albeit few expect the growth rates to reach the magnitude of East Asia.

The diversity of performance has motivated many researchers. Currently, the predominant view is that liberalization and stabilization policies were crucial. Stabilization of the macroeconomy is a precondition for growth. Its failure contributed to the prolonged recession in the former Soviet Union. However, liberalization that frees market forces and entrepreneurial initiative is essential to resume economic growth. The international institutions, that is the World Bank [1996] and the EBRD [1996], stress the positive correlation of their respective liberalization indices with economic growth. This view is supported by a number of empirical cross-country studies [Fischer, Sahay and Végh 1996, De Melo and Gelb 1997, Selowsky and Martin 1997]. On the other hand, the advances in transition are strongly related to the countries' starting points. Therefore, Kekič [1996] finds that performance depends significantly on initial conditions and the absence of (civil) war. Yet liberalization indices remain insignificant in his regression analysis. In comparision with China and Vietnam, the output drop and the sluggish growth can be attributed to the structure of the socialist economies: while most of CEE was overindustrialized, China and Vietnam were still largely agrarian in Asia [Parker, Tritt and Woo 1997].

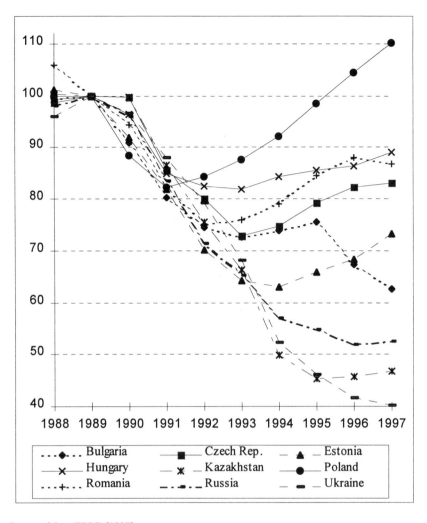

Source of data: EBRD [1997]

Figure 2.1 Index of real GDP (1989 = 100)

BUSINESS IN CENTRAL AND EASTERN EUROPE

Six aspects of the economic environment in the transition countries are of particular interest to international business partners: the process of economic restructuring, large scale privatization, an evolving institutional framework, the reorientation of international trade, virgin markets, and low labour costs.

Microeconomic Transition and Industrial Restructuring

In the centrally planned economies, the state formally owned virtually all production facilities, with the exception of agriculture in Poland and some small businesses in Hungary. All economic activity, in particular factor allocation, was centrally coordinated through the central plan. Production targets replaced prices as key coordination mechanisms. The system implied not only a different mode of resource allocation, but also many structural differences. This includes the pattern of industry, the role of enterprises and the routines of individual behaviour [for instance Ellman 1989, Gregory and Stuart 1988].

The conditions varied considerably across the region due to historical structures and reform attempts during the past decades, notably in Hungary and Poland. Yugoslavia had since the 1950s gone its own way based on the principle of labour-managed firms. The system of central planning had been implemented most comprehensively in the Soviet Union, but also in the Czech Republic and Bulgaria. Some important microeconomic features of the system were:

- Manufacturing was overdeveloped, especially heavy machinery, at the expense of consumer goods and service industries due to a development policy led by industrialization and a lack of mechanisms for structural change. This also led to the continued existence of firms creating negative value added, if world market prices had been applied [Hughes and Hare 1992]. Most production operations were large-scale with a high degree of vertical integration. They were created with the objective of utilizing economies of scale and simplifying planning. However, they were inappropriate for creating domestic competition.
- The fulfilment of the central plan dominated all other objectives at the enterprise level due to the nature of incentives set with the plan. This led to the production of large volumes of low-quality standardized products irrespective of consumer demand. Moreover, externalities of any kind were disregarded, leading to serious environmental contamination especially in the mining and the chemical industries.
- Few incentives encouraged innovation and technological progress. Nor were there any suitable mechanisms for the improvement of factor allocation in the central plan in response to technological progress. Furthermore, the acquisition of technology was constrained by export restrictions. Consequently, capital stock and production technologies were very dated by 1989.
- No effective mechanisms enabled the undistorted collection and transmission of information on many important economic indicators, such as value, productivity, demand, capacity or impact of innovation.
- The role of management was primarily to execute orders received through

the plan. In a strictly hierarchical system, there was no role for either leadership in a Western sense or risk-taking entrepreneurial activity. Therefore, essential human capabilities for a market economy were not developed.

- Enterprises were not subject to binding financial constraints. Even after the onset of transition the government provided finance for firms in need, a phenomenon known as 'soft budget constraints' [Kornai 1986].
- Enterprises employed far more people than necessary to achieve their output because managers had incentives to hoard labour as a resource and overemployment provided a convenient means of preventing open unemployment. Employment relationships were effectively based on life-time employment, and enterprises provided many social needs of both current and retired employees.
- International trade was was mostly limited to the CMEA area and was conducted by specific external trade units, often using barter trade due to lack of prices. At the enterprise level, there was therefore no expertise in negotiating and conducting international business (with the exception of Hungary where international transactions were crucial for the early lead in attracting foreign investors after 1989).

The task of microeconomic restructuring is to adapt CEE industries to the conditions of a market economy. The details of the institutional framework to be built were widely debated. Some authors advocated the Anglo-Saxon version of free capitalism (or its idealized image in the minds of American trained economists), others recommended a German-Austrian style of social market economy. Even a 'third way' was suggested by some representatives from within the region. However, a widespread consensus emerged that the new economic order should be market-led. Thus, the structural differences need to be resolved. While macroeconomic reforms could be implemented in a big-bang style, microeconomic reform and institution-building is a more time-consuming process. The transformation of state-owned firms into competitive private firms is a complex task that requires more than establishing the right macroeconomic conditions and the institutional framework, and to date progress has been mixed [Ernst, Alexeev and Marer 1996, Commander, Fan and Schaffer 1996].

Privatization

A major, if not the main, task of microeconomic restructuring is the transfer of enterprises from state ownership to private ownership. The objectives of privatization are both economic and political [Estrin 1994a].[1] The economic motive is to increase efficiency of production through private ownership. Neoclassical theory shows efficient equilibria to be independent of ownership if only markets are competitive. However, several economic considerations suggest that private ownership improves efficiency.

Principal-agent conflicts can emerge between the government as owners and the managers of enterprises. Managers may follow their own objectives which may diverge from profit maximization. This can be particularly harmful in enterprises where major restructuring is required, such as the reduction of over-employment or the need to upgrade the power of finance, accounting and marketing departments. Privatization should ensure that managers are subject to market discipline which is generally equated with control by outside owners [Frydman and Rapaczynski 1993]. A different argument for private ownership arises from Schumpeterian views of competition where permanent innovation with the rise and fall of entrepreneurs is the driving force for economic growth. The claim to the residual surplus creates a powerful stimulus for entrepreneurial management.

Privatization in CEE differs from Western experiences by the scope of the task, by the absence of efficient capital markets, and by the lack of private domestic savings that could be invested in privatization. Therefore, alternative means of privatization have been discussed. The basic choices concern methods and envisaged future owners. The main methods are sale and free distribution. Owners are distinguished as insiders, the population at large, former owners, and outside investors [Estrin 1994a, World Bank 1996]. The trade-offs in designing a privatization scheme include fairness of distribution, creating effective corporate governance, government revenues, and speed. Rapid privatization was desirable to limit the time-period of 'drifting' and to make the transition process irreversible in view of a potential reversal of political power.

Mass privatization has been promoted as an opportunity to redistribute the wealth of the economy to its citizens in a 'fair' way. However, the organization of a voucher-based auction is a complex task and can result in dispersed ownership and no effective control. To create effective corporate governance, investment funds may play an important intermediate role [Frydman and Rapaczynski 1993]. For foreign investors, such schemes offer opportunities to acquire local firms only after privatization has been completed. Privatization through sale to foreigners can be faster than distribution schemes and generates revenues for the government budget. However, it is often less popular because it does not create widespread local ownership, and additionally firms may be sold below market value due to information asymmetries.

The actual privatization process has often been a mix of many methods.[2] The interplay of political forces and interest groups has determined the methods of privatization and their timing. Arguments of economic efficiency and social fairness have often been secondary. Small firms, such as shops, have usually been privatized first using direct sales or auctions. Privatization of large enterprises has been more complex.

In the Czech Republic, a voucher scheme was implemented in which investment funds took an unanticipated dominant role by accumulating vouchers from individuals [Singer and Svejnar 1994, Coffee 1996].[3] In Hungary, early privatization often took the form of spontaneous privatization in that insiders took control of enterprises. Large-scale privatization involved many enterprise sales to foreign investors. The state property agency may or may not have retained a minority share. By 1995, Hungary moved on to privatizing telecommunications and other network operating companies [Canning and Hare 1996]. The focus on privatization by means of foreign investment was to some extent copied by Estonia. In Poland, large privatization was delayed due to political conflicts. Eventually, in 1996, a voucher scheme was instituted that gave designated investment funds a central role. In Russia, mass privatization was carried out in 1994, creating a high degree of insider ownership or at least insider control [Boyko, Shleifer and Vishny 1995].

For foreign investors, this diverse privatization process offers opportunities as well as obstacles. Through acquisition by privatization, investors can instantly acquire market shares with local brand names and distribution networks. Although the technology and existing capital stock has mostly been of minor value, firms have possessed valuable team-embedded knowledge such as R&D teams and local networking contacts. Negotiations on acquisitions have become rather complex because many parties have been involved in the process. Privatization agencies have followed a variety of objectives including employment and investment guarantees, and a preference for JVs as well as revenue maximization. Managers of the local firms have taken an active role in the negotiations with their own objectives [Rojec and Jermakowicz 1995]. Additionally, lack of experience and unclear responsibilities of the Eastern partner had made negotiations more tedious. Some investors may have found opportunities to take advantage of inexperienced negotiators.

A major constraint for enterprise transformation became the systems of corporate governance. After the central planning system broke down, state-owned enterprises found themselves in a quasi-market environment with government agencies as nominal owners. At this stage, managers had extensive control over the enterprise. State agencies had neither the means nor the incentives to create effective systems of corporate governance. Workers' councils attained considerable influence over management, de facto or de jure, especially in Poland. A common fear was that managers and workers would follow short-term objectives and decapitalize the firms for their own benefit. The actual evidence does not support this view. Although there are cases of 'asset-stripping' and 'self-privatization', most studies find evidence of changes of firm behaviour towards economic restructuring prior to privatization.[4] Output and input have been adjusted to conditions of demand and supply; trade has been reoriented towards new markets, exposure to bad debt has been reduced, and labour and management costs have been kept under control. The adjustment of state-owned or privatized firms has primarily taken the form of cost-cutting rather than output expansion. Apparently, the new competitive environment, hard budget constraints and managers' desire to qualify for the new post-privatization job market have created sufficient incentives. Problems have persisted in the areas of innovation and marketing as relevant managerial capabilities have been scarce. Successful privatization and economic turnaround depends on the level of politicization and intensity of organizational politicking, on the effectiveness of new corporate governance, and the availability of new resources [Antal 1995].

Even after privatization, corporate governance systems are incomplete and their future is uncertain. The privatization process has created various kinds of new ownership patterns in the region. In very few cases, Anglo Saxon style corporate governance has emerged with the majority of shares traded on the stock exchange and dominant owners taking control. Investment funds play an important role as effective owners of enterprises, be it by default (Czech Republic) or by construction (Poland). Government agencies have retained a minority share in many enterprises to be privatized later. In Poland, workers have also obtained minority shares. Especially in Russia, most firms are effectively insider-owned after privatization. Many authors have major concerns that insider control inhibits restructuring unless equity markets soon evolve.[5] So far, by most criteria the empirical evidence does not show significantly inferior performance of insider-owned firms [Estrin and Earle 1995, Mygind 1997].

While the former state-owned enterprises are gradually reforming, most economic growth after the transitional recession is found in newly established firms. This pattern has been described particularly in Poland where privatization effectively began with the crowding-out of the state sector [Johnson and Loveman 1995, Borish and Noël 1996] The slow privatization arose by default as the economic framework was liberalized but large state-owned companies were not (yet) transferred to the private sector. The most dynamic units of the economy are the new enterprises without the burden of an organizational inheritance from state-owned predecessors. In Russia, a similar trend can be observed although the independent private sector is starting from a much lower level [Richter and Schaffer 1996] For foreign investors, these young growing firms may provide more interesting partners. They have more flexible organizational structures and may be both eager and capable suppliers, distributors, or even JV partners.

The interesting question for this research is whether differences in the privatization processes across countries affect the volume and characteristics of incoming DFI. Apparently, investors have been attracted to Hungary because of the high priority given to foreign investment in the privatization process. This may also affect the mode of entry and equity ownership. Privatization may provide opportunities for acquisition replacing greenfield projects and induce investors to accept JV ownership. Yet, the acquisition of a formerly state-owned firm also faces specific costs for the complex negotiations and the restructuring of the enterprise.

Institutional framework

Under the central planning regime, the economies of CEE were following a policy of autarky that closed them to multinational business activities. However as early as 1971 (Romania) and 1972 (Hungary) countries began to introduce joint-venture laws that permitted DFI [Gutman 1993]. These laws did not stimulate large investment inflows as legal permission alone was insufficient to create an attractive business environment. The legal and economic environment of a planned economy could not incorporate a privately owned and independently managed foreign firm [McMillan 1992]. Even when this systemic conflict was overcome, substantial resources and time had to be invested to set up a foreign venture. Foreign investment law was complex, the general legislative framework was unsuitable, and local authorities were inexperienced in dealing with potential investors. Of particular concern were the issues of profit repatriation, protection against expropriation, the obtainment of property rights, protection of intellectual property, contract enforcement and the hiring and firing of workers [Gray and Jarosz 1993].

Countries removed restrictions on foreign ownership and allowed majority ownership starting with Hungary in 1988. Investment picked up only after this and other obstacles were removed and a market-friendly environment was created. An important step has been the move from a discretionary bureaucratic approach to a rules-oriented system of regulation of DFI. This was accomplished by most countries by 1991 when new foreign investment laws were established. In the Visegrad countries, DFI is now fairly unregulated apart from registration requirements and some sectors being closed to DFI [EBRD 1994]. In Russia, however, obstacles persist in the laws regulating DFI, including de facto constraints on ownership. These institutional constraints reduce the number of investors, and those investing have to adapt to the regulatory environment. This implies less investment in wholly-owned affiliates and, if acquisition of real estate is constrained, fewer greenfield projects.

However, not only DFI regulation affects DFI, but also a weak general political, institutional and legal framework. Political instability is a major issue in most countries of the former Soviet Union. Central European countries appear to be committed to the transition path despite the election of reform communist parties to power in several countries. Most countries have carried out fiscal reform including the introduction of value-added tax and the overhaul of corporate and personal income tax systems. Reform of the legal system has made substantial progress in all countries with again the Visegrad countries leading ahead of the former Soviet Union. Nevertheless, some serious deficiencies in legal structures and law enforcement remain. Murrell [1996: 34] summarizes the current situation:

> the quality of laws is quite low, in many cases lacking internal consistency and completeness. Moreover, these laws are often a facade without foundation. Missing are the appropriate structured agencies, effective courts, the customary practice of enforcing private rights, the professionals, the scholarly and judicial opinion, and the web of ancillary institutions that give substance to written law. In the large majority of countries, especially in the former USSR, it will take a generation, or more, for the legal system to buttress capitalism in the manner imagined by the drafters of the many new laws. Although these laws are beginning to affect behaviour, they are presently of no more than marginal significance.

The weak legal institutions discourage the use of the courts to settle disputes and permit corruption, notably in Russia and less in Poland [Frye and Shleifer 1997]. Western business operations in those economies is further inhibited by different business ethics that for instance permit the breaking of a law that is considered non-sensible [Puffer and McCarthy 1995]. Last, but not least, crime and corruption are increasing, notably with the rise of the Russian mafia. Their rule deters many business entrants, local and foreign.

International trade
Prior to 1989, the countries of CEE traded mainly within their regional trading bloc, the CMEA (Table 2.1). All transition economies suffered from the collapse of these traditional trade links with the collapse of the CMEA and the Soviet Union. Between 1989 and 1992, some CEE countries reoriented their external trade to new markets and new sources.

The international trade regime in Central Europe is overshadowed by rapid opening, in line with the 'Europe Agreements' with the EU [see Nuti 1994, Baldwin 1994]. These agreements aim at creating a free trade area (except for agriculture) in two successive five-year stages and require the abolition of most tariffs and the adaptation of the regulatory framework to EU rules. This reduces opportunities for protecting import-substituting investment, although there are exceptions. The agreements offer easy access to EU markets and should thus attract export-oriented investments.

On the other hand, the EU itself is undergoing a structural adjustment process in which overcapacities in agriculture, textiles, steel and chemicals are gradually reduced in a highly regulated fashion. As the countries of CEE have overcapacities in the same industries, they would take part in this exercise of capacity reduction, were they members of the union. This serves to justify that these sectors have not been liberalized in line with other industries as part of the

Europe Agreements.[6] Hence, in sectors where CEE may currently have comparative advantages, EU protectionism may prevent them from taking advantage. It is, however, an open question whether CEE can gain long-term competitiveness in the sectors where it currently has overcapacities [Nuti 1994].

The actual trade data show a strong export performance of CEE economies in OECD markets and Western Europe in particular. Yet the extent to which they have succeeded in trade reorientation varies. While former Czechoslovakia increased its trade with OECD countries at an average annual rate of about 20 per cent in the period 1988-93, Romanian trade grew at a modest 2 per cent annually in the same period. In the former Soviet Union the main concern is the re-establishment of many trade links interrupted by the break down of the SU and the common currency. Differences in trade performance are related to the progress in economic transition [Kaminski, Wang and Winters 1996]. Comprehensive trade liberalization has been essential for successful trade performance [de Menil 1997]. The growth of East-West trade overcomes the distortions of the previous trade patterns. International trade now approaches the 'natural patterns' described by gravity models.

Virgin Markets

Markets in CEE are potentially attractive for many businesses in Western Europe. First, consumers in CEE had no access to many consumer goods that are readily available to consumers at similar levels of per capita income in other parts of the world. This catch-up emerged immediately after trade liberalization. The high esteem for Western goods at the time of opening was in part a result of Western media penetration which was sustained through effective advertising and brand building in the liberalized local media. For consumer durables and manufacturers of fast-moving consumer goods, this opened growth opportunities for firms whose established markets in the West were saturated.

Second, the Visegrad countries reached high economic growth, and the region has the potential to achieve sustainable high growth rates with growing markets for several years to come. Recent economic forecasts predict high growth rates for several years as CEE narrows the gap with Western Europe as a result of liberalization, stabilization, and prospective integration into the EU market. This creates opportunities not only for consumer goods manufacturers, but for any business supplying machinery or building infrastructure in the, hopefully, rapidly upgrading economies.

West European businesses discover new opportunities for expansion. First, firms facing barriers to growth in their present markets due to saturation or intense competition can move onto a new growth path. Second, multinationals in oligopolistic industries may be induced to invest in accordance with their strategic positions *vis-à-vis* their global competitors. Dominated firms may see new markets as an opportunity to gain competitive advantages, while global leaders wish to prevent such challenges and the emergence of new competitors from within the region. MNEs established in both Western and Eastern Europe may be in a superior position to exploit opportunities of price discrimination, product differentiation or vertical integration [Estrin, Hughes and Todd 1997]. In industries with major network externalities, such as consultancy and financial services, presence in the region may be necessary for global competitiveness.

Thus the question of entry becomes a 'how' and 'when' rather than 'whether'. Many early investors cited benefits of first-mover advantages as a motive to invest early [Lankes and Venebles 1996]. This includes expected long-term benefits from brand recognition or access to distribution channels, preferenced relations with local suppliers and contacts to governments. They may even be able to influence the local regulatory environment in their favour. Early entry has been observed for many MNEs in industries with an oligopolistic market structure [Marton 1993, Kogut 1996, Estrin, Hughes and Todd 1997]. On the other hand, first-movers may create spill overs in favour of followers. They improve local agents' understanding of the needs of MNEs and invest in training and promotion. These positive spill overs have enabled many 'fast-second' entrants to take over as market leaders [Estrin and Meyer 1998].

Low Labour Costs

Under distinct economic systems, the industrial structure of the economies in Eastern and Western Europe developed apart, despite geographic proximity. While the socialist countries focused on scale-intensive, heavy industries, Western Europe moved on to knowledge-intensive industries and services. This resulted in a large gap in productivity and real wages as CEE industry used outdated technology and infrastructure. Additionally, wages were kept low by politically imposed constraints that emphasized equality over incentives. As the Iron Curtain fell, there were two widespread expectations:

- Higher wages in the West would attract cheap labour from the East and lead to massive economic migration.
- Low wages in the East would motivate Western businesses to relocate their production lines, and thus to move jobs from the West to the East.

Economic migration has been constrained by the political and language barriers facing migrants in the West. It has, however, accelerated the pace of German unification, as these barriers did not apply between East and West Germany.

The relocation of production was seen as a great potential for the transition economies and also a threat to current employment and high levels of social security in Western Europe. Economic theory of location suggests that substantial DFI would enter Eastern Europe in search of lower labour costs [Ozawa 1992, Arva 1994]. Production processes using medium-level technical skills would be moved to CEE with DFI facilitating the enhancement of efficiency in the local production. A comparison of CEE with East Asia led to similar suggestions [Meyer 1996, UN 1995 chap V]. The region should have strong comparative advantages within intermediate-level technical skills as the level of education in the region is relatively high. Factor-cost advantages also arise from low costs of some raw materials, especially in Russia. Unit labour costs rose considerably in CEE but are still far below West European, especially German, levels. Economic policy strengthened this advantage by an effective undervaluation of the exchange rate and incomes policy such as constraints on wage increases, for example the Polish wage increase tax.

However, productivity is often low despite the workforce being well qualified. Technical skills are not matched by managerial skills, entrepreneurial culture and willingness to take business risks. Although rapid improvements are reported, finding a local partner with the necessary business skills may still be difficult. Further costs arise from the weak infrastructure, especially the road network and telecommunications, from an outdated capital stock, social costs, and the regulatory environment. Investors may also be concerned with the viability of the East-West wage gap. Especially projects with long time horizons may be inhibited by uncertainty surrounding future labour costs.

TRENDS OF DIRECT FOREIGN INVESTMENT

This section reviews and interprets available statistical information in order to obtain an overview of actual DFI in CEE since the beginning of the transition. However, it is first necessary to assess the quality of the available statistics.

Foreign Investment Data

DFI is defined as a flow of investment in the form of financial capital or other resources into another country with the intention of influencing the policy of the foreign firm. Economically, DFI is a mechanism to transfer a bundle of resources, including financial capital as well as technology and human resources across national borders while keeping it under the control of the parent company. In practice, the definitions of this bundle may differ for different purposes and limit themselves to equity as it is more easily measured. Control of the foreign business unit distinguishes DFI from portfolio investment.[7]

For some research questions, the stock of DFI as the foreign controlled business units in a country is the relevant unit of analysis. This reflects the fact that DFI creates international production [Dunning 1988], that is value adding activities in different countries under the common governance of one firm called a transnational or multinational enterprise (MNE). Thus, two concepts are referred to as DFI: the foreign-owned capital stock of companies with a controlling foreign stake in their equity, and the cross-border flow of capital to and from such foreign-controlled enterprises.

The *flow* of DFI is measured in the balance of payment (BoP) statistics collected by central banks and the IMF. These data are generally reported on a net basis, that is discounting 'outflow receipts', that is disinvestments. This can, in special cases, lead to a seemingly 'wrong' sign. BoP data are based on recorded transactions and cover transfers of capital in the form of equity, reinvested earnings and short- and long-term loans. According to IMF guidelines, they should also cover reinvested profits, but many emerging markets do not collect these profit data.[8] Furthermore, they do not capture in-kind contributions such as technology transfer. The limitations in the data collection are apparent since the recorded DFI inflows worldwide exceeded the corresponding recorded outflows in 1994 by US$ 10.5 billion (5% of outflows) following surplus outflows in previous years. Guidelines from the IMF and the OECD should theoretically ensure that data are collected worldwide in a comparable way. However, national statistical offices use diverse technical definitions of DFI and different survey or reporting systems to obtain data from enterprises [OECD 1993].

The flow of DFI is approximated by data on 'registered DFI' which are provided for example in the database of the UNECE [UN 1996, UNECE 1996]. These data are collected during the approval and registration of DFI projects by investment promotion agencies or administrations. For cross-country comparisons, these sources are of limited use, because:

- Registration requirements vary. In the Czech Republic and Hungary, DFI is registered *after* the payment of the statutory capital and with the cash inflow as recorded for the BoP. In Romania, DFI is registered prior to being set up [Hunya 1992]. The Polish Investment Agency uses a wider definition of DFI.
- The valuation of in-kind contributions, especially knowledge transfer, is unavoidably arbitrary.
- Reported DFI capital may refer to foreign equity contribution, total equity, or include equity and loan capital.
- Data may be distorted by incentives to register as a JV in order to enjoy tax advantages or gain access to convertible currency, for which there is substantial anecdotal evidence, for example in Russia and Romania.
- Some statistics cover JVs only, omitting wholly foreign-owned ventures.

The *stock* of inward and outward DFI is ideally measured by a survey of all relevant enterprises. A mandatory reporting system on existing foreign capital stock would provide the most comprehensive overview, capturing all DFI that an analyst would like to include. In Germany and Austria, central banks regularly publish such survey data. However, they cannot fully cover small businesses and while BoP data become available within weeks, survey-based data are published with time-lags of about 18 months. The Hungarian Statistical Office has a comprehensive database of all enterprises based on their tax reports, which seems to meet most wishes [Lane 1994].

The stock of DFI is not equal to the cumulative flow because of revaluation effects. Nevertheless, the stock of DFI is often approximated by cumulative BoP flows, by cumulative registered DFI, or using data on 'committed DFI'. The latter usually rest on company announcements that reflect investment intentions, and are thus unsatisfactory for most academic research questions.

Working with DFI data, several potential biases have to be considered: BoP statistics suffer from incomplete coverage and focus on capital transfers only, thus tending to underestimate actual DFI, particularly inflows. Statistics on 'committed DFI' or journalistic sources tend to overstate actual investment. Registration data may have biases in either direction depending on their timing and coverage of registration requirements: registration generally precedes implementation, sometimes even the payment of the investors' contribution and may reflect more potential rather than actual investment. At some stage only 20 per cent of JVs in Russia were actually operational. On the other hand, registration data is collected on registration only, which implies that:

- the cumulative total of registered DFI flows disregards any changes to existing projects, discontinuations as well as increases in invested capital,
- investments which are not required to register are therefore not covered. For instance, Hungarian registration data are collected only for newly founded firms and thus do not capture JVs with an existing Hungarian partner [Lane 1994].

As a rule of the thumb, registration data tends to overstate DFI in recently emerging investment locations if implementation lags are long and if obstacles such as bureaucracy or political instability induce potential investors to abandon projects after their registration. However, these data capture only a fraction of actual DFI in a mature host country without formal approval procedures. In addition, statistical offices and data collection systems in CEE only recently and gradually obtain a satisfactory coverage of the private sector.

Hence, great caution and consideration of the method of data collection are necessary in interpreting DFI data and in aggregating data from different sources. BoP statistics are generally the most reliable and consistent sources of data for cross-country analysis - despite their incomplete coverage. Fortunately the discrepancies between data from different sources are declining. Brewer [1994] concludes diplomatically, that for each purpose a different data set may the most suitable, and combined they may best reflect actual DFI.

Before discussing the general pattern of DFI in the region, let us briefly review the data for Hungary to illustrate the data quality issues (table 2.2). DFI inflows to Hungary are reported by various data sources that, however, show a similar general trend for the invested capital: DFI inflows soared in the early years of economic transformation and continued to enter in large volume but with considerable volatility over time.

Table 2.2 Various measures of DFI in Hungary

	DFI Stock in Hungary			Flow of DFI into Hungary				
	(1)	(2)	(3)	(4)	(5)	(6)	(7)	(8)
1974	2	...	...	...	...	...	...	...
1980	6	...	...	...	...	...	...	...
1984	27	...	...	...	...	...	...	...
1986	62	...	...	17	...	...	...	...
1988	227	188	14	104	97	...	...	14
1989	1357	504	229	1130	1123	...	316	215
1990	5693	1475	583	3814	4343	...	970	354
1991	9117	2838	2045	5642	3424	733	1363	1462
1992	17182	5087	3524	4101	8065	543	2248	1479
1993	20999	6144	5776	4286	3817	502	1057	2350
1994	23557	7530	6920	4431	2558	302	1386	1144
1995	25096	9354	11439	3720	1539	219	1824	4519
1996	...	...	13300	4088	...	200	...	1900

Notes:
(1) Number of foreign-owned firms recorded by the tax office.
(2) Foreign capital paid by firms recorded by the tax office, in million US$.
(3) Cumulative inflow of DFI recorded in the balance of payments, see (8), in million US$.
(4) Number of newly-registered DFI firms.
(5) Increase of foreign-owned firms by number, change in (1).
(6) Foreign capital paid by newly registered firms, in million US$.
(7) Increase of foreign-owned firms by capital, in million US$, change in (2).
(8) Balance of Payments, in million US$.

Sources: Hungarian Statistical Office, IMF, Meyer [1995].

DFI capital inflow as reported by the BoP data reached US$4.5 million in 1995 (col. 8) with lower levels in years without major privatization projects, notably in 1994 and 1996. The cumulative total of BoP-recorded DFI adds up to US$ 13.3 billion in 1996. These BoP data exceed the foreign capital reported by the tax office in the latest available year, 1995. This contrasts with earlier years when the tax office data exceeded the balance of payments data. This may be a result of fewer contributions in kind as well as peculiarities connected to the privatization of utilities in 1995.

Foreign capital contributions reported by the registration data are far lower than the BoP data, with only US$0.2 billion of new investment in Hungary in 1995 and 1996. This continues a decline in real terms over previous years. DFI now occurs increasingly by taking over existing enterprises or by increasing capital contributions in existing JVs or subsidiaries. However, registration data are the only available ones disaggregated by sector. Unfortunately, the discrepancies between data from different sources are not diminishing over time as a new discrepancy emerges for 1995. Notably, the major receipts of privatization have apparently not made their way into the tax office database.

The number of DFI firms is reported by registration and tax office data which give different impressions of the establishment of new DFI (cols 4 & 5). The number of newly registered firms peaked in 1991 at 5642 and then settled at a level of about 4000 annually. However, the tax office database recorded the largest inflow in 1992, and declining increases since. Lane [1994] suggests that many newly registered firms in 1991 failed to report to the tax authorities in that year but did so in 1992. The recent overshooting of the registration data probably reflects the fact that many enterprises do not actually take up business or discontinue operations. By the end of 1995, some 25,000 enterprises with foreign equity filed tax documents (col. 1).

Volume of Investment

Countries of destination in the region
The annual inflow to the Central European transition economies increased from 1989 onwards and reached some US$5 billion in 1993 (Table 2.3). It dropped slightly in 1994 but increased to more than US$11 billion in 1995 and US$7 billion in 1996. The stock of DFI in the region has reached US$29 to 32 billion by 1996 - estimated from the cumulative total of flows. These are quite remarkable investment flows, comparable to other emerging market regions. The Economist Intelligence Unit [1996] forecasts a stock of US$64 billion by the year 2000.

Yet in the early years of transition, the inflow of investment capital was below expectations. CEE attracted, in aggregate, much less DFI than emerging markets in East Asia or Latin America: DFI flows to developing countries

Table 2.3 DFI inflows to CEE
Balance of payments data, excluding reinvested profits, in million US$

Year	88	89	90	91	92	93	94	95	96
Albania	...	...	...	-1	20	58	53	70	90
Bulgaria	...	...	4	56	42	55	105	90	115
Croatia	...	...	...	...	...	74	98	81	349
Czech Rep.[a]	...	171	120	511	983	654	878	2568	1435
Hungary	14	215	354	1462	1479	2350	1144	4519	1982
Poland	15	11	69	241	524	1516	1493	2771	4254
Romania	...	...	112	40	77	94	341	419	263
Slovakia[a]	...	86	53	82	72	199	203	183	280
Slovenia	...	...	...	41	111	113	128	176	186
Total	...	483	712	1927	3308	5113	4398	10877	8954
Estonia	...	...	...	...	73	135	172	186	132
Latvia	...	...	...	...	29	45	214	180	293
Lithuania	...	...	...	...	10	30	31	65	128
Armenia	...	...	...	...	...	...	8	19[b]	18
Azerbaijan	...	...	...	...	...	...	22[b]	284[b]	661[b]
Belarus	...	...	...	...	7[c]	10[c]	10[b]	7[b]	75[b]
Georgia	...	...	...	...	...	...	8[b]	6[b]	25[b]
Kazakhstan	...	...	...	...	100[c]	165[c]	635[b]	859[b]	1100[b]
Kyrgystan	...	...	...	...	...	6[c]	38	96	46
Moldova	...	...	...	...	17[c]	14[c]	12	64	41
Russia[e]	...	...	...	-100[d]	700[c]	700[c]	637	2017	2479
Tajikistan	...	...	...	...	9[c]	12[c]	12[b]	13[b]	13[b]
Turkmenistan	...	...	...	...	...	...	103[b]	233[b]	108
Ukraine[e]	...	...	...	...	170[c]	200[c]	159	267	500[b]
Uzbekistan	...	...	...	...	40[c]	4 [c]	73[b]	-24[b]	50[b]
Total CIS	...	...	...	...	...	...	1700	3800	5000
China	...	3393	3487	4366	11156	27515	33787	35849	40180

Sources: International Financial Statistics (IMF), except: [a] separation of Czech and Slovak Republic 1989-92 based on PlanEcon, [b] net DFI-inflows, estimate by EBRD [1997], [c] Economic Reviews (IMF), [d] net DFI [World Bank 1992], [e] includes reinvested earnings.

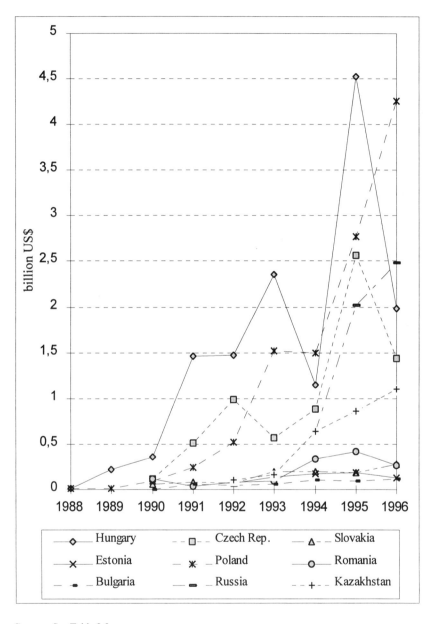

Sources: See Table 2.3.

Figure 2.2 DFI flows to Central and Eastern Europe

Table 2.4 Alternative measures of DFI

	cumulative DFI 1989-96	registered DFI 1.7.1995	DFI per capita (US$) 1993-95	DFI as % of GDP 1993-95
Albania	300	...	18	2.8
Bulgaria	500	514	10	0.4
Czech Republic	7,100	3,431	130	3.7
Hungary	13,400	9,990	259	6.5
Poland	10,000 [a]	3,910	50	2.1
Romania	1,600	1,406	13	0.9
Slovakia	1,000	585	37	1.6
Slovenia	750	1,347	70	0.6
Estonia	750	524	110	3.6
Latvia	650	380	59	0.5
Lithuania	225	253	12	0.4
Russia	...	3,808	8	0.3
Ukraine	...	566	4	0.2

Notes: DFI per capita and as a percentage of GDP are three-year averages 1993-95 to eliminate effects of annual volatility. [a] Author's estimate.

Sources: Cumulative DFI from Table 2.3, registration data: UNECE [1996], population and GDP from World Development Report 1996.

increased continually from US$12 billion in 1986 to US$108 billion in 1995 by BoP definitions. However, this DFI is distributed very unequally as a few very dynamic economies in East Asia (China, Singapore and Malaysia) and countries with major liberalization and privatization programmes in Latin America (Argentina and Mexico) are taking the largest shares [Meyer 1996]. Until 1994, the leading East-Asian recipients received more DFI than the CEE region as a whole.

Hungary has been the leading destination for investors in the early years of transition. The country received almost half of all DFI into the region until 1993 and regained its lead in 1995 with US$3.4 billion after being second to Poland in 1994. The leading position is illuminated by the US$259 per capita and the 6.5 per cent DFI as percentage of GDP (Table 2.4). These size-adjusted figures are among the highest in the world. Among emerging markets, only Singapore (US$1963, 8.3%), Malaysia (US$256, 7.2%) and Hong Kong surpass Hungary's performance. Hungary is established among the top emerging markets for DFI, comparable to Brazil, Taiwan or Indonesia in absolute volume. The pre-1989 economic reforms, the earlier opening to international business and the outward-oriented privatization policy contributed to this performance.

DFI in *Czechoslovakia* took off with the VW-Skoda project in 1991, making it the second-largest recipient of DFI in the region. In 1992, the number of JVs already reached 6000, and US$1.1 billion DFI inflows were recorded in the BoP. After the divorce in January 1993, the Czech Republic suffered a set-back but soon recovered. After the voucher privatization programme was completed, new opportunities for foreign investors emerged. Inflows accelerated to US$2.5 billion in 1995, including US$1.3 billion in the telecom privatization. This result has not been repeated in 1996. Slovakia reported almost US$200 million annually which translates to above average DFI/GDP percentages. This is more than one might predict, considering the weak stance of economic reform and the political environment in Slovakia.

Poland received some US$10 million of DFI annually throughout the 1980s, mainly in the form of investment by Polish expatriates, restricted in size and regulated by a special law [Gutman 1993]. Although Poland is a much larger economy, has been successful in macroeconomic stabilization and has been the first country to overcome the recession, it came only third as a recipient of DFI until 1992 - and only sixth in per capita terms. It was not until 1993 that investors finally moved into Poland on a large scale. Then, inflows grew more than threefold to US$1.9 billion in 1994 and US$2.8 billion in 1995.[9]

Hungary, Poland and the Czech Republic also opened their stock exchanges to foreign investors. These emerging equity markets attract considerable net portfolio investment. In 1993, the IMF BoP data for the first time reported portfolio investment for Hungary and the Czech Republic. They received US$3.9 billion and US$1.8 billion respectively. In subsequent years the inflows were lower, for instance in 1995 Hungary received US$2.2 billion and the Czech Republic US$1.7 billion. Poland reported portfolio investment for the first time in 1995, US$1.3 billion. No other country in the region has reported portfolio investment of a comparable magnitude.

The countries of South-Central Europe show a very disappointing performance in attracting DFI. Inflows were less than US$100 million in both *Bulgaria* and *Romania* until 1993. However, Romania surprised by the number of registered JVs, reporting 29,115 by the end of 1993 - most of which, however, were very small. In 1994, DFI rose substantially with Korean Daewoo accounting for a major share, and in 1996 it exceeded US$550 million. Bulgaria had no comparable take-off due to the prolonged economic and political crisis. Investment in *Albania* was small, but comes to a small economy with a very low income level. The Albanian DFI/GDP ratio is, if confidence can be placed in the data, second only to Singapore among emerging markets. A few large resource-exploration projects explain this performance.

Yugoslavia attracted investors throughout the last two decades, reaching a cumulative total of US$3 billion by 1991. The largest inflow was recorded in 1990 with US$1.4 billion, of which 21.5 per cent went to *Slovenia* [UN 1992]. However, due to the civil war DFI projects in the former Yugoslavia have been discontinued, thereby reducing the invested capital stock. Recent DFI inflows are concentrated on Slovenia where, by the end of 1993, 3300 enterprises were recorded with foreign investment of US$1.2 billion. However, the registration data for Slovenia by far exceeds recent balance of payment data, which shows some US$ 100 million annually, with an increasing trend. This makes Slovenia an average performer in per capita terms, but since it has a much higher level of income, its DFI/GDP-ratio is disappointing.

DFI into the then *Soviet Union* started to increase after it was made legal in 1987 and reached a peak earlier than Central Europe at US$640 million of DFI inflows in 1989, but fell in 1991 to US$480 million [estimates, World Bank 1992]. After the break-up of the Soviet Union, the Baltic States emerged as the most successful recipients of DFI. *Estonia* started receiving large amounts of DFI from 1993 onwards, followed and now overtaken by *Latvia*. DFI in *Lithuania* picked up in 1995-96. Since these economies are small, their size-adjusted DFI figures are high (Table 2.4): as a percentage of GDP, DFI in Estonia is on a par with that of the Czech Republic.

For the *Commonwealth of Independent States* (CIS), comprehensive data is not available. For 1992, following registration data, the IMF reports an (estimated) inflow of US$700 million to *Russia*. The World Bank [1992] reports a *net* flow of US$200 million, which accounts for substantial outward DFI as a means of capital flight. The IMF Economic Review reported about US$700 million from 1992 to 1994. The annual DFI inflow in the early 1990s to the CIS was thus in the range of between US$0.5 billion and 1 billion annually. Recently some CIS countries have accelerated their DFI inflows. The International Financial Statistics report DFI into Russia for 1995 with very remarkable US$2.0 billion, and even more in 1996. Russia, *Kazakhstan* and *Azerbeidjan* now receive long expected investment in oil, gas and other resource exploration projects. Yet other CIS countries still lack major investment flows. Notably, the second-largest CIS country, *Ukraine,* receives very little DFI relative to its size (Table 2.4).

The poor performance of the CIS is confirmed by Western outflow data. The reported outflow of DFI to the former Soviet Union was negative for several countries for individual years (see Table 2.5, note f). This suggests that investors withdrew investment funds on a large scale, although accounting or revaluation effects may have contributed to this effect. The data on DFI in Russia are further distorted by substantial 'round-tripping', that is investment by Russian-owned businesses located abroad, for instance in Cyprus (which according to Goskomstat is source for 6% of DFI in Russia).

Table 2.5 DFI in CEE: countries of origin
Stock and flow, in million US$ and as percentage of home-countries DFI.

	Stock of DFI		Flow of DFI (net)					
	1994	share [a]	1991	1992	1993	1994	1995	share [a]
Austria	2,869	30.9%	505	470	587	509	...	42.5%
Belgium	...	...	288[g]	41[g]	320	30[g]	...	0.1%
Canada	127[c]	...	2[c]	72[c]	1[c]	...	...	...
Denmark	...	...	9	17	52	54	...	1.4%
Finland	174	1.4%	...	37	35[f]	38	105[c]	0.9%
France	625	0.4%	245	401	273[g]	250	...	2.3%
Germany	4,943	2.3%	837[f]	1,137	1,647	2,157	2,831[c]	13.0%
Italy	1,213	1.0%	35	97	433	142	...	2.8%
Netherlands	1,101	0.7%	178	648	518	371	1,261[c]	2.2%
Norway	47	0.3%	...	...	...	38	...	1.7%
Spain	...	...	8	3	9	23	...	0.5%
Sweden	...	...	17	26	79	78[f]	...	1.2%
Switzerland	822	0.8%	46	105	110[f]	241	...	2.2%
Turkey	...	...	1	8	10	10	...	4.9%
UK	659	0.2%	27	272[f]	68[g]	342[g]	...	1,2%
USA	4,270	0.7%	272	509	1,665	809	...	1,5%
sum [d]	16,850	--	2,470	3,843	5,807	5,092	...	--
total CEE [d]	20,000	--	2,500	4,500	6,500	6,000	14,000	--

Notes: [a] DFI stock/flow in CEE as a share of the total outward DFI stock/flow *from this home country* in 1994, [b] 1992, [c] from national statistics, [d] the sum refers to the available data only, the total is estimated from table 2.3, [e] approximate share in worldwide DFI, [f] net flow reduced by net withdrawal from Russia/Soviet Union, [g] net flow reduced by net withdrawal from countries other than Russia.

Sources: OECD [1995], national statistics (Statistics Canada, Bank of Finland, Deutsche Bundesbank, De Nederlandse Bank).

Countries of origin

Where does the investment come from? The most striking country pattern of early DFI data is proximity. Table 2.5 shows the outflow of DFI to CEE from OECD source countries. The largest flows originate from Germany, the US and from Austria. The latter is not a typical investment country which is reflected in the high proportion of CEE investment in its overall investment stock. For most other countries, CEE is of minor importance as an investment location. From several host country sources, based on their respective DFI registrations, Table 2.6 of leading investors has been assembled. Germany and Austria emerge as the main investors measured by invested capital in CEE, and even more so if the number of projects is considered.

Austria became a major source of DFI in the region and CEE became the major destination for its investors. Austrian DFI stock in CEE increased from virtually nothing to almost US$3 billion in 1994 (Table 2.5). The country distribution of Austrian outward DFI-stock reflects the special relationship with Hungary, which in 1994 accounts for 17 per cent of its worldwide outward DFI-stock. As a region, CEE accounts for 30.9 per cent of its stock and even 42.5 per cent of flows. For no other country, CEE is of comparable importance - not even for other neighbours such as Finland or Turkey. On the other hand, Austria was of major importance for all its direct neighbours, accounting for more than 20 per cent of their inward DFI by number of projects [Hunya 1996].

Austria has a special relationship with the region based on personal ties and historical links. Many Austrian enterprises have a competitive advantage based on their superior knowledge of their neighbours, existing business contacts and expatriates from the region living in Austria [Bellak 1997]. During the early 1990s, this special role was strengthened by multinational enterprises locating their regional headquarters in Vienna and from here formally undertaking their DFI in, say, Hungary. Vienna offers an attractive geographic location for supplying local markets and coordinating activities in Central Europe, plus a superior infrastructure and cultural environment. However, by the mid 1990s, Austria has been taken over by other source countries - and Vienna only partially capitalized on its geographic advantage.

Germany was the first or second-most important investor in all Central European countries (Table 2.6) by number and by statutory capital. Deutsche Bundesbank reports German DFI outflows to the region of US$2.8 billion in 1995 and US$2.9 billion in 1996.[10] Of total inflows into the region, Germany accounts for more than 20 per cent every year since 1991, with a peak of 33 per cent in 1991. CEE is more important for German business than any other country, except Austria, accounting for 13.0 per cent of outflows in 1994. German flows to the transition economies continued a modest growth even in the recession of 1993, when worldwide outflows from Germany halved to DM 19 billion from its 1991 level of DM 40 billion. In 1995, DFI to CEE grew to new record levels.

British firms have, despite their strong position in global business, only a minor role in Eastern Europe. None of the countries covered by the stock statistics in Table 2.5 report a smaller proportion of DFI in CEE, not even the

Table 2.6 Cross-country patterns of DFI flows
Ranking: what is the most important source country in the CEE countries?

Origin	ALB	BG	CR	HU	PL	RO	SLN	SVK	EST	LAT	LIT	R
Germany	4	1	1	2	2	2	1	2	7	2	2	3
Italy	1	...	...	9	3	3	3	8	...	10	...	2
France	5	...	3	6	4	4	4	5	...	...	...	6
Netherlands	...	2	...	4	5	6	...	7	...	...	...	...
Belgium	...	4	4	10	10	...	...	...	...	...	...	...
UK	...	5	...	7	8	7	...	...	6	9	7	10
Ireland	...	...	...	...	...	...	...	...	5	...	9	...
Denmark	...	...	...	...	11	...	...	...	9	...	...	...
Greece	2	...	...	...	...	...	...	...	...	...	...	...
Austria	3	6	5	1	9	...	2	1	8	...	5	4
Switzerland	...	3	...	8	6	10	5	11	...	...	8	7
Sweden	...	...	...	...	7	...	...	6	2	5	1	5
Finland	...	...	...	...	...	...	...	...	1	11	...	8
USA	...	...	2	3	1	5	...	4	4	3	3	1
Canada	...	...	...	...	12	...	...	10	...	8	...	...
Japan	...	...	...	11	...	...	...	...	...	...	...	12
S. Korea	...	...	...	...	...	1	...	9	...	...	...	...
British Virgin Isl.	...	...	...	...	...	...	...	...	...	...	10	...
Turkey	...	...	...	...	...	8	...	...	...	...	...	...
Bulgaria	...	...	...	...	...	...	...	...	...	...	...	11
Czech R.	...	...	-	...	...	...	...	3	...	...	...	...
Poland	...	...	...	...	-	...	...	...	...	4	6	...
Yugoslav.	...	...	...	...	...	-	...	...	...	...	...	9
Russia	...	...	...	5 [a]	...	...	...	...	3	1	4	-
Ukraine	...	...	...	...	...	...	...	...	...	6	11	-
Belarus	...	...	...	...	...	...	...	...	...	7	...	-

Interpretation: ranks refer to the relative importance of source countries in the host country. For example in the Czech Republic (CR), Germany is the most important investor, USA second, France third, etc. up to twelve ranks.
Abbreviations and sources see next page.

ALB = Albania: cumulative flow 1990-1993 [Germany Ministry of Economics]
BG = Bulgaria: cumulative flow 1990 [Germany Ministry of Economics]
CR = Czech Republic: cumulative flow 1989 to 1993 [Czech National Bank].
HU = Hungary: DFI stock registered end 1992 [Hungarian CSO]. [a] Russia refers to CIS.
PL = Poland: registered stock of DFI of more than US$500,000, Sept. 1994 [PAIZ].
RO = Romania: registered DFI stock end of 1995 [Romanian Development Agency].
SLN = Slovenia: registered DFI stock end 1993 [Slovene National Bank].
SVK = Slovakia: registered DFI June 1994 [Ministry of the Economy].
EST = Estonia: registered DFI, July 1995 [Estonian Investment Agency]
LAT = Latvia: registered DFI, June 1992 [World Bank].
LIT = registered DFI, 1.1.1995 [UNECE 1996].
R = Russia: registered DFI, end of 1991 [World Bank].

Table 2.7 Regional distribution of German and UK DFI within CEE Stock of DFI at the end of 1994, in million US$ and in %

	BG	CR	HU	PL	RO	R	SVK	Other[a]	Total
German	24	1,788	1,803	731	54	165	312	364	5,224
DFI	*0.5*	*34.2*	*34.5*	*13.7*	*1.0*	*3.2*	*6.0*	*7.0*	*100%*
British	41	86	370	94	17	45	0	4	659
DFI	*6.2*	*13.0*	*56.2*	*14.2*	*2.6*	*6.9*	*n.a.*	*0.9*	*100%*
Total [b]	262	3,317	7,014	3,869	663	n.a.	695	n.a.	20,000[c]
DFI	*1.3*	*16.6*	*35.0*	*19.3*	*3.3*		*3.5*		*100%*

Notes: [a] = mainly former Yugoslavia, [b] = cumulative flow of DFI, [c] = author's estimate.

Sources: Deutsche Bundesbank, Office for National Statistic, table 2.3.

US. Partly, this is due to lack of proximity: the relative role of CEE as a business partner declines with geographic distance. However, the inferior British position may also be due to longer implementation lags in the energy sector, a traditionally important activity of British investors. The strongest UK positions arise from telecommunication projects in the Baltics and oil exploration in Russia.

Table 2.7 reports additional information for the two countries considered in this study, Germany and the UK, for 1994, the point in time of the survey (Chapter 5). German stock of DFI is concentrated in Hungary and the Czech Republic. In 1995, the Czech Republic (35.2%) actually overtook Hungary (30.2%) as the most important location. Poland follows with 15.9 per cent in 1995. All other transition economies are of minor importance for German economy. The total stock of German DFI in Russia increased to a still relatively small position of US$0.5 billion in 1995. At the time Russian DFI in Germany stood at US$1.1 billion, presumably due to capital flight! British investors have their main position in Hungary, relatively more investment in Bulgaria and

Romania, and weaker positions in the Czech and Slovak Republics.

The proximity pattern also appears for small countries, for example comparing the former EFTA countries: while Austria and Switzerland are important in Central Europe, the Nordic countries are prominent in the Baltic states (Table 2.6). Proximity also strengthens special relationships including Finns in Estonia [Borsos 1995], or Swedes in Poland and the Baltics. Italy and France have a relatively stronger presence in South-Eastern Europe. Turkey emerged as a notable investor for the first time, primarily in Central Asia and around the Black Sea. Proximity is generally more evident in the number of projects than in the contributions of capital, because it is more important for small businesses than for large MNEs. Firms from neighbouring countries were also particularly active in the privatization process [Lane 1994]. However, the pattern of proximity is diminishing over time. Recent data report less dominance of investment from EU and EFTA countries.

US and *Canadian* investors are more evenly spread across the region and have a relatively more important role in the states of the CIS. Using registration data, it appears that the USA and Germany are neck and neck [Csáki 1993, Szanyi 1995, Hughes 1995]. They have a very strong position in Poland where more than 30 per cent of registered capital is of American origin. However, source country data, notably those compiled by the OECD, suggest that Germany is far ahead [Table 2.5, Sels 1996, Lane 1995]. Also data on operational DFI suggest that the US has implemented less investment [Quaisser 1995]. US investments tend to be by large firms in large projects with majority ownership.

Investors from Asian countries are rare in the transition economies. *Japanese* investment is minor. The notable exception is a project by Suzuki in Hungary. *Koreans* have overtaken the Japanese with major projects in the automotive industry in Romania and Poland. Their chaebols appear to follow a strategy of entering European markets from a lower cost base in Eastern Europe.[11] None of the newly industrialized countries of the South-East Asian region are present with significant capital. This may be because their economies are dominated by small businesses. The low representation of Asian investors in the region is quite significant considering their dominant role in the surge of worldwide DFI in the late 1980s.

Sectors of investment

The distribution across sectors of industry is available from registration data, although their coverage may be incomplete and changes over time in business activities may not be recorded. Comparability is further constrained by the use of different industrial classification schemes. Over time, these data show considerable volatility as a single large project can dominate the data of any particular year. Table 2.8 provides a cross-country comparison of general industrial patterns. The main features are a strong position of manufacturing, a growing role of services that attract many small projects, and a minor role of agriculture and mining activities.

Table 2.8 DFI by sector of investment, in % of total DFI

	Destination Countries					Countries of Origin	
	CR	HU	PL	R	RO	Germany [a]	UK [b]
Food & tobacco	9.3	16.3	18.3	2.6	32.6	...	50
Light industry	...	6.0	2.7	1.3	...	...	1
Chemicals	5.7	6.5	10.0	19.3	1.4	4.5	10
Metals	...	3.1	4.0	2.3	...	...	2
Engineering	27.5	13.2	6.8	24.1	26.5	36.8	9
Other manufacturing	...	4.8	22.3	15.9	...	16.8	13
Total manufacturing	...	49.9	64.1	65.5	...	58.1	76
Construction	12.7	4.7	3.3	8.5	17.6	...	...
Utilities	...	...	...	...	...	...	7
Trade	...	...	...	...	...	9.1	9
Transport & communications	...	8.2	4.1	3.2	...	...	1
Financial services	...	...	...	...	...	6.5	1
Other services	16.4	35.5	28.2	28.0	...	...	...
Other, n.a.	28.4	1.7	0.3	...	21.9	21.2 [c]	-1

Notes: East European sources refer to registration data end of 1994. West European data refer to statistics on DFI-stock: Germany stock 1994, UK stock 1993.
[a] = German data include China, [b] = UK data were too generously rounded to provide more precise percentage figures, [c] = mainly investment in holding companies.

Sources: UNECE [1996a], Deutsche Bundesbank, Office for National Statistics (UK).

Manufacturing received the major share of DFI capital across all countries, exceeding its share in the host countries' GDP or worldwide DFI flows. In Poland and Russia, manufacturing received even two thirds of DFI capital. Traditional industries such as machinery and chemicals were the most attractive industries. Sels [1996] argues that DFI does not occur in traditional sectors of DFI such as scale- and resource-intensive industries, but in industries that are both advertising- and research-intensive.

The food, beverage and tobacco-processing industry received high proportions of investment, reaching 30 per cent in Hungary 1992. This includes many Western investors in confectionary (Nestlé, Cadbury), alcoholic beverages, soft-drinks (Coca-Cola and Pepsi), coffee, tobacco, and other branded goods, but few in basic foods products such as meat or milk [Kiss 1995, Möller 1996]. On the other hand,the food and beverage industry has not yet moved into Russia at a comparable scale. Many leading brands have established themselves early, but capital investment is held back.

Leading car manufacturers have established themselves in Hungary (for example Audi, Opel, Suzuki, Ford), the Czech Republic (VW-Skoda and many suppliers) and Poland (Fiat, Daewoo). They have acquired all major local producers and even moved into regions without related industrial tradition. In the car industry, the creation of cross-European production networks is already at an advanced stage [van Tulder and Ruigrok 1997].

Despite the factor-cost advantages, there is no trend to typical low-cost industries such as textiles or electronics. The construction sector attracted 12.7 per cent of DFI in the Czech Republic, but far smaller shares in other countries, which might reflect different classifications. Utilities attracted substantial investment due to the privatization of large electric utilities in Hungary.

The service sector, underdeveloped under the previous socialist system, has been leading throughout the region in terms of the number of DFI projects. This sector received almost three out of four projects in Hungary. Among services, trade was most important, measured by number of projects, by share of foreign firms in total enterprise population, or by invested capital. This includes sales-related activities by Western industry as well as wholesale and retail investments. Some other service activities attracted large capital inflows in particular years: in Hungary in 1993, a few large projects increased the proportions of the transportation and the post and telecom sectors to 23.1 per cent and 13.8 per cent, respectively, of all registered capital. In response to deregulation and privatization, also the financial sector received large amounts of capital.

Western data on the sectoral distribution show the same emphasis on manufacturing. They naturally reflect the strength of any country in industries with national comparative advantages. Some industries are more sensitive then others to proximity and thus come particularly from neighbouring countries. A particular concentration can be observed for the British food, drinks and tobacco industry, almost exclusively in Hungary. In 1991, investment by the German automobile industry into the region jumped from a negligible amount to 37.5 per cent of all investment in the region, due to the VW investment in the (then) CSFR. This is much higher than the general share of the automobile industry in German outward DFI of 5.8 per cent. Comparing the sectoral structure of German DFI stock in CEE to worldwide German DFI, manufacturing receives a much higher share (58.1% over 39.3%) and conversely the financial sector takes a far lower share (less than 6.5% compared with 22%).

CONTEMPORARY RESEARCH IN THE EMERGING FIELD

Soon after DFI was permitted in the region, research activities flourished in economics and business disciplines. This condensed summary of the literature shows in which direction research has developed in the five years since it emerged with the fall of the Iron Curtain.[12] Transition economists are primarily concerned with the systemic transition from a centrally planned economy to a market-led economy. Their research on DFI describes recent trends, analyses its potential impact on host economy, and aims to develop suggestions for government policy towards multinational enterprises.

International business scholars are interested in the interaction of the special transition environment and the multinational enterprise from the firms' perspective. They explore if and where the environment offers opportunities for business, how corporate strategies adapt to the environment, and how this differs from other regions of the world. The transition environment also provides opportunities to test general theories in the field and to observe recent developments of strategies by MNEs. Indeed, the novelty of DFI in CEE may enable the observation of phenomenona which are not observable elsewhere. In this way, the study of DFI in this region is interesting for the advancement of knowledge on a wider level, beyond the region itself.

Table 2.9 Selected country studies

Country	Studies
Hungary	Marton 1993, Csáki 1993, Török 1994, Hamar 1994, Szanyi 1995, Arva 1994, Lane 1994, Hunya 1992, 1996
Czechoslovakia	Bakal 1992, Hosková 1992, Drábek 1993
Poland	Bochniarz and Jermakowicz 1993, Brezinski 1994, Quaisser 1995
Slovenia	Rojec and Svetlicic 1993, Rojec, Jasovic and Kusar 1994
Baltics	Borsos and Erkkilä 1995, Mygind 1997a
Bulgaria	Bobeva and Bozhkov 1996, Marinov and Marinova 1997
Romania	Radulescu 1996
Soviet Union, CIS & Russia	Gutman 1992, Adyubei 1993, McMillan 1993b, 1994, Bradshaw 1995, Andreff and Andreff 1998
China	Chan, Chang and Zhang 1995, Zhan 1993, UN [1995]
Vietnam	Dodsworth et al. 1996, Freeman 1994

Survey Studies

Research on DFI in transition economies began with several studies that interpret the data on DFI flows with respect to host countries, source countries, sectoral structure, JVs versus fully-owned affiliates, and entry modes. Also, the evolution of the legal framework received much attention at this stage. Many early studies reviewed the experience and potential of one country (Table 2.9).

This research merged in cross-country comparative studies that discuss DFI in a broader context. Although many of the issues are similar, the local environment varies considerably across the region, leading to a wide variation of investment performance. Comprehensive and concise surveys are given by EBRD [1994 chap.9], Meyer [1995] and UN [1995 chap. 2]. The main trends described in the survey studies have been presented in the previous section.

Determinants of Investment

Theoretical work has pointed to the importance of factor-cost advantages [for instance Ozawa 1992, Arva 1994], as have comparisons of CEE with East Asia [Urban 1992, Meyer 1996]. DFI was expected to utilize lower factor costs in the CEE region and invest in export-oriented production facilities. Eastern Europe and the CIS still have very low labour costs compared with Western Europe although higher than some locations in South-East Asia. In the early years of transition, economic policy strengthened this advantage by effective undervaluation of the exchange rate and through incomes policy. However, the cost advantage was eroded by low manufacturing productivity, due to outdated capital stock, weak infrastructure and an underdeveloped legal and institutional framework. Nevertheless, the region should be able to develop strong comparative advantages for intermediate level technical skills as the level of education in the region is relatively high. Factor cost advantages may also arise from low costs of raw materials, which are still subsidized in some countries, notably Russia.

The issues of investment motives has been of prime interest in a long series of survey studies among Western firms with investments in CEE and among JVs within the region (Table 2.10). They consistently report that markets are the main attraction of the region. Even most of the early country-specific studies recognize that. For instance, in the OECD study, of 162 interviewees, 71 gave 'access to large domestic markets' as their prime reason for attractiveness of the partner country, followed by 'market share' (42), 'market potential' (18), 'low cost of production' (15), and 'source of raw materials' (11) [OECD 1994, table 4]. The attraction of the markets arises from the catch-up demand to Western levels of consumption and the expectation of sustainable economic growth.

Table 2.10 Selected enterprise surveys on DFI in CEE

Authors (and sponsors)	Time of study	method, respondents and response rate	Main focus of the study
Genco, Taurelli & Viezzoli 1993	1991 to 1992	questionnaire, 87 Western firms (48 investors w. 107 projects) 27%	obstacles to and problems of DFI
Gatling 1993 (Business International)	July 1992	questionnaire, 34 Western firms operating 82 projects in CEE, plus interviews	characteristics of investment projects, business strategies
Engelhard & Eckert 1994	fall 1992	questionnaire, ca. 269 German companies known to be active (19%)	entry processes: sequence of organizational modes
Lyles 1993	1991 to 93	interviews managers of 201 JVs in Hungary	performance of JVs
Möllering et al. 1994 (German-Czech CoC)	Aug to Sept 1993	questionnaire, 300 German firms, 149 investors (20 %)	type of activity, motives and performance
OECD 1994	Nov 1993	interviews with 291 managers of Western companies (162 investors)	characteristics, motives, obstacles, support by institutions.
Duvvuri et al. 1995 (German-Hungarian CoC)	summer 1994	questionnaire, returned by 101 German parents (30%) and 58 affiliates in HU (15%).	type of activity, motives and performance
Ali & Mirza 1996	Jan 1995	questionnaire, 67 British firms active in PL & HU (15%).	entry mode, and performance
Lankes & Venebles 1996 (EBRD)	1995	interviews 145 projects.	motives & obstacles, control modes, esp. host country variations
Laurila & Hirvensalo 1996 (Bank of Finland)	1995	questionnaire 345 Finnish companies	pattern of Finnish DFI in CEE
Knight & Webb (1997)	late 1995	questionnaire, 151 UK firms with business in CR or PL 51%	motives, experience
Pye (1997)	spring 1996	questionnaire, 334 affiliates of Western firms (27%)	characteristics, motives, control modes, changes over time.

Note: For each study only one publication with summary results is reported. See NERA [1991], McMillan [1991], Pfohl et al. [1992], Collins and Rodrik [1991], Wang [1993], Wimmer and Wesnitzer [1993], Benito and Welch [1994], Hoesch and Lehmann [1994], Klavens and Zamparutti [1995] and Sharma [1995] for further survey studies.

Cases of production relocation are observed in textiles, clothing, furniture or musical instruments manufacturing [Savary 1992, Borsos 1995, Estrin, Hughes and Todd 1997, Graziani 1998, Boudier-Bensebaa 1998] especially for intermediate rather than final products [Estrin and Richet 1998, Møllgaard 1997]. The aggregate evidence suggests that these are industry-specific exceptions from the main pattern [Meyer 1995a, Andreff and Andreff 1997]. An interesting outlier suggests that almost as many Italian firms were interested in low labour costs as in markets [Mutinelli 1994]. Other evidence suggests that the factor cost aspect gained more importance over time [Lankes and Venebles 1996]. It appears more important for small firms and for firms from the directly neighbouring countries Germany [Möllering et al. 1994, Kurz and Wittke 1997], Austria and Italy [Szanyi 1995]. The cost differential is also utilized by outward-processing trade, where an Eastern firm manufactures a labour-intensive stage of the production process. It may be organized through DFI or contractual arrangements [Graziani 1998, Lemoine 1997, Pellegrin 1997].

Correspondingly, the survey studies confirm that market size and expected growth are the most important determinants of DFI, along with political and economic stability. Factor costs, especially labour costs, are reported as a secondary aspect in attracting foreign investors.

The most frequently reported obstacles to investment relate to the high investment risks in the region. Risks are associated with the uncertain political and legal environment and a volatile economy; with unpredictable changes in relative prices in the liberalization process; with uncertainty on the value of property rights and with unclear export market access, particularly to the European Union. Typical risks of developing countries such as expropriation were perceived less important. The risks vary hugely across the region, with Hungary and the Czech Republic being perceived as relatively low-risk [see for example Lankes and Venebles 1996]. Möller [1996] reviews risks affecting investors in the food and beverage industry in CEE and presents a mathematical model that enables a comprehensive risk assessment.

The second category of obstacles is the underdeveloped legal infrastructure and the bureaucracy. The bureaucracy did not develop smooth administrative routines for their relations with foreign investors. Over time, the legal framework has developed, usually but not always, towards consistency and market orientation. Yet their smooth implementation has been constrained by capabilities of the bureaucracy and the development of a respected court system. Bureaucracy-related problems arise from inconsistent guidelines for decision-makers within the bureaucracy as well as from interests of the local administration and, in some countries, corruption. The legal framework has been adapted towards the rules and regulations of the European Union. However, this often complicates procedures as the administration is not trained to implement these rules smoothly. The problems for investors lie less in the rules themselves than in the documentation firms have to provide to show what exactly they are doing [Møllgaard 1997].

Thirdly, investors were deterred by low productivity and the lack of infrastructure in telecommunications and transportation. As discussed above, these are the more visible consequences of misguided industrial development during central planning.

Entry Strategies

Recent research has observed a number of strategic motives affecting the investment decision, the characteristics of the project or the timing of entry. The starting point for most research exploring strategic motives is the empirical observation that DFI in CEE is particularly common in industries with worldwide oligopolistic market structures. For instance, Böckenhoff and Möller [1993] compare privatization in various sectors of the food industry in Hungary. They found that foreign investors focus on concentrated industries, where acquisition gives 'comparably easy access to a significant market share and high barriers to entry ... will deter new entrants'. Also, industries that require less interaction with local suppliers were more attractive for foreign investors.

DFI in CEE is an outcome of the global strategy of the investor. As such it has been analysed in case studies [Estrin, Hughes and Todd 1997, Sander 1995, Mirow 1996]. Global oligopolistic competition spills over into Eastern Europe. DFI in CEE may ease Europe-wide strategies of price discrimination or product differentiation, or prevent competitors from following such strategies [Estrin, Hughes and Todd 1997]. As a typical strategy, Kurz and Wittke [1997] point to firms producing a specific product segment in CEE which fits both the CEE markets and the lower market segment in Western Europe. A pan-European multinational can utilize a network of operations using different resources and thus achieve higher degrees of specialization and flexibility.

For many American MNEs present in West European markets, CEE is just another market which they integrate into their worldwide or European product manufacturing and branding strategies. Some companies also appear to invest in the region to gain or secure entry to the EU market. This is particularly the case with American and, recently, Korean investors. In contrast, most European investors take a country-specific approach [Gatling 1993, OECD 1994]. This applies notably for the many small and medium-size firms active in the region.

After deciding to become involved in CEE, firms face the choice of various entry strategies. In the early years, investors often followed foothold strategies that would give them entry to a market, but delay commitment of substantive amounts of capital investment [McMillan 1991, EBRD 1994]. Such 'platform investment' [Kogut 1983] provides them with opportunities to learn about the local environment and prepare for upcoming opportunities. Learning and positioning were important motivations at very early stages in Hungary [Marton 1993] and in the Soviet Union [Samonis 1992, Fey 1995].

In order to gain a long-term advantage, many investors pursue 'first-mover advantages'. In the survey by Lankes and Venebles [1996], such advantages were perceived to be important by about half the market-oriented investors in the region. Pye [1997] reports first-mover advantages as the most important of several strategic motives. First-movers expect long-term benefits from brand-building and access to distribution channels. They may be able to acquire the sole local distributor in their industry or favourably influence the new regulatory framework.

On the other hand, first-movers face high investments in training and promotion. Followers may benefit from more educated local partners, officials and customers and avoid mistakes made by the leader. Many cases have been observed where a fast-second was able to overtake and establish itself as the market leader [Estrin and Meyer 1998]. The second-mover advantages can, theoretically, lead to a 'waiting game' where oligopolists wait for the rival to break the market [Sels 1996, Konings 1996].

Other investors are asked to invest by a major customer that has established local operations and wishes to procure supplies or services with their industry-standard of quality. This motivates investment by suppliers of services or intermediate goods, for example in business services and the financial sector, and in the automotive industry [Harwitt 1993, van Tulder and Ruigrok 1997].

Bridgewater, McKieran and Wensley [1995] further distinguish entry strategies as first-mover, client-follower, option-taker (high risk projects) and deal-maker (projects with short pay-back periods).

Ownership and Mode of Entry

When DFI was first permitted in 1971 (Romania) and 1972 (Hungary) investment was constrained by many regulations, including a requirement of JV-ownership. Before 1989, generally no majority foreign-owned operations were permitted. Thus, for many early investors a JV was the only feasible mode of establishing a local operation. Since then, regulations have been relaxed gradually. By 1992, DFI was fairly unregulated in Hungary, Poland and Czechoslovakia, and in most other countries soon afterwards [EBRD 1994]. However, in Russia many regulations still remained [McMillan 1994].

Thus, the share of JVs used to be high, especially in manufacturing. However, there has been a massive shift towards fully owned affiliates, both by new investors and old investors increasing their equity share. Recent surveys report a higher share of WOS than earlier studies [Möllering et al. 1994, Duvvuri et al. 1995, Sharma 1995]. JVs established earlier may or may not have been converted into wholly-owned affiliates.

Recently, a trend towards greenfield projects is observed in manufacturing [Svetličič 1994, Rojec and Jermakowicz 1995]. The Johanson-Vahlne model of increasing involvement in the internationalization process receives support, but many firms move in very quickly, even establishing WOS as their first activity [Engelhard and Eckert 1994, Ali and Mirza 1996]. One form of entry which has been specific to the region has been called 'brownfield': investors acquire a local firm but replace the existing physical capital stock almost completely, retaining only intangible assets such as brand names or the workforce [Estrin, Hughes and Todd 1997].

The choice between JVs, acquisition and greenfield projects depends on industry-specific factors such as labour intensity, concentration, supplier and distribution networks and restructuring costs [Dunning and Rojec 1993, OECD 1994]. In the early years, acquisition in transition countries generally required participation in the privatization process. Variations in entry modes have been observed across industrial sectors [Rolfe and Doupnik 1996] and host countries [OECD 1994, Lankes and Venebles 1996, Pye 1997]. Differences between countries of origin emerge between firms based in close proximity, such as German, Austrian or Dutch firms, and those further away, especially British and American firms. Sharma [1995] and van Dam *et al.* [1996] stress the importance of risk aversion of American investors choosing low control modes. The determinants of entry modes and forms of ownership are analysed more systematically in chapter eight.

Non-equity forms are used as an alternative mode of entry. Surveys show many cases of licensing and franchising in East-West business, sometimes in combination with equity investments [OECD 1994, Möllering et al. 1994]. Subcontracting selected stages of production is particularly popular with German [Naujoks and Schmidt 1994, Dyker 1996] and Italian firms [Graziani 1998]. Contractual alternatives to DFI are considered in chapter seven.

Performance

Hooley et al. [1996] present a very comprehensive comparative study of the performance of foreign-owned and local firms. They distinguish six types of ownership in Hungary for data collected around 1991: cooperatives, state-owned, state-private JVs, privately owned, state-foreign JVs and private-foreign JVs. They find performance differences across categories which by some criteria distinguish the foreign from the local firms, but some criteria show different dividing lines. For instance, firms with foreign ownership are more likely to have implemented a long-term strategy, focus on market share, develop new products, and focus on high-quality-high-price products.[13] Only foreign-private JVs aspire towards market domination and entry into new markets. Export-orientation is higher for state-foreign JVs, followed by, surprisingly, state-owned firms and private-foreign JVs. Profits and return on investment are highest for JVs with foreign participation, but closely followed by domestic private firms. Among the other ownership forms, the cooperatives appear to have most difficulties in adjusting to the new environment.

The performance of foreign investment projects has also been analysed on the basis of enterprise level statistics by for instance Lane [1995], Kubista [1995] and Hunya [1996]. Typical findings are that foreign-owned firms are more export- and import-oriented, and are less labour-intensive than local firms. The results concerning profitability are inconsistent. Interestingly, the performance of JVs and fully foreign-owned firms appears to differ with respect to their profitability and their export performance. In the subjective assessment of questionnaire respondents, wholly owned operations are judged to perform better in the investors' own opinion [Lyles 1993, Möllering et al. 1994].

More detailed understanding of successful JVs are obtained in interview surveys of both domestic and foreign partners of JVs. Such survey studies have been conducted in for example Hungary [Lyles and Baird 1994, Meschi 1995], Russia [Fey 1995, 1996, Thornton 1997] and Kazakhstan [Charman 1996, 1996a, Szymanski 1996]. The success of a JV depends mainly on issues such as the compatibility of the objectives of the parents and the establishment of mutual trust. International business experience of the local partner is important, as is the Western partner's management training. Empirical studies suggest that shared management with considerable influence of both the local and the foreign partner has a positive impact on both JV performance [Lyles and Baird 1994] and the acquisition of knowledge [Lyles and Salk 1996]. Furthermore, JV performance has been studied at the organizational level. Puffer [1996] and Michailova [1997] have found many organizational conflicts arising from incompatible corporate culture of the parent firms. The organizational culture and individual attitudes in CEE have been shaped by the experience of central planning and do not easily adopt to the needs of a market-driven enterprise.

The results suggest that careful preparation and partner selection are important for the performance of a JV. Many successful entrants have chosen to form a JV with a partner they knew from previous business experience. Alternatively, and especially in Russia, reputation effects and self-enforcing contracts are important when overcoming the weaknesses of the institutional framework [Thornton 1997]. Preparation includes not only the negotiations on the formation of a JV, but also discussions between the partners on the objectives of the project, and the agreement and commitment of mutual responsibilities of the parents. However, Western partners frequently report that the negotiations on the establishment of JVs have often been lengthy and tedious, especially with state-owned partner firms. They are inhibited by the Eastern partners' frequent lack of experience in international business and by their unclear lines of responsibility [Antal 1995, van Zouweren *et al.* 1996].

Impact on the Transition Process

DFI contributes to the transition and development of CEE economies through several microeconomic and institutional effects besides the well-known macro-economic effects [McMillan 1993, Estrin, Hughes and Todd 1997]. Initially, the need for additional foreign capital for the economic restructuring was emphasized [IMF et al. 1991]. Formal modelling of potential macroeconomic effects focuses on the impact on international trade and the balance of payments [Abel and Bonin 1992, Devreux and Roberts 1997]. Except for Hungary, the inflow of capital was low in the early years of transition when capital was needed the most. Continued large DFI inflows enable the servicing of the large external debt in Hungary [Hamar 1994, Hunya 1996]. For other countries, concerns were raised that the inflow of too much foreign capital, of which DFI is a major component, contributes to monetary expansion and thus inflationary pressures [Nuti 1995] or encourages consumption rather than investment [Calvo, Sahay and Végh 1995].

Theoretically, the impact of DFI on trade balances is ambiguous. Foreign-owned firms export more than domestic firms, but also import a larger share of their inputs. Especially at an early stage the net impact on host countries in CEE was negative because of: (a) a large number of marketing and sales-only projects; (b) the import of capital goods to establish local production facilities; (c) the lack of local suppliers, which have developed only over time. MNEs may emphasize the integration of acquired firms into their global network at the expense of the maintenance and growth of local supplier relations. On the other hand, they make an important contribution to international trade becoming increasingly diversified and upgraded through access to advanced technologies and international markets [Naujoks and Schmidt 1995].

Data on exports by foreign affiliates are available for several countries and show that foreign affiliates export a larger share of their production than do local firms [for example Quaisser 1995]. However, data on imports are rarely published in a comparable format and consequently the net-effect on the trade balance is difficult to assess. The UN takes the very optimistic view that 'beginning with 1993 DFI contribution to the trade balance of most CEE countries has been positive' [UN 1995, p. 112]. In Hungary, JVs as a group ran a trade deficit half the size of Hungary's total trade deficit [Hamar 1995, Hunya 1996]. With the largest DFI stock, Hungary had the largest trade deficit in the region in the first half of the 1990s.

Direct effects on employment tend to be small as DFI contributes more to output and capital formation than to employment [Borsos 1995, Hunya 1996] and privatization-related DFI often requires lay-offs of a large number of employees.

A wide consensus suggests that the most important contribution of DFI is the transfer of know-how. This includes technological know-how and, especially important in CEE, managerial knowledge in finance, marketing and organization [McMillan 1993, Murrell 1992a, Kogut 1996, Svetlicic 1994a, Quaisser 1995]. Casson [1994] emphasizes the transfer of cultural values of entrepreneurial behaviour. MNEs transfer values and norms that are conducive with success in a market economy, such as entrepreneurial risk-taking and cooperative behaviour in teams. Hopefully, their example spills over to local entrepreneurs. Thornton [1997] finds a different kind of intangible contribution: a US investor guarantees quality control and, through their reputation, enables international market access.

Case and survey evidence suggests that investors invest heavily in training their local workforce and even local suppliers [for example Sereghyová 1995, Thornton 1997]. In many cases, for example in the automobile industry, the technology implemented in CEE is world-leading [Harwitt 1993, Dyker 1996, Estrin, Hughes and Todd 1997]. Imported technological know-how through DFI or otherwise makes an important contribution to the development of human capital and thus productivity. The argument made in the development economics literature [Bhagwati 1985, Ozawa 1992, Lall 1996] easily extends to the transition economies. An important aspect of technology transfer is its diffusion beyond the foreign affiliate, via forward and backward linkages [Svetlicic 1994, Woodward et al. 1995] or the movement of employees. However, DFI is only one mode of acquiring modern technology, contractual arrangements offer alternative modes [Urban 1992, Radice 1995a, Dyker 1996].

Some authors question whether DFI actually contributes to the development of indigenous technological capabilities [Dunning and Rojec 1993, Sugden and Thomas 1994]. MNEs usually centralize R&D activities and have thus been seen to reduce R&D in their locally acquired companies [Sereghyová 1995a, Papánek 1995]. Expectations of Russian research institutes that their foreign JV partner would help gaining access to Western markets have frequently been disappointed [Fey 1995]. On a positive note, foreign-owned firms report higher R&D spending than domestic firms in Hungary [Hunya 1996].

A different contribution of DFI specific to the transition context is their involvement in restructuring formerly state-owned enterprises. Estrin and Earle [1993] classify the main tasks of enterprise transformation as: (a) depolitization, that is breaking the link between governments and firms, (b) restructuring the organization, (c) restructuring employment and other inputs, and (d) social criteria. Foreign acquisitions are superior to domestic ownership, state or private, by the first two criteria due to the foreign investors' corporate culture and know-how. The restructuring of employment may be more rigorous under foreign control than under insider control, which evolved in many CEE countries. However foreign investors avoid enterprises in need of major labour shedding. Also they tend to be less sensitive to social sensitivities in the host economy [Estrin, Hughes and Todd 1997]. Foreign-owned firms have restructured more actively than domestically owned firms [UN 1995, Meyer 1997]. They are in a better position to induce corporate restructuring because they can contribute essential financial and managerial resources, they have a clearer vision of the objectives of restructuring, and immediately command effective governance.

DFI also contributes to increased competition through entry, linkages and by being an example, and to institution-building through the establishment of Western practice and lobbying [McMillan 1993, Kogut 1996, Radice 1995, 1995a]. A related contribution is the signalling effect of DFI on the credibility of reform. DFI inflow is by some used as an indicator of the medium-term perspective of the local economy. Therefore, it provides a signal that is important because of the role that self-fulfilling expectations can have for the success of transition and for the second wave of foreign investors [Gál 1993].

Negative effects of DFI may arise for instance if foreign firms negotiate protection for their locally produced goods [EBRD 1994, Svetlicic 1994a], by crowding out local competitors, by involvement-concentrated industries [Vissi 1995] or in sectors with highly distorted economic incentives [Booth and Record 1995].

Policy Issues

To attract DFI, the most important aspects of government policy are not DFI-specific measures, but the commitment to systemic transformation and the general economic policies implemented to ensure macroeconomic stability, infrastructural development and the establishment of a market-oriented legal framework [for example Agarwal et al. 1995a, Borsos and Erkkilä 1995]. Macroeconomic stability made major progress in most countries, as did the improvement of the infrastructure although starting from a low level.

Several papers discuss policies that should be adopted *vis-à-vis* foreign investors. If the objective is to achieve particular goals of technology transfer or competition, the authors argue in favour of an active policy [van Brabant 1993, Dunning and Rojec 1993, Cantwell 1993, Guerrieri 1995, Hunya 1996]. However, regulation should allow MNEs to experiment and to introduce new ideas of corporate governance [Kogut 1996]. Incentives such as tax incentives are generally rejected as costly and ineffective [for example Agarwal et al. 1995]. There are doubts whether or not CEE institutions can follow a flexible industrial policy with similar successes as in East Asia [Radice 1995a]. Also, an active competition policy similar to the practice in the West is recommended [Estrin and Cave 1993, Fingleton et al. 1996].

Some disagreement emerged about the desirable degree of openness of the trade regime. On the one hand, infant industry may require temporary protection [for example Dunning and Rojec 1993]. On the other hand, distortions could be exploited by MNEs in their favour. The openness of the trade regime is an important part of the transition process, especially for price liberalization, and induce import competition and to increase the credibility of the reforms. The trade policy of CEE in the early 1990s is mainly determined by the Europe Agreements.

The most important tool of industrial policy is, often unacknowledged, the privatization policy. The way the state-owned firms are privatized and restructured has major implications for the industrial structure of the economy in the long term. Already major differences are emerging between the economies of CEE which are somewhat related to different historical conditions, but to a greater extent a result of different policies followed during the past years. The Polish economy has recovered with the force of many new small businesses while the Czech economy is highly dependent on the large enterprises privatized through the voucher scheme. The Hungarian economy is dominated by firms that are at least partly foreign-owned. tese differences are a result of different privatization policies and will have major implications for the future industrial structure of the countries [Comisso 1997].

Privatization through sale to foreigners is an option that contributes to the speed of transition, and to government revenues, but also has some drawbacks [Dunning and Rojec 1993]. The experiences of the privatization process are far more complex than any theory would suggest. The process of 'foreign privatization' has been studied using a case method [Rojec, Jasovic and Kusar 1994, Estrin et al. 1995]. DeCastro and Uhlenbrock [1997] compare privatization from the acquirers' perspective between post-communist, developing and industrial countries. Interestingly, they find more required investment commitments and fewer JVs in post-communist economies.

DIRECTIONS FOR THIS RESEARCH

The literature synopsis shows that the patterns of DFI have been established in broad terms. Therefore this study focuses on determinants of investment decisions and characteristics of DFI projects. The following three research questions have motivated this research:

- Why was DFI so low in most countries until 1994?
- How does the special environment of CEE influence volume and characteristics of DFI?
- How does the pattern of activity differ between German and British firms?

The first question is concerned with the economic determinants of direct investment. The aim is to understand not only why companies engage in the region, but also why many others do not invest. Therefore, the empirical part of the study covers firms with and without DFI in the region, and focuses on their decisions to become involved in various forms of West-East business, including DFI.

The second question relates to the interaction of the local environment with the strategies of foreign businesses. The analysis focuses on observed patterns of activity with respect to similarities and differences in patterns described in the international business literature. It includes more specific questions such as the relative importance of market and factor-cost related investment motivations and their evolution over time. Is DFI driven by market attraction or by factor costs? What determines investors' choice of DFI over other forms of international business? Why do investors frequently choose JV entry? Who is entering via acquisition of local firms? Who participates in the privatization process?

To analyse the issues, the host countries that the empirical study focuses on have been selected to reflect a variation in both the host country policy environment and in observed DFI in the early years of transition. These are Hungary, Poland, the Czech Republic, Russia and Romania.

A special feature of this study is the comparison of enterprises from two countries of origin that have different patterns of activity in the region. Three main lines of argument suggest that German firms would be more active: (1) they have had closer relationships with the region throughout the past decades, and often established direct contacts through acquisitions in former East Germany. (2) They are geographically closer which reduces transportation costs and thus eases exports and subcontracting, and (3) they face higher labour costs due to the real appreciation of the Deutschmark and high social costs that make production relocation a more attractive option.

The second part of the book reviews theoretical and empirical research on DFI in other parts of the world. From this work, propositions will be developed for factors expected to determine DFI in CEE. The empirical analysis in Part three will investigate whether or not these determinants also drive DFI in CEE - and how the special environment affects DFI.

NOTES

1. On objectives and options for privatization also see Lipton and Sachs [1991], Borensztein and Kumar [1991] and Welfens and Jasinski [1994].
2. The actual privatization processes are reviewed in Estrin [1994], Boyko, Shleifer and Vishni [1995], Brada [1996] and Estrin and Stone [1996].

3. Various concepts for mass privatization and their advantages over other forms of privatization are discussed by Bolton and Roland [1992], Frydman and Rapaczynski [1993] and Nuti [1994].

4. See any of the survey studies, many sponsored by sceptical observers at the World Bank: Pinto, Belka and Krajewski [1993], Estrin, Brada, Gelb and Singh [1995], Fan and Schaffer [1994], Brada, Singh and Török [1994], Estrin, Gelb and Singh [1995], Pinto and van Wijnbergen [1994], Earle and Estrin [1996], and Earle, Estrin and Leshchenko [1996], Basu, Estrin and Svejnar [1997], Pohl et al. [1997], Smith, Cin and Vodopivec [1997].

5. See for instance Aghion and Carlin [1997], Frydman and Rapaczynski [1997] and Woo [1997]

6. Rollo and Smith [1993] and Baldwin, Francois and Portes [1997] show that the actual costs of openness to the EU are fairly small as the adjustments required by Western industry and agriculture are within the range of normal economic adjustment processes.

7. Some authors from within the region prefer the term 'strategic investor' over direct foreign investor. They wish to emphasize that the investor takes a long-term interest in the firm. The control-based definition for DFI includes the 'long-term' aspect, though the term does not make that explicit. However, the concepts are identical.

8. Of the CEE countries, few report reinvested profits. In 1995, Poland reported US$888 million, Estonia US$15 million and Lithuania US$7 million. Table 2.3 *excludes* reinvested profits to enable cross-country comparisons.

9. Data on DFI are available from the National Bank of Poland in BoP-statistics earlier than the IMF figures referred to in the main text, but they use a far narrower definition of DFI reporting only 284, 580, 542 and 1,134 million US$ for the years from 1992 to 1995, respectively. Using these data, the EBRD reports far less DFI in Poland than other sources.

10. The common practice of reporting DFI data in US$ does not reflect the trends appropriately for intra-European investment. The depreciation of the DM versus the US$ leads to an understatement of the increase in local currency of the German (and other West European) investment.

11. Korean investment has been given considerable attention in the business press, especially the projects by Daewoo [for example *The Economist* 27.1.1996, *Financial Times* 18.8.1995, 10.2.1996, *Business Eastern Europe*, May 1997].

12. For a more extensive list of references see Meyer [1997].

13. Lyles, Carter and Baird [1996] find that local single-owner firms are most likely to follow a low-price strategy, local partnerships follow a premium-price strategy with US-Hungarian JVs taking an intermediate position by both criteria. The foreigners' superior knowledge of low-cost production (assumed by the authors) is counterweighted by their better access to capital.

PART TWO

The Theory of Direct Foreign Investment

3.   Determinants of Direct Investment: A Review of the Literature

A comprehensive review of the literature on direct foreign investment (DFI) invariably becomes a *tour d'horizon* of the field of International Business. Disciplines from Economics and Finance to Strategic Management, Marketing and Organizational Behaviour have contributed to the present understanding of DFI. This chapter reviews the literature on DFI with focus on determinants of DFI.[1] It considers DFI at different levels of aggregation, including macroeconomic flows of DFI-capital, industry and firm level analysis, as well as individual decisions by firms.

Early research analysed DFI as a financial flow. As researchers recognize the specific characteristics of direct, rather than portfolio, investment, they focus on three issues: the location of production, the sources of firm-specific advantages, and the reasons for integrating different business units in one firm. John Dunning's OLI paradigm incorporates these three issues. It is now the most common analytical tool for the determinants of DFI and it is applied in this study.

The limitation of the framework is its ability to explain dynamic processes. Therefore, this review pays special attention to recent advances of economic theory addressing the dynamics of DFI. Dynamic models focus on particular types or aspects of DFI and thus are less general than the OLI paradigm. The most familiar dynamic approach is that of the internationalization process models based on the work of the Uppsala school in the 1970s. Recent advances include the rediscovery of economic geography in the work of Paul Krugman and Michael Porter, the integration of MNE into models of international trade by James Markusen, Elhanan Helpman and, again, Paul Krugman, as well as the game-theoretic analysis by the Leuven school. The appendix presents another dynamic approach to DFI, the developmental model. It relates economic development of a country to the characteristics of DFI outflows.

Table 3.1 summarizes economic theories by their level of analysis and whether they focus on static or dynamic analysis. This categorization serves as orientation only. In some cases dynamic theories have developed from static theories, as is the case with the developmental model. In other cases the pairs reflect contrasting views. Internalization and internationalization theories account for some of the most lively encounters at academic conferences. Table

3.2 lists the multitude of theories with their main analytical concepts, original contributors and recent reviews or extensions.

Table 3.1 Theories of direct foreign investment

Unit of analysis	Static analysis	Dynamic analysis
Financial flow of DFI	Capital markets approach, Macroeconometric analysis	Exchange rate analysis
Location of production	Theory of location (L), Institutional analysis	Developmental model, Economic geography
Firms and competition	Resource based view, Ownership advantages (O)	New international trade theory, Game theory
The scope of the firms	Internalization theory (I)	Internationalization process models

DFI AS CAPITAL FLOWS

On an aggregate level, DFI is analysed as a flow of capital between countries. Theoretical research on this level has evolved from financial market analysis and the aggregation of microeconomic theory. Recent research focuses on dynamics of DFI flows which includes exchange rate effects. Available aggregate data permits extensive empirical analysis which is not feasible at lower levels of aggregation.

Capital Markets Approaches

The first response by economists to the emergence of DFI was to observe the new phenomenon 'through the filters least disturbing to reigning paradigms of the profession' [Vernon 1994: 138]. Considering Thomas Kuhn's 'The Structure of Scientific Revolutions' [1962], Vernon [1994] finds it all but surprising that capital market approaches to DFI have been dominant in the 1960s.

The basic premise is that MNEs face differentials in international capital rents and use DFI to overcome barriers to international capital flows. They finance themselves in countries with a relatively high capital endowment and hence lower interest rates. They invest in countries with a relatively low capital endowment and high capital costs. DFI serves as international capital arbitrage. In this framework, international return differentials determine DFI stocks whereas changes in relative return determine DFI flows. As DFI also transfers other resources than capital, these resources also have to yield a higher return abroad to make DFI profitable. This differential rate of return hypothesis has been analysed empirically but has often been insufficient in explaining DFI [see Agarwal 1980 for review]. It can, however, explain DFI in the nineteenth century due to high transaction costs in capital markets at that time [Hennart 1991].

Table 3.2 Core concepts and major contributors

Theory	Early contributors	Recent work and reviews
Capital markets approach	Aliber 1970 Agmon & Lessard 1977	--
Exchange rate analysis	Logue & Willet 1977 Batra & Hadar 1979	Froot & Stein 1991 Kogut &Kulatilaka 1996
Macroeconometric analysis	Scaperlanda & Maurer 1969	Clegg 1995
Theory of location	Mundell 1957	Dunning 1993
Institutional analysis	Kobrin 1987 Guisinger et al. 1985	Stopford & Strange 1991 Loree & Guisinger 1995
Developmental cycles	Vernon 1966 Kojima & Ozawa 1984 Dunning 1986	Ozawa 1992 Narula 1995 *see appendix 3.1*
Resource based view	Hymer 1960/1976 Kindleberger 1969	Yamin 1991 Dunning 1993
Industrial organisat./ game theory	Knickerbocker 1973 Dixit 1980 Krugman 1983	Markusen 1995
Internalization theory	Caves 1971 McManus 1972 Buckley & Casson 1976	Dunning 1993 Casson 1995 *see chapter 4*
Economic geography	Marshall 1920 Krugman 1991	Krugman & Venebles 1994, Malmberg, Sölvell & Zander 1996
Internationalization process model	Johanson & Wiedersheim-Paul 1975 Luostarinen 1979	Johanson & Vahlne 1990 Nordström 1991 Andersson 1993
Eclectic paradigm	Dunning 1977	Dunning 1993, 1995

Aliber's [1970] widely cited hypothesis of optimal currency areas assumes that MNEs can finance themselves in hard currency countries. They earn a 'currency premium' by utilizing the interest differential between hard currency and weak currency countries because their creditors do not recognize the risk of devaluation associated with DFI in weak currency areas. Therefore they pay lower capital costs than competitors in local markets, whose capital costs are increased by a risk premium to compensate the creditor for the expected devaluation.

The financial market approach became more comprehensive when the trade-off between yield and risk was incorporated. Firms maximizing yield and minimizing risk diversify their investment portfolio by international investments, as do financial investors. If the systematic risk profiles of the home and foreign markets are less than perfectly correlated, then the risk of an internationally diversified portfolio is lower than that of a purely national portfolio. The capital asset pricing model has been extended to become an international asset pricing model. It can explain diversified DFI as a reaction to barriers and costs pertaining to international portfolio capital flows. By lowering these barriers, MNEs contribute to the integration of international capital markets [Agmon and Lessard 1977, Errunza and Senbet 1984]. For private investors, investing in an MNE becomes an alternative to investing in an inter-national investment fund.

The empirical support for the ability of portfolio investment models to explain direct investment is weak [see Agarwal 1980, Stehn 1992 for reviews]. In recent years, the international liberalization of financial markets has made this motive for DFI increasingly irrelevant with respect to investment between industrialized countries which accounts for most DFI.

Dynamic Macroeconomic Analysis

DFI flows are a function of firms' desired capital stock in given foreign locations, according to their long-term plans. Individual investment decisions determine the timing of a given DFI project. This timing is sensitive to changes, anticipated changes and volatility of major environmental variables, as well as uncertainty. DFI flows react very sensitively because generally they are irreversible. Sunk costs are high due to plant-specific investment, personnel recruitment and training, market research, and negotiations with foreign partners and governments.

Changes in the environment can create temporary cycles of DFI flows as MNEs adjust to new levels of desired foreign holdings. Such changes arise in tax and tariff policies, innovations in corporate finance markets, liberalization of service sectors, or privatization processes. Once the finite number of firms which can make use of new business opportunities have invested, DFI flows drop to their previous level - at a higher level of stock. The reaction to change may involve substantial adjustment costs. Implementation lags may drive a temporary wedge between desired capital stock abroad and the actual capital invested. Also anticipated changes of for example investment incentives, can lead to a rush or delay of DFI and thus cause cycles.

On the other hand, due to so-called 'hysteresis effects' [Dixit 1990, Pindyck 1991], temporary influences such as taxation and exchange rate revaluations, can have long-run implications for the permanent stock of DFI even though the temporary influence has long disappeared. An enterprise investing during an incentive program or a favourable exchange rate constellation will not necessarily withdraw if these cost factors become less favourable, such that the country in question would not attract similar projects again. Divestment decisions depend on expected future cash flow only and ignore sunk costs. Therefore volatile exchange rates and exchange rate expectations will induce investment flows that follow different cyclical paths as increasing investment during a devaluation is not matched by an equivalent divestment during a revaluation. Baldwin and Krugman [1989] made this argument for international trade, showing how entry and exit decisions during a temporary shock can lead to a different equilibrium after the shock although the cause of the shock has been removed. Kogut and Kulatilaka [1996] apply this approach to DFI.

Exchange Rate Analysis

The issues arising from volatility and uncertainty of environmental variables have been discussed in most detail for exchange rates. In perfect capital markets the revaluation of exchange rates does not affect investment flows as both domestic and foreign investors have access to the same financial markets. Three independent lines of arguments have been made why this may not be so.

A devaluation of foreign currency reduces the share of foreign assets in an investor's portfolio. With an unchanged risk evaluation, the share of foreign assets should remain constant. Thus a 'portfolio rebalance effect' induces selling of domestic and buying of foreign assets [Logue and Willet 1977]. Froot and Stein [1991] reach a similar conclusion by assuming imperfect capital markets with information asymmetries: since investors are better informed than bankers on a given project, financing will always require a contribution of an equity share from their own wealth. If a temporary devaluation changes the value of the investors' wealth in foreign currency, this 'wealth effect' will enhance the ability to invest abroad: the same funds buy more foreign assets.[2]

Third, only changes in real exchange rates affect decisions on location of production. Changes in nominal exchange rates influence only the timing of DFI, not the general trend. A real devaluation of foreign currency reduces relative foreign labour costs and thus leads to more DFI. Local production replaces exports from the home base [Kohlhagen 1977], possibly smoothly, as the adjustment to desired capital stock is lagged [Goldsbrough 1979]. However, this result does not necessarily hold if constant marginal cost functions are not assumed to be constant [Batra and Hadar 1979]. Empirical tests of the influence of the wealth-effect versus the labour cost argument on DFI into the US found support for the wealth effect [Klein and Rosengren 1994].

Exchange rate risk can be hedged in financial markets if it is short- or medium-run and in a commonly traded currency. In this case it 'only' causes transaction costs (TC). To reduce TC and to minimize unhedgeable risk the firm may change its investment decisions. It can reduce 'exposure', that is the net cash flow in foreign currency. Models of MNEs with exchange risk generally find a positive relationship between DFI and exchange risk, as DFI replaces exports. The reason for this relationship is that, when engaged in DFI, only repatriated profits are exposed to exchange risk. As regards exports, all sales revenues are received in foreign currency while costs arise in domestic currency [Itagaki 1981, Batra and Hadar 1979, Calderón-Rossel 1985]. Cushman [1985, 1988] empirically supports this line of argument. These results contradict pure portfolio models [Hartman 1979] that predict a negative correlation.

Exchange risk furthermore induces firms to invest in more locations to be able to react flexibly to changes in real local costs of production [see Kogut and Kulatilaka 1996, Aizenman 1992]. Also, an initial investment can serve as a platform for subsequent entry where the timing of entry is triggered by movements in the real exchange rates [Kogut and Chang 1996].

Macroeconometric Analysis

The diversity of DFI is a major obstacle to macro-level analysis, both to modelling and to empirical research. Macroeconometric research combines financial data, such as those discussed above, with microeconomic determinants of DFI derived from firm-level theoretical work. The most commonly tested variables include market size, market growth, factor costs, trade barriers, as well as interest rate differentials and exchange rate movements. This research has used three different kinds of data set: cross-country inflows of DFI from a source country, cross-industry data of DFI inflows, or time-series of DFI into a particular country. The time-series approach is most popular as capital flow data is readily available and econometric techniques are well-developed. The dependent variable is DFI as measured in the balance of payments or changes in recorded DFI stock.

Market size and growth are considered in all these studies, as penetration of foreign markets is a major motive for DFI. GDP and the change in GDP are the most common proxies and generally significant.[3] Low labour costs are generally presumed to attract DFI as they reduce costs of production. However, it is difficult to show this empirically because low labour costs are associated with low income and thus low local demand.[4]

Exchange rate effects are tested but empirical results are on the whole as inconclusive as the theoretical research [for example Cushman 1985, Stevens 1993, Clegg 1995]. Relative interest rates reflecting the cost of borrowing were however frequently significant [for example Cushman 1985, 1988, Pain 1993 and Clegg 1995, but not Culem 1988]. Institutional aspects can often only be captured by dummy variables that indicate the presence of condition. For instance, dummies for tariff discrimination and the time of membership in the European Union were significant [Culem 1988 and Bajo-Rubio and Sosvilla-Rivero 1994]. Economic risk of macroeconomic instability is related to the inflation rate and reduces investment [Bajo-Rubio and Sosvilla-Rivero 1994].

THE LOCATION OF PRODUCTION

Theory of Location

The traditional basis for analysis of international economic activity in the real (rather than monetary) sector is the neoclassical theory of international trade. However, it provides however no framework for explaining the existence or development of DFI. It explains international trade in terms of comparative advantages of the participating countries based on the assumption of perfect competition. Certain resources or factors are immobile, production functions and consumer preferences are identical, and specialization is incomplete. Countries specialize in production which uses factors of production that are relatively abundant. Trade leads to an equalization of factor prices (Heckscher-Ohlin Theorem). In this model the assumption of perfect competition eliminates MNEs.

Early attempts to model DFI use a modified factor endowments-based model of international trade. An early popular hypothesis was Mundell's [1957] 'factor endowment theory' that showed that, under certain assumptions, capital flows can substitute trade if barriers prevent the free flow of goods. This type of DFI allocates factors of production in a trade-reducing and inefficient way as it does not utilize comparative factor-cost advantages.

Trade theory suggests that location of international production is based on comparative advantages of factor costs. If firms use DFI to minimize costs, it will move to the location where production costs are lowest. However, empirical evidence shows that trade barriers and labour costs are a very incomplete framework to analyse the location of DFI. The concept of 'locational advantages', as reviewed by Caves [1982] and Dunning [1993], covers many influences. While popular debate still focuses on production costs, research suggests that the attractiveness of the local markets is at least as important.

Production cost advantages are an important component of locational decisions in industries with low transportation costs. Their DFI depends on costs of production in alternative countries, in particular productivity-adjusted labour costs. Thus factors influencing productivity are determinants of DFI. This includes transportation and telecommunications infrastructure, quality of the human capital, for example education and employee motivation,[5] and quality, reliability and costs of local supplies. Facilities processing natural resources naturally depends on the existence of natural resources.

Market-related advantages are increasingly replacing factor costs as the prime determinant of DFI. Proximity of the production to the market becomes the overriding consideration in any of the following situations:

- Protectionism (tariffs, quotas, administrative barriers to trade) can be bypassed by DFI. It can jump tariff barriers and obtain or maintain market access, and even extract rents generated by trade barriers. Also, DFI can be a means to prevent or preempt anticipated protectionist measures and to establish presence in a trading bloc.[6]
- Transportation costs are a natural barrier to trade. They are diminishing in relevance due to modern transportation technology but are still relevant for bulky goods and fresh food.
- Production and sales activities may be indivisible, especially in service industries (hotels, banking, trade, consulting). DFI in the service sector is of increasing importance, but has often been neglected by academic research focused on manufacturing [McCulloch 1988].
- The interaction between production and sales activities may require local production. This includes cooperation with downstream firms, such as just-in-time delivery or long-term reliable supplies. Local production can improve performance by increasing flexibility, after-sales service, or access to market information or technological know-how, which in turn influence innovation, product design or marketing.
- Investment in distribution channels may complement exports to the host economy. Acquisition of existing distribution networks from local competitors or adaptation of established local brand names are fast market penetration strategies [Sölvell 1987].

Investment of these types is becoming more important along with modern management in production and marketing. It depends primarily on the potential market, that is market size and growth, plus costs of local production. This provides a theoretical rationale for empirically established positive effects of host country market size and growth on DFI.[7] However, according to Dunning [1993: 142] the potential loss of a market is the paramount driving force behind market-oriented investment and is of greater importance than gaining entry into new markets.

Developmental Model

Comparative advantages of nations evolve with the process of economic development. On this basis, stages models relate the product cycle [Vernon 1966, 1979] or the economic development of the source country [Dunning 1986, Ozawa 1992, Narula 1995] to outward DFI. Simultaneously, research has focused on differences of DFI within East-Asia and other regions of the world [for example Kojima 1978, Lee 1990, Ramstatter 1991]. This stream of literature ise reviewed and extended in appendix 3.1 with the objective of developing a model of the interaction between changing comparative advantages and inward and outward DFI flows.

Economic Geography

The location of economic activity in geographic space has largely been analysed independently of mainstream economics in the field of economic geography. Krugman [1991] highlights the importance of this work for the explanation of regional concentration of economic activity. Alfred Marshall [1890/1916] already points out the causes of economic agglomeration:

- the pooling of markets for specialized skilled labour,
- the development of subsidiary trade and suppliers of intermediate inputs,
- the flow of information, especially technological know- how, between firms.

Krugman's work focuses on modelling the agglomeration process, especially external economies of scale in labour and input markets. Fixed costs in the industry, regional dispersion of the markets and transportation costs determine the cumulative process of concentration. The locational patterns can change very suddenly: once a critical mass of capital and industry-specific infrastructure is accumulated, investment moves to new centres that may evolve by historical accident or temporary protectionism [Krugman 1991].

Krugman [1992] formalizes the tensions between scale-related 'centripetal' and market-related 'centrifugal' forces of locational decisions. In simulations he shows the agglomeration of economic centres with given economies of scale, transportation costs, immobile farmers, and mobile production workers. The same argument applies to DFI. It is the international allocation of mobile capital in the presence of immobile workers and complex barriers to trade. Research extending this approach primarlily uses simulation techniques [for example Krugman and Venebles 1994, Markusen and Venebles 1995].

These arguments imply that the existing industrial structure can be a major determinant of inward DFI. Suppliers of intermediate goods and a technologically specialized labour force are locational advantages for related firms and competitors.[8] The effects are especially observable for DFI because of specific externalities:

- Service industries such as banks and consultants follow their customers [Erramilli and Rao 1990], but once established they provide services and information to other potential investors.
- Local individuals and institutions adapt to the needs of foreign MNEs: managers may learn foreign languages, governments set up foreign investment agencies and change the legal framework, and local businesses upgrade their quality standards.
- Suppliers of intermediate goods follow their customers, as widely reported in the automobile industry.

Other research focused on the third aspect of externalities: the exchange of knowledge. Innovation processes tend to be localized, and knowledge is highly tacit at early stages of development and tends to stick to the local milieu [Aydalot 1986, Malecki 1991]. Intense innovative activity in an area contributes not only to firms' competitiveness [Porter 1990] and the evolution of multinational firms [Sölvell, Zander and Porter 1991]. It also attracts additional investors who wish to participate in the innovative activity.

Access to localized knowledge is increasingly important for the advancement of technological competence of MNEs [Cantwell 1989]. Thus, especially the location of R&D activities follows patterns of similar or complementary technological competence in the local environment, leading to a cumulative process. The Swedes Malmberg, Sölvell and Zander [1996] call it the 'Greta-Garbo-effect' after the Swedish actress who was attracted to Hollywood and later herself attracted more business related to the movie industry. This approach can explain apparently paradoxical phenomena such as Korean DFI in the Californian semiconductor industry: by becoming insiders they gain access to the knowledge pool in Silicon Valley for the benefit of their own innovation and development.

Institutional Analysis

The general institutional framework in both source and host countries influences the volume of DFI and its characteristics. This consists of the social environment as well as the legal, institutional and general policy environment ('Ordnungspolitik'). Research has mainly focused on host country policies rather than on countries of origin, presumably because most countries take a neutral attitude towards outward DFI [Meyer, Ambler and Styles 1994]. Exceptions are Japan in the 1970s when outward DFI was supported actively [Ozawa 1979b], and Sweden [Blomström and Kokko 1995].

Empirical evidence suggests that the general policy framework plays a more important role in attracting DFI than fiscal measures specifically designed to attract DFI. This includes the openness of the economy [Li and Guisinger 1992], approval procedures and bureaucracy, tax regime, environmental regulation and other aspects of business law. The nature of regulative environment may become a significant advantage over alternative locations or the home location if the latter is tightly regulated in specific industries, for example by environmental standards. For instance, negative effects of the social or institutional environment can arise with uncooperative bureaucracy, restrictions on foreign ownership and profit remittance, or a high degree of unionization and union bargaining.

At best, specific fiscal incentives and tax allowances geared towards DFI play a marginal role although they may influence the choice of location within a country or region. This evidence is regularly found in studies of DFI into developing countries [Guisinger et al. 1985, Hill 1990] as well as industrial countries [Safarian 1993].[9] However, specific incentives and requirements for DFI influence the performance of DFI, for example the local content of inputs or the share of exported output.[10] The impact of governmental policy on the competitive structure of markets and DFI, however, differs between industrialized and developing countries [Brewer 1993].

In the increasingly interrelated world economy the relationships among companies, among host and home governments, and between companies and government are increasingly intertwined and complex [Stopford and Strange 1991]. Major investment projects are increasingly subject to individual negotiations between investor and host country agencies, not only in the case of privatization-related DFI. The relative bargaining power of the MNE *vis-à-vis* its host government has been used successfully to explain the organizational form of DFI as weaker MNEs have to accept a JV partner [Kobrin 1987, Gomes-Casseres 1991]. Game-theoretic models have been developed to analyse some of the emerging interaction between institutions and MNE [for instance Vannini 1995, Haapanranta [1996].

A peculiar aspect of the institutional framework is political risk. It arises with potential changes in the legal framework of any of the countries involved which affect the return on investment of DFI. It includes the impact of political violence or revolutions as well as the changes in the structure of taxes, tariffs and the regulatory environment. All these can induce major changes in relative prices. Thus small changes may have a major impact on the profitability of foreign investments.

Political risk is generally reported as a major deterrent of DFI in survey-based studies. The econometric evidence is weak, however, mainly due to problems defining political risk and finding appropriate proxies.[11] Studies using indices based on the quantity and intensity of political events are not very successful in explaining DFI flows. They show the relevance of political variables, but their impact on DFI was small compared with economic variables: Nigh [1985] finds significant effects of inter-country conflict and cooperative events and - in developing host countries - of internal political events. Schneider and Frey [1985] compare various models and obtained best performance of a model that included several both economic and political variables. Edwards [1990] uses indices by Cukierman, Edwards and Tabellini [1992] for the probability of change in government and for political violence but found significant impact on DFI only by the former. Chase, Kuhle and Walther [1988] use commercial risk indices to proxy political risk and find no support for the hypothesis that country risk is compensated by a higher return on investment.

INDUSTRIAL ORGANIZATION

DFI is most prominent in industries with large economies of scale, intangible assets, high product differentiation and worldwide oligopolistic market structures. This is mainly horizontal DFI among high income economies rather than vertical DFI that would take advantage of factor cost differentials [Markusen 1995]. Oligopolistic competition strongly suggests that at least the short-term dynamics of DFI and the timing of investment, if not the location decision as such, are influenced by strategic motives. Multinationals consider their strategic positions *vis-à-vis* their main rivals in their most important markets to decide on market entry and investment projects. This section considers which advantages may induce DFI, how strategic interaction affects DFI in oligopolistic markets, and why firms internalize international business.

Sources of Competitive Advantage

A major school of thought views incomplete markets as the main reason for DFI. Foreign investors have a competitive disadvantage relative to local competitors due to lack of information on local market conditions and higher costs of communication and transportation. To overcome these disadvantages and to operate profitably in foreign markets, they must have some kind of firm-specific advantage. This explanation of DFI as a function of firm-specific or 'ownership advantages' is related to the 'resource-based view' of the firm [Penrose 1959/1995, Wernerfelt 1984, Conner 1991] in the management literature.

Since Hymer [1960/1976] and Kindleberger [1969] many sources of firm-specific advantages have been analysed. In order to induce DFI, the advantage has to be both transferable within the MNE and specific to the firm. Thus the firms have to possess some degree of monopolist power.[12] In addition - as argued in the transaction cost approach - internal transfer has to be superior to an external transfer [Caves 1971]. In this framework multinational firms are mainly exporters of the services of firm-specific assets [Markusen 1991, 1995]. Dunning [1993] distinguishes three firm-specific, or 'ownership', advantages:

* resources based on the assets of the firm, including property rights and intangible assets,
* advantages of common governance of the established firm over a de novo entrant,
* advantages of common governance arising because of multinationality.

Relevant corporate assets include physical assets, intellectual property rights and intangible assets embodied in the human capital of the firm, such as management, engineering, marketing and financial capabilities. In terms of Prahalad and Hamel [1990], competitive advantages arise from 'core competencies' such as technological know-how, and 'value-creating activities' such as total quality control and just-in-time manufacturing systems. In other cases, firms may possess assets that arise from the regulatory environment, for example preferred access to natural resources.

Advantages of common governance arise from economies of scale on firm level rather than on plant-level. This includes centralized R&D and marketing or favourable access to resources. Advantages of multinationality arise from market power, worldwide accumulation of technology, and business contacts and knowledge of managing a worldwide network of activities. Operating in a variety of environments exposes MNEs to many challenges and innovations which stimulate the development of specific competencies and learning opportunities which are not available to purely national firms [Bartlett and Ghoshal 1989]. Therefore ownership advantages become increasingly specific to the firm and independent of the asset base and economic structure of the home economy [Narula 1995]. Advantages of multinationality can have a reinforcing 'experience effect'. Firms established internationally are best positioned for further expansion because acquisition of knowledge is a cumulative process of interaction between the creation of technology and its application in production [Pavitt 1987, Cantwell 1989].

Empirical studies have focused on the identification of relevant firm-specific advantages. The review of this research by Dunning [1993: 142-3, 148-53, 160-4] suggests that the most important advantages are technology-related, including capabilities of generating technological know-how, as well as brand names and marketing knowledge. The effect of multi-plant industries conferring back advantages to their owners, receives some support, while the experience effect is empirically difficult to separate from other effects. However, the empirically significant firm-specific advantages vary widely across source countries. For instance technology[13] and marketing assets were of great significance for US firms, but not for Japanese [Hennart and Park 1994].

Strategic Competition

The analysis of oligopolistic competition among MNEs has for a long time considered two effects: Graham's 'exchange of threats' hypothesis, and Knickerbocker's 'follow the leader' hypothesis. More recently game-theoretic models consider DFI as a strategic move within oligopolistic competition in order to obtain first-mover advantages. Formal models have also been developed by international trade economists introducing market imperfections and firm-level economies of scale into their models.

Graham [1975, 1978] models intra-industry DFI resulting from the 'exchange of threats' between rivals. In his model firms finding their domestic market invaded by a foreigner will retaliate by attacking the monopolistic position of the rival in his home market. This strategy is particularly relevant for capital-intensive production processes with significant economies of scale. The basis of the argument is a model of Cournot-type competition between two firms, both enjoying monopolies in their home market but with different marginal costs. Graham identifies conditions that trigger an entry into the rival's market. The argument is further refined by considering experience curve effects that reduce marginal cost as the volume of production increases, creating incentives to increase output at an early stage in order to slide down the experience curve sooner than the competitors. He concludes that the exchange of threats maintains competition, but in a less cut-throat form than between enterprises with large production facilities and low marginal costs. Graham [1985] extends the argument by suggesting that this cross-investment would accelerate new product development and make collusion less likely.

Knickerbocker [1973] suggests that dominated firms in an oligopoly imitate the strategy of the leader to prevent him from gaining an early lead advantage by establishing a position in the market and factually raising entry barriers. Scharfstein and Stein [1990] model this 'follow the leader' pattern: with managers of the follower being assessed in their performance through comparison with the leader. With an imitation strategy their downside risk is to miss a major opportunity. Investing in a project similar to the leader may be more risky in absolute terms but not relative to the position of the leader.

The hypothesis implies that DFI increases with industry concentration. Knickerbocker [1973] and Flowers [1976] detect a concentration of entry by firms in the same industries. The phenomenon increases with industry concentration, but decreases with very high concentration which they interpret as indicating tacit collusion in very narrow markets. The hypothesis receives further empirical support by Yu and Ito [1988] who compare DFI in a competitive and an oligopolistic industry, and Li and Guisinger [1992] who analyse service MNEs. However, the phenomenon may be explained in an alternative way: (a) followers may assume that the leaders have undertaken proper market research and his investment thus 'signals' an investment opportunity; (b) the leaders contribute to the local infrastructure by their externalities which make the location more attractive for suppliers, customers, and, subsequently, competitors;[14] (c) the effect may be spurious as both competitors react to a common external stimulus such as market liberalization.

Porter [1990] focuses on push factors arising from the competitive nature of the home market. He argues that domestic competition strengthens firms' competitive advantages because it creates permanent challenges for improvements. This competitive strength makes firms 'fit' for international competition where they may compete with a competitor from the same region of origin [Porter 1990: 117-22]. Dominated firms in oligopolistic competition may actually lead the move abroad because they face limits to expansion in their domestic markets [Mascarenhaas 1986, Ito and Pucik 1993].

Other researchers focus on the interaction between the foreign investor and local agents. Dixit [1980] presents a game-theoretic model to analyse the interaction between an MNE and a potential competitor. DFI can be a strategic move to deter entry: by choosing the DFI option the MNE can deter a local competitor from emerging, as his post-investment decisions are based on the lower marginal costs of local production. Extending the model, Smith [1987] and Jacquemin [1989] show that DFI can replace exports even in the absence of tariff barriers: DFI simultaneously reduces transaction costs and increases market power through a commitment of sunk costs because the locational decision is irreversible.

Further models of strategic motives inducing DFI have been developed by what should be called the 'Leuven school' of DFI. For instance, Motta [1992] shows how the decision between exports and DFI becomes non-monotonic because of the interaction with the potential local competitor. In Motta [1994], he shows how DFI can crowd out an existing local competitor as well as a competing MNE exporting to the country. Veuglers [1995] presents a model in which firms are induced to become multinational by their domestic rivals' (potential) DFI, because they may incur competitive disadvantages in their home markets. Sels [1996] considers a waiting game between two potential entrants with externalities from the first mover.

Modern International Trade Theory

The neoclassical theory of international trade assumes perfect competition. Only by dropping this assumption can it explain issues related to DFI which include intra-industry trade and locational decisions of MNEs. Models have been developed to illustrate locational decisions of multinational firms and, building on these models, alternative patterns of multinational firms under different policy regimes.

Locational decisions of firms in imperfect markets have been modelled on the basis of intra-industry trade models. Krugman [1983] presents two models of horizontal and vertical MNEs with firm-specific advantages. Horizontal MNEs are modelled as a response to product differentiation. Costs of producing locally are assumed to be higher than at home, but if marginal costs of exporting exceed the marginal costs of local production, the firm shifts its production to the market. Vertical MNEs are explained in a model of a monopsonistic downstream firm that can eliminate the distortions of monopsonistic markets by international backward integration. Along similar lines Helpman [1984, 1985] and Helpman and Krugman [1985] analyse locational decisions for single plants in general equilibrium trade models with increasing returns on the level of the firm and a given non-competitive market structure with differentiated products. Markusen [1984] and Horstmann and Markusen [1987a] consider multiple plants under a single headquarter.

The next generation of models by Horstmann and Markusen [1992] and Brainard [1993] has endogenous market structures in which they show the emergence of MNEs. Both models have firm-level activities with joint inputs across plants, plant-level economies of scale, and tariffs or transportation costs between the two countries in the model. MNEs emerge in equilibrium if firm-level fixed costs are large and tariffs and transportation costs dominate plant-level scale economies. MNEs are more likely to exist if both countries are large and, in Brainard's [1993] model, if the countries have similar relative factor endowments. Horstmann and Markusen [1992] also show that small changes in the underlying locational advantages, for example taxation, can cause major shifts in the market structure because of movements between different Nash equilibria resulting in jumps in prices and output.

Markusen and Venebles [1995] use this model as the basis for simulations showing that, for countries of similar size, multi-plant MNEs displace international trade. Markusen et al. [1996] and Markusen [1997] analyse alternative trade and investment regimes and suggest that, under full liberalization, MNEs may locate one function in each country replacing the multi-plant MNEs. Between countries of similar size and factor endowment, no MNEs emerge. New international trade theory has been combined with game-theoretic models of the Leuven school by Motta and Norman [1996] and Sanna-

Randaccio [1996] in order to analyse the effects of economic integration. Their models show how the removal of trade barriers triggers market-seeking DFI.

Similar models have been used to analyse licensing versus DFI decisions. The internalization theory (discussed in Chapter 4) has explored incentives in great detail but international trade economists have provided more formal models. Ethier [1986] considered market failure due to informational asymmetry with respect to the value of the technology being licensed. Horstmann and Markusen [1987b] consider incentives of franchising contracts where the franchisor has to monitor the quality of the local franchisee to protect his reputation. Ethier and Markusen [1996] and Saggi [1996] consider the potential diffusion of knowledge that may create third market competition. Horstmann and Markusen [1996] use an agency model to analyse the incentives between a licensor and a licensee who has superior information on the local market. They show how DFI is motivated by the unwillingness to share rents with a local licensee. Temporary licensing may be preferred if costs of investment mistakes due to unfamiliarity with the market are high.

THE SCOPE OF THE FIRM

Internalization Theory

Internationalization theory explains the emergence of multinational enterprises from the failure of markets. Its roots are in the transaction cost (TC) approach initiated by Coase [1937] but it has largely been developed independently of the well known work on TC by Williamson [1975, 1981, 1985]. Early contributions are Caves [1971], Buckley and Casson [1976], McManus [1972], Swedenborg [1979], Rugman [1981] and Hennart [1982].

The views of researchers of internalization theory do not differ in substance from those of transaction costs economists, but in emphasis: whereas Williamson's arguments focus primarily on market failure due to lock-in effects arising from asset specificity, internalization theory focuses on market failure in markets for information. Many assets transferred by MNEs to their affiliates partially have a public-good nature such that market transactions fail due to information asymmetries. Chapter 4 reviews the concepts of this literature and develops a synergetic model. Some authors, in particular Rugman [1981, 1985] and Hennart [1995], argue that internalization is a sufficient explanation for the existence of MNEs. This view contrasts with Dunning's OLI paradigm where all three conditions, ownership, location and internalization, are necessary to explain DFI. In this study Dunning's view is adopted.

Transaction cost economics (TCE) treats decisions on engaging in a transaction and its internalization as distinct and is therefore a static approach.

Some dynamic approaches to TC have aspired to overcome this limitation: Buckley [1988, 1990, Buckley and Casson 1985] incorporates dynamic aspects of corporate expansion and strategic actions, which are taken not to overcome market failure, but to create or exploit it. Internalization incentives arising from strategic positioning have been incorporated in one 'internalization theory'. This approach takes an opposite line of reasoning: rather than deriving internalization incentives from market failure, it defines them as the motive that may lead to an internalization decision. Langlois' [1992, 1995] dynamic view of transaction costs sees boundaries of firms entirely determined by capabilities of the firm rather than market failure. He argues that in an uncertain environment, common ownership of multiple stages of production is a superior institutional arrangement for coordinating systemic change.

Kogut and Zander [1993, 1995, Zander and Kogut 1995] depart from the market-failure approach of TC arguing that the transfer of tacit knowledge explains internalization. Markets are not considered to be a feasible alternative because of the need for an organizational mode to transfer tacit knowledge. Thus the creation, accumulation and transfer of tacit know-how determine the evolutionary growth of firms.

Internationalization Process Model

The theories reviewed so far consider DFI as determined by characteristics of the firm and its environment. Researchers on internationalization processes analyse the international business of a firm as a gradual process. Based on the early contributions by Johanson and Wiedersheim-Paul [1975] and Johanson and Vahlne [1977], this research is frequently called the Uppsala school. Other early contributors are Luostarinen [1979] in Finland, and in the American literature Bilkey and Tesar [1977], Cavusgil and Nevin [1981].

The model by Johanson and Vahlne [1977, 1990] is rooted in the behavioural theory of the firm following Cyert and March [1963] and Aharoni [1966] as well as the growth theory of the firm by Penrose [1959/1995]. The gradual increase of firms' international involvement is explained by an interplay between the development of knowledge on foreign locations and operations in the countries, and, on the other hand, an increasing resource commitment. Knowledge on foreign markets is 'experiential knowledge' which cannot be taught. It can only be acquired through experience and active involvement in the country. Such knowledge is essential for resource commitment because it enables recognition of business opportunities and reduces market uncertainty. Therefore, past commitment and accumulated country-specific experience determine current activities as well as future resource commitments and involvement on a higher level. American researchers modelled the process analogous to innovation adaptation as incremental increases of experience and learning over multiple stages [Cavusgil 1980, Reid 1981].

This understanding of the internationalization process has three implications. Firstly, firms will typically follow an 'establishment chain' moving from lower to higher modes of involvement. This has led to a number of stages models: the Swedish school suggests an initial phase with no regular export activities, then exports via independent representatives, then sales subsidiaries, and eventually local manufacturing [Johanson and Wiedersheim-Paul 1975, Johanson and Vahlne 1990, Nordström 1991]. Other models have additionally introduced contractual business such as licensing and JVs as stages of the internationalization process [Root 1987, Young et al. 1989, Kay 1991].

The second implication is that firms enter markets in a sequence starting in countries in close 'psychic distance'. This term, first used by Beckermann [1956], includes not only geographical but also cultural, political and linguistic communalities between the home and the host economy [Johanson and Wiedersheim-Paul 1975]. Traditional business ties also reduce unfamiliarity and thus increase present DFI. Luostarinen [1979] argues that even similarity of the economic conditions and market size favour an early entry.[15] Thirdly, initial investments in a country can serve as a platform for learning about a market or to allow customers to develop brand loyalty. A platform creates an option for further DFI and taking advantage of emerging opportunities [Kogut 1983, Kogut and Chang 1996].

Case study research frequently found support for the sequential entry pattern.[16] However, the pattern was established primarily for firms at an early stage of internationalization [Forsgren 1989]. The relative importance of psychic distance appears to have declined since the 1970s as economic conditions are becoming more important, for example industry- specific barriers to entry [Sölvell 1987], market potential and industry structure [Nordström 1991]. Also, firms move more rapidly from low to high involvement modes and may even leap-frog some stages of the traditional model [Nordström 1991, Engelhard and Eckert 1994].

The limitations of the internationalization process models are, first, a weak delineation of theoretical boundaries, that is the underlying assumptions and scope of the models; second, weak explanatory power and, third, insufficient congruence between the theoretical and operational level [Andersson 1993].

A SYNTHESIS: THE ECLECTIC PARADIGM

John Dunning [1977] integrates many theories surveyed in this chapter into a general paradigm of international production. He extends the framework repeatedly [1981, 1988, 1993], most recently to explain strategic alliances [Dunning 1995]. The basic premise is that DFI is undertaken if three conditions are met simultaneously. If not, exporting or licensing may be superior strategies. Based on the acronyms of the three components, this approach is commonly known as the 'OLI-paradigm'.

- The investing firm needs 'ownership advantages', that is specific assets to obtain a competitive advantage over local competitors. They include property rights and intangible assets, named 'Oa advantages', as well as advantages arising from common governance, named 'Ot advantages'. Oa advantages include advantages due to abilities that facilitate the generation of new assets, especially knowledge. Ot advantages are capabilities of organizing Oa advantages with complementary assets. They include (i) those of branch plants of established enterprises over *de novo* firms, and (ii) those arising specifically from multinationality.
- The host country must possess 'locational advantages' which include factor cost advantages, proximity to the market, the existing economic structure, and the legal, social and political frameworks.
- 'Internalization incentives' must make it more efficient for the MNE to use its competitive advantage by selling components internally rather than in the market place. These advantages may arise from market failure as discussed in the transaction cost and internalization literature (see Chapter 4), but may also arise because of distortions in the regulatory environment.

This chapter has given a condensed summary of the various streams in the literature that contribute to the explanation of DFI. It sets the scene for two lines of theoretical work that shall be extended in the next chapter: the internalization or transaction cost approach.

NOTES

1. Dunning [1993, chapter 4] gives a comprehensive survey of the theory of DFI in a mainly microeconomic context. Pitelis and Sugden [1991] present a collection of papers on current issues related to the theory of the multinational firm, of which Cantwell [1991] gives a comprehensive discussion of the state of the art. Markusen [1995] reviews modern international trade literature related to DFI. Also see Lizondo [1991] and Meyer and Rühmann [1993]. Agarwal [1980] surveys earlier theoretical and empirical literature.
2. The model assumes that the long-term expected value of foreign assets in home currency is independent of current exchange rates.
3. GDP and/or GDP growth have been tested by, inter alia, Hultman and McGee [1988], Culem [1988], Barrel and Pain [1991], Bajo-Rubio [1991] as well as Bajo-Rubio and Sosvilla-Rivero [1994]. Clegg [1995] found a surprisingly negative effect. O'Sullivan [1993] and Millner and Pentecost [1992] defined the relevant market beyond the host country, by refering to the European Union.
4. This applies to time-series studies [Goldsbrough 1979, Cushman 1988, Barrel and Pain 1991, Pain 1993, 1996, Bajo-Rubio and Sosvilla-Rivera 1994] as well as cross-country studies [Swedenborg 1979, Kravis and Lipsey 1982, Schneider and Frey 1985, Woodward and Rolfe

1993, Yamawaki 1993, Thiran and Yamawaki 1995, Döhrn 1996].

5. Educational and technological infrastructure was shown to be significant in attracting DFI by Swedenborg [1979], Cantwell [1989] and Yamawaki [1993]. For this reason some studies found a positive association between endowments with skilled labour [Svensson 1996], or the wage level, and DFI [Swedenborg 1979, Thiran and Yamawaki 1995].

6. Pain [1996] and Döhrn [1996] estimate the impact of the integration in the European Union on DFI flows and find a significant positive effect on flows to the countries of the union.

7. See cross-country studies by Swedenborg [1979], Kravis and Lipsey [1982], Dunning [1980], Veuglers [1991], and Svensson [1996], time-series studies cited above, and reviews by Lizondo [1991] and Stehn [1992].

8. Svensson [1996] found empirical support for an industry agglomeration index attracting DFI.

9. The impact of general tax legislation and specific tax allowances on DFI has been analysed empirically by Root and Ahmad [1978, 1979], Lim [1983] and Woodward and Rolfe [1993] for DFI in developing countries, and Grubert and Mutti [1991], He and Guisinger [1992] and Loree and Guisinger [1995] for outward DFI from the US.

10. This arises in Guisinger et al. [1985], Wells [1986], Hill [1990],and Loree and Guisinger [1995].

11. Recently, Brunetti and Weder [1997] established the effect of various indicators of institutional risk on the (domestic) investment rate.

12. The monopolistic nature of firm specific advantages has been of major concern to Hymer [1960/1976], Kindleberger [1969, 1984] and others because of the potential extraction of monopolistic rents from the host economy. For instance, Newfarmer [1985] and Cowling and Sugden [1987] are concerned with collusion between MNEs that may become more likely if they develop similar international structures and more easily can agree on any collusive action. See Yamin [1991] for a review of research following the market-power approach in Hymer's work. Most researchers of MNEs apply a Schumpeterian view of competition where monopolistic advantages are temporary and create incentives for innovation and dissemination of new products.

13. Technological capabilities are commonly measured by the ratio of R&D expenditures in turnover. Empirical research established a positive relation between R&D expenditure and the propensity for DFI [for example Caves 1974, Mansfield, Romeo and Wagner 1979, Grubaugh 1987, Hennart and Park 1994, Wagner and Schnabel 1994, Kogut and Chang 1996, Svensson 1996].

14. The empirical studies use broad industry classifications which cannot distinguish between 'follow the leader' and 'follow the customer' as is commonly the case for automotive suppliers and services.

15. Casson [1995] presents a formal model of entry decision-making and shows which conditions would favour sequential entry, including expected similarities between alternative foreign markets, and their differences to the home market, low costs of deferred entry, and high costs of learning combined with low costs of communicating experience from the first to the second foreign country.

16. See for example Johanson and Wiedersheim-Paul [1975], Luostarinen [1979], Larimo [1985], Buckley, Newbold and Thurwell [1979], Davidson [1980], Veuglers [1991] Jansson [1993], Chang [1995]. Contradictory findings emerge from Hood and Young [1983]. The entry sequence pattern does not seem to apply to service industries such as advertising agencies [Terpstra and Yu 1988]. A possible explanation is that the internationalization of business service firms is driven typically.

APPENDIX 3.1: A DEVELOPMENTAL MODEL OF DIRECT FOREIGN INVESTMENT

Developmental Approaches to DFI

The developmental approach to DFI is discussed in this appendix in detail as it has special relevance to the East European case. To begin, the various contributions in the recent literature are summarized, subsequently a model is presented that illustrates the forces driving DFI between countries at different stages of their economic development. It relates the economic conditions of the home and host economies to the pattern of DFI.

The economies in CEE are middle-income economies in geographic proximity to the industrialized countries of Western Europe. This situation demands an analytical framework that can explain the role of DFI between countries at different levels of economic development. This framework should guide the search for the determinants of DFI from advanced into less advanced economies and describe its special characteristics. Using John Dunning's terminology: what home or firm-specific O-advantages would induce firms to take advantage of the low labour cost L-advantage of CEE?

Developmental approaches draw on various streams of literature on the interaction between DFI and economic development. The basic premise is that the structure of the economy influences DFI which in turn influences economic structures and development. In the process of development, some industries become uncompetitive in more advanced countries. They move to less advanced countries where the factor endowment is more appropriate for their production technology, and where they contribute to the accumulation of human capital. The model in the next section describes the mechanisms underlying this interactive process of development and DFI.

The intellectual antecedents of the model are the product-cycle hypothesis by Vernon [1966], the 'Japanese-type DFI' observed by Kojima [1978], and the relationship between stages of economic development and the pattern of inward and outward DFI first described by Dunning [1981a, 1986].

Vernon [1966] first proposed a dynamic model of DFI by relating it to the stages of the product cycle. Firms locate their innovative activities in countries where technological know-how is available, high income increases demand for high quality products, and a shortage of unskilled labour supply increases incentives for innovations. Innovators enjoy a temporary monopolistic position, which allows them to charge prices above marginal cost. Close co-operation between R&D and production activities enables the transfer of technology to the production line during the innovation phase of the product. Thus production in the industrialized home country supplies the home market.

As the product matures, competitors emerge in the domestic market and the innovator starts exporting to other industrial countries to maintain his leadership. Increasing demand and intensified competition with standardized products in the mass production phase leads to a relocation of the production to less advanced countries with comparative advantages in manual labour. Thus DFI emerges as part of a strategy that allows the innovator to maintain a competitive advantage over potential competitors throughout the product cycle. This hypothesis could explain American DFI abroad in the 1950s and 1960s when the USA was the only major source of DFI. However, as Vernon himself recognized [1979], this approach is less useful for explaining technological competition between Europe, Japan and the USA in the 1980s.

Kojima [1978] argues that Japanese DFI would be different from American DFI in that it is trade-creating rather than trade-replacing. He found that Japanese investors in Asia to made more use of the differences in comparative advantages of different locations. Ozawa [1979a] describes Japanese investment in Asia as a result of industrial upgrading in Japan itself: as the economy has advanced towards skill-intensive sectors, labour-intensive production processes and environmentally sensitive industries have moved to South-East Asia. The shortage of unskilled labour in Japan has led to investment in labour-intensive production in the economies of South-East Asia where labour costs were low. Recent research on DFI from the newly industrializing economies of Korea, Taiwan and Hong Kong found similar features [Whitmore, Lall and Hyun 1989, Lall 1991, Wells 1993].

Dunning [1981a] takes a more general perspective. His investment-development cycle draws connections between the character and composition of DFI outflows and the national stage of development of the home country. Early DFI tends to be resource-oriented, at first towards raw materials, later using cheap labour. DFI from mature industrial countries is more likely to be market-oriented and thus determined by the international competitive situation in the marketplace [also see Dunning 1986 and Tolentino 1987, 1993]. Using a similar approach, Ozawa [1992] relates the accumulation of physical and human capital of economic development to inward and outward DFI. In the factor driven first stage of development, inward DFI is factor-seeking while outward DFI is diminutive. In the second, investment-driven stage, inward DFI becomes market-seeking while outward DFI seeks low-cost labour. In the innovation-driven third stage both inward and outward DFI are market and technology-seeking.

Narula [1995] analyses the dynamics of the interaction between the competitive advantages of firms and the immobile locational advantages of countries in more detail. In the early stages of development, countries have mainly natural assets and their outward DFI is determined by this asset base and the economic structure at home. In the final stage, the asset base consists mainly of created assets such as human capital and infrastructure. The O-advantages of firms become increasingly independent of their home country as assets are created and acquired at many locations in the world. The created assets of any country at a given point in time are path-dependent on prior technological accumulation which depends on, among other things, inward DFI [see also Cantwell 1989, Kateseli 1991].

The stages model approach is useful as a descriptive tool. Yet, as with all stages theories its explanatory and predictive power is limited. This is particularly the case when applying it to a region with a very different economic structure. Therefore, this discussion focuses on forces driving DFI at a given stage in the process.

Structural Change and DFI

Economic development is a process of accumulation of physical and human capital. In this process economies move towards more sophisticated production technologies by acquisition of the necessary resources. In particular, higher levels of human capital enable higher productivity and thus higher income. The factor endowment of the economy becomes more capital and human capital-intensive. The industrial structure of the economy gradually changes towards the more skill-intensive sectors. (This is a simplification as other factors of production may also become prohibitively expensive such as real estate or environmental goods - due to regulation. The focus on human capital does not however change the general implications.)

Western Europe is at an advanced stage where, in Narula's [1995: 30-31] words, L-advantages 'increasingly take the form of the ability of countries to create and efficiently organize technological and human assets and to tap new markets'. O-advantages are increasingly firm-specific rather than derived from host country structures because they 'become globalized, their nationalities become blurred'. However, many small and medium-size enterprises (SMEs) are more appropriately described by intermediate stages. They primarily seek production factors or new markets. CEE is at an early stage of the process in that it possesses mainly natural assets and low-cost labour with some created assets such as technological expertise in selected areas.

In this situation DFI can emerge as a consequence of developmental adjustment processes in the advanced economy (Figure 3A.1). The evolution of locational advantages and especially of comparative cost advantages creates the environmental conditions that favour factor-cost oriented DFI. Some countries lose competitive advantages in sectors that other countries try to attract [Markusen 1991]. In the course of this structural change, certain stages in the value chain or whole production processes become unprofitable as they face competition from imports. The supply of untrained labour declines as workers have opportunities to increase their skill levels. This shortage of low-skilled labour, combined with maximum spreads of wages between the skilled and unskilled, undermines the international competitiveness of production processes based on unskilled labour. The core of untrained workers moves to sectors that are not exposed to international competition, in particular the service sector.

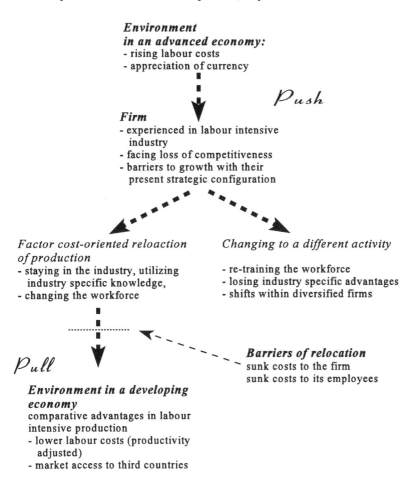

Figure 3A.1 Economic forces driving the 'Asian model' of DFI

Rising labour costs, often in connection with an appreciation of the currency, create strong push factors for labour-intensive firms. If they are unable to redesign their production processes by substituting low-skill labour with capital and knowledge-intensive technologies, they face barriers to growth in their present environment and lose international competitiveness. Nevertheless, they possess valuable assets that can be utilized through restructuring. Businesses in this situation face two strategic alternatives to put their assets and capabilities to best use:

- they can move into another sector, acquiring new technological knowledge and retraining their labour force, but losing their industry-specific assets, especially knowledge-based intangibles such as employee experience or exclusive technological knowledge, or
- they can move their production facilities - or the labour-intensive parts of the production process - abroad, utilizing their industry-specific assets but changing the labour force as they close domestic operations in the long run, and use the locational advantages of the host economy [Kojima and Ozawa 1984].

The choice between these alternative strategies depends on

- the attraction of potential low-cost locations,
- the nature of the firm's core competencies, and
- the sunk costs of implementing the relocation strategy.

The attraction of a potential foreign location for production creates the pull factors that draw factor-cost oriented investment. They depend on local labour costs, adjusted for labour productivity, and a wide range of secondary factors affecting production costs. For instance, the costs of local supplies vary due to access to raw materials and existence of local supplier network for intermediate products. The costs of bringing the products to the market depend on the geographical proximity to important markets, the trade regime, and the infrastructure. Additionally, the regulatory environment, including the tax regime and bureaucratic procedures, may raise costs substantially.

The nature of the core competencies of a firm is always a core determinant of corporate strategy. Diversified enterprises with mainly financial assets or capabilities embodied in employees that are not mobile, may prefer to shift to new industries. On the other hand, if assets are highly industry-specific and intangible they may prefer relocation, as this strategy can profitably combine lower local factor costs abroad with existing capabilities. Such capabilities include technological and managerial know-how, including knowledge about markets and reputation with customers [Wells 1993]. Due to their intangible or tacit nature they can often not be transferred via markets, as markets for knowledge-based assets are highly imperfect (Chapter 4).

DFI induced by structural change involves established MNEs as well as small and medium-size enterprises (SMEs) moving abroad for the first time. Since structural change creates very strong push factors it can induce major changes in corporate strategy such as the first step in the internationalization process of an enterprise. Thus structural change induces relatively many first-time investors and SMEs. As their investment behaviour differs from established MNEs, this will influence the characteristics of DFI. These investors have a strong preference for locations in close proximity to their home base where gathering experience is less costly.

Relocation involves, however, one-off expenses that are often unrecoverable sunk costs. Fixed costs are incurred by the firm as well as its employees and have to be weighed against the net present value of reduced production costs. Firms incur costs from exploring potential new locations and setting up new production facilities. Machinery may be immobile and has to be written off. In addition, labour legislation may require high redundancy payments to former employees. The human capital of laid-off workers is lost and new employees need firm-specific training.

Workers in the relocating firm face a loss of their human capital as their industry-specific training becomes worthless (sunk costs) at home after the structural change has been completed. As they are usually immobile they have to invest in education and training or face 'structural' unemployment. This explains the strong resistance of labour unions to structural change and thus inertia in the process. The job-specificity of qualifications and the inter-sectoral labour mobility thus affect the costs of the individuals and indirectly of the firm that has to restructure its workforce. These costs are highly dependent on the institutional environment in the home country.

The factor-cost oriented DFI described in this model is a special case of Dunning's [1993] general paradigm: structural change threatens the ownership advantages of certain firms in their established location. They can continue to use their ownership advantages in a less advanced country that has complementary locational advantages, especially labour supply. However, only DFI allows them to internalize the markets for their intangible assets.

Many scholars researching DFI in developing countries expressed the expectation that inward DFI could play a catalytic role in the process of economic development. For instance, Markusen [1991] argues that, via its 'linkages and leakages', know-how transferred by the foreign investor diffuses throughout the host economy and thus strengthens its locational advantages, especially the quality of the human capital. Externalities arising from the mechanisms described in the model lead to an often very positive assessment of the impact of this type of DFI.

This structural-change related DFI is by its motivation 'comparative advantage augmenting' in that its complementarity to the domestic human and capital resources makes its externalities particularly useful. It is considered 'desirable from the viewpoint of the developing countries' factor endowment' [Ozawa 1979b] and contributes to a balanced economic growth. Therefore an

MNE is not only 'a facilitating institution which helps to organize world production to optimally exploit comparative advantage' [Markusen 1991], but its externalities contribute to 'DFI facilitated development' [Ozawa 1992]. However, the empirical evidence for these arguments is mixed [Meyer 1996].

Since Western and Eastern Europe are at different stages of their development process the model may be applicable here. The model predicts that a certain type of DFI will emerge which has some desirable impact on economic development, and the following characteristics:

- Factor costs are a major motivation for DFI.
- Industries in the process of restructuring due to a loss of competitive advantages in their home location move their production activities to less advanced countries. Thus, firms facing barriers to growth in their established markets will be more active.
- This DFI comes from industries that are labour-intensive by the standards of the home country, but technology-intensive by the standard of the host economy. Firms with labour-intensive production will thus be more active.
- A relatively high share of this DFI comes from SMEs which prefer locations in close proximity to the home economy.

4. Transaction Cost Analysis of Direct Foreign Investment

Since the work of Coase and Williamson, transaction cost economics (TCE) has developed in many directions. In an international context it has been advanced simultaneously, but largely independently, as 'internalization theory' following Caves [1971], McManus [1972], Swedenborg [1979], Buckley and Casson [1976], Rugman [1981] and Hennart [1982]. In subsequent literature various complementary interpretations of the concept have emerged, including several empirical studies in an international context.

This chapter reviews and extends the transaction cost approach to analyse the research questions of this study, in particular the choice between DFI and other forms of international business. This decision is of concern because DFI in CEE was well below expectations in the early years. Aggregate flows of DFI do not seem to match the opportunities of new markets and factor-cost differentials. Thus, the objective of the study is to explain not only why firms invest, but also why many others do not invest. Therefore, a firm-level analysis covers both investors and non-investors.

The underlying framework is the OLI paradigm [Dunning 1993]. It suggests that firms become more active in the region if they have ownership advantages that can be combined profitably with locational advantages in the region. They engage in DFI if they have the incentive to internalize such business. Thus the analysis has to consider specific locational characteristics as well as relevant ownership advantages and internalization incentives.

A general framework is developed for the analysis of the internalization decisions. It grows out of a synergy of prior theoretical and empirical work and demonstrates how much TCE can incorporate, including some arguments brought forward by its critics.

This chapter presents normal science, in that it modifies an existing paradigm in order to confront it with empirical evidence [Kuhn 1962: 30]. The economic transition of CEE offers the opportunity to apply existing paradigms to a different and changing environment. In turn, the evaluation of the theoretical and empirical results should provide feedback with the purpose of advancing the underlying paradigms. Thus mid-range theories are developed to guide the empirical inquiry. That is, 'theories that lie between the minor but necessary working hypotheses ... and the all inclusive systematic efforts to develop a unified theory that will explain all the observed uniformities' of the objects of inquiry [Merton 1968: 39].

THE INTERNALIZATION DECISION

Transaction costs (TC) are the unobservable costs of using the price mechanism. They appear in many forms, including directly attributable costs such as 'costs of negotiating and concluding a separate contract for each transaction' and 'discovering what the relevant prices are' [Coase 1937: 390]. They also appear as opportunity costs of a sub-optimal factor allocation, for example due to time lags or acceptance of a second best offer as expected search costs exceed expected efficiency gains. In other words, they are the costs arising from the loss of efficiency in factor allocation due to less than perfect markets.

The trade-off between these costs of the market and those of internal organization determines the optimal organizational form for a given transaction, and thus the boundaries of the firm. This analysis is concerned with the choice of organizational form in an international context: when do companies prefer to internalize their foreign operations? A model of *international* TC should explain the internalization of transactions between business units located in different countries, while considering the costs of trans-border transactions and of operating in different social and economic environments.

The choice of organizational form for a transaction depends on the TC of alternative modes. In the international context, the trade-off is between the costs of using international markets for goods and services and the costs of the internal organization of a DFI project. The costs of organizing a transaction, both internally or externally, depend on the potential market failure for the goods and services transferred. Characteristics that make them sensitive to market failure are here referred to collectively as 'sensitivity'. The causes of sensitivity are discussed below as asset specificity and information asymmetry.

Figure 4.1 illustrates the basic relationships. Both external and internal TC increase with growing product sensitivity. External TC are shown as a linear function of sensitivity, $TC(e)$. Internal organization requires certain fixed costs, F, that are independent of the characteristics of the products. In the international context, these would be the costs of setting up and operating a DFI project. Yet the internal TC curve, $TC(i)$, has a flatter slope as internal organization allows enterprises to overcome market failure.

The bold line illustrates the TC-minimizing organizational mode. External transactions are preferred for products with low sensitivity, for example homogeneous goods in competitive markets. A critical point is reached at s_1 where $TC(i)$ and $TC(e)$ intersect. If external TC exceed internal TC, DFI is preferred to a market exchange of the same transaction. The benefits of a

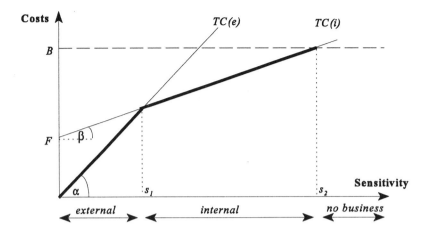

Figure 4.1   The internalization decision

transaction are equivalent to the difference of sales revenues and production costs. No business will occur if the costs of a transaction exceed its benefits (B). This is the residual of sales revenues (R) and production costs (PC), that is to the right of s_2. These relationships can be expressed formally: starting from the profit maximization function:

$$Profit = R - PC - TC \qquad (4.1)$$

It follows that profit maximization requires the minimization of TC. Assuming that the choice of organizational mode does not change revenues or production costs, then

$$Mode = \left\{ \begin{array}{ll} \text{external} & \text{if } TC(i) > TC(e) \\ \text{internal} & \text{if } TC(i) < TC(e) \text{ and } TC(i) < (R - PC) \\ \text{no business} & \text{if } TC(i) > (R - PC) \end{array} \right. \qquad (4.2)$$

Hence, for all business that can be observed, that is profitable under either condition, the internalization condition is:

$$\text{Internalization} = \text{yes, if } TC(i) / TC(e) < 1 \qquad (4.3)$$
$$= \text{no, otherwise}$$

The expression can be rewritten as:

$$TC(i) / TC(e) = (\alpha S + F) / (\beta S) = (\alpha + F/S) / \beta \qquad (4.4)$$

where β, α are the slope coefficients of $TC(e)$ and $TC(i)$ respectively, and S is an index of sensitivity. The probability of a transaction being internalized in a DFI-project is thus positively related to α and S, and negatively to β and F:

$$P \ (DFI = \text{yes}) = P \ (TC(i) \ / TC(e) < 1) = f \ (\beta^-, \ \alpha^+, \ F^-, \ S^+). \qquad (4.5)$$

The next section introduces the factors influencing the elements of the basic model, making extensive use of prior empirical analysis. Therefore a brief introduction to this empirical work is in order. Empirical studies on TC face the challenge that it is by definition impossible to quantify and measure TC. The discrepancy between managers' perceptions of TC and actually measured costs [Buckley and Chapman 1995] is a major obstacle but not the only one. Empirical research has proxied TC with their presumed determinants. With statistical significance it is shown that the proxy influences TC and that TC influences the internalization decision under consideration.

A common way to test transaction cost models is a binary-dependent variable model of internal versus contractual transfer. For instance, Davidson and McFetridge [1985] use a Logit model, defining the dependent dummy variable as one for transfers to wholly owned subsidiaries (WOS) and zero for licensing. Alternatively, Contractor [1984] and Shane [1994] define their dependent variable as the 'ratio of royalties earned from licensing to unaffiliated foreigners' to different measures of direct investment income, as a proxy for the share of business which has been externalized. Table 4.1 summarizes the methodology used in empirical research of TC in an international context. The theory presented here is based on this empirical research. Mid-range theory is advanced through the synergy of many specific empirical studies. The empirical foundations are reported in extensive footnotes pertaining to the theoretical arguments. (To ease the presentation, empirical tests are referred to in such a way that all 'positive' effects refer to a higher preference for internalization, that is DFI, and 'negative' effects to a higher preference for market transactions such as licensing.)

Product Sensitivity

Transaction costs are a function of characteristics of products being transferred, aggregated above as sensitivity to market failure. The characteristics of goods and services that make them susceptible to market failure are asset specificity and information content, discussed in the literature on problems of 'hold up' and 'information asymmetries'.

Table 4.1 Methodology of empirical research

Author, year	Model	Dependent variable	Sample (country, data source, sample size, unit of analysis)
Horst 1972	LPM	MNE - domestic firm	US
Grubaugh 1987	LPM, Logit	MNE - domestic firm	US, n=186 firms
Davidson 1980	rank correlat.	Entry sequence	US outward, Harvard MNE project, n=20 host countries (180 firms)
Contractor 1984	OLS	Share of royalties over DFI income	US outward, department of commerce survey 1977-80, n=30 countries
Kumar 1987, 1990	OLS	share of DFI / royalties over sales	India inward, domestic sources, n=49 industries
Davidson & McFetridge 1984, 1985	Logit	DFI - licensing	US outward, Harvard MNE project, n=1226 technology transfers
Kogut & Singh 1988	M-Logit	greenfield - JV - acquisition	US inward, various sources, n=228 entries
Gatignon & Anderson 1988	Logit M-Logit	WOS - JV	US outward, Harvard MNE project, n=1267 affiliates
Chu & Anderson 1992	M-/O- Logit	WOS - JV	replication of Gatignon and Anderson 1988
Gomes-Casseres 1989, 1991	Logit	WOS - JV	US outward, Harvard MNE project, n=1532 affiliates
Hennart 1991	Logit	WOS - JV	Japanese in US, questionnaire, n=158 parent affiliate couples
Agarwal & Ramaswani 1992	M-Logit	no biz - export - JV - WOS	US in Japan, Brazil, UK; Q-survey 97 firms (18%[a]), n=285 firm-country relations
Kim & Hwang 1992	M-Logit Manova MDA	licensing - JV - WOS	US outward, questionnaire (15%[a]), using Likiert scales, n=96 firms
Benito & Gripsrud 1992	OLS	Entry sequence	Norwegian outward, Norge Bank data, n=201 affiliates
Kogut & Zander 1993	Logit	WOS - licensing, WOS - JV	Swedish outward, questionnaire (16 of 20 firms[a]), using Likiert scales, n=82 technology transfers

Table 4.1, continued

Author, year	Model	Dependent Variable	Sample (country, data source, sample size, unit of analysis)
Hu & Chen 1993	Logit Manova	Min. JV - Maj. JV	China inward, China Investment guide 1984/86, n=1456 JVs.
Shane 1994	OLS	Share of royalties over DFI income	US outward, department of commerce survey 1977 and 82, n=86 and 166 industries
Aswicahyona & Hill 1995	OLS	Share of DFI in output	Indonesia inward, domestic sources, n=37 industries (31%[a])
Denekamp 1995	OLS	DFI Stock	US outward, official sources, n = 61 industries 1982 / 85 / 89
Hennart & Larimo 1996	Logit	WOS - JV	Japanese and Finnish outward, various sources, n= 401 entries
Erramilli 1996	Logit	non-equity - Min. JV - Maj. JV	US outward, advertising industry data, n =337 subsidiaries
Padmanabhan & Cho 1996	Logit	WOS - JV	Japan outward, Toyo Kaizai data, n=839 affiliates

[a] = ratio of used observations to firms contacted. n = number of observations.

Asset specificity

Asset specificity is the core determinant of internalization in the TC framework by Williamson [1985]: it motivates vertical integration. Asset specificity refers to investments by either partner specific to the business relationship. These are sunk costs, that is unrecoverable costs in the case of a change of partners [Klein, Crawford and Alchian 1978].

If two or more agents sign a contract requiring relationship-specific investment they become mutually dependent. After the investments are made, market forces will not punish opportunism and maladaptation as in the case of perfect markets; and therefore, agents become vulnerable to misbehaviour by the partner. If both partners depend on each other, a situation of bilateral monopoly evolves that may or may not be resolved efficiently. However, if only one partner depends on the other, the lock-in situation may be exploited by the stronger partner. A long-term contract can theoretically resolve such situations [Demsetz 1988]. However, if contracts are not enforceable because of limitations in the legal framework, or if contracts are highly incomplete due to uncertainty over final outcomes, internalization may occur. In this line of argument asset specificity is neither a necessary nor a sufficient condition, as information asymmetry suffices and imperfect contracting is needed.

In international business transaction-specific investments are higher than in a national environment due to higher costs of negotiating, coding and measurement, partner search costs, bargaining and coordination. Asset specificity arises with investment in physical assets or human capital, notably if resources are committed to product or process customization:

- Products customized to one buyer or supplier require higher coordination costs and possibly investments in equipment specific to the business relationship [Williamson 1981, Anderson and Gatignon 1986]. Such sunk cost investments constitute asset specificity in a narrower sense.
- Production processes specialized in the use of a particular input quality may be dependent on one source for their raw material. Such dependence arises particularly in industries processing natural resources. Hennart [1988] showed how this led to higher vertical integration in the aluminium industry than in the tin industry.
- Training individuals specifically for a business relationship is a form of transaction-specific investment [Monteverde and Teece 1982, Anderson and Schmittlein 1984]. Such costs arise in particular with the transfer of 'tacit knowledge' [Teece 1977]. Training costs rise for transfers to countries with a lower level of education and less sophisticated technological expertise and thus imply a preference for internalization.

Empirical researchers face problems finding suitable proxies for asset specificity because it emerges in many variations. It varies not only between firms but also between individual transactions for any firm. None of the international studies reviewed had proxies for product customization, but process customization was shown by Gomes-Casseres [1989, 1991] and Hennart [1991] using measures of intra-firm trade and resource-industry dummies. More evidence exists showing a positive relationship between local technical capabilities and the preference for contracts or joint-ventures (JVs).[1]

Information content
The price mechanism generates an optimal allocation of goods if all agents have full information. If, however, information about the traded goods is incomplete, or information itself is the traded item, then various forms of market failure arise [Arrow 1971]. Such 'demand externalities' [Williamson 1985] include information asymmetries [Akerlof 1970], the free-rider potential for users of brand-names who may degrade the quality of standards [Davidson 1982, Anderson and Gatignon 1986] and externalities from the 'public good character of knowledge within the firm' [Caves 1971: 4]. Like public goods, knowledge is non-rivalrous in consumption in that its use by one agent does not reduce its utility for other agents. These market failures are conceptually distinct from

asset specificity because they arise from the non-specific nature of intangible assets [Kay 1992].

Here the framework departs from Williamsonian TCE which aggregates information and market failure related to asset specificity [Williamson 1985, Anderson and Gatignon 1986]. Information-related issues are more important in an international context and therefore receive more attention in the internalization literature on MNEs [for example Casson 1987, 1995]. While asset specificity is mostly related to transfers of goods and vertical integration, information asymmetries arise mainly for technology transfer and horizontal expansion. However, exports can be subject to informational asymmetries, for instance over the quality of goods, and licensing agreements can be subject to asset specificity if the licensee has to invest in specific physical assets.

In the international environment informational market failures are more prevalent because less efficient formal and informal information channels make information asymmetries more likely and more persistent. The diffusion of transferred knowledge is more likely as licensors can less observe the misuse of intellectual property and control externalities. Transactional problems proliferate because international law is less specific and more costly to enforce. Thus the 'appropriability regime' permits only weak enforcement of property rights and thus reduces control of externalities [Rugman 1981, Teece 1986]. Multinational firms can safeguard their intangible assets by other means than the legal system, for instance by operating the business themselves or by choosing not to train local employees more than necessary for their particular jobs functions.

Imperfections in the markets for information thus imply that product sensitivity to TC increases with:

- Buyer uncertainty regarding the quality of goods related to product diversification and human capital intensity [McManus 1972, Casson 1982]. Information asymmetries may require multiple quality and quantity controls and thus increase measurement costs [Hennart 1982].
- The transfer of information, such as marketing, general management, and technological knowledge, especially of recent origin [Williamson 1981]. Product sensitivity also increases with the transfer of product innovations which are more difficult to evaluate than process innovations [Brada 1981, Hennart 1989] and with the transfer of 'unstructured, poorly-understood products and processes' [Anderson and Gatignon 1986].
- The transfer of goodwill, especially by permitting local partners to use a brand name. Goodwill is conceptually different from marketing knowledge, as the former is the value of a brand reputation, and the latter refers to management capabilities.

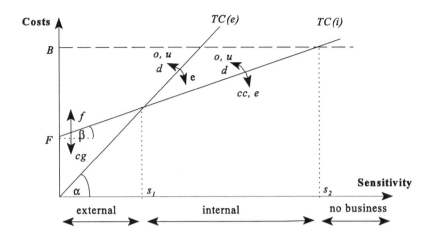

Figure 4.2   Changes in transaction costs curves

A different kind of market failure arises if knowledge is 'tacit' [Polanyi 1958]. Knowledge may still be a public good in that its use is not rivalrous. However, access to knowledge is not costless because it requires a learning process. The recipient acquires knowledge through experience, rather than by reading factual information. Therefore concerns about externalities from uncontrolled diffusion are secondary. Diverse cultures, formal and informal communication networks, and different languages in particular, inhibit the transfer of tacit knowledge as teaching and the exchange of experience becomes more difficult. The transfer is facilitated by the codifyability of the technology [Kogut and Singh 1988], by the transfer experience of the transferor, and by the technical expertise of the recipient [Contractor 1981, Pavitt 1985]. Kogut and Zander [1993] argue that the transfer of tacit knowledge requires an organizational mode of transfer because a market transaction is not feasible [see also Love 1995].

Empirical studies support to the effect of information intensity. Research[2] and advertising[3]-intensive firms are frequently found to internalize relatively many business operations. Proxies for human capital were positive and significant in Contractor [1984], Kumar [1990] and Aswicahyona and Hill [1990]. A diversification proxy that incorporates aspects of intangible assets interacted positively with contract risk in Agarwal and Ramaswani [1992].[4] Furthermore, internalization is more likely for foreign operations that are close to the firms' core business activities because an uncontrolled diffusion of know-how may be more harmful.[5] However, the conditions vary for firms from different origins as they compete on the basis of different kinds of core competences. Less empirical evidence exists to support the sensitivity of reputation, since marketing knowledge and goodwill are difficult to separate empirically and advertising intensity has been used as a proxy for both.

Whether the preference for internalization by information-intensive firms is attributable to the public good character or the tacit nature of knowledge has only recently received attention. Kogut and Zander [1993] show empirically that tacitness increases the likelihood of an internal mode of technology transfer.

Moderating Influences on TC

Transaction costs are subject to two moderating influences: uncertainty about the outcome of the transaction and potential opportunistic behaviour of the business partner. These moderating influences induce the curves $TC(e)$ and $TC(i)$ to turn upwards as indicated by arrows (o, u) in Figure 4.2. It is generally presumed that the effect of these influences is stronger on external TC than internal TC, leading to a shift of s_I to the left, that is internalization becomes more likely. In fact, the ability to cope with opportunism and to adjust more effectively to a volatile environment has been the rationale for the superiority of internal organization in Williamson's original work.

This section discusses the logic underlying the moderating effects, outcome uncertainty and the likelihood of opportunism. A note on necessary and sufficient conditions for TC to evolve, follows.

Uncertainty
International business is subject to various sources of uncertainty. It arises from the unpredictable impact of environmental or organizational variables on corporate performance or inadequacy of information [Miles and Snow 1978, Pfeffer and Salancik 1978]. Uncertainty includes not only a probabilistic distribution of outcomes but also unknown types of events that may influence business results in an 'unpredictable' way.

Uncertainty reduces the possibility of writing complete contracts while increasing the probability of situations arising in which the partners need a joint reaction in response to changes in the environment. Therefore higher uncertainty, and higher risk aversion [Chiles and McMackin 1996], increase preferences for internalization. This is because risk-sharing may (i) reduce effects on the outcome of the joint project, and (ii) eliminate effects on the terms of trade between the partners.

(i) Risk may be shared through equity holding or contractual arrangements. The ability of firms to bear risk is related to business size, and two partners may jointly engage in business that would not happen otherwise. If risk-sharing contracts are not feasible because they are unenforceable, or the uncertainty makes even the type of event that might affect the business unpredictable, then internalization may be preferred.

(ii) Re-negotiation over the distribution of rents and complex coordination mechanisms may substantially slow the adjustment of interdependent partners linked by a contractual relationship. With interdependence a hierarchical mode of coordination within a common organization may be more efficient [Williamson 1991]. On the other hand, if the market is perfect spot markets are the quickest medium to adjust to a new equilibrium price.

Thus higher industry uncertainty induces the internalization of markets where product characteristics are sensitive to market failure, while simple and homogeneous goods are traded on spot markets. Dunning [1993, p. 177] refers to these uncertainties as 'contract risk', Anderson and Gatignon [1986] as 'external uncertainty'. Under some conditions, they lead to higher degrees of integration.

Industry uncertainty arises in input markets, for instance by changes in quality or shifts in market supply, as well as output markets, for instance by changes in demand due to changes in tastes or the availability of complementary or substitute goods [Miller 1992]. Industry uncertainty also arises from the competitive nature of the output market. Some TC literature refers to this situation as the small-numbers problem. Furthermore, uncertainty increases with the duration of an envisaged project, because the longer the planning horizon the less predictable is the environment at the time near the conclusion of the contract [Coase 1937: 391].

Showing the impact of industry uncertainty convincingly in an empirical study is almost impossible. Kim and Hwang [1992] include constructs for demand uncertainty and intensity of competition as proxies for economic uncertainty in the market. In a domestic study, Anderson and Schmittlein [1984] use a deviation-from-forecasts variable to proxy uncertainty. Neither study found significant results.

Opportunism

Williamson explains TC as a result of opportunistic behaviour: if transactions 'are subject to *ex post* opportunism ... [then] appropriate safeguard measures can be devised *ex ante*', by organizing them inside the boundaries of the firm [Williamson 1985, p. 48]. Contrary to Williamson, others do not consider opportunism a necessary condition for internalization.

Casson [1995] and Ghoshal and Moran [1996] suggest including opportunism as a distinct attitudinal variable. Individuals' propensity to behave opportunistically depends on their attitudes and the costs of opportunistic behaviour. Cultural values shape attitudes to opportunism but also change with institutional settings and the perceived behaviour of others. The costs of opportunism include social or legal consequences of detected cheating: a social network acts as a means of preventing opportunism, as each individual has a reputation at stake which is vital for continued business [Granovetter 1985]. A clear legal code and contract enforcement at no or low costs limit the scope for opportunistic re-negotiation.

The institutional structure of a society, including its norms and value systems, affects TC. Therefore the economic performance of countries depends on the trust in their society which in turn depends on culture [Casson 1995, Hill 1995]. For instance, socialization mechanisms influence the individual's sense of obligation and duty and can prevent opportunistic behaviour [Ouchi 1980]. A culture that emphasizes respect and self-respect relative to status will face less cheating and thus lower TC. On the other hand, TC will be high in a country that lacks middle-class social networks that are neither infested by corruption nor absent due to revolution (as can be the case in some countries of CEE).

Internationally, fewer social networks exist and partners often do not know each other. A damaged reputation abroad may not matter as much as it would in the local community because businesses in different countries are less likely to communicate such information efficiently. The reputation of new partners are more difficult to establish and it takes longer to establish mutual trust. Thus international transactions are subject to TC related to lack of trust. However, these TC vary across partner countries. The presence of high levels of trust and co-operative behaviour in a foreign country affect the TC of business with that country, and thus the preference to internalize international transactions.

- High trust countries experience lower levels of internalization [Hofstede 1980, Hedlund 1980]. Their international transactions would use more licensing if their business partners also trusted them more.
- For international business, not only the trust within a society but also trust between two countries is important: political friction between countries reduces the latter without affecting the former.
- International law enforcement is often more costly as partners operate under different legal codes, and interaction with the legal system in a foreign country may be cumbersome. Of particular concern is the weak protection of intellectual property [Anderson and Gatignon 1986, Clegg 1990]. This increases internalization in certain environments and industries.

Shane [1994] tests the trust proposition empirically and finds that US companies in high trust countries uses more licensing compared with investment.[6] Denekamp [1995] uses a 'legal intensity index' to show empirically that industries where lawyers constitute a high share of the employees are more likely to internalize. Other aspects of international variations in trust and constraints on opportunism have not been tested in a comparable way.

Necessary and sufficient conditions

The literature fails to agree on the necessary or sufficient conditions for TC, and how various determinants interact. Based on the review of the theoretical arguments, the following propositions are suggested:

- The existence of at least one of these two product market imperfections, asset specificity or information asymmetries, is a necessary condition.
- Uncertainty is a necessary condition.
- Opportunism increases the magnitude of TC, but is not a necessary condition.

These propositions are based on the following considerations:

(i) In a highly uncertain environment, the ability to adjust to changes in the environment is essential for market performance. With neither asset specificity nor information asymmetries, as on currency markets, spot markets are used as coordination mechanisms. If adjustment processes by related agents are interdependent, many co-ordination problems arise, and internal adjustment mechanisms are superior [Williamson 1991]. The same arguments hold with respect to opportunism.

(ii) In the absence of uncertainty, complete contracts overcome interdependence between partners [Demsetz 1988], and information asymmetries do not arise by definition. As uncertainty increases contracts will become incomplete and thus raise TC. In particular, it has been argued that complexity aggravates a product-specific market failure problem [Masten, Meehan and Snyder 1991, McFetridge 1995]. Similarly, Anderson and Gatignon [1986] argue that 'external uncertainty' affects internalization only if interacting with asset specificity or technology transfer.

(iii) Opportunism is a necessary condition for firms to exist in the original framework of TC by Williamson [1981]. He retains this position [Williamson 1995] despite a growing number of critics, including Demsetz [1995] and Coase. Certain interaction between individuals may be accomplished only within an organization, not across markets, even in the absence of opportunism. This includes teamwork [Alchian and Demsetz 1972] and the transfer of tacit knowledge [Kogut and Zander 1993]. An alternative counter-argument states that internalization does not resolve the problems of opportunistic behaviour [Granovetter 1985]. Extensive monitoring may actually reduce co-operative attitudes and thus increase opportunistic behaviour and, consequently, TC [Ghoshal and Moran 1996].

Internal Transaction Costs

Within organizations hierarchies replace prices as co-ordination mechanisms. Management co-ordinates individual activities, gives directions and monitors agents. Many of its activities revolve around the collection, communication and evaluation of information [Casson 1997]. The costs of managing across borders exceed those of a national firm. Firstly, this is due to specific administrative costs of international production [Hirsch 1976], and secondly, monitoring is more costly. Thus, both the intercept and the slope of the TC(i) curve are higher for international business.

However, firms may reduce these costs of internal organization if they can utilize economies of common governance (*cg*), corporate culture (*cc*), experience (*e*), low psychic distance (*d*) and, in imperfect financial markets, superior sources of funding (*f*). These influences affect the shape of $TC(i)$ and are indicated in Figure 4.2.

Costs of governance
International business has major cost components that are sunk costs, that is incurred at entry and unrecoverable, or fixed costs and independent of turnover. Examples for the latter are the costs of headquarter functions of international corporations. Country-specific sunk costs are incurred upon entering a foreign country when investors need to study the legal, social and economic framework and to establish contacts with local partners and government authorities. Goods have to be adapted to local tastes, legal requirements and the specific properties of inputs. Subsequent transactions can use existing facilities and thus have lower set-up costs which consequently makes them more likely to be internalized.

These economies of common governance exist both for international business *per se* as well as for business with any partner country. Firms with a larger turnover are able to utilize such economies and incur lower (marginal) costs when adding an additional operation to their portfolio. The internal TC per unit thus decline with increasing turnover. Williamson [1985] described this effect by pointing out that the more frequently transactions incur, the lower are the internal TC per transaction. These effects reduce fixed costs F and thus shift TC(i) downwards, making internalization more likely.

Firms differ not only with respect to their sensitivity-independent fixed costs, but also in their ability to manage sensitive transactions. Capabilities that increase an organization's ability to reduce uncertainty and opportunism of internal transactions turn the TC(i) curve downwards. A good example of such an effect is corporate culture, as analysed by Casson [1995]: Firms may be able to instill a higher level of trust among their employees than exists in the society outside the enterprise. Therefore internal transactions are subject to lower TC, as indicated by the arrow (*cc*) in Figure 4.2.

Psychic distance and experience

As the costs of business in a foreign country increase, the more distant and different this country is from the environment in which the company is used to operate. This effect increases both internal and external TC.

Understanding of other cultures requires an extra effort that is often not undertaken, and consequently cultural distance becomes a constraint on rationality. Risk assessment is hampered because the investor is not used to the nature of many sources of risk and political influences on trans-border transactions [Caves 1982]. The costs of establishing a business in a distant country increase with the need to gather information, train local staff and adapt management to the local cultural and legal environment. These costs are caused by lack of information, difficulties in exchanging information (due to language barriers), higher legal enforcement costs, and a lack of reputation as an entrant. All these aspects are captured by the concept of 'psychic distance' which covers geographic, cultural, legal, religious, linguistic, historical, economic and ethnic aspects of the differences between two locations of business activity [Johansson and Wiedersheim-Paul 1975].

Companies can reduce the costs of distance if their management is familiar with the local environment through personal experiences and contacts [for example Gomes-Casseres 1989]. Cultural distance may decline with the presence of a foreign business community as it fosters an environment that adapts to the need of foreign firms [Anderson and Gatignon 1986]. On the aggregate level, familiarity can be expected to follow historical relationships, such as political cooperations, or expatriate communities. The increasing costs of psychic distance have three implications:

- The choice of organizational form for a given transaction depends on the differential impact of psychic distance on costs of markets and internal organization. Clegg [1990] stresses that distance increases the problems of controlling the use of knowledge transferred by licensing, that is TC(e) turns upwards. In contrast, Root [1983] and Davidson and McFetridge [1985] argue that internal costs increase more than external TC, turning, and possibly shifting, TC(i) upwards. Thus, psychic distance increases the preference for licensing. Anderson and Gatignon [1986] argue that either a high or a low control mode is preferred for business across great socio-cultural distance, but not an intermediate. Thus, whether s_l shifts left or right is an empirical question.
- Companies prefer to enter countries closer to home early in their internationalization process. Firms without international experience prefer expansion to the nearer country if faced with the choice between countries that differ only with respect to their psychic distance.
- Cultural gaps raise obstacles to integrating acquired firms. Considering

organization costs, greenfield investments are preferred to acquisitions if post-acquisition costs of matching organizational structures are high. These costs rise if the 'organizational fit' of the firms is low [Jemison and Sitkin 1986]. Furthermore, firms nearby have personal contacts and may find it easier to find suitable partners with whom to form a successful JV. Therefore, Kogut and Singh [1988, p. 414] hypothesize: 'The greater cultural distance between the country of the investing firm and the country of entry, the more likely a firm will choose a JV or ... greenfield over an acquisition'.

Experience in international business at large helps to overcome the obstacles of psychic distance and reduces operating costs. Experience is gathered in every business context and may be transferable to related business projects and permits continuous reductions of production costs. Specific experience effects apply to the mode of business [Padmanabhan and Cho 1996a] and to the partner country: (i) experience in transferring technology by licensing reduces the future cost of licensing; (ii) experience in managing foreign subsidiaries reduces the cost of additional operations; (iii) any experience in a country reduces the costs of future projects in that particular country or similar countries. The accumulation of experience leads to continuous reductions in transaction costs. Both TC curves turn downwards, compensating the effect of distance.

Empirical evidence strongly supports the view that firms start internationalization in nearby countries and subsequently move on to more distant countries (Chapter 3). Several studies found that large distances favour low involvement modes.[7] Using a Hofstede index for cultural distance, Kogut and Singh [1988] find a preference for JV over acquisition for increasing distance, while Shane [1994] finds contrary evidence as distance favours licensing.[8] Contrary to their expectations, Kogut and Singh also find that investors from distant places of origin favour acquisitions. However, this effect is reversed after removing Japanese firms from the sample.

The effects of experience have been confirmed in several empirical studies.[9] For instance, Hennart [1991] finds that manufacturers of consumer goods which have been the US for a long time, and older affiliates are more likely to be in full ownership.

Costs of capital
Internalization decisions are frequently interdependent with investment decisions and thus with the commitment of the investor to bear country-specific investment risk. TCE often ignores this aspect because it does not arise in perfect capital markets: either a risk-sharing contract is established, or each partner receives a share in the integrating company to reverse the impact on the risk portfolio of each individual.

However, international capital markets are not perfect, especially in emerging and transition economies. An enterprise wishing to internalize its business in a foreign country has to contribute a major share of capital. If local capital markets are underdeveloped, this capital may have to be raised on international capital markets rather than locally. Hedging such currencies is expensive or impossible. Thus, the investor has to bear the country risk associated with the project because he has to invest at least some equity as lenders otherwise would not be willing to finance foreign operations. The risk can be reduced by shifting it to a local partner [for example Brouthers 1995]. This reduces internalization as a JV or licensing replaces WOS. The alternative would be non-involvement or even withdrawal from the market. In either case, country risk reduces the extent of internalized cross-border business. Thus, in less complete capital markets more low-control modes and non-involvement are to be expected.

Country risk arises primarily from environmental uncertainty, but also from industry and firm uncertainty. Environmental uncertainty covers changes in political regimes and government policy, macroeconomic changes in economic activity and prices, social movements and the natural environment, such as rainfall or earthquakes [Miller 1992]. This suggests that internalization is less likely in developing countries.

However, uncertainty has now been introduced in the model twice with opposite implications:

- interacting with asset specificity and information, uncertainty raises TC and thus the preference for internalization,
- increasing country risk, uncertainty reduces investment and internalization.

Unfortunately the literature does not provide distinct concepts of uncertainty that fit this model. Presumably, internalization effects are mainly associated with industry uncertainty, whereas the business deterrent effect is associated with environmental risk. This separation is helpful for analytical purposes. The trade-off between different kinds of risk implies that agents may be willing to accept higher levels of industry risk if country risk is low.

In empirical research country risk is rarely shown to influence DFI unless measures of managers' perceived risk are used.[10] Economic development influences several determinants of the model, including country risk, but also including the technological capabilities of the recipients of technology transfer (and thus costs of training), the development of financial markets and the regulatory environment. This can lead to correlations between various country-specific variables and surprising effects in regression analysis.[11]

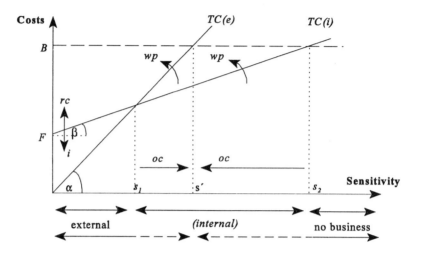

Figure 4.3   Influences of the institutional environment

The Institutional Environment

Governments in a considerable number of countries employ a variety of measures to constrain the activity of multinational enterprises, or to induce them to perform in a way deemed beneficial for the host economy. In particular, ownership is constrained as expected spill-overs to the national economy are larger if the business is run in partnership with a local company. Some potential effects of government policy and the institutional environment on internalization decisions are illustrated in Figure 4.3. These effects occur in imperfect or restrictive regulatory frameworks, as is the case in the transition economies.

(i) governments may constrain foreign ownership by prohibiting DFI in selected industries. Such regulation was common throughout CEE until about 1992. This implies that the internalization option is not available (*oc*). Thus the $TC(i)$ curve vanishes from the menu of available options. The model retains only one critical point, s', between market transaction and no business. Firstly, this implies that some businesses that would have been internalized are now externalized, as intended by regulators. However, business of higher sensitivity between s' and s_2, is not profitable under this constraint and therefore not implemented. Since this includes sensitive technology transfer, such constraints may prevent some of the most attractive projects.

(ii) regulatory constraints (*rc*) can increase the fixed costs of operation. This can be a weakness in the institutional framework, for example if the bureaucracy is incompetent. However, many governmental policies deliberately raise the cost for investors, for instance by local content or export share requirements, limited profit remittance, or taxation. Any such extra costs are independent of product sensitivity and shift the $TC(i)$ curve upwards. Thus less DFI occurs as some transactions are externalized and others are not implemented.

(iii) a weak protection of property rights (wp) may increase the scope for opportunistic behaviour and thus turn the TC curves upwards. This condition is likely to occur in transition economies where many property rights have only recently been codified and law enforcement costs may be high. Since internal organization enables to overcome some of these hazards, $TC(e)$ is likely to turn more. This shifts s_1 to the left, and increases the likelihood of DFI at the expense of contractual knowledge transfer.[12] Yet it also reduces the upper benchmark s_2 and thus the number of transactions occurring. In this way the model suggests that enforceable property rights encourage more international business, using both external and internal modes. A crucial point in this argumant is the cost of law enforcement. If legal fees are expensive, this may have the same deterrent effect as lack of legal protection.

Because of governmental regulation of DFI, one stream of literature argues that the choice of organizational form depends on the relative bargaining power of MNEs *vis-à-vis* host governments [Fagre and Wells 1982, Lecraw 1984, Kobrin 1987].[13] Gomes-Casseres [1991] combines this argument with TC, arguing that the decision on the organizational form of business can be divided into two stages; the determination of the firm's preferences, and the negotiations with the local government. He finds empirical support for some interaction effects. Several other studies find support for specific aspects of the regulatory framework as an exogenous constraint on the choice of ownership form.[14] Figure 4.3 suggests that the bargaining power of MNEs is high in sensitive businesses that are profitable only if organized internally. Governments may be more successful in negotiating externalization in the range between s_1 and s'.

An Equation

The components of the TC model can be brought together in one equation which is the basis of the empirical analysis in Chapters 7 and 8. The abstract variables influencing the choice between DFI and market transactions in equation (4.5) have subsequently been explored in more detail. Merging all the elements, a more detailed relation is proposed. In the notation, plus and minus signs are used again to indicate the sign of the first derivative, that is the direction of the influence. The slope coefficients α and β of the TC(e) and TC(i) curves depend on uncertainty, opportunism, psychic distance, weaknesses in property-right protection, experience and corporate culture:

$$\beta = f(\, u^+,\, o^+,\, d^+,\, e^-,\, cc^-\,) \tag{4.6}$$

$$\alpha = f(\, u^+, \, o^+, \, d^+, \, e^-, \, wp^+ \,) \tag{4.7}$$

The fixed costs F of internal TC depend on common governance, availability of financial resources, and on constraints and incentives set by host government regulation:

$$F = f(\, cg^-, f^+, \, rc^+, \, i^- \,) \tag{4.8}$$

The concept of sensitivity has been defined as a non-measureable index of asset specificity (*AS*) and information contents (*IC*). Inserting equations (4.6) to (4.8) into equation (4.5) the analytical framework is summarized in one equation. This equation establishes a relationship between the probability of a business choosing DFI as an internal mode of transaction instead of a market mode, and the independent variables discussed in this chapter:

$$P\,(DFI{=}1) = f(\, AS^+, \, IC^+, \, u^+, \, o^+, \, d\,?, \, e^+, \, cc^+, \, wp^+, \, cg^+, f^-, \, rc^-, \, i^+ \,) \tag{4.9}$$

In the case of the variables *u, o* and *e*, the arguments in previous research are adapted with respect to the relative impact on the *TC*(*e*) and *TC*(*i*) curves. For psychic distance *d*, the literature disagrees on the relative impact.

MARKETS, HIERARCHIES AND INTERMEDIATE FORMS

The discussion so far has compared two distinct modes of operation, internal and external. In recent literature the notion of organizational forms that mix elements of markets and hierarchies has received considerable attention. Some researchers of TCE treat contractual arrangements, explicit or implicit, as intermediate forms of internalization between markets and hierarchies. For instance, Williamson [1991, p. 280] describes intermediate forms such as 'various forms of long-term contracting, reciprocal trading, regulation, franchising and the like' as hybrid modes. They are 'located between markets and hierarchies with respect to incentive adaptability and bureaucratic costs'. Shelanski and Klein [1995, p. 337] review TCE and state that 'governance structures can be described along a spectrum'.

Hennart [1993] presents a model that 'locates contracts in the continuum between markets and firms'. He assumes convex total costs and suggests that intermediate forms are cost-efficient. Also the interpretation of out-sourcing with long-term contracts as a 'move-to-the-middle' [Clemons, Reddi and Row 1993] suggests an understanding of the market and firms as end points of a one-dimensional scale. Figure 4.4 illustrates this line of argument.

An alternative interpretation of the dependent variable is to treat different

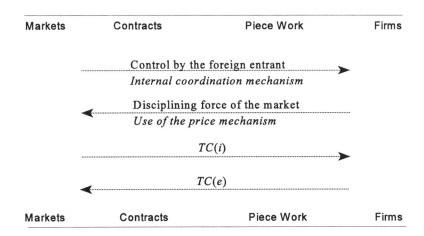

Figure 4.4   Markets versus hierarchies

organizational modes as alternatives with no implicit order. Buckley [1985a: 52] argues that 'a simple spectrum running from wholly-owned foreign subsidiary to "simple contracts" is an inadequate representation of the nuances and complexities of the different arrangements.' Buckley and Casson [1996] show that licensing is preferable if high volatility combines with large market size, which appears to fit the case of Russia (Figure 4.5). In their model licensing is less attractive *vis-à-vis* 'no business' or DFI, if patent rights are poorly protected or the value of the technology is highly uncertain. JVs become less attractive for business across high cultural distance because of coordination problems. Root [1987] located exports and DFI at opposite corners of a box diagram with the dimensions 'risk' and 'control'. In this framework contracts are characterized by zero risk and some degree of control.

These interpretations consider contracts as a distinct mode of transaction. Firms would make internalization decisions between contractual relations and DFI, as well as between trade and DFI. The relevance of different aspects of the TC framework varies however. Licensing involves technology transfer and is therefore likely to face problems of information asymmetry. For exports, information asymmetry related to quality control and asset specificity may cause market failure.

The choice between contracts and DFI has been analysed in research on the transfer of technology in the theoretical internalization literature [for example Buckley and Casson 1976] and the corresponding empirical analysis [for example Davidson and McFetridge 1985]. The choice between trade and DFI choice is comparable to research on transfer of goods, such as out-sourcing [Monteverdi and Teece 1982].

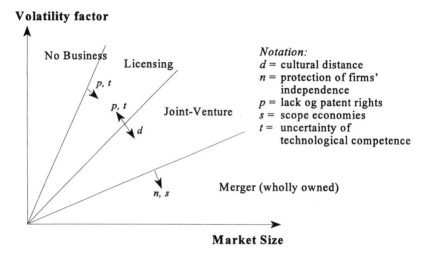

Source: Buckley and Casson [1996], with modifications

Figure 4.5   A two-dimensional perspective

THE NATURE OF CROSS BORDER INTERFACES

So far the TC approach has been presented for *given* transactions. However, decisions on the organizational mode and the transaction itself are related. For the empirical analysis, it is necessary to distinguish various cross-border transactions that may be found between Western and Eastern Europe. Only similar transactions in terms of the underlying choices on location of production and markets may be compared with the TC approach.

Figure 4.6 illustrates seven stylized patterns of cross-border transactions between a 'home country', say Western Europe, and a 'host country', say Eastern Europe. The first distinction is with respect to the markets that the project is to serve ultimately. In the lower half of the figure, projects are illustrated that use local production facilities in the host country to serve global markets. The simplest mode of obtaining local produce is to buy it from a local producer, a market transaction, and to import it to the parent's plant. There it may be further processed for sale in the global markets, including home, host and third countries.

Alternatively, DFI could establish a local production facility, using technological know-how and, typically, intermediate goods supplied by the parent firm. With the re-import of (semi-) finished goods, the parent is linked to the affiliate by bilateral flows of goods and services. The same kind of

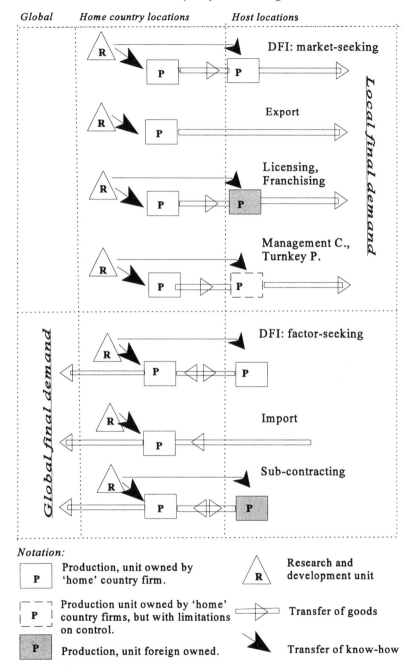

Figure 4.6   Cross-border interfaces

relationship can be established with an independent subcontractor. Again, goods are transferred in both directions and the 'home' firm can supply the local firm with production technology. The subcontracting arrangement is an intermediate form while DFI is an internalized mode. Imports are usually considered as market transactions, although they include long-term supplier relationships.

Business focussing on the local market can also be organized by exporting, contractual arrangements or DFI. Exports are market transactions, usually involving only transfer of goods and not supported by transfer of know-how. The buyer could be a local partner with an exclusive relationship, an independent sales agents, or the final customer.

A licensing agreement transfers the know-how to an independent local producer. He may receive intermediate and raw materials in addition to technology. Similarly a franchising agreement transfers goods, services and marketing know-how to an independent downstream partner engaged in the final stages of production, sales and distribution. If a firm wishes to serve a market, without locating major parts of the production at the location, franchising offers an alternative to arm's length exports and direct investment.

Special cases are management contracts and turnkey projects which are designed to accommodate the indivisibility of production and sales location in services and construction industries (Figure 4.6). In a management contract, the home firm operates a business on the premises of a local partner. Intangible assets required to run the operation are internalized and business risks can be shared with a local partner. This mode, which is common in the hotel industry, gives management firm control of its sensitive know-how, but not of the

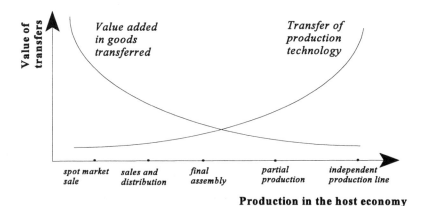

Figure 4.7 Extent of local production: international transfers and organizational modes

physical property [Contractor and Kundu 1996]. A turnkey project also enables a manufacturer to internalize the production know-how while operating abroad. A plant is built on premises owned by a local firm, but is transferred to local control only after completition. With the complete 'turnkey' plant, only how-to-operate knowledge is transferred, not how-to-build knowledge.

A DFI internalizes stages of the production chain located in the host country. This may involve a full local production or only the local distribution of goods. Figure 4.7 illustrates that the further down the production chain the cut-off is between home and local production, the more value-added is transferred in the goods, and the less production technology know-how is required locally. If the local partner does not have production knowledge, additional transfers of know-how are required. For projects covering only the sales and distribution stages, marketing know-how becomes an important transfer - especially in CEE.

CONCLUSION

Equation (4.9) integrates many aspects of the TCE literature. The synergy shows the eclectic nature of TCE: many quite different arguments have been made in its name and fit under the common umbrella of TCE. Most empirical work on TC in the international context takes a partial view focusing on selected determinants and specific kinds of business transactions. Thus it appears well-established that, for instance, intangible assets are preferably internalized because markets for information are imperfect. A number of other determinants have also been shown in specific studies. However, some of the core concepts remain to be shown empirically, including asset specificity, uncertainty and opportunism. Also, interaction effects have frequently been proposed but rarely supported empirically. This also applies to TCE literature on topics other than MNEs [Shelanski and Klein 1995].

Which of these objectives can be achieved in this study? Since the prime objective is to explain DFI in the context of economic transition, the sample has been selected accordingly. In addition, industry-level data for the host economies are of too poor a quality to yield any interesting results. Thus the task is to make the best use possible of available information while applying the framework as broadly as feasible.

In Chapter 7, market transactions of international trade and contracts are analysed as an alternative to DFI. Special tests feature the interaction of product sensitivity with environmental variables and contracts as intermediate form between markets and hierarchies. Chapter 8 applies TCE to the choices of entry mode and of joint ventures (JVs) versus wholly owned affiliates. In the latter decision the internalization incentives favour full ownership since JVs are an intermediate form which is more sensitive to market failure.

NOTES

1. Contractor [1981, 1984] finds negative effects on internalization by indigenous capabilities, proxied by R&D expenditures and research personnel. Kumar [1987, 1990] finds a negative effect of R&D expenditures in India on incoming DFI versus licensing. A similar study in Indonesia finds an insignificant positive effect [Aswicahyona and Hill 1995]. Gomes-Casseres [1989] uses the size of the host country's industrial sector to proxy the experience of local firms and finds a significantly negative effect on DFI. Hallwood [1990] shows how the lack of capable Scottish licensees induced suppliers to use DFI in the emerging off-shore oil-industry. Evidence against the proposition comes from Davidson and McFetridge [1985] who find a positive effect of literacy on DFI than on licensing.

2. R&D expenditure is commonly used as proxy for technology intensity. It is significant for international internalization decisions, for example in Davidson and McFetridge [1985], Gatignon and Anderson [1988] and Denekamp [1995] (using industry level data on R&D). Grubaugh [1987] finds R&D expenditure to have a significant effect on the likelihood of a firm being multinational rather than domestic.
    Hennart [1991a] does *not* find this variable to be significant for Japanese MNEs, suggesting that their core competencies and intangible assets are other than technological

3. Marketing intensity is commonly proxied with advertising expenditure. Gatignon and Anderson [1988] and Gomes-Casseres [1989] find a positive significant effect using industry level data on advertising expenditure. Grubaugh [1987] finds a positive but insignificant effect of advertising intensity. Hennart [1991a] found *no* significant effects for Japanese MNE, in the case of consumer good industries even a 'wrong', that is negative, sign. Kumar [1987] finds positive effects of advertising intensity on DFI and licensing of which the former was significant. A similar proxy is significant in Aswicahyona and Hill (1995).

4. Their product diversification proxy which includes the perception of innovation potential and the quality of training programs is surprisingly negative and significant, but positively significant as an interaction term with contract risk. This suggests that diffusion of knowledge is only of concern, and prevents DFI, if contract law is weak [Agarwal and Ramaswani 1992].

5. A dummy indicating whether the partner or affiliate is the same industry as the parent is significantly negative in Davidson and McFetridge [1985], and Hennart [1991]. Gomes-Casseres [1989] found product innovation to favour wholly owned affiliates only if the affiliate was in the core business of the MNEs whereas process innovations had no significant impact. Padmanabhan and Cho [1996] found relatedness to have a negative effect before 1985, but a positive effect thereafter.

6. He uses Hofstede's [1980] 'power distance scale' and a Confucian Connection 'integration index' as proxies for the level of trust within different societies.

7. For British firms, Buckley and Davis [1981] find DFI more likely the closer the host country is culturally to the UK, particularly for countries within the Commonwealth. Also see Stopford [1976]. Davidson and McFetridge [1985] find that countries bordering to the US (as country of origin) receive more DFI relative to licensing. They also find a positive significance for dummy variables in the case of countries with the same language and religion as the investor's country (USA).
    Gatignon and Anderson [1988] use multiple dummies for four clusters of partner countries outside the Anglo social-cultural sphere which are significantly *negative* in some model specifications. Gomes-Casseres [1989] derives a familiarity index from Davidson's [1980] entry sequences and finds that WOS are more likely in familiar countries. A similar result is obtained by Padmanabhan and Cho [1996] but Kim and Hwang [1992] find a significant *negative* effect.

8. Both use a composite index based on the deviation of each country from the US as country of origin by ranking along four cultural dimensions developed by Hofstede [1980]. The same index is not significant for entry sequences of Norwegian firms in Benito and Gripsrud [1992].

9. Experience is considered by counting related activities, for example the number of previous transfers [Teece 1977], number of worldwide DFI projects [Davidson and McFetridge 1985], the number of previous foreign entries [Gatignon and Anderson 1988, Barkema, Bell and Pennings 1996], thenumber of countries where the MNE has subsidiaries [Kogut and Singh 1988] and years of prior presence in the host country [Hennart and Larimo 1996]. Agarwal and Ramaswani [1992] also find that 'scale and experience' significantly influence the choice between joint and wholly owned ventures, but not between exports and DFI. In contrast, Erramilli [1996] finds a negative effect.

10. See for instance Kobrin [1982] or Nigh [1986]. Gatignon and Anderson [1988] include a country risk dummy for medium and high-risk countries, of which the high-risk dummy was significant. Kim and Hwang [1992] find a significant negative influence by managers' perceived country risk. Erramilli and Rao [1990] find that DFI by service multinationals which is motivated by following the customer, is more likely to be internalized than market-seeking DFI because the latter faces higher market uncertainties.

    Agarwal and Ramaswani [1992] include constructs for perceived contractual risk and perceived investment risk. Contractual risk is found to encourage exports and discourage DFI (but with no effect on the choice between JV and WOS). Investment risk discourages all forms of business, in the case of JV and WOS significantly. Some interaction effects with other variables were also significant.

11. Contractor [1984] includes GDP per capita and the share of manufacturing in GDP as proxies for level of development, both of which were shown to favour DFI. Davidson and McFetridge [1985] had various proxies for economic development, some of which had surprising signs. Dunning [1988] found a U-shaped relationship with only intermediate countries prefering licensing over DFI. This effect could, however, be removed by including other country variables.

12. A similar effect can occur with regulatory constraints on licensing or other forms of contractual cooperation and spot markets.

13. Relative bargaining power of MNEs *vis-à-vis* local governments is analysed empirically by Beamish [1985], Lecraw and Morrison [1991], Grosse and Behrman [1992] and Loree and Guisinger [1995].

14. Shane [1994] measures investment barriers and incentives as the proportion of US firms reporting various government regulations in the US Department of Commerce benchmark survey. Using factor analysis, these variables are reduced to a single variable. Contrary to his expectations, Shane finds that it has a positive effect. He explains this by the 'national level correlations between barriers to foreign investment, barriers to licensing, and level of economic development' [Shane 1994: 63].

PART THREE

Empirical Analysis

5.   The Enterprise Survey

The review of statistical evidence shows a dearth of reliable quantitative information on DFI in CEE that would be useful for analytical purposes (Chapter 2). The discussion of theoretical issues suggests that enterprise level data may be more suitable than data at higher levels of aggregation (Chapter 4). Therefore, a special database for this research was created using a questionnaire survey.

This is the first large enterprise survey that draws on a (stratified) random sample of Western companies. In order to explore reasons both for and against involvement in the region the survey covers firms with, as well as firms without, investment in the region. The focus is on the characteristics of their business relationships, including trade, investment and contractual arrangements.

This chapter contains the details of the questionnaire survey. The next section summarizes the data collection method. More details and the full text of the questionnaire are reported in the appendices to this chapter. Section three introduces the descriptive statistics for the key variables of the data set. In section four, the factor cost hypothesis is evaluated based on descriptive statistics, and the fifth section discusses the attractions and obstacles for foreign investors. The final section sets the direction for the empirical analysis.

SURVEY METHOD

The study focuses on (West) Germany[1] and the UK as contrasting cases of countries that are, respectively, unusually active and unusually inactive in their DFI activity in CEE - compared with their worldwide DFI activities. The questionnaire covers five transition countries: the Czech Republic (CR), Hungary (HU), Poland (PL), Russia (R) and Romania (RO). These countries are large enough to potentially attract the attention of multinational businesses while representing a variation of economic and political conditions in the region. The Visegrad countries (CR, HU and PL) are the most advanced but differ in their policy towards DFI and in their privatization processes. According to local sources Russia attracts substantial DFI, to a very different local environment. Romania was selected as a contrasting case that, until the time of the survey, received only a small amount of DFI. In addition, respondents were asked to provide information on a 'write-in' country of their own choice.

A compromise was made to focus on industries of interest from both the theoretical and policy analysis perspective. The base population for the survey covers manufacturing companies. This choice is based on the comparatively important role of manufacturing investment in the region. In addition, the theoretical frameworks have been developed for manufacturing industries. Three industries which cover more than half of all manufacturing firms in the two countries have been selected so as to reduce variation but retain policy relevance:

- Food, beverages and tobacco ('Food'),
- Chemicals industry including pharmaceuticals, petroleum refining ('Chem'),
- Machinery including electrical and transport equipment ('Mach').

DFI in machinery and automotive industry constitutes a higher share of investment in CEE than worldwide. Also, the food industry is very active in the region, beyond its share in worldwide DFI. The chemicals industry, on the other hand, appears as yet under-represented in the region in terms of capital invested (Table 2.8). The theoretical requirement of variation in technology and marketing intensity applies to all three industries, as they all include consumer goods industries and, except for the food industry, high-tech firms. Labour intensive production is important in some machinery industries but not in the food or the chemicals industry.

The data have been collected using a stratified random sampling method. The sample has beern stratified based on categories of companies by size according to turnover:

- Large firms with turnover more than £750 million
- Medium size firms with turnover of £100 to £750 million, and
- Small firms with turnover of £3 to £100 million.

In addition, some firms reported by chambers of commerce to be active were included. In total, 677 companies were contacted, slightly more in Germany than in the UK in anticipation of different return rates. The return rate of 39.3 per cent is quite high relative to similar studies (table 2.10). This is a result of a thorough questionnaire design and administration (see appendix 5.1).

Table 5.1 gives the absolute number of respondents for each size group for both the UK and Germany. The return figures include responses from companies that explained that they are not active in the region. Three respondents did not refer to the requested business unit, but instead to the European headquarters of a multinational enterprise. In addition, 27 (4%)

mostly large firms replied that they were not willing to complete the questionnaire, mainly as a matter of corporate policy due to too many requests to complete questionnaires. Two questionnaires contained inconsistent responses and have been excluded from the analysis and the return statistics.

Of 269 responding firms, 40 had to be excluded because they either had their main activities outside the predefined sectors of industry, or they were affiliates of multinational companies oriented solely towards the domestic market. Table 5.2 reports the structure of the sample across industries, size groups and home countries. The regression analysis in Chapters 6 to 8 is based on fewer firms because for some observations values of independent variables were missing.

Table 5.1 Questionnaire returns

Group	Turnover million £	British sample number	%	German sample number	%	Total number	%
Large	> 750	55[a]	53.4	44	41.1	99	46.6
Medium	100 - 750	34	35.0	38	35.5	72	34.8
Small	3 - 100	37[a]	36.0	36	33.6	73	34.8
COC	3 - 750	11[a]	38.5	11	40.7	22	39.6
parents	> 750	2	n.a.	1	n.a.	3	n.a.
Total		139	41.3	130	37.4	269	39.3

Note: [a] includes a response referring to a business unit not in the original base population. These three cases have not been included in the calculation of the reported return rates.

Table 5.2 Number of observations, by sector and size of the firm

	British Large	Medium	Small	CoC	German Large	Medium	Small	CoC	Euro-HQ
Food	10	5	9	-	5	8	7	2	-
Chem	13	5	2	1	16	6	6	2	1
Mach	19	12	22	10	20	21	20	5	2
Total	42	22	33	11	41	35	33	9	3

Note: CoC = chamber of commerce list.

Table 5.3 Business activity, in % of sample firms

	Large	Medium	Small	CoC	Total
Active	88	82	44	100	76
of which					
trade	84	75	44	95	72
contracts	41	33	18	45	34
DFI	58	46	8	75	43
Total no.	86	57	66	20	229
	Food	Chem	Mach	British	German
Active	57	92	77	69	83
of which					
trade	52	88	73	63	81
contracts	13	31	42	32	36
DFI	26	58	44	35	51
Total no.	46	52	131	111	118

χ^2 - tests	Propensity of Activity	Type of Activity
Size	40.909 (2) ***	8.182 (4) *
Industry	17.425 (2) ***	5.285 (4)
German vs. British	5.941 (1) **	0.653 (2)

Notes: Totals are absolute numbers of firms. Boxes refer to sections of the table tested with χ^2 tests. χ^2 statistics are for tests of independence, that is whether the entries in each cell of a table are correctly predicted by the proportions of the full sample. Levels of significance: * =10%, ** = 5%, *** = 1%. CoC = chamber of commerce list.

THE PATTERN OF BUSINESS ACTIVITY

This section presents the descriptive statistics for the activities observed in the sample. At this stage, few interpretations are provided as this is reserved for the in-depth empirical analysis of the following chapters. A simple technique is used to illustrate the significance of differences in the pattern of activity: a contingency table analysis tests for the significance of the proportions observed in a table [see Aczel 1993: 678-83 for details]. These χ^2 tests of independence of the variables are based on the difference of the value expected for each cell E_{ij} and the actually observed value O_{ij}. The χ^2 statistic is

$$\chi^2 = \Sigma^c_{i=1} \, \Sigma^r_{j=1} \, (\, (\, O_{ij} - E_{ij} \,)^2 \text{ and } E_{ij} \,) \qquad (5.1)$$

where the double-sum $\Sigma \, \Sigma$ refers to the sum across all columns c and all rows r. The χ^2 has $(r-1)*(c-1)$ degrees of freedom. If this test statistic is significant, then the values in the cells of the table are influenced by cell specific determinants, i.e. the two dimensions of the table are not independent.

Activity of Sample Firms

The firms in the sample show patterns of activity that differ significantly for their home countries, their industries and their size classes (Table 5.3). Of 229 firms included in the sample, 175 (76%) have active business relationships with the economies in transition in the form of international trade, direct investment or contractual arrangements.[2] These are referred to as active firms. Their share is higher for large firms than for medium or small firms, higher for the chemical industry than for the machinery and food industries and higher for German firms than for British firms. These differences are highly significant as shown by χ^2 tests. The firms drawn from the chamber of commerce sources are, as expected, all active and have been excluded from the formal test for size groups.

The pattern differs between the two home countries (not tabulated). More than 90% of large firms and of the chemical industry from both countries are active in the region. In the other industries and among the medium and small firms, German firms have a far higher propensity of activity. For instance, 93 per cent of medium-size German firms are active compared but only 68 per cent of their British counterparts. Among the small firms, almost twice as many German as British firms are active (58% versus 30%). Across industries, the largest home country difference emerges in the food and beverages industry (68% versus 46%).

Major differences can also be observed for the types of activity. Including multiple activities, 72 per cent of firms are engaged in trade, 43 per cent have DFI, and 34% have contractual relations. The differences again vary across categories, but mostly insignificantly. The propensity to engage in trade follows the pattern of activity as most active firms are involved in trade as part of their business. Contracts are particularly common in the machinery industry amongst both German and British firms. They are most common among large British firms, but medium and small German firms make use more contracts than their British counterparts.

DFI is undertaken by more than half of the active companies. Once more, the highest proportions of active firms are observed among large enterprises (58%), firms in the chemicals industry (58%) and firms of German origin (51%). The difference between British and German firms is particularly evident among the small firms where not one British DFI has been identified, compared with five (15%) investing small German firms. The food industry is the least active with only 36 per cent of German and 17 per cent of British firms investing in the region. The industry differences reflect the large economies of scale in the chemicals industry, and the high transportation costs in the food and beverages industry, which account for different degrees of internationalization of the industries.

Not only are more German firms active in the region, the region is also more important to them. Table 5.4 shows the East European business as a share of the firms' worldwide operations, in terms of turnover, assets and employment. By all three measures, CEE accounts for a substantially larger share of business for German firms. The leading UK companies are less active than the leading German companies. One German beverage company already employs half its personnel in Hungary.

Table 5.4 CEE business as a percentage of worldwide operations

CEE business	>20%	10% - 20%	5% - 10%	2% - 5%	0% - 2%	0%	n.a.	total
By turnover								
British	-	-	4	18	78	-	-	100
German	-	7	19	40	33	1[a]	-	100
By assets								
British	-	-	1	1	44	53	1	100
German	-	4	1	9	34	49	3	100
By employment								
British	-	1	6	10	26	36	21	100
German	3	4	4	12	20	49	8	100

Notes: Respondents in each category, as percentage of active firms. Categories are by share of CEE activities in world wide activitities. [a] = a company is importing but not exporting.

Characteristics of Active Business Relationships

The questionnaire collected information on business relationships with five countries in CEE: Poland, Hungary, Czech Republic, Russia and Romania. The variation of business across these countries can be analysed using the firm-country relationship as the basic unit of analysis. Of these, there are 1145 observations (229 sample firms times five countries). The number of active business relationships with the countries is 656 (57.3%).

In Table 5.5, the pattern of activity is tabulated for various categories of sub-samples: home countries, host countries, industries and firm size. The propensity of activity and the pattern of broad categories of activity are similar on the firm-country level to those described in Table 5.3 at the firm level. Activity data for home country, industry and size groups thus need no further comments, except to note that increased sample size increases significance levels.[3]

Table 5.5 Types of business activities
(in % of maximum possible business relationships)

Category	UK	D	CR	HU	PL	R	RO	Total
Active	47.9	66.1	62.9	57.6	65.1	58.1	42.8	57.3
Trade	43.4	61.7	56.3	52.0	59.4	55.5	41.0	52.8
Contracts	14.8	15.1	17.9	14.8	18.3	16.6	7.0	14.9
DFI	13.2	24.1	26.2	23.1	25.3	13.5	5.7	18.8
Export	43.1	60.0	54.4	51.3	59.4	54.1	39.7	51.8
Import	4.5	17.6	15.7	13.5	14.8	9.2	3.1	11.3
Licensing	4.7	7.1	4.4	5.7	7.4	9.6	2.6	5.9
Franchising	3.2	-	2.6	1.3	1.7	0.9	1.3	1.6
Subcontracting	2.5	7.3	8.3	7.0	6.1	3.1	0.4	5.0
Management C.	3.2	1.4	3.1	1.7	3.1	1.7	1.7	2.3
Turnkey project	3.2	2.9	3.5	1.7	3.9	4.8	1.3	3.1
Other contracts	5.2	2.9	3.9	2.2	4.8	7.4	1.7	4.0
Total no.	555	590	229	229	229	229	229	1145

Category	Food	Chem	Mach	Large	Med.	Small	CoC
Active	37.8	76.5	56.5	77.0	59.3	25.8	71.0
Trade	32.6	73.8	51.6	71.4	53.3	23.6	68.0
Contracts	4.3	11.5	20.0	22.1	11.9	5.8	23.0
DFI	11.3	28.5	17.6	29.1	18.2	3.0	28.0
Export	33.0	72.3	50.2	69.5	53.0	23.3	66.0
Import	2.2	13.5	13.6	18.6	7.7	3.6	15.0
Licensing	0.9	7.3	7.2	9.5	3.5	0.9	14.0
Franchising	1.7	-	2.1	1.4	2.5	0.3	4.0
Subcontracting	0.4	3.5	7.2	7.0	4.2	3.3	4.0
Management C.	0.9	0.8	3.4	4.2	2.8	-	-
Turnkey project	0.4	1.2	4.7	5.6	1.1	0.3	7.0
Other contracts	1.7	3.5	5.0	7.2	3.2	0.9	3.0
Total no.	230	260	655	430	285	330	100

χ^2-tests	Home C.	Host C.	Industries	Size
Propensity of activity	38.604 (1)***	28.316 (4)***	75.153 (2)***	200.521 (2)***
Type of activity	7.790 (2)**	23.542 (8)***	27.314 (6)***	13.363 (6)***
Import	49.262 (1)***	25.108 (4)***	23.804 (2)***	47.144 (2)***
Type of contract	43.471 (5)***	27.977 (20)	25.407 (10)***	24.544 (10)***

Level of significance: * = 10%, ** = 5%, *** = 1%.

Across the five host countries, a significant variation can be observed. In terms of the share of companies reporting business, Poland leads (65.1%) followed by the Czech Republic (62.9%), Russia (58.1%), Hungary (57.6%) and at distant fifth place Romania (42.8%). The non-tabulated underlying differences between German and British firms suggest that Germans are more active than their British counterparts in all countries, except Russia. British firms have a slight preference for Poland, especially in terms of the first business contact, which is reflected in the slight Polish lead in the proportion of active firms.

The pattern of trade, contracts and DFI is broadly similar to that of aggregate activity and varies significantly among host countries. Romania lags behind more in terms of contractual relationships and DFI than in trade contacts. Russia attracts only little more than half the number of investors that each of the Visegrad countries attract. These two observations suggest that the less attractive environments especially affect the extent of foreign investment, but also, to a lesser degree, international trade. Surprisingly, the Czech Republic has the largest number of foreign investors, ahead of the early opened Hungary and the large market of Poland. This small (and insignificant) difference reflects German business, while British firms prefer Poland. Other surveys also found a similar propensity of business across the Visegrad countries (see Chapter 2). However, the survey evidence differs from aggregate capital flows, according to which Hungary lead by a large margin. This may reflect the industries other than those sampled, or, more likely, it is a result of large volumes of DFI being attracted by a few large projects such as telecom-privatization [Canning and Hare 1996].

Trade as the basic form of international business is, not surprisingly, the most common form of business reported by the sample firms. A substantial imbalance appears between imports and exports. Export is part of most business relationships, while imports are reported by only 11.3 per cent of firm-country relationships. This result holds across all sectors and size groups. The imbalance is in part a result of the sampling frame that focuses on manufacturing firms since imports are to a larger extent undertaken by trading companies.

The import data show interesting features of trade in manufacturing. Imports are more likely in machinery industry and in large companies, and less in small and medium food processing companies. This holds true for the share of firms importing as well as for importing firms relative to active firms. The discrepancy between export and import is more substantial for British companies. Only 4.5 per cent of firm-country relations involve imports to the UK, compared with 17.6 per cent for German firms. The Visegrad countries are the main source of imports, especially for German firms. Russia lags behind, while Romania so far seems almost negligible as a source of imports. These differences in the propensity to import are statistically significant as shown by χ^2-tests.

Table 5.5 furthermore reports the kinds of contracts used by sample firms. 14.9 per cent of firm-country relations recorded contractual arrangements as their sole form of activity in the region or combined with other contracts or investment. Such dual relationship may or may not refer to the same business partner. The most common types are licensing (5.9%) and subcontracting (5.0%). The use of contracts varies significantly across industrial sectors, firm size, and between German and British firms, but has only a small variation among the Eastern countries.

German and British firms show a similar propensity to use contracts, but prefer different types of contracts. Germans use licensing and subcontracting, but never franchising while British firms use a variety of different contracts. The German preference for subcontracting confirms earlier research [Naujoks and Schmidt 1994]. Licensing, turnkey projects and other contracts are most common in Russia, followed closely by Poland, presumably due to the attraction of the markets. These contracts can reduce the investment risk of a market entry. Subcontracting is most common in the Czech Republic and in Hungary, which corresponds with the German preference for this form of business.

The machinery industry is most actively using contracts, as 20 per cent of firm-country units involve contracts, compared with only 4.3 per cemt in the food industry. The most common types of contracts in the machinery industry are licensing and subcontracting, while the chemical industry makes an over-proportionate use of licensing. No type of contract attains importance in the food industry. Contracts are more commonly used by large firms, even relative to the number of their active business relationships. Contracts do not seem to be used by small and medium firms to overcome their limited financial and managerial resources. Only subcontracting is used over-proportionately by small and medium firms.

Characteristics of Direct Foreign Investment

DFI is defined as investment in equity to influence management operations in the partner company. For this research, a lower limit of 5 per cent in equity has been implemented in the questionnaire to define a minority JV. A DFI is recorded for all respondents indicating minority or majority JVs or a wholly-owned subsidiary or branch in question 1. Of all firm-country relationships, 18.8 per cent include DFI projects (Table 5.5).

Table 5.6 reports the characteristics of these 215 DFI projects with χ^2-tests of independence for sections of the table. The table reports, firstly, the equity ownership chosen by the investors. It varies significantly across home and host countries but not for industries or size groups. The overwhelming majority of 77.1 per cent of investors have wholly owned affiliates, while 27.1% have majority JVs and 14.0 per cent have minority JVs. Many firms have multiple

Table 5.6 Characteristics of DFI projects

Category	UK	D	CR	HU	PL	R	RO	Total
Minority JV	20.5	10.6	6.8	5.7	12.1	38.7	20.8	14.0
Majority JV	16.4	32.6	30.5	22.6	24.1	35.5	23.1	27.1
Wholly-owned subs.	74.0	78.7	79.7	86.8	81.0	58.1	53.8	77.1
Greenfield	62.0	48.2	55.9	54.0	57.9	40.0	41.7	52.9
Acquisition	22.5	32.4	31.0	32.0	35.1	10.0	25.0	29.0
JV-entry	15.5	23.9	12.3	18.0	15.8	50.0	27.3	21.0
JV-acquisition	19.7	18.7	17.5	18.0	14.0	33.3	18.2	19.0
Market motive	94.5	98.6	98.3	98.1	98.2	93.5	92.3	97.2
Factor cost motive	23.3	35.5	35.0	28.3	33.3	29.0	23.1	31.3
Both	19.2	34.0	33.3	26.4	31.6	25.8	15.4	29.0
Exporting to CEE	78.1	85.0	83.1	80.8	82.8	87.1	76.9	82.6
Importing from CEE	20.5	27.5	28.3	28.3	29.3	12.9	7.7	25.1
Total no.	73	142	60	53	58	31	13	215

Category	Food	Chem	Mach	Large	Med.	Small	CoC
Minority JV	15.4	12.2	14.9	17.6	7.7	22.2	7.1
Majority JV	26.9	17.6	33.3	28.0	25.0	33.3	25.0
Wholly owned Subs.	69.2	86.5	72.8	77.6	80.8	55.6	75.0
Greenfield	38.5	70.4	45.0	48.8	61.2	40.0	60.7
Acquisition	38.5	32.4	24.5	35.0	22.4	10.0	21.4
JV-entry	19.2	12.7	26.9	23.5	18.4	33.3	10.7
JV-acquisition	19.2	14.1	22.2	22.7	14.3	11.1	14.3
Market motive	100.0	98.6	95.7	96.8	96.2	100.0	100.0
Factor cost motive	24.0	18.9	40.9	30.6	30.8	40.0	32.1
Both	24.0	18.9	36.5	28.2	26.9	40.0	32.1
Exporting to CEE	73.1	90.5	79.6	88.8	72.0	40.0	89.3
Importing from CEE	11.5	16.2	33.9	27.2	13.5	20.0	39.3
Total no.	26	74	115	125	52	10	28

χ^2-tests	Home C.	Host C.	Industries	Size
Ownership	7.915 (2) **	24.138 (8) ***	5.548 (4)	3.406 (4)
Entry mode	4.633 (3)	23.791 (12) **	12.641 (6) **	5.999 (6)
Factor cost motive	3.314 (1) *	1.196 (4)	10.791 (2) ***	0.393 (2)
Import	1.226 (1)	5.715 (4)	10.397 (2) ***	3.969 (2) **

projects with different ownership arrangement such that the percentage figures add to more than 100 per cent.

German investors have a higher share of wholly or majority owned investments. 30 per cent of British investments include minority JVs compared with only 10 per cent of German DFI. In Poland, Hungary, and the Czech Republic most DFI are wholly owned, while JVs are established by about one in three investors. This is surprising as JVs have been reported widely as the most common form of investment, and until recently full foreign ownership was not permitted. On the other hand, JVs are still far more common in Romania and Russia. The chemicals industry has a high share of wholly owned affiliates while the share of JVs is higher among small firms. Yet these differences are not significant.

The ownership structure is related to the mode of entry for which four alternatives had been suggested in the questionnaire, following Gatling [1993] and OECD [1994]:

- greenfield, that is start-up ventures that are more than 95 per cent foreign owned,
- acquisition, that is the purchase of all or part of an existing enterprise,
- joint venture acquisition, that is the formation of a new entity where the local partner contributed assets from the existing enterprise, and
- joint venture entry, where a new entity is set up with one or more local partners.

Again, substantial variations can be observed that are significant across host countries and industries. Greenfield investments are the most common mode of entry, accounting for more than 50 per cent of projects, followed by acquisitions, JV-entry and JV-acquisition.[4] The high proportion of greenfield projects is surprising given the worldwide trend towards entry via acquisitions [for example UN 1992]. Greenfield entry is especially common for British firms, the chemicals industry and for projects in the Visegrad countries. Acquisitions are more common for large parent firms, the food industry, German firms, and investments in the Visegrad countries. On the other hand, acquisitions account for only 10 per cent of investments in Russia. JV-entry and JV-acquisitions are the dominant mode of entry in Russia, and are comparatively important in the machinery industry.

The data across firm size indicate few variations of ownership or entry mode because of the small number of DFI projects by small firms, and different trends for medium and small firms: medium firms seem to prefer greenfield entry and full ownership while small firms have a relatively high share of minority JVs and JV-entry. Due to the unequal distribution over size categories, the χ^2-statistics in the fourth column are mostly insignificant.

For the same question in the EIU study [Gatling 1993], respondents were to indicate one option only. 29 per cent of investors reported greenfield projects and 56 per cent JVs or JV-acquisitions. In the OECD [1994] study, German and British investors have above average preferences against greenfield projects. Considering UK and German respondents only, 17 per cent reported greenfield investments and 67 per cent JVs or JV-acquisitions. The outlier in that study is Poland that had already received more than half its projects as greenfield projects. Comparing the results of that study with this study, it is even more remarkable that a high share of greenfield investments and a low share of JV has now been reported (Table 5.7). Two subsequent surveys, Knight and Webb [1997] and Pye [1997], also found higher proportions of greenfield investment.

Table 5.7 Mode of entry in different studies

	D	UK	a	total [c]	%	PL	HU	CR	R	RO	b
						OECD 1994					
greenfield	4	4	29	37	23	16	10	2	3[e]	1	4
acquisition	4	7	28	39	24	4	16	13	1	-	3
JV-acquis.	10	14	36	60	37	7	15	7	11	2	14
JV-entry	3	4	23	30	19	4	12	6	4	-	3
other	-	2	6	8	5	1	-	5	1	-	-
total	20	26	126	162	100	30	52	30	19	2	24

	EIU / Creditanstalt [Gatling 1993]								This Study	
	PL	HU	CR	SU	RO	d	total	%	total	%
greenfield	7	7	8	5	2	2	31	29	110	53
acquisition	1	2	4	-	-	-	7	7	60	29
JV-acquis.	3	4	4	3	1	1	16	15	43	19
JV-entry	6	9	5	14	2	8	44	41	39	21
n. a.	3	-	1	2	-	3	9	8	7	3
total	20	22	22	24	5	14	107	100	215	100

Notes: a = Austria (34), France (34), Japan (7) and USA (41); b = Slovakia (9), Bulgaria (4), Ukraine (4), Kazakhstan (3) and Baltic States (3); c = Totals from Western and Eastern countries do not add to the same totals for unknown reasons; d = Bulgaria and Yugoslavia; e = typo in the original corrected.

Sources: tables 10a to 10k in OECD [1994], table A1.17 in Gatling [1993], and Table 5.6 above.

The high share of greenfield projects is however in accordance with an observed trend towards greenfield entry and full ownership in the region [Möllering *et al.* 1994, Rojec and Jermakowicz 1995]. This pattern raises the question, why are greenfield entries so popular in CEE - in opposition to worldwide trends? The differences can be attributed to the industries surveyed, and the time of the study. Both Gatling [1993] and OECD [1994] include other industries, such as trade and services.[5] This could explain a bias towards JVs. The timing of the studies however suggests a highly plausible interpretation: JVs were a popular form of entry at very early stages of DFI in the region, a time of regulatory constraints and lack of knowledge on the local environment. Over time, constraints have been eased and multinationals gathered local experience such that greenfield entry and full ownership becomes feasible.

INVESTMENT MOTIVATIONS

In appendix 3.1, it was proposed that low labour costs may be an important motivation for DFI in the region, given the cost differential between Western and Eastern Europe. This is also suggested by Arva [1994], Acocella [1995] and UN [1995, chap. V]. The proposition can be analysed using descriptive statistics on questionnaire data only. For a formal hypothesis test see Meyer [1995a]. The questionnaire includes two direct questions on investment motives:

Q8.   It is said that CEE offers interesting new market opportunities. Did you invest in the region to supply the local markets?

Q9.   It is said that CEE offers opportunities for low-cost production for export to Western markets because wages are substantially lower than in Western Europe. Did you invest in the region to utilize such opportunities?

The responses are included in Table 5.6. The data show that 97.2 per cent of investors are following a 'market motive'. Almost three out of four projects are attracted solely by new markets, with 29.0 per cent following both motives simultaneously, combining the access to a new market with exports of goods. This confirms the dominance of the market-seeking motive observed in earlier studies (see Chapter 2). Remarkably, only five companies (2.3%) are investing in the region solely following a 'factor cost motive'.[6] These are different machinery firms, and include a company who wanted to use local scenery to cast a movie. They are by coincidence equally distributed with one case in each host country. The factor-cost motivation has been indicated by 31.3 per cent of respondents, but mostly in combination with market orientation. Factor-cost differences are only realized if also an attractive local market exists. Only when the local market is saturated, will the local production operations develop competitive strength for world markets and develop its export potential.

The share of companies with dual motivation is significantly higher for

German (34.0%) than for British investors (19.2%). Dual motivation varies insignificantly between the host countries with the highest share among investors in the Czech Republic and lowest for Romania. The machinery industry makes significantly more use of factor cost differentials (40.9%), as would be predicted because the food industry (24.0%) faces trade barriers in agriculture and higher transportation costs, and the chemical industry (18.9%) is capital and scale intensive. Thus, the importance of factor-costs is an industry specific phenomenon. Note that this study does not cover the textile and clothing industry, in which the low factor costs are likely to be important.

A second indicator for the utilisation of factor-cost differences is the extent to which DFI projects are connected with imports to the Western home country. Only 25 per cent of investors import from the region, compared with 83% exporting to CEE. As noted above, this difference may be a result of selecting manufacturing firms as the base population. However, the variation of the import propensity confirms the pattern found for factor-cost orientation. Investors in machinery industry are far more likely to import from the region than either chemicals or food industry. Also, large firms are significantly more likely to import. A higher propensity to import is also found for German firms and projects in the Visegrad countries.

In conclusion, the evidence does not support the view that the developmental model (appendix 3.1) would appropriately describe West-East European DFI during the early years of transition. Only a few West European industries such as electronics and textiles are competing in world market on the basis of price and using cheap labour. Over recent decades labour intensive industries have lost competitiveness in Western Europe and are no longer strongly a major component of their economies.

ATTRACTIONS AND OBSTACLES FOR INVESTORS

Investors reported the main determinants of their locational decisions separately for market and cost-oriented projects in questions 8 and 9. Table 5.9 reports the responses in an aggregate form that merges related arguments. Also, write-in responses have been taken into account and the scores have been adjusted for the varying number of responses indicated by each respondent.

Market-oriented investment depends on the attraction of the local market (24.7%), which is mainly related to the population (14.4%) and income levels (7.3%). Investors take advantage of the unsatisfied demand in virgin markets. In addition, several investors reported demands specific to their industry, such as coal mines requesting specific machinery in Poland or wine connoisseurs appreciating importes wines in Hungary. Factor-cost related arguments were of secondary importance for market investment.

Factor-cost oriented investment depends, naturally, foremost on labour costs and qualifications (47.2%). Market access was also important, though access to regional markets (13.5%) was reported more frequently than access to the European Union markets (5.1%).

Table 5.8 Attractions and obstacles of local environments

Attractions	Market projects (Question 8a)	Factor cost projects (Question 9a)
Market attraction	24.7%	18.6%
Factor costs	8.3%	47.2%
Institutional framework	26.5%	18.8%
Partner and people	23.7%	14.2%
Competition	12.4%	none
Other	11.5%	4.2%
Obstacles	Market projects (Question 8b)	Factor cost projects (Question 9b)
Investment risk	9.3%	11.7%
Market attraction	11.9%	none
Factor costs	2.8%	6.5%
Institutional framework	14.2%	11.9%
Partner and people	4.6%	14.5%
Other	6.9%	6.0%
Company specific	34.8%	28.1%
Industry specific	15.6%	21.7%

Note: Each respondent counts for one unit in the weighted score, such that a respondent ticking five options would add 0.2 to each item. The tables report the percentages of this weighted score for groups of responses.

Both kinds of DFI are encouraged by the development of the institutional framework. This includes foremost the stability of the political environment and secondly the development of the legal system. Specific aspects of the framework suggested in the questionnaire, such as Europe Agreements, were rarely ticked. Interesting to note is the importance attached to the the presence of specific business partners and personal contacts (23.7% in Q8a / 14.2% in Q9a). This includes prior contacts to future JV partners (15.3% / 9.3%) that are based upon existing trading relationships as well as personal contacts, for example by expatriates.   Also presence of other foreign investors, and, for factor-cost oriented investment, the quality of locally available intermediate goods was important. These personal aspects are often overlooked in economic analysis. Lastly, the fact that few competitors were present also attracted many market seeking investors.

The responses to the question, 'why did you not invest', often indicated that Eastern Europe was outside the scope of the firm's corporate strategy for company or industry-specific reasons (Table 5.9). The write-in answers under this category include firms focusing exclusively on the domestic market, often affiliates of MNE,[7] and firms reporting an existing overcapacity in the industry. Factor-cost oriented investment was often not undertaken, as relocation was not considered a strategic option, given the nature of the production process. This relates to the industry-specific nature of the labour cost argument. Many consumer goods are nowadays produced in Western Europe in capital and scale intensive production lines. All these firms are not potential investors and thus not of interest for the current analysis.

The obstacles related to the host economies reflect first the weak institutional framework. Many respondents considered the general economic risks in the region too high (9.3% / 11.7%). Even more frequently, the weak political and legal framework was cited (14.2% / 11.9%). These general concerns were more important than any specific aspects of the framework that were proposed in the questionnaire, for example trade barriers. This reflects the slow progress in establishing the institutional framework that guarantees the functioning of a market economy.

Many non-investors could serve the market from outside, or considered the local demand too low to justify DFI (11.9%). Factor cost investment was inhibited by local costs being too high (6.5%) due to the lack of infrastructure and qualification as well as the expected future labour costs. Some investors are also concerned about the viability of the East-West wage gap. Especially projects with long time horizons are inhibited by uncertainty over future labour costs and real exchange rates.

The obstacles in the partner and people category include the costs of restructuring local firms, lack of suitable local partners, and unsatisfactory quality of locally procured inputs. These arguments relate to the quality of local businesses, and are not typically found in investor surveys. They are specific to the CEE region and reflect the problems that arise when dealing with the structures of local business inherited from 40 years of socialism.

DIRECTIONS FOR THE EMPIRICAL ANALYSIS

The empirical analysis focuses on the decision process of firms contemplating investment in a transition economy. The theoretical basis is the OLI paradigm

(Chapter 3) with special emphasis on the internalization aspect. Three stages of involvement are analysed separately. First, firms decide whether or not they wish to engage in business with the region. Second, they decide whether or not they wish to invest in the region, and finally they decide upon their preferred mode of entry and ownership (Figure 5.1).

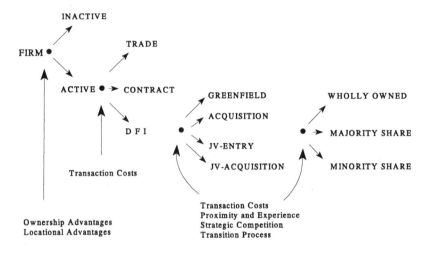

Figure 5.1 Stages of the empirical analysis

At the first stage, firms consider their firm-specific advantages and how these will combine with the specific locational advantages of the host economy. These two components of the OLI framework should explain the propensity to engage in West-East business. In Chapter 6, firm-level regression equations are estimated for the probability of a firm being active in the region, active in any of the selected countries, and active in multiple countries simultaneously.

The type of business activity is chosen at the second stage. The resulting pattern of trade, contracts and DFI (Table 5.5) is analysed in Chapter 7. Internalization incentives are predicted to determine the propensity to engage in DFI. The empirical tests on the level of firm-country relationships consider internal and external transaction costs as determinants for the choice between a market transaction (trade, contract) and internalization by DFI.

At the third stage, firms decide upon the equity ownership and mode of entry of the investment project summarized in Table 5.6. This decision is again subject to transaction costs, but also to other firm and industry effects such as experience and proximity. The analysis also considers the involvement of investors in the privatization process, which is the main option for acquiring local firms in the transition economies.

This analysis of DFI decisions is novel in that multiple decisions in the entry process are analysed with the same data set. By using a three-step approach, the determinants of business activity are explicitly separated from the determinants of DFI, and the determinants of entry mode and ownership. For this analysis, it has to be assumed that the decisions at the three stages are independent of each other. This assumption can be rationalized by arguing that decisions concerning involvement (stage 1) and DFI (stage 2) are made at different times in the internationalization process of the firm. However, it is sufficient if they are distinct decisions, which is a less exposed assumption. The separation of decisions concerning DFI (stage 2) and mode of entry (stage 3) is implicit in the transaction cost dichotomy of markets and hierarchies.

NOTES

1. Including East Germany would have added an additional layer of complexity to the study. Therefore, the sample includes only West German firms and investment in other transition economies. (One exception is a firm which relocated its corporate headquarters from West to East Germany.) For legibility, the word West is henceforth omitted.

2. The interpretation has to consider that a self-selection bias is likely to operate in favour of active companies because managers without a business interest in CEE are more likely to ignore the request to complete the questionnaire. However, differences in the proportions of active firms across sub-samples would reflect differences in base population.

3. The data set includes multiple observations for each firm. This leads to 'repeated measures' in the home country, industry, and size categories which lead to overstatements of statistical significance.

4. For the analysis, all projects described as representative offices were excluded. This includes some DFI projects reported as WOS or JV in the ownership question. In this way, the analysis covers only substantive investment projects.

5. Gatling [1993] and OECD [1994] do not explain their base population making any direct comparison of the data difficult. Their data sets are smaller than the one used here and have been collected in 1991 and 1993 respectively while the data set used in this analysis was collected in winter 1994/95.

6. One respondent replied 'no' to both questions.

7. These firms have been excluded from the empirical analysis, see appendix 5.1.

APPENDIX 5.1: METHODOLOGY OF THE SURVEY

The questionnaire has been designed according to the following objectives:

- To collect information on the dependent variables, that is the business activities of the sample firms in the countries of CEE (questions 1, 5).
- To collect information on the business characteristics that according to theory would be relevant for the choice of organizational form (questions 2, 3, 4, 6, 7, 8, 9).
- To collect firm-specific data relevant for the decisions concerning activity and organizational form that are not generally available from databases and annual reports (questions 11, 12, 13).
- To collect exploratory information on attractions and obstacles to investment, separating market and factor-cost DFI (questions 8a, 8b, 9a, 9b, 10).
- To build a database of contact persons for further research.

The full text of the questionnaire is reproduced in appendix 5.2.

Base population
The base population has been selected in view of the two research objectives understanding DFI flows to CEE, and testing theory of the multinational enterprises. These two objectives are to some extent conflicting. Transition economists, and policy advisors, would prefer to use a very broad sample to get as close as feasible to explaining the aggregate flows of DFI. To be relevant for economic policy, the selected industries should be relevant for the host countries, and typical or representative for investment at large. Thus,

- sample firms should be active in CEE with a variety of organizational forms;
- sample firms should be representative of selected industries,
- the sample should contain a matched sample of German and British industries for comparative analysis.

The analysis of theoretical propositions on the other hand requires focus on some selected industries only to reduce variations from influences other than those analysed in the theory. The tests of the propositions arising for transaction cost economics and the developmental model further require for the sample that

- it should exclude industries facing major trade barriers such as textiles,
- it should include technology and goodwill intensive industries as variation of these characteristics is important to analyse TC propositions,
- it should include labour intensive industries such as textile or electronics to be able to test propositions derived from the developmental model.

On these considerations, three industries have been selected, defined as follows:

Food   Food, beverages and tobacco (USSIC codes 20, 21),
Chemicals   Chemicals industry including pharmaceuticals, petroleum refining
              (USSIC 28, 29),
Machinery   Machinery including electrical and transport equipment (USSIC
              35, 36, 37).

The base population was retrieved from a company database (Fame-Amadeus) using their own selection routine.[1] These databases are the most comprehensive databases available and cover more than stock market quoted enterprises. They also provide data on company accounts needed for further analysis. In addition to the random sample, some companies have been contacted, who, from sources of the chambers of commerce (CoC), were known to be active in the region. These all have annual turnovers below £750 million and are active *via* investments or contractual arrangements. They add information on the preferred form of business by small and medium firms without being representative of German or British industry.

Earlier studies have not used random samples, but lists of companies known to be active, for instance from Chambers of Commerce [Wang 1993, Engelhard and Eckert 1994, Ali and Mirza 1996]. Others remain vague about the method of selection of their sample firms [Gatling 1993, OECD 1994], which may, but need not, have major implications for the validity of their conclusions.

Sample stratification
The data have been collected using a stratified random sampling method. The stratification by company size is based on the turnover in the latest available year (usually 1993):

Large   turnover more than £750 million,
Medium   turnover of £100 to £750 million, and
Small   turnover of £3 to £100 million.

In the 'Large' group, all companies have been contacted, while in the 'Medium' and 'Small' groups a random sample was selected. The purpose of this stratification was to include a complete list of the largest investors, as they account for most of the business volume with the region, but also to include medium and small companies in the sample, as they make a major contribution in some industries and react differently to the same incentives. The stratification has been designed such that the proportions of firms contacted in each size group were equivalent to the proportions of firms known to be active from a list from Chamber of Commerce sources.[2] Also, the lower limit of £3 million was motivated by the smallest firms in this list. The sample was not stratified by industry. The number of firms contacted in each industry thus reflects their proportion in the base population. The sample should thus be a good representation of potential investors from the selected industries.

Preparation and administration

The design of the questionnaire paid special attention to the ease of completion, potential sensitivity of information and avoidance of quantitative questions to enable a high return rate and thus a good representation of the base population. The German translation was prepared by the researcher himself and has been thoroughly checked by another native German speaker experienced in the design of research questionnaires.

The questionnaire has been piloted on a sample of 30 British companies in July 1994, followed by a reminder letter. Of them, five (17%) returned a completed questionnaire. The pilot study led to changes in questionnaire design, formulation of questions and the definition of the base population. The preparation of the final questionnaire included interviews with individuals experienced in questionnaire design as well as potential respondents. After this process, the researcher felt confident that questions were correctly understood and not ambiguous, and that the main options had been included in the suggested responses.

Administration included several tasks necessary to achieve good quality replies and a representative response rate: identification of contact persons from various data bases and some telephone calls, mailing the questionnaire with a prepaid return envelope, and mailing a reminder letter with a new copy of the questionnaire to non-respondents after two weeks. The cover letter on LBS letterheads contained a strong statement of confidentiality. The questionnaire was sent out in October and November 1994 to the British companies and in February 1995 to the Germans. German responses were collected at University of Bonn (Prof. Dr. Dieter Bös), although the questionnaire was sent from the UK due to substantial postage cost differentials. Respondents who had indicated their interest received a thank-you letter with a LBS CISME Centre brochure and an executive briefing of the nontechnical data analysis.

Sample section bases

The return rates are consistently high across size groups, home countries and sectors, with more than 30 per cent for each category considered (Table 5.1) and highest returns for large firms. British firms were expected to have a higher return because of experiences by other researchers and the reputation of London Business School within the UK. This may have increased returns by large British firms, but no difference was observed for medium and small firms. In anticipation, the number of German firms had been increased. Active firms were expected to be more likely to respond than firms without business with CEE because they would have greater personal interest in the research.

Comparing the return by CoC-list firms with the other medium and small firms indicates that such a bias exists, but is not substantial. Advertising intensive firms were suspected to have a lower return because of greater concern about confidentiality. This does not seem to be the case either: of 22 top advertising firms in the sample, 12 returned a completed questionnaire, which implies a return rate comparable to that of large firms in the full sample.[3]

Across industries, little variation was observed except for a low return of 32 per cent from the German food industry. This is in part explained by the only major self-selection effect observed: only two of nine tobacco manufacturers responded, both exclusively supplying the domestic market. This may be a result of secrecy in this industry. It was solved by redefining the industry as 'food and beverages, USSIC code 20' only. Overall, none of the potential biases seems to affect the general representativeness of the sample with respect to the base population.[4]

Intra-firm variation
The questionnaire requested mainly factual information about business activities rather than perceptional or motivational data. Therefore, it was expected that responses from different individuals within a firm would not vary much. This 'intra-firm variation' could be checked based on 10 companies returning two responses, which did not reveal major differences for the main questions. Exceptions are the motivations and obstacles questions 8a, 8b, 9a, 9b that are not used in the analysis. The position of the respondent was not requested in the questionnaire unless he or she would be willing to participate in an interview, or requested a copy of the result. From this information, it can be inferred that most respondents were managers in charge of coordination of business with Eastern Europe reporting to the board, plus a substantial number of board members or Chief Executives.

Adjustments of the sample
Two problems arose in the creation of the database with the questionnaire responses:

* The database contains enterprises that have their main business activity in an industry other than the three specified branches of manufacturing.[5] These firms have been removed from the sample to avoid distortion by industry-specific effects and to maintain comparability of the German and the British subsamples.
* The database contains business units of MNEs from third countries. These are an indigenous part of the British or German industry and therefore had been included in the base population. However, respondents indicated in 21 cases that their firms' strategic responsibilities do not include business or investment with CEE. Mostly, they were limited to supplying the domestic

market. For the empirical analysis, they had to be excluded because they are not potential investors.

In total, 40 firms were thus removed from the analysis (Table 5.A1).[6] Since ideally these firms would not have been in the base population, this does not affect the return rate.[7] Potential sample selection biases should be reduced by their exclusion. The remaining 229 firms are from now on referred to as the sample.

Table 5.A1 The respondents

Firms	Respon- dents	Firms in sample
By industry		
Food and beverages (and tobacco)	50	46
Chemical industry including pharmaceuticals and petroleum refining	59	52
Machinery industry, incl. electrical machinery and transport equipment	140	131
Other industries: mainly construction and services	20	--
By firm size		
Large firms, annual turnover more than £750 million	99	83
Medium firms, annual turnover £100 - 750 million	72	57
Smaller firms, annual turnover below £100 million	73	66
Medium firms known to be active from Chambers of Commerce	22	20
Respondents referred to European headquarters of company contacted	3	3
Total	269	229

Notes to appendix 5.1

1. It was necessary to clean the resulting list for instance to exclude firms in liquidation or receivership, and to avoid contacting both parent and affiliated company. Thus holding companies have been excluded if affiliates accounting for more than 50 per cent of turnover were also in the list - unless the affiliates were functional sales affiliates.
2. Without stratification, the sample would have been dominated by small firms most of which have no investment in CEE.
3. Based on a list 100 top advertising firms in the UK published by *Marketing Week* [14.4.1995] which included 22 firms of the base population.

4. Note however that in the empirical analysis in Chapters 6 to 8, missing accounting data led to exclusion of small and medium German firms in 'private' ownership.

5. These companies have activities in three specified industries according to the selection routine provided by database, that however turned out to be only a small part of their business. They include from the UK eight construction and building materials companies, three utility distributors, three companies in paper and related industries, two telecommunication companies, two plastic manufacturers, a textile company, a trading company, and a shipping company, and from Germany a trader in raw materials, and a mining company.

6. In Meyer [1995b] the summary statistics including all respondents have been reported.

7. Assuming that the proportion of ineligible respondents among respondents is equal to the proportion of ineligible respondents among firms contacted.

APPENDIX 5.2: TEXT OF THE QUESTIONNAIRE SURVEY

CISME Centre, London Business School, 1994

Business with Central and Eastern Europe - Questionnaire
U.K. version

Company: _____

This questionnaire asks for characteristics of enterprises in the U.K. and Germany, and their business activities in Central and Eastern Europe (CEE). The countries considered are:
Albania, Bulgaria, Czech Republic, Hungary, Poland, Romania, Slovakia, Croatia, Slovenia and other states in the former Yugoslavia, Estonia, Latvia and Lithuania, Russia, Ukraine, Belarus, Moldova, as well as the Central Asian and Caucasian states of the former Soviet Union

The information obtained for this research will be used for research purposes only. Do you have any specific requests with respect to confidentiality?

The questionnaire has three sections:
  1. Business in and with Central and Eastern Europe
  2. Motivations and obstacles to investment in Central and Eastern Europe
  3. General information on your company

If you have any questions about this questionnaire, please contact me under the telephone or fax numbers listed below:

Tel.: (071) 262 5050, Extension 3485   Fax: (071) 724 7875

When completed, please return this questionnaire in the provided envelope to:
    Klaus Meyer
    CISME-Centre
    London Business School
    Sussex Place, Regent's Park
    London NW1 4SA

Thank you very much for your cooperation

Section 1: Business in and with Central and Eastern Europe

If you <u>do not</u> have business with the region, please start on <u>page 5</u>.

Please respond to the following questions in respect to your business in <u>Poland</u>, <u>Hungary</u>, the <u>Czech Republic</u>, <u>Russia</u>, and <u>Romania</u>. Additionally, please use the 'write in' column to add another country in Central and Eastern Europe (CEE) where your company has business interests.

1. **What type of business links do you have with/ in Central and Eastern Europe?** Please tick:

	Poland	Hungary	Czech R.	Russia	Romania	write in
1. exporting to CEE	☐	☐	☐	☐	☐	☐
2. importing from CEE	☐	☐	☐	☐	☐	☐
3. licensing to CEE,	☐	☐	☐	☐	☐	☐
4. franchising to CEE,	☐	☐	☐	☐	☐	☐
5. outward processing or 'subcontracting' to CEE	☐	☐	☐	☐	☐	☐
6. management contract	☐	☐	☐	☐	☐	☐
7. turnkey project	☐	☐	☐	☐	☐	☐
8. other contractual forms of cooperation or technology transfer	☐	☐	☐	☐	☐	☐
9. minority share in joint-venture (5-50%)	☐	☐	☐	☐	☐	☐
10. majority owned joint-venture (51-95%)	☐	☐	☐	☐	☐	☐
11. wholly owned subsidiary or branch (more than 95% share in equity)	☐	☐	☐	☐	☐	☐

2. **<u>When</u> did you first establish your business links with Central and Eastern Europe?** Please give year:

Poland	Hungary	Czech R.	Russia	Romania	write in...
____	____	____	____	____	____

3. **What kinds of transfers is your Western company supplying <u>to its</u> <u>Central and East European</u> partner or subsidiary?** please tick

	Poland	Hungary	Czech R	Russia	Romania	write in
a. final goods	☐	☐	☐	☐	☐	☐
b. intermediate goods	☐	☐	☐	☐	☐	☐
c. raw materials	☐	☐	☐	☐	☐	☐
d. technology transfer						
(i) patented technology	☐	☐	☐	☐	☐	☐
(ii) unprotected technology	☐	☐	☐	☐	☐	☐
e. marketing know-how	☐	☐	☐	☐	☐	☐
f. general management know-how	☐	☐	☐	☐	☐	☐
g. permission for using brand names	☐	☐	☐	☐	☐	☐
i. other, please specify _____	☐	☐	☐	☐	☐	☐

4. What kinds of transfers does the Western company receive from its Eastern European subsidiary or partner? please tick

	Poland	Hungary	Czech R	Russia	Romania	write in___
a. final goods	☐	☐	☐	☐	☐	☐
b. intermediate goods	☐	☐	☐	☐	☐	☐
c. raw materials	☐	☐	☐	☐	☐	☐
d. technology transfer						
(i) patented technology	☐	☐	☐	☐	☐	☐
(ii) unprotected technology	☐	☐	☐	☐	☐	☐
h. 'consultancy' on the local	☐	☐	☐	☐	☐	☐
environment e.g. information						
on legal or cultural aspects						
of doing business in the partner country.						
i. other, specify _____	☐	☐	☐	☐	☐	☐

5 What characterises your investment projects (wholly owned and joint-ventures)? please tick, or give the number of projects if more than 1)

	Poland	Hungary	Czech R	Russia	Romania	write in___
a. Greenfield	☐	☐	☐	☐	☐	☐
(Start-up venture, more than 95% foreign owned)						
b. Acquisition	☐	☐	☐	☐	☐	☐
(purchase of all or part of an existing enterprise)						
c. Joint-venture acquisition	☐	☐	☐	☐	☐	☐
(the formation of a new entity where the local partner						
contributed assets from the existing enterprise)						
d. Joint-venture	☐	☐	☐	☐	☐	☐
(where a new entity was set up with one or more local partners)						
e. Representative office	☐	☐	☐	☐	☐	☐
f. Investment	☐	☐	☐	☐	☐	☐
(other than any of the above)						
g. No investment	☐	☐	☐	☐	☐	☐

If acquisition or joint-venture acquisition:

6. Was the acquisition part of a privatization program? (please tick)

yes	☐	☐	☐	☐	☐	☐
no	☐	☐	☐	☐	☐	☐

7. How important is your business in Central and Eastern Europe relative to your worldwide activities? (please tick)

By investments:
☐ no investments in the region
☐ up to 2% of total assets
☐ 2% - 5% of total assets
☐ 5% - 10% of total assets
☐ 10% - 20% of total assets
☐ more than 20% of total assets

By sales:
☐ no sales in the region
☐ up to 2% of total sales
☐ 2% - 5% of total sales
☐ 5% - 10% of total sales
☐ 10% - 20% of total sales
☐ more than 20% of total sales

Section 2: Motivation and Obstacles to Direct Investment in Central and Eastern Europe

Please tick the most appropriate responses (maximum: 5) for these questions, and briefly explain your situation or possible other reasons. Please, use the back pages if you need more space.

8. It is said that CEE offers interesting new market opportunities. Did you <u>invest</u> in the region to supply the local markets?
      ☐ Yes   ☐ No

**8a. if <u>yes</u>, in which countries:_____
what was important for your <u>choice of the country</u> for investment in the local market?**

☐ availability of information
☐ prior contacts to future partner

☐ physical infrastructure
☐ political environment
☐ development of the legal system
☐ offers by privatisation agencies
☐ ease of negotiations with local authorities
☐ presence of other foreign investors
☐ other, *please explain:*

☐ level of income, indicating demand for your goods
☐ size of population of the country, indicating demand
☐ few competitors present in the market
☐ entry by competitors
☐ protection of trademarks
☐ trade barriers of CEE countries

8b. if <u>no</u>, <u>why</u> have you not invested to serve these markets?

☐ economic risks are too high
☐ insufficient information
☐ no appropriate partner was found
☐ financial constraints
☐ political environment too uncertain
☐ lack of physical infrastructure
☐ legal system is too ambiguous
☐ negotiation with local authorities too difficult
   please explain your situation:

☐ markets can be served from facilities outside CEE
☐ expected demand for your goods too low
☐ insufficient protection of trademarks
☐ competition too intense
☐ trade barriers of CEE countries
☐ costs of local production too high

9. It is said that CEE offers opportunities for <u>low-cost production for export</u> to Western markets because wages are substantially lower than in Western Europe.
Did you invest in the region to utilize such opportunities?

      ☐ Yes   ☐ No

9a. if <u>yes</u>, in which countries:_____
what was important for your <u>choice of the country</u> to locate your production facilities?

☐ availability of information
☐ prior contacts to future partner
☐ physical infrastructure
☐ political environment
☐ development of the legal system
☐ presence of other foreign investors
☐ offers by privatisation agencies
☐ ease of negotiations with local authorities
☐ other, *please explain:*

☐ labour costs
☐ costs of raw materials
☐ quality of local suppliers
☐ qualification of local workforce
☐ incentives for exports
☐ access to regional markets
☐ access to European Union markets
☐ Europe Agreements with the EU

9b. if <u>no</u>, <u>why</u> does your company not produce in Central and Eastern Europe for export?

☐ economic risks are too high
☐ insufficient information
☐ no appropriate partner was found
☐ financial constraints
☐ political environment too uncertain
☐ lack of physical infrastructure
☐ legal system is too ambiguous
☐ negotiation with local authorities too difficult

☐ production processes cannot be relocated
☐ qualification of local workforce insufficient
☐ labour costs too high
☐ predicted future labour costs too high
☐ quality of local suppliers is insufficient
☐ long-term development of costs too uncertain
☐ trade barriers for important markets
☐ environmental liabilities
☐ restructuring costs of local facilities too high

please explain your situation:

10. Did you have business relationships in the past that have been terminated?
      ☐ Yes   ☐ No

if yes, please briefly explain why:

Section 3: General Information on your (British) company

11. Is your company itself a subsidiary of a multinational enterprise?
Yes □ No □

If yes, which unit, and at which location, within your multinational enterprise is coordinating business with Central and Eastern Europe?

12. Please give an approximate international breakdown for 1993 of the number of persons employed by your company, and of the proportions of your turnover in %:

	no. employed	turnover
a. UK	_____	_____%
b. other Western Europe	_____	_____%
c. OECD countries outside Europe	_____	_____%
d. developing countries	_____	_____%
e. Central and Eastern Europe	_____	_____%
total =	_____	100%

13. How much does your company spend on the following activities? Please give as an (estimated) percentage of turnover 1993:

a. research and development	_____%
b. advertising and promotion	_____%
c. training of personnel	_____%

Thank you very much for completing this questionnaire!
In the second stage, this research shall deepen the analysis of business in Central and Eastern Europe in a series of interviews with managers. These interviews with individuals actively involved in business with the region will take about 30 minutes and focus on your actual business activities and investment motivations. We would very much appreciate your cooperation in this research, and will provide participants with its results.

Would you or a suitable colleague be willing to participate in an interview for this research?
Yes □ No □   If yes, please provide your details:

company:	_____
contact person:	_____
title:	_____
address:	_____
telephone:	_____
fax:	_____

If you do not want to participate in an interview, you do not need to provide this information!

APPENDIX 5.3: DEFINITION OF VARIABLES

This appendix lists all variables used in the empirical analysis for further reference. The enterprise data are obtained mainly from the questionnaire, appendix 5.2, and from company accounts. In some cases additional sources have been utilized.

BALTIC — Dummy, taking the value of one if the firm is located within 100 km from the Baltic Sea. From the contact address of the firm.

BAVARIA — Dummy, taking the value of one if the firm is located in Bavaria. From the contact address of the firm.

CE_EUROPE — Percentage share of turnover in CEE in total turnover of the firm. From (i) annual reports of the firm, (ii) question 12, (iii) follow-up questionnaires, (iv) question 7 using interval means.

CHEM — Dummy, taking the value of one if the firm has its main activity in the chemical or petroleum industry (USSIC codes 28, 29). From the Fame and Amadeus database.

COC-L — Dummy, taking the value of one if the firm has been added to the base population from the list of firms known to be active from chamber of commerce sources.

CZECH — Dummy, taking the value of one for responses referring to business with the Czech Republic.

DIVER_TO — Number of USSIC codes plus UK-CIS codes reported in the AMADEUS database, divided over turnover. This variable neutralizes some bias that any one coding system may have, and is adjusted to size to avoid multicollinearity with the SIZE variable.

EMPL_TO — Ratio of employment over turnover in £1000 sterling, calculated with the data from the Fame and Amadeus database.

EUROPEAN — Dummy, taking the value of one if the firm is an affiliate of a multinational with headquarters in a European country other than the firm contacted, (i) question 11, (ii) from the Fame/Amadeus database.

FACTOR_C — Dummy, taking the value one if respondent answered 'yes' in question 9.

FIRST — Dummy, taking the value of one if turnover in CEE accounts for more than 40% of the firm's international turnover, calculated from CEE_TO and INTL_TO.

FOOD — Dummy, taking the value of one if the firm has its main activity in the food and beverages industry (USSIC code 20). From the Fame and Amadeus database.

GERMAN — Dummy, taking the value of one if the contacted firm is in Germany.

GLOBAL — Percentage share of employment outside the home country in total employment, from (i) annual reports, (ii) Dun Bradstreet and Hoppensteadt directories, (iii) question 12.

GROWTH — Percentage change of company turnover in 1993 compared to 1992, calculated from Fame and Amadeus database and annual reports.

H_GROWTH — Percentage growth of the industry in the Eastern Country from 1991 to 1994, standardized for each country with mean zero and standard deviation one. Calculated from Polish Central Statistical Office, PlanEcon (for CR and RO), Hungarian Central Statistical Office, and

IMF Economic Review Russia. (The original variable for industry growth was highly correlated to the country dummies for Poland (+0.6) and Russia (-0.6). The differences are attributable to different growth pattern as well as differences in data collection. By standardisation of the variable to have zero mean and unit standard deviation for each host country, industry and country specific effects can be separated.)

H_GROW_D   Deviation of H_GROWTH from its country specific average.

H_RECESS   Percentage growth of the industry in the Eastern Country from 1989 to 1991, standardized for each country with mean zero and standard deviation one. Source: UN Industrial Statistics Yearbook 1991, Vol. 1.

HUMAN_CAP Ratio of personnel expenditures in £ sterling over employment, from (i) Fame /Amadeus database, (ii) calculated from annual reports or (iii) follow up questionnaire.

HUNGARY   Dummy, taking the value of one for responses referring to business with Hungary.

INTL_TO   Percentage of employment outside the home country in total employment, from (i) annual reports, (ii) Fame and Amadeus, (iii) Dun Bradstreet and Hoppensteadt directories, (iv) question 12.

MACH   Dummy, taking the value of one if the firm has its main activity in the machinery industry (USSIC codes 35, 36, 37). From the Fame and Amadeus database. Usually used as base case.

NONEUR   Dummy, taking the value of one if the firm is an affiliate of a multinational with headquarters in a country outside Europe, from (i) question 11, (ii) from the Fame and Amadeus database.

NON_FOOD   Dummy, taking the value of one if the main activity of the firm is in consumer goods industries including pharmaceuticals but not food and beverages. From the activity description in the Fame and Amadeus database and annual reports.

ONLY_PROJ Dummy, taking the value of one if the DFI project is the only project the respondent reported in the questionnaire.

PHARMA   Dummy, taking the value of one if the firm is in the pharmaceutical industry (USSIC code 283).

PLC   Dummy, taking the value of one if the firm is in the legal form of PLC in the UK or AG in Germany, as opposed to Ltd in the UK and GmbH, KG, OHG and eG in Germany. From the Fame and Amadeus database.

POLAND   Dummy, taking the value of one for responses referring to business with Poland.

ROMANIA   Dummy, taking the value of one for responses referring to business with Romania. Usually used as base case.

RUSSIA   Dummy, taking the value of one for responses referring to business with Russia.

R&D   Percentage ratio of research and development expenditures to turnover, from (i) annual reports, (ii) 'The 1993 UK R&D Scoreboard' [Company Reporting Limited], (iii) question 13 of the questionnaire, (iv) follow-up questionnaires, (v) predicted values of a regression equation using only variables not employed elsewhere in this research.

SIZE   Number of employees of the firm, from (i) Fame and Amadeus database, (ii) annual reports, (iii) Dun Bradstreet and Hoppensteadt directories,

                (iv) question 12. For regression analysis divided by 10^5.

SIZE_SQ	Square of EMPLOYM. For regression analysis divided by 10^{10}.
SLOVAK_BG	Dummy, taking the value of one for write-in responses referring to DFI in Slovakia or Bulgaria.
SLOVENIA	Dummy, taking the value of one for write-in responses referring to DFI in Slovenia.
T_FIN_ETAL	If the firm has downstream business (see section 7.2) and transfers final goods in addition to intermediate goods or raw materials, then this dummy takes the value of one.
T_MANAG	Dummy, taking the value of one if the respondent indicated transfer of managerial and or marketing know-how to the Eastern partner and affiliate. From question 3.
T_NONE	If the firm has downstream business (see section 7.2), but does not transfer any goods to the partner country, then this dummy takes the value of one.
T_O_FIN	If the firm has downstream business (see section 7.2) and transfers final goods, but no intermediate goods or raw materials, then this dummy takes the value of one.
T_TECHN	Dummy, taking the value of one if the respondent indicated transfer of patented and/or unprotected technological know-how to the Eastern partner/affiliate, from question 3.
UP&DOWN	If the firm has both upstream and downstream business (see section 7.2), this dummy takes the value of one.
UPSTREAM	If the firm has only upstream and no downstream business (see section 7.2), this dummy takes the value of one.
YEARS	Number of years since the firm established its first business contacts with the partner country, calculated from question 2.

General notes:

1.   Multiple sources with Arabic numerals indicate the priority of sources if multiple sources were used to obtain data on a variable.

2.   All accounting data refer to 1993, the year preceding the survey.

3.   Short follow-up questionnaires have been sent to firms with missing values for important variables. Some 30 companies have been contacted in two rounds, with about eight useful responses together.

6. The Determinants of West-East Business

This is the first of the three chapters analysing the entry process of Western businesses into Central and Eastern Europe (CEE). The first step is to analyse the propensity to engage in West-East business. The determinants of activity in CEE are a function of firm-specific assets that enable firms to internationalize, and of their interaction with the special condition of the transition economies.

West-East business is a part of firms' international business. Special features emerge due to the relatively recent entry, or major upgrading of activity, after 1989 and the special economic conditions of the transition economies. Firms engage in international business if they have assets demanded elsewhere such as physical and intangible resources. These would enable them to manufacture goods for export or to set up production facilities locally. In terms of Dunning's OLI paradigm (Chapter 3), Western firms are active if they have ownership advantages (O) that they can combine with locational (L) attractions of the Eastern partner country. The locational attraction includes demand for goods and services, as well as favourable conditions for local production, for example for licensing or DFI projects. This chapter is exclusively concerned with firms incidence of engaging in international business, without consideration of different forms of business. Therefore, internalization advantages (I), which would favour direct investment over other forms of business, are discussed only in the subsequent chapters.

The concept 'West-East business' is analysed as a dependent variable of the empirical analysis using four alternative definitions:

- the incidence of a firm having business anywhere in CEE,
- the incidence of a firm having business with a particular country of CEE,
- the number of countries in which a firm is active, and
- the categorical variable 'not active - some activity - active in all countries'.

The chapter is structured as follows: in the next section, hypotheses are developed from a review of relevant ownership advantages and their interaction with the local environment in CEE. The third section discusses the methods of empirical analysis and the regression equations. Section four reviews the evidence of the analysis for each hypothesis, and section five concludes.

THEORETICAL BASIS AND HYPOTHESIS

In chapter three, the theoretical foundations of multinational business have been discussed based on the literature in the field. On this basis, this section develops hypotheses on the determinants of multinational business in CEE. To avoid repetition, only the key arguments and references are given, and related to the variables used in the empirical analysis. For further details refer to Chapter 3, especially the sections on 'industrial organization' and 'the scope of the firm'.

Ownership Advantages

Dunning [1993] uses a very comprehensive definition of ownership advantages that includes property rights and intangible asset advantages as well as economies of common governance. In addition, relative advantages of psychic proximity, and threats to existing O-advantages due to barriers to corporate growth are considered.

Property rights and intangible assets

O-advantages arise from specific assets in the firm's possession, such as superior production technology, product innovations and innovative capabilities. A firm with superior technological resources and capabilities can maximize its revenues by serving the largest accessible markets, and by combining its resources with a wide range of complementary assets found at other locations. As markets and complementary assets are found abroad, this becomes a motive for international business. Thus, technology intensive firms can be expected to be more active. In line with prior empirical research on exports [Ito and Pucik 1993] and DFI, technology is proxied by R&D expenditures and predicted to increase activity:

H1:   The more technology intensive a firm, the more likely it has business with CEE.

The second major group of intangible assets relates to marketing and strategic competition. O-advantages exist as property rights on established brand names and the intellectual organizational capacities to design and implement successful marketing strategies. CEE had virgin markets previously not supplied with many Western Goods. Their opening may induce early activities especially by firms in internationally oligopolistic industries, because the timing of their entry may determine the position *vis-à-vis* their main competitors and thus the value of their O-advantages.[1]

Foremost, the advantages of early moving strategies are important in consumer goods industries. Large unsaturated demand surfaced at the time of liberalization, and early establishment of a market share could, through brand loyalty, contribute to a leading position in the long run and deter potential later entrants. Consumer goods manufacturers would thus move into the new markets sooner than producers of industrial and investment goods. Thus, the dummies for the food and beverage industry (FOOD) and for non-food consumer good manufacturers (NON_FOOD) are predicted to have a positive effect.

H2:   Consumer goods manufacturers are likely to be more active

Marketing related assets and capabilities are often measured by a firm's advertising expenditures [for example Caves 1974, Pugel 1981]. This measure is not available for the sample.[2] Therefore, a broader concept of human capital is used as a proxy. Managers in marketing or other highly qualified positions such as finance are paid higher salaries. Their human capital is a major intangible asset of the modern corporation. Thus, the average remuneration is used as a proxy for the qualification of employees and thus the existence of human capital (HUMAN_CAP).[3]

H3:   The higher its human capital, the more likely that the firm is active.

Advantages of common governance
Advantages of common governance arise from multi-plant economies of the established firm over a de novo entrant, and from international experience as such. They emerge in particular if the new business is an extension of a product specialization strategy.

Industries with large economies of scale are more internationalized. This applies to both economies of scale at the plant level, and common governance of multiple plants. Plant level economies of scale relative to transportation costs imply fewer locations of production and thus more international trade with their output. At firm level, a large corporation can economize on headquarters functions, such as marketing and finance. In this way, economies of common governance of multi-plant firms create advantages for MNE that arise in direct relation to their size.

Firms using advantages of common governance can integrate new operations in CEE into their organization at low additional costs. Thus, large firms are predicted to be more active in CEE than smaller firms. Size is measured by the firm's employment numbers, which enter the equations in linear and quadratic form (SIZE and SIZE_SQ).

H4:   Large firms are more likely to be active

Multinational firms have competitive advantages that arise from the fact that they are multinational. These advantages include, for instance, international accumulation of know how, arbitrage flexibility for production shifting, and international diversification of risk. Following the arguments in Chapter 3, firms with international experiences can thus be expected to

- know better how to make best use of new opportunities in CEE,
- have lower costs of entry as they utilize synergies with other international business,
- increase the value of their network by covering more countries, in addition to the value enhancing effect that the network provides to a given local operation.

International experience of firms is measured by the share of turnover obtained outside the home country (INTL_TO), and is expected to increase firms propensity to engage in West-East business.

H5:   Internationally experienced firms are more likely to be active in CEE.

Furthermore, the nature of firms' competences determines potential common governance. Diversified companies have managerial competences in the coordination of different activities, often specific to the economy in which they operate [for example Hitt, Hoskisson and Ireland 1994]. If they face competitive pressures for a given product, they may primarily consider redesigning their product portfolio. Uncompetitive products are phased out as new competitors gain market shares. Other firms have technological and managerial capacities that are very specific to a specialized range of goods. Many SME maufacturing firms in Germany are successful through their product specialization and a worldwide market leader strategy [Simon 1996]. Their managerial competences are product or industry specific, with two implications for their international strategy:

- Their marketing strategy is based on worldwide presence, or leadership, in their narrow product range. Thus they would enter CEE early once local demand emerges.
- If they face competitive pressures, they consider strategies of redesigning or relocating the production process rather than changing to different kinds of productive activity. They would thus be more likely to utilise lower labour costs in CEE by sourcing or relocation (appendix 3.1).

Thus, for two reasons, a negative association between diversification, adjusted for size (DIVER_TO), and the propensity to engage in CEE business is to be expected.

H6:   Diversified firms are less likely to be active in CEE

Furthermore, this hypothesis can be developed from a perspective of risk management: diversification across product groups and across regional markets are alternative strategies to diversify financial risk. As firms choose either strategy or a mix thereof, product and international diversification should be negatively related.

Proximity
The arguments for the need of O-advantages originally arose from the view that without them foreign firms would be at a competitive disadvantage *vis-à-vis* local competitors. This competitive disadvantage of foreignness is however lower for firms based in nearby or similar countries in 'psychic proximity'. They are therefore more active, *ceteris paribus*, than their counterparts from distant origins. It is a common strategy for internationalizing firms to enter markets in close psychic proximity first. Of the countries of origin selected for this research, Germany is not only geographically closer but has closer cultural and historical links to the region. Thus,

H7:   German firms are more active in the region than British firms.

The GERMAN dummy captures the proximity effect along with other home country effects. The hypothesis can be extended by including the location within the home country in the analysis. More personal or cultural contacts exist in areas close to the border. They are strengthened by the pattern of post World War II refugees within Germany, in particular Sudentendeutsche in Bavaria and Ostpreußen in the Northern parts. Dummies named BAVARIA and BALTIC are used to capture these effects. Within-country proximity has not been considered in previous research.

H8:   Firms from an area close to Germany's Eastern borders are more likely to establish business relationships eastwards.

Threats to existing O-advantages
Threats to existing ownership advantages can be as much a driving force of internalization as expansion based on growing advantages. Firms facing constraints to growth, or threats to survival, with their present strategic configuration are forcefully pushed into exploring opportunities. Barriers to growth arise in current markets as well as in procurement sources and production locations. If markets are saturated or a recession reduces competitiveness in established markets, this constrains firms' growth paths and creates strong factors towards restructuring, relocating and searching for new

markets. This suggests that firms most affected by the 1993 recession as well as firms experiencing slow growth are more likely to engage in new activities.

The developmental model (appendix 3.1) emphasized push factors arising from barriers to growth on the supply side as well as from loss of competitiveness. Firms reaching growth barriers with their present strategic configuration, are more likely to restructure their sourcing strategy. This applies to firms with declining sales during the German post-unification recession. Both effects affect the sales turnover of the firm. The change of turnover in 1993 over the previous year is used as a proxy for growth during the recession (GROWTH).

H9: Firms with slow growth of sales are more likely to engage in new business with CEE, be it in search of new markets or lower production costs.

On the other hand, rapidly growing firms have opportunities to accumulate internal cash flow and have better access to financial markets. They have more resources to redeploy and would thus be more likely to expand to new regions. This provides an alternative to the hypothesis H9.

The relative comparative advantages of the region are labour intensive production processes, especially medium skilled, because labour costs are far below West European levels. The developmental model stresses the importance of local production for export in such an environment. If the model is applicable to CEE, sourcing of intermediate inputs and even relocation of production would be a major motivation for business activity. Firms with labour intensive production processes are most likely to procure in the region and to set up local productions for exports. The high wage costs in Germany in the early 1990s put particular competitive pressures on labour-intensive production. If relocation was a major force to international business, then the net effect on the propensity to engage in international business would be positive. Thus, following literature emphasizing the importance of labour costs for decisions over location of production in CEE, the following hypothesis tested:

H10: Firms with labour intensive production processes are more likely to import from the region, and are thus more active.

Control variables
Economies of scale and transportation costs are at the centre of the new theory of international trade. This literature would suggest differences across the three sectors of industry considered in the analysis: food and beverages, chemicals, and machinery. The food and beverage industry has high transportation costs and tariff barriers while, in many sectors, producing with relatively

unsophisticated technology. The chemical industry is scale and research intensive. Therefore, the chemical industry can be expected to be more, and food industry less, active in trade with CEE. On the other hand, the local competitiveness varies across industries. Thus, no hypothesis is proposed, but an additional chemical industry dummy, CHEM is included as control variable.

Firms with foreign parents have access to more resources and their business development would exceed that of a domestic firm of equal size (which is implicit in using the local firms accounting data for size). For instance, an American MNE may instruct its British affiliate to undertake business in CEE. On the other hand, firms may find their international business restricted by constraints imposed by the global strategy of the parent, in particular not to compete with other affiliates of the company. The predicted signs for dummies for foreign parents are therefore not clear, be they from outside Europe (NONEUR) or a different European country (EUROPEAN).

The sample contains some firms that were not sampled randomly but drawn from a chamber-of-commerce-list of active firms. To control for any bias arising from this subsample, dummy COC_L is included. It should be positively signed since it was known *ex ante* that these firms had business with at least one country of the region.

Matching Ownership and Locational Advantages

The OLI paradigm suggests that ownership advantages combined with locational advantages of the host economy are necessary conditions for international business. Therefore it should be possible, albeit never done before, to develop specific hypotheses about which O-advantages would be relatively more important in a given country. The five countries considered in this study vary by several aspects relevant to potential Western business partners (Chapter 2, especially Table 2.1). This includes markets, production costs, technological capabilities, administrative structures and political risks as well as cultural and geographic proximity to Western Europe. This section relates the O-advantages to the specific local environments.

Market size and growth are major determinants of international business. The largest market, in terms of number of potential customers, is surely Russia. However, the level of income was low and declining at the time of the survey. Only a small proportion of the 148 million people were able to buy Western consumer goods. The Czech Republic and Hungary have the highest per capita income. Poland combines a large market with relatively high income. In addition, she is the first country that overcame the transition recession and achieved highest growth rates in the period 1993 to 1996. Market oriented businesses would thus primarily focus on Poland, followed by Hungary, Czech Republic and Russia.

Market attraction is most relevant for firms with intangible assets to sell in the region, primarily consumer goods manufacturers (NON_FOOD, FOOD) and firms with high human capital (HUMAN_CAP). Firms facing barriers to growth in existing markets (GROWTH) would also consider the largest markets first. Thus, first the interaction hypothesis is

I1:   Consumer goods manufacturers, human capital intensive firms, and firms with slow growth prefer larger markets and therefore Poland.

The level of local education is a major determinant of productivity. It is particular important for technology intensive firms who need to train their local employees. The better the general education and industry specific training the lower are the costs of technology transfer. In the region, the Czech region has a tradition in industrial production that dates back pre-1939 and has the highest secondary school enrolment. Technology intensive firms thus would locate there to utilize the trained workforce.

I2:   Research intensive firms prefer the Czech Republic.

All five countries made progress in the process of systemic transformation from socialist to market economy. The three Central European countries advanced further. Russia is lagging behind, for instance with the reform of the legal and institutional framework and the banking sector. Delayed reforms increase business risk. Also other types of environmental risks are high in the region, which deters foreign investment. The inflation rate and the Euromoney index suggest that business risk would be highest in Russia (Table 2.1).

Firms which are internationally diversified or have a large volume of business would more capable of coping with country risk as they can hedge with other international operations. Firms specialized in a narrow range of products would be more willing to accept the risk as their product specific ownership advantages can best be exploited by penetrating all accessible markets. These firms would also be more capable of overcoming the costs of psychic distance between their home and the investment location.

I3:   Firms with advantages of common governance, as indicated by international experience, size or low diversification, are relatively more active in Russia.

Psychic proximity particularly favours the countries bordering Germany or related to her by historical links. German firms should thus be relatively more active in Poland, Czech Republic and Hungary. As the relationship with Poland has historically been subject to tension, and since the British prefer Poland, the

predicted sign for the coefficient for Poland is ambiguous. If the role of
proximity also applies to regional, rather than national level alone, then specific
effects would also be observed for BALTIC or BAVARIA firms.

I4:   *German firms are more active than British in the Czech Republic and in*
        Hungary.
I5:   *Firms from Bavaria prefer the Czech Republic and Hungary, while firms*
        from regions near the Baltic Sea, including Hamburg, prefer Poland and
        Russia.

Table 6.1 Expected coefficients

	Active	Every where	CR	HU	PL	R	RO	Hypo-theses
Intangible Asset Advantages								
R&D	+	+	++	+	+	+	+	H1, I2
HUMAN_CAP	+	+	+	+	++	+	+	H3, I1
NON_FOOD	+	++	+	+	++	+	0	H2, I1
FOOD	?	?	+	+	++	+	0	H2, I1
Common Governance Advantages								
SIZE	+	++	+	+	+	++	+	H4, I3
SIZE_SQ	-	- -	-	-	-	- -	-	
INTL_TO	+	++	+	+	+	++	+	H5, I3
DIVER_TO	-	-	-	-	-	-	-	H6, I3
Barriers to Growth								
GROWTH	-	-	-	-	- -	-	-	H9, I1
LABOUR	++	+	+	+	+	++	++	H10, I3
Proximity								
GERMAN	++	+	++	++	?	0	0	H7, I6
BALTIC	+	0	0	0	++	++	0	H8, I7
BAVARIA	+	0	++	+	0	0	0	H8, I7

Table 6.1 summarizes the variables proposed for the empirical analysis, and
their expected signs. If an effect is expected to be stronger in one equation than
in others it is indicated by double-plus or double-minus signs. The table also
distinguishes effects on the probability of being active in CEE, and the
probability of establishing business everywhere in the region. For instance,
consumer-goods manufacturers have good incentives to establish a presence

throughout the region, whereas labour-intensive firms may be looking for one or a small number of local suppliers or production relocations.

METHODS OF EMPIRICAL ANALYSIS

The empirical tests analyse different conceptualizations of 'active business relationships':

- Who is active in CEE?
- Who is active in any of the five countries?
- Who is active in several or all countries?

For the first two concepts, the dependent variable is binary, taking the value of one if the firm has any business relationships with the region, or the particular country considered. In the third case, the dependent variable is the number of countries in which a firm is active, which takes the values of zero to five, and a categorical variable taking three values.

For binary dependent variables, both Logit and Probit models are commonly used. Their empirical results do usually not differ substantially, in particular for values of ß'x near zero, that is $P = 0.5$. Greene [1993: 638] suggests that they give similar probabilities for values of ß'x between -1.2 and +1.2. For this research, a Probit specification is used because the subsequent ordered dependent variable model was not estimable using a Logit specification.

Limited dependent variable models, such as the Probit, are rationalized using index functions. Decision makers have a utility function with an unobservable variable y^* as the dependent variable and x as vector of the independent variables. If the unobserved utility obtained from a positive choice passes a threshold limit, the decision is in favour of one, here in favour of engaging in business with CEE. Thus,

$$ACTIVE \ = 1 \text{ if } y^* > 0 \qquad\qquad (6.1)$$
$$= 0 \text{ if } y^* <= 0$$

with $y^* = ß'x + \epsilon$ where y^* is the unobserved utility and ϵ are the residuals, which in the case of a Probit are assumed to be normally distributed. ß'x is called the index function. The Probit is modelled as the density function of a normal distribution [Greene 1993: 637]:

$$P(ACTIVE=1) \ = \ _{-\infty}\!\int^{ß'x} \phi(t)\, dt \ = \ \Phi\, (ß'x) \qquad\qquad (6.2)$$

where x is a vector containing firm and industry specific variables. In this chapter, the binomial Probit is used to analyse the firms' propensity to engage in the region in general, and in each of five countries. They show whether or not, and how, determinants of activity vary within the region.

If the dependent variable takes more than two values that are ordinal but not cardinal, then the utility function contains several thresholds. As the utility from activity in CEE increases, firms would engage in a higher order of business activity, that is start business with more countries. The observed dependent variable #COUNTR thus takes six different values from zero to five that stand in an ordinal relationship.[4] They are presumed that to be related through an unobserved utility y^* as follows:

$$
\begin{aligned}
\#COUNTR \quad &= 0 \quad && \text{if } y^* < 0 && (6.3)\\
&= 1 \quad && \text{if } 0 <= y^* < \mu_1 \\
&= 2 \quad && \text{if } \mu_1 <= y^* < \mu_2 \\
&= 3 \quad && \text{if } \mu_2 <= y^* < \mu_3 \\
&= 4 \quad && \text{if } \mu_3 <= y^* < \mu_4 \\
&= 5 \quad && \text{if } \mu_4 <= y^*
\end{aligned}
$$

with

$$ y^* = \beta'x + \epsilon . $$

The threshold parameters μ_j have to be estimated with the model. As before, error terms ϵ are assumed to be normally distributed. The second regression model estimates the Ordered Probit with 6 categories for #COUNTR. The model is subsequently simplified by defining a more parsimoneous dependent variable:

$$
\begin{aligned}
ACTIVE\_3CAT &= 0 \quad && \text{for } \#COUNTR = 0 \\
&= 1 \quad && \text{for } 0 < \#COUNTR < 5 && (6.4)\\
&= 2 \quad && \text{for } \#COUNTR = 5
\end{aligned}
$$

This variable captures the same ordinal relationship as the #COUNTR, yet distinguishes only no-business, some-business, and business-in-all-countries. Thus, four different models are estimated to capture alternative interpretations of the concept West-East business: a binomial model for the incidence of activity, an ordered model on the number of countries, an ordered model with only three categories, and binomial models for each of the five CEE countries. The three categories model is furthermore tested for subsamples by home country and industry.

Table 6.2 reports the descriptive statistics for the independent and alternative dependent variables. Note that employment and employment-square have been scaled for readability of the results tables. Table 6.3 shows the correlations of the independent variables. The human capital proxy HUMAN_CAP is highly correlated to both the GERMAN dummy ($r = 0.60$) and to LABOUR ($r = -0.50$), and moderately to BALTIC and CHEM. It therefore has to be excluded from the analysis, and analysed separately in a subsequent test (Table 6.8). CHEM and NON_FOOD are naturally related as most chemicals firms produce consumer goods. The effects of these two dummies thus have to be interpreted together.[5]

Table 6.2 Descriptive statistics

	Unit of measurement	Mean	Standard error	Median
Dependent Variables				
#COUNTR	count	2.99	1.98	4
ACTIVE_3CAT	3 categories	1.14	.75	1
Independent Variables				
SIZE	10^{-5}	0.1113	0.1898	0.0361
SIZE_SQ	10^{-10}	0.0484	0.1584	0.0013
R&D	per cent	3.55	3.66	2.82
HUMAN_CAP	£ per employee	25.79	10.49	25.14
INTL_TO	ratio	0.4204	0.2937	.4348
GROWTH	per cent	5.35	15.86	3.34
DIVER_TO	ratio	0.00012	0.00024	0.00001
LABOUR	ratio	10.73	6.87	9.90

Note: the median of binary independent variables is zero in all cases. Details of variable definitions are in appendix 5.3.

The regression models were estimated with the independent variables, excluding HUMAN_CAP (Tables 6.4, 6.6). The regresssions over subsamples (Table 6.7) were based on a reduced set of variables, excluding five variables that were consistently insignificant. This was necessary to avert degree of freedom problems. For the Ordered Probits, the squared expression of the employment variable has been taken out because otherwise the model would not deliver sensible results.[6]

The overall performance of the empirical models is quite satisfactory. The χ^2 statistics of the Binomial and Ordered Probit models are highly significant. The critical values at 1 per cent are 24.725 for 11 degrees of freedom (df) and 32.000 for 16 df. The reported χ^2 statistics are substantially higher indicating that the models as a whole make a significant contribution to explaining the dependent variable. The correct predictions are very high for all models. They should be assessed relative to the proportions of correct predictions in a random draw. Relative to this benchmark, the share of correct predictions of the model is more than 20 percentage points higher in each model specification.

Table 6.5 details the model predictions. The ACTIVE and ACTIVE_3CAT models show a very good predictive ability of the model and for each actual value, the majority of predictions are correct.[7] This is not true for the #COUNTR model. Almost all observations in category zero or five are correctly predicted. Yet the model is unable to provide a reasonable prediction for the

Table 6.3 Correlations of the independent variables

		1	2	3	4	5	6	7	8	9	10	11	12
1	SIZE	1.0											
2	SIZE_SQ	.92	1.0										
3	R&D	.03	-.01	1.0									
4	HUMAN_CAP	.03	.05	.22	1.0								
5	NON_FOOD	.19	.17	.17	.13	1.0							
6	INTL_TO	.33	.25	.25	.07	.17	1.0						
7	GROWTH	.00	.01	-.13	-.18	.01	-.01	1.0					
8	DIVER_TO	-.28	-.15	-.02	-.28	-.11	-.24	.03	1.0				
9	NONEUR	.01	.02	.03	.09	.04	.08	.05	-.09	1.0			
10	EUROPEAN	-.09	.02	.03	.01	-.05	.04	-.08	.06	-.09	1.0		
11	BALTIC	-.09	.06	.06	.30	.13	.21	-.01	-.07	.02	-.05	1.0	
12	BAVARIA	-.01	.04	.08	.10	.08	.02	-.09	-.08	-.08	.04	-.04	1.0
13	COC_L	-.12	.08	.01	-.10	.05	-.04	-.05	.10	.06	.08	.14	-.07
14	GERMAN	-.12	-.08	.01	.60	.04	-.04	-.22	-.22	-.17	.04	.21	.25
15	FOOD	-.10	-.07	-.26	-.16	-.23	-.38	-.01	.01	-.10	-.01	-.03	.06
16	CHEM	.15	.14	.20	.34	.44	.20	-.07	-.12	.13	-.08	.09	-.07
17	LABOUR	.03	-.04	.02	-.50	-.10	-.05	-.07	.30	-.14	.03	-.11	-.02

continued		13	14	15	16
13	COC_L	1.0			
14	GERMAN	-.06	1.0		
15	FOOD	-.11	-.04	1.0	
16	CHEM	-.04	-.04	-.28	1.0
17	LABOUR	.10	-.22	-.20	-.21

Note: correlations are significant at 5% level if they are > 0.14.

Table 6.4   General models

Dependent model categories	ACTIVE Probit 2	#COUNTR Ordered Probit 6	ACTIVE_3 Ordered Probit 3
R&D	.0479 (.064)	.0434 (.037)	.0499 (.391)
NON_FOOD	.1317 (.547)	.2194 (.325)	.2124 (.330)
FOOD	- .2863 (.387)	- .1351 (.262)	- .0794 (.290)
EMPLOY	3.8204 (2.55)	2.7478 (.591)*****	3.0280 (.648)*****
EMPL_SQ	-3.8967 (2.73)	--	--
INTL_TO	1.7018 (.598)****	1.8750 (.375)*****	1.9601 (.403)*****
DIVER_TO	-2750.7 (873.5)****	-600.35 (579.7)	-600.49 (607.4)
GROWTH	- .0279 (.010)****	- .0157 (.007)**	- .0143 (.007)**
LABOUR	- .0006 (.023)	- .0196 (.016)	- .0160 (.017)
GERMAN	.8167 (.358)**	.7947 (.211)****	.7896 (.223)****
BALTIC	.2790 (.866)	.1839 (.731)	.1106 (.823)
BAVARIA	.0480 (.818)	.7158 (.582)	.5402 (.592)
CHEM	.5273 (.541)	.2323 (.275)	.1886 (.300)
NONEUR	2.0774 (1.46)	.2323 (.303)	.3993 (.362)
EUROPEAN	.8373 (.727)	- .3991 (.463)	- .1495 (.529)
COC_L	5.0186 (38.1)	.8020 (.395)**	.8508 (.543)
Constant	- .0984 (.548)	- .1956 (.373)	- .3485 (.402)
MU(1)	--	.3952 (.104)****	1.7762 (.190)*****
MU(2)	--	.7503 (.132)*****	--
MU(3)	--	1.1694 (.149)*****	--
MU(4)	--	1.7662 (.168)*****	--
χ^2-statistic	106.220	143.933	137.873
log-likelih.	-49.21	-251.29	-141.57
correct pred.	87.37%	51.01%	67.17%
random pred.	66.57%	19.73%	35.57%

Notes: Levels of statistical significance: * = 10%, ** = 5%. *** = 1%, **** = 0.5%, ***** = 0.005%.   -- = Variable not included.

Table 6.5 Predicted versus actual outcome

ACTIVE	Predicted			ACTIVE_3	Predicted			
Actual	0	1	Total	*Actual*	0	1	2	Total
0 not-active	25	17	42	0 not-active	26	16	1	43
1 active	8	148	156	1 active	5	60	19	84
Total	33	165	198	2 active in all	1	23	47	71
				Total	32	99	67	198

#COUNTRIES	Predicted						
Actual	0	1	2	3	4	5	Total
0 not-active	35	0	0	0	2	6	43
1 country	11	0	0	0	1	3	15
2 countries	6	0	0	0	1	9	16
3 countries	10	0	0	0	0	12	22
4 countries	7	0	0	0	2	22	31
5 all countries	6	0	0	0	1	64	71
Total	75	0	0	0	7	116	198

four intermediate categries. The statistical reason for this is that most observations are in the tails of the distribution of the unobserved utility function y^* and the intermediate intervals are very narrow. Therefore, the ACTIVE_3CAT model was developed.

The subsamples have been analysed using the 3-categories Ordered Probit model (Table 6.7). This approach was moderately successful: although a reduced data set was used, only few significant effects can be shown, results from the machinery industry being an exception. The small number of observations in the sub-samples do not permit the obtaining of significance. Nevertheless, the χ^2-statistics were significant and the correct predictions were high for all sub-samples.

HYPOTHESIS TESTS

Intangible Asset Advantages

Ownership advantages of intangible assets were hypothesized to encourage internalization by R&D intensive firms, (H1: R&D), for consumer goods manufacturers (H2: FOOD, NON_FOOD) and human capital intensive firms

(H3: HUMAN_CAP).

Research-based intangibles increase the propensity of firms' activity, but are not statistically significant. The effect of the R&D variable is positive but insignificant in each of the general models (Table 6.4), and for both home countries and both industries (Table 6.8). The alternative hypothesis of no contribution cannot be rejected although the coefficient is not small considering that R&D is measured in percent.

Consumer goods manufacturers show no persistent pattern of more activity. The empirical evidence shows few significant effects for either the FOOD or the NON_FOOD dummy. FOOD includes some highly internationalized sectors with branded goods, but also others with high transportation costs and low internationalization. These opposite effects may explain the small negative effects for the FOOD dummy in the aggregate equation. The NON_FOOD dummy is mostly positive yet insignificant. Negative coefficients emerge for subsamples of British firms as well as for the food and chemicals industry with correspondingly larger effects for German firms and the machinery industry. This indicates an interesting country and industry difference that, however, is statistically insignificant and thus requires further research. Thus, non-food consumer goods manufacturers appear to be more active in the region, with interesting differences between the countries and industries.

The broader defined concept of human capital could not be tested in the original set of empirical models because of multi-collinearity. Therefore, the proxy HUMAN_CAP has been tested separately by incorporating it in a reduced version of the model. It is correlated with the GERMAN dummy since labour costs per employee are substantially higher in Germany than in the UK. In this way, HUMAN_CAP accounts for the effect of human capital after accounting for home country differences. The contribution of HUMAN_CAP is illustrated by the difference in the χ^2-statistic between the base model and the new model (Table 6.8). The coefficient on HUMAN_CAP is never significant in the general models, though the 6-categories model is significantly improved according to the chi-square test. However, human capital significantly increases the propensity of a firm to be active in Poland.

Overall, it is possible to detect significance for the intangible asset coefficients, but they appear to be dominated by other influences. The hypothesis that intangible assets increase firms' propensity to engage in East-West business cannot be rejected but does not receive statistically significant support either.

Advantages of Common Governance

Ownership advantages arising from economies of common governance were hypothesized to increase firms' propensity to be active. As a measure of

Table 6.6 Host country models

Country	Czech R.	Hungary
R&D	- .0250 (.041)	.0412 (.040)
NON_FOOD	.5291 (.400)	- .0832 (.371)
FOOD	- .6825 (.337)**	- .2144 (.331)
SIZE	5.1807 (2.21)**	5.1272 (2.01)**
SIZE_SQ	-4.4771 (2.49)*	-4.5026 (2.11)**
INTL_TO	1.4645 (.487)****	1.6843 (.468)****
DIVER_TO	-1027.0 (736.4)	-1467.6 (722.3)**
GROWTH	- .0216 (.008)**	- .0096 (.008)
LABOUR	- .0242 (.021)	- .0071 (.019)
GERMAN	1.2110 (.304)****	.8338 (.275)****
BALTIC	- .2888 (.726)	- .1867 (.587)
BAVARIA	.0772 (.657)	.8325 (.720)
CHEM	.2854 (.364)	.0927 (.322)
NONEUR	.4293 (.409)	.2614 (.345)
EUROPEAN	- .3769 (.468)	- .8227 (.510)
COC_L	.8531 (.424)**	.6832 (.376)*
Constant	- .4692 (.469)	-1.0092 (.441)**
χ^2-statistic	106.337	93.883
log-likelih.	-74.84	-86.63
correct pred.	87.37%	77.27%
random pred.	54.59%	56.25%

Notes: see Table 6.4.

common governance, firm size (H4: SIZE), international experience (H5: INTL_TO) and diversification (H6: DIVER_TO) are tested. All hypotheses receive strong support.

The size variable is usually highly significant. In some cases, a quadratic expression has been more successful in illustrating the influence than a linear variable. All measures of assets have been controlled by firm size. Even so, larger firms have advantages of common governance that reduce the costs of engaging in business with CEE. Surprisingly, the size effect is larger and more significant for German than for British firms, which is contrary to the expectation that size would help in overcoming distance. This effect may be

Table 6.6, continued

Poland	Russia	Romania
.0049 (.045)	.1194 (.045)***	.0854 (.038)**
.5137 (.453)	.1932 (.394)	- .0690 (.349)
- .0827 (.347)	.0657 (.330)	- .0593 (.333)
5.3162 (2.20)**	5.4996 (2.01)***	3.5874 (1.89)*
-5.6448 (2.36)**	-5.1808 (2.11)**	-2.2960 (2.17)
1.7898 (.493)****	.9968 (.462)**	1.6402 (.461)****
-1497.0 (788.6)*	-2909.7 (842.2)****	-872.57 (750.5)
-.0338 (.009)****	- .0165 (.008)**	- .0172 (.008)**
- .0430 (.026)	- .0180 (.018)	- .0391 (.026)
.5266 (.299)*	.0612 (.265)	.4706 (.259)*
.0109 (.742)	1.1729 (.735)	.1659 (.610)
.5464 (.724)	.8842 (.716)	.7455 (.552)
- .5776 (.403)	.2763 (.327)	- .0317 (.302)
- .0357 (.403)	.0763 (.357)	- .2939 (.346)
- .3129 (.448)	.0021 (.496)	- .8630 (.517)*
1.4070 (.499)****	.7047 (.421)*	.9868 (.385)**
- .1676 (.496)	- .5001 (.438)	-1.0998 (.466)**
103.889	92.655	83.664
-72.65	-85.98	-94.592
83.33%	78.79%	74.24%
51.84%	52.47%	50.41%

caused by a few, very large British firms in the sample without activity in the region. In contrast, almost all major companies in Germany are present in the region.

The variable INTL_TO is significantly positive throughout all model specifications. It attains the highest level of significance of 0.005 per cent, marked by five *s, in several model specifications. The coefficients show little variation between the models. Neither do significant differences emerge between firms from differing home countries and industries.

The coefficient on the diversification proxy is always negative, as hypothesized. However, the size of this effect varies for the different models.

Table 6.7 Home country and industry samples: model with 3 categories

	German	British	Food&Chem	Machinery
SIZE	12.153 (4.29) ****	2.0069 (.783) **	2.6908 (1.53) *	2.8798 (.843) ****
R&D	.0592 (.073)	.0266 (.046)	.1405 (.095)	.0180 (.555)
NON_FOOD	1.0541(.960)	- .0816 (.401)	- .1410 (.588)	.6382 (.484)
INTL_TO	2.1697 (.693) ****	1.9920 (.467) *****	2.2078 (.655) ****	1.9677 (.569) ****
GROWTH	- .0165 (.014)	- .0138 (.010)	- .0068 (.024)	- .0148(.008) **
DIVER_TO	-193.0 (1201)	-660.1 (743.7)	-729.0 (1197)	-491.4 (786.6)
GERMAN	=	=	.7448 (.383) *	1.0690 (.299) ****
NONEUR	- .1604 (.707)	.6920 (.435)	.6676 (.486)	.3551 (.534)
EUROPEAN	.4864 (1.06)	- .3300 (.586)	- .5051 (.943)	- .1518 (.724)
COC_L	1.1554 (.805)	.6363 (.811)	.9263 (1.06)	.7829 (.596)
Constant	.0569 (.414)	- .4415 (.302)	- .5717 (.392)	- .5973 (.422) **
MU(1)	2.3539 (.403) *****	1.6076 (.246) *****	1.8815 (.333) *****	1.7272 (.243) *****
Observations	90	108	86	112
χ^2-statistic	68.265	67.911	69.785	70.995
log-likelih.	-51,214	-82.867	-56.777	-83.328
correct pred.	70,00%	65.74%	66.28%	68.75%
random pred.	41,56%	34.45%	35.40%	35.71%

Notes see Table 6.4.

ACTIVE is negatively related to diversification, but this effect does not translate to the decision to become active in several or all countries considered. The coefficients in the Ordered Probit are less than a fourth that of the binomial model, and statistically insignificantly different from zero. The result suggests that specialized firms are more likely to enter at least some countries of the region, but that they are not seeking presence in every single market. British firms and the food and chemicals industries show a stronger relationship than German firms and the machinery industry. However, coefficients in subsamples are rarely statistically significant due to the small sample size. Thus, the inverse relationship between product and regional diversification is confirmed. The relationship is more important for British firms and the food and chemicals industries. It is also more important in inducing firms to engage in business than inducing them to become active throughout the region.

Table 6.8 Introducing HUMAN_CAP into the model: new coefficients, with standard errors, based on the parsimonious model version

Model	GERMAN	HUMAN_CAP	new χ^2 [a]	difference[a]
ACTIVE	.4196 (.421)	.0330 (.021)	106.439	2.524
#COUNTR	.7446 (.223)****	.0190 (.012)	141.264	3.406***
ACTIVE_3CAT	.7482 (.240)***	.0142 (.012)	135.791	.247
Czech Rep.	1.0656 (.334)****	.0177 (.016)	100.748	1.231
Hungary	.8409 (.303)***	.0072 (.013)	92.214	.290
Poland	- .0205 (.355)	.0662 (.019)****	109.886	14.377***
Russia	-.0365 (.310)	.0244 (.015)*	88.868	2.852*
Romania	.2726 (.291)	.0326 (.013)**	84.617	6.041**

Note: the models in Tables 6.4 and 6. 6 were re-run including additionally HUMAN_CAP as the independent variable, while omitting five variables that were not significant (analogue to Table 6.7 on subsample analysis). This table records only the coefficients on HUMAN_CAP and GERMAN, with which it is correlated. The difference of the χ^2 refers only to the change from adding HUMAN_CAP. [a] The new χ^2-statistics have 12 degrees of freedom, the differences have one degree of freedom.

In conclusion, significant effects are found for all proxies suggested for common governance ownership advantages. Size and international experience are the most important determinants of firms' activity, more influential than various measures of intangible assets. Product specialization encourages involvement in West-East business, and interesting differences are shown as it has more influence on decision to be active than on the extent of activity throughout the region.

Proximity

German firms, in particular those located near Germany's Eastern border, are predicted to be more active due to their psychic proximity to the region (H7, H8). Also, priorities within the region are expected to vary according to country and region of origin (I4, I5), and firm capabilities, in overcoming psychic distance (I3). Thus, ownership and interaction hypotheses should both be considered to assess the impact of proximity. Most hypotheses receive support, although the pattern of psychic proximity is more complex than hypothesized.

The GERMAN dummy is significant in all general models with coefficients of similar magnitude. In the machinery industry, this home country effect is more significant than in the food and chemicals industries.

The proximity effects vary considerably across the five host countries (Table 6.6): the specific German effect is largest for the Czech Republic, followed by Hungary. Poland and Romania take an intermediate position, while in Russia the coefficient is very small and insignificant. This general pattern is confirmed by the tests that include the human capital proxy HUMAN_CAP (Table 6.8). Thus, the psychic distance between the two home countries differs most *vis-à-vis* the Czech Republic and Hungary. In Poland the difference is smaller, presumably as a result of a combination of the British preference for Poland and tensions in the German-Polish political and economic relations. This is an example of diverging patterns of psychic and geographic proximity.

The two dummies for regions within Germany, BALTIC and BAVARIA, are not significant. However, an interesting result emerges for the business relationship of North German firms which have a relative preference for Russia (hypothesis I5). The coefficient for BALTIC is large and positive in the Russia equation, but small or negative in the others. Thus, these firms are not more active in the region, but when they are active they focus more on business with Russia. However, the number of BALTIC firms in the sample is too small to obtain a significant effect to prove the proposition. On the other hand, no such preference for Poland exists among BALTIC firms, neither does it exist among Bavarian firms for the Czech Republic. In fact, the BAVARIA coefficient is positive for all five CEE countries, but *smallest* in the Czech model. However, the sample does not contain firms from the Bavarian Forest region close to the Czech border, courtesy of the random sampling. Thus, a special border effect cannot be tested with this data set.

Furthermore, it was proposed that firms with advantages of common governance arising from size, international experience and product specialization would be better equipped to enter the more distant and uncertain markets in Russia (I4). The empirical results in Table 6.6 do not lend much support to these hypotheses: the size effects are of a similar magnitude across host countries. International experience even has a pattern opposite to that hypothesized: it is more relevant for lower psychic distance and low risk countries. The coefficient in the Russia model is *smaller* than for all other countries. This difference is indeed significant between Russia and Poland.[8] This surprising result suggests that internationally experienced firms are expanding to both Central Europe and Russia. However, the experience is relatively less important for Russia where a different kind of ownership advantage must therefore be more important. This might be product specialization: the third aspect easing entry over long distance is found to be more important for Russia.

The effect of DIVER_TO is twice as large with respect to business with Russia as it is for business with Central European countries, and lowest and insignificant for Romania. This confirms that a product specific leadership strategy may induce firms to accommodate high costs and risk in Russia.

Thus, evidence in favour of the proximity hypothesis is confirmed by the GERMAN dummy, and its variation across the five CEE countries. There may be other reasons for British-German differences, but only psychic proximity would explain this pattern. Yet, psychic distance is not easily overcome by large or internationally experienced firms, but by those specializing in a narrow product range. Their strategy of disseminating a narrow range of products worldwide even takes them into Russia.

Barriers to Growth and Control Variables

Firms facing barriers to growth in their established strategic configuration were hypothesized to be more active in the region. They would be characterized by low growth of turnover (H9: GROWTH) or labour-intensive production (H10: LABOUR).

The GROWTH variable is consistently negatively signed and significant for all models, except for Table 6.7 where sample sizes are small. Poland and the Czech Republic appear to be these depressed firms' preferred countries. The effect is larger for the machinery industry. Thus, firms experiencing slow growth, or even a fall in output in recent years, are more likely to be active in the region, especially in Poland. Business with CEE appears to offer an opportunity to overcome barriers to growth, though the effect varies across the region.

The production relocation argument suggested that labour-intensive firms would be more active because they can take advantage of labour cost differences. The results show no support for this hypothesis. The coefficient on LABOUR is negative, though insignificant, in every single model specification. Thus, capital- and human-capital intensive firms are relatively more active. Exports based on comparative advantages dominate over procurement and relocation in labour-intensive production. The negative effect is smaller for the ACTIVE model than for the other models in Table 6.4. This would, plausibly, suggest that capital- or human-capital intensive firms are active throughout the region, while labour-intensive firms are also active but in fewer countries. Production relocation requires only one new location while market-oriented firms are more likely to spread out their activity in order to supply all markets. This confirms the analysis of motives for DFI (Chapter 5): labour cost seeking is not a major force inducing firms to engage in East-West business.

Taking the two variables on barriers to growth together, there is little evidence that constraints on the supply side, in particular labour cost, would account for a major wave of business in CEE. However, barriers to growth in present markets are being overcome by entering the new markets in the East.

In addition, the analysis includes four control variables. The industry dummy CHEM is mostly insignificant, despite significant variation in the descriptive statistics. Two parent dummies, NONEUR and EUROPEAN, account for differences in corporate strategy imposed by parent firms. NONEUR has a positive effect while EUROPEAN has a negative effect; both are mostly insignificant. The COC_L dummy controls for a mixed sampling framework. These firms have been added to the sample with the prior knowledge that they are active in the region, and the coefficients are thus positive.

Locational effects

The OLI paradigm suggests that ownership advantages will combine with the locational advantages of the host economy to induce multinational business. Therefore, some hypotheses have been developed, in a novel fashion, as to how the impact of ownership advantages varies for DFI across host countries. They have been tested with country-specific Probit models (Table 6.7).

The larger market in Poland was predicted to attract more market-oriented business than Hungary or the Czech Republic. This effect would lead to larger effects of consumer goods, human capital intensity and barriers to growth in established markets. The coefficients of NON_FOOD are largest for business with the Czech Republic and Poland, but negative for Hungary. Contrary to the hypothesis, the FOOD dummy is negative in most country models. Thus, a special preference of consumer good manufacturers emerges only for non-food products, and the differences between countries are not significant.

Firms facing barriers to growth and those with high human capital have more business with all five CEE countries, but are most likely to engage in business with Poland and least likely to do so with Hungary (where the coefficients of GROWTH and HUMAN_CAP are smallest and insignificant). In both cases, the difference between Poland and Hungary is statistically significant and supports the view that large markets are a prime attraction for slow growing firms.[9] Thus, as proposed in I1, the larger market in Poland attracts some firms more than others. These are human capital-intensive firms, firms facing barriers to growth in existing markets, and, though with weaker evidence, non-food consumer goods manufacturers.

Surprisingly, the effect of R&D is larger and positive than in all other equations, and statistically significant for business with Russia and Romania. This suggests that business with these two more distant countries is driven by the kind of intangible assets that have frequently been found important for business around the world. However, the business relationships with the Central European countries are driven by other determinants. Note that the coefficient even turns negative for the Czech Republic. This is surprising given that it was hypothesized that R&D-intensive enterprises would primarily engage in business with countries of high technological standards as the need for local training and adaptation would be lower. A possible explanation is that opportunities to exploit natural resources especially attract R&D-intensive firms.

In conclusion, the analysis reveals few significant differences in the investment pattern other than those of psychic distance and firms' ability to overcome distance. While the evidence suggests that slow-growing firms focus primarily on Poland, as the country with the largest market in the region, research-intensive firms, surprisingly, appear to prefer Russia and Romania.

CONCLUSIONS

The evidence supports all four groups of hypotheses: intangible assets, common governance, barriers to growth and proximity all have a role in determining firms' propensity to engage in business with CEE. However, the evidence is weakest for the frequently cited intangible asset advantages, and strongest for variables often not considered in empirical analyses of ownership advantages.

The common governance variables show high statistical significance. They show that large, internationally experienced and specialized firms are more active in the region. With the advantage of proximity, German firms are more active especially in the Czech Republic and in Hungary. On the other hand, the results were mostly insignificant for the R&D and consumer goods variables. Consistent support also emerges for the negative association of sales growth and propensity of West-East business. Barriers to growth in the home market thus appear important in inducing firms to seek new opportunities in the East. This result is somewhat surprising since the alternative hypothesis that growing firms are more active because of better access to financial resources is a strong argument from a resource-based or financial perspective.[10]

The analysis reveals some differences in the determinants of business with the Visegrad countries. Slow-growing firms and human capital-intensive firms focus on the larger Polish market. More substantial differences emerge between the Visegrad countries and Russia, where research intensity is, surprisingly, more important while diversified firms abstain, to an even greater extent than usual, from entering the country. The pattern of determinants of international business is more in accordance with predictions in the case of Russia. This applies especially with respect to research intensity and production specialization strategies. Firms with very specific and technologic ownership advantages appear most willing to cope with the distant and highly uncertain environment. On the other hand, CEE also attracts numerous businesses without the hypothesized specific advantages. For firms with international experience, this region seems a natural extension to their global strategy.

Diversification is the only variable that significantly varies between the binomial and the ordered model. Thus, specialization induces firms to engage in business in the region - even in the distant Russian market - but it does not foster a presence in all accessible markets. Product leadership requires positioning in important markets, but not in all markets.

Together, these results indicate the importance of advantages of common governance, termed Ot-advantages by Dunning, over the more frequently discussed Oa-advantages of intangible assets and property rights. The dominance of common governance variables over intangible assets suggests that international business is increasingly a matter of multinational enterprise. Their capabilities are of an organizational rather than a technological or a product-specific nature. Corporations acquire technological and organizational knowledge from their various locations but retain home country-specific abilities and strategies as the difference between British and German firms in this sample illustrates. Empirical research should thus pay more attention to ownership advantages, other than intangible assets and property rights, as motivators for international business activity.

NOTES

1. Most specific strategic motivations cannot be analysed at the level of aggregation of this study, as detailed information on the competition in the market for each firm and country is not available.
2. It had been requested in the questionnaire but too many respondents did not provide it.
3. Svensson [1996] uses a similar measure and found a significant effect on DFI.
4. This is not a cardinal relationship because the variable is truncated at zero and the selection of countries has been constrained in the questionnaire.
5. The regression models were also estimated using a reduced dataset, omitting five variables that were mostly insignificant. This removes the moderate collinearity, for instance between CHEM and NON_FOOD. The results did not deviate in substance from those reported in the text.
6. For the binomial Probit models, a better fit was obtained with an additional squared employment variable. Coefficients to SIZE are reported multiplied by 10^5, and SIZE_SQ by 10^{10} to facilitate readability of the tables.
7. One firm had business with the CEE region reported in the questionnaire but not in any of the five countries for which specific information was requested. Therefore the zero category of not-active firms has 42 and 43 observations respectively in different models.
8. Using the values of the parsimonious model (Table 6.8), the difference of the coefficients in the Russian and Polish model is 2.0013 - 0.8149 = 1.1864. The standard error of the difference is the square root of the sum of the variances of the coefficients which is 0.5782. Thus the t-statistic for the difference is 2.25.
9. For GROWTH, the difference is 0.0242, its standard error 0.0120 and t=2.01.
10. Haiss and Fink [1995] also report that weaker firms would be more actively investing in CEE.

7. Determinants of Direct Investment: Testing Transaction Cost Theory

In Chapter 6, we established which types of firms are active in CEE. In this chapter the choice between DFI and other forms of business is analysed, applying and testing the transaction cost (TC) model developed in Chapter 4.

In the theoretical model, the choice between DFI and market transactions depends on the relative TC of internal and external organization. Both are functions of product sensitivity, that is their information content (IC) and asset specificity (AS). The internal TC curve has a fixed cost component independent of the sensitivity, and a flatter slope. DFI would be preferred if sensitivity exceeds a benchmark set by the intersection of the two TC curves (Figure 4.2). The model illustrates how the pattern of the TC curves over product sensitivity is influenced by several environmental and firm variables, including uncertainty (u), psychic distance (d), and international experience (e). Thus, the probability of choosing DFI over an alternative mode can be expressed as,

$$P\,(\,DFI=1\,)\;=\;f\,(IC^{+},\,AS^{+},\,u^{+},\,d^{\prime},\,e^{+}) \tag{7.1}$$

Equation (7.1) is a simplified version of equation (4.9). It is tested empirically in this chapter. The chapter begins by laying out the hypothesis by explaining the dataset and the method of analysis. The empirical analysis is based firstly on a multinomial Logit model. This is extended to an empirical test of interaction effects of product characteristics with environmental and firm characteristics, notably psychic distance and experience. Furthermore, the view that contracts can be analysed as an intermediate form between markets and hierarchies is assessed by comparing a multinomial and an ordered Logit model.

TESTING TRANSACTION COSTS

Propositions

The first stage of the empirical analysis considers the impact of variables proposed in the TC model on the propensity of DFI. This section introduces the variables and their proxies based on the theoretical arguments in Chapter 4. Variables include information intensity, uncertainty, psychic distance, common governance and experience. Since the data-set contains mainly market-oriented businesses, the analysis focuses on the final stages of the product chain, and the interfaces between production and sales.

Information intensity
A major cause of market failure is asymmetric information on properties of the product to be transferred. Related phenomena are externalities from the 'public good character of knowledge' within the firm, the costs of transferring tacit knowledge, and the free-rider potential for users of brand-names who may degrade the quality of standards. These properties of knowledge inhibit the use of contracts for its transfer. Therefore, information asymmetries and related market failures are a rationale for the existence of multinational enterprises. Therefore the first hypothesis is:

H1:   *Firms potentially subject to information asymmetry are more likely to internalize downstream business in CEE.*

Ownership advantages based on knowledge are a motivation both for becoming international and for internalizing the business. Therefore firms with knowledge-based assets are more active *and* more likely to internalize as they would prefer to control their produce until it reaches the customer. This includes research and human capital-intensive firms: research-intensive industries face particular information asymmetries in the transfer of production technology. At interfaces further downstream, information asymmetry affects the market opportunities for innovative products and the training of sales and service personnel. Other forms of human capital, notably in finance and marketing, similarly affect all transactions. Their relative importance can be expected to vary for different interfaces along the product chain. Research intensity (R&D) is proxied by R&D expenditures over turnover, and human capital intensity (HUMAN_CAP) by personnel costs per employee.

Secondly, the marketing and distribution of consumer goods is more information intensive. The unit coordinating local marketing, and possibly local distributors, exchanges sensitive strategic marketing information with headquarters. Furthermore control of product quality is essential to maintain the reputation of a worldwide brand. Therefore, manufacturers of non-food consumer goods (NON_FOOD) and food (FOOD) would be likely to internalize at least a unit of their local distribution.

Uncertainty
Uncertainty reduces the possibility of writing complete contracts while

increasing the probability that situations arise in which the partners need a joint reaction in response to changes in the environment. Therefore industry uncertainty increases preferences for internalization. This is because risk sharing can reduce effects on the outcome of the joint project, and eliminate effects on the terms of trade between the partners. Hierarchical structures allow smoother adjustment because fewer agents' interests need to be coordinated.

Industry-specific uncertainty is difficult to assess in CEE. Concentration ratios are not available, and may not be applicable because the industry structure is influenced by import competition. Most uncertainties arise as a result of government policy including the privatization process. Uncertainty is greater in high-growth sectors and in those sectors most affected by transition recession in CEE. The latter have extremely negative growth rates and are most in need of restructuring. Thus, the larger the difference between an industry growth rate and the average growth (H_GROW_D), the higher is uncertainty, and the higher is the expected propensity to internalize.[1]

H2:   *Industrial sectors with average growth have a lower degree of internalization than those with either above or below average growth.*

Psychic distance

Psychic distance has a theoretically ambiguous effect in the TC model because it increases costs of both internal and external modes of business. Psychic distance increases both internal and external transaction costs. Distance reduces the ability to control the use of knowledge transferred by licensing. On the other hand, internal costs may increase more than external TC. Thus, TCE does not suggest a clear net effect of psychic distance on internalization.

Country dummies act as controls for the variation of distance in the sample. They include the home country dummy GERMAN and the host country dummies CZECH, HUNGARY, POLAND and RUSSIA. Accordingly, UK firms and Romania are the base case. The hypothesis can only suggest an effect, without giving its direction:

H3:   *Psychic distance affects the propensity of internalization.*

If distance favoured internalization, then the GERMAN, CZECH, HUNGARY, and POLAND dummies should all have a negative sign. If proximity favoured internalization, then the signs would be opposite. The latter case would imply that proximity reduces internal costs by more than external TC.

By the distance argument, the coefficient for the RUSSIA dummy should be opposite to those for the Visegrad countries. In addition, it may have a positive effect due to higher potential opportunism. The scope for opportunistic behaviour can be constrained by ethical business practice, social networks, and the development of the legal code. Visegrad countries are more advanced than Russia in all of these three criteria. Table 2.1 shows the EBRD assessment of Russia's lagging position in the legal and banking reform. This implies that foreign businesses in Russia have high incentives to maintain control over their local operations.

Economies of common governance and experience

In the model developed in Chapter 4 experience and economies of common governance reduce internal TC. International business has a major fixed cost component. Larger firms can use economies of scale and of common governance because the per unit internal TC decline with increasing turnover. Firms with related activities and experiences are thus more likely to choose DFI:

H4:   *Firms that can utilize experience or economies of common governance are more likely to internalize their downstream business.*

In the regression analysis, the effects of firm size, as well as international and regional experience are analysed. Firstly, large firms are more likely than small firms to engage in DFI because the marginal costs of adding a new operation are lower. Thus, the larger the parent firm the more likely it is to internalize the business. Firm size is proxied by its employment (SIZE).

Secondly, the more international experience a firm has, the lower are the internal TC of the CEE operations. Experience can be gathered by operating international production in general, measured as the share of employment outside the home country (GLOBAL). This experience is more relevant for new investments than international turnover which was used in Chapter 6. Thirdly, common governance effects bring synergies with other operations in the region, which are proxied by the share of turnover in CEE in total sales (CE_EUROPE). Due to the nature of the available proxies, experience and common governance effects cannot be separated: a firm with extensive international business has both experience in such business and can utilize certain headquarters' functions for multiple business activities.

Summary, and control variables

All hypotheses, their respective proxies and the expected signs on DFI are summarized in Table 7.1. Some of the independent variables have proxies also used in Chapter 6. However their role in this model differs. Rather than considering their value as ownership advantage, the analysis now focuses on their sensitivity to asset specificity and information asymmetry. For instance, human capital intensity creates ownership advantages (O) that motivate a firm to engage in international business. This advantage is however intangible and thus difficult to sell through markets. Therefore there is also an incentive for internalization (I). The stepwise analysis enables the distinction between the O- and I-properties.

Table 7.1 Hypotheses and variables

Hypothesis	Proxy	Expected Sign	Level of analysis
H1: Information	R&D	+	firm
	HUMAN_CAP	+	firm
	NF_CONS	+	firm
	FOOD	+	firm
H2: Uncertainty	H_GROW_D	+	host industry
H3: Distance	GERMAN	?	home country
	CZECH	?	host country
	HUNGARY	?	host country
	POLAND	?	host country
	RUSSIA	?	host country
H4: Experience	SIZE	+	firm
& Common	GLOBAL	+	firm
governance	CE_EUROPE	+	firm

In addition, some control variables are required. To test the effect of research intensity, controlling for the pharmaceuticals industry (PHARMA) is necessary. This industry has the highest R&D ratios, but their know-how is, at least in CEE markets, codified by the time new products are brought to the market. Pharmaceuticals can only be sold if they pass comprehensive approval procedures which follow patenting. Thus, copying is more observable and can either be prevented by enforcing the patent or, less efficiently, by keeping production know-how internal. Furthermore the industry is highly dependent on government policy since the health sector, its predominant customer, is a highly regulated service. Therefore investment decisions are influenced by government-industry negotiations.

Another control dummy deemed necessary is for firms affiliated to non-European MNEs (NONEUR). In addition to the firm-level variables, it is necessary to introduce variables to control for the different types of transactions included in the sample. In the base sample, only two control dummies are used based on the kinds of knowledge transfers reported in the questionnaire. These are management and marketing know-how (T_MANAG) as well as patented and unprotected technological know-how (T_TECHN).

In the downstream sample (explained below), the different types of goods transferred need to be controlled for. Thus, dummies for final goods only (T_O_FIN), final and other goods (T_FIN_ETAL), and for market seeking business without exports (T_NONE) are added. In the full sample, dummies for upstream business (UPSTREAM) and for business with both upstream and downstream orientation (UP&DOWN) are added.

METHOD OF ANALYSIS

This empirical test analyses the type of business decision as a trilateral choice made by the active firms. Western firms choose between DFI, trade and contracts in CEE. The model analyses the probability of a firm choosing either mode over the two alternatives. The empirical model is a multinomial logit, an extension of the binomial Logit. The latter is defined as the log of the odds ratio in the following form:

$$\log (P/(1-P)) = \text{\ss}'\mathbf{x} \tag{7.2}$$

where P stands for the probability of the dependent variable taking the value of one, $\mathbf{x}$ for the independent variables, and $\text{\ss}$ for the regression coefficients. This can be transformed as follows with the probability as the dependent variable [Maddala 1983]:

$$P (Y=1) = (e^{\text{\ss}'\mathbf{x}})/(1 + e^{\text{\ss}'\mathbf{x}}) = \Lambda (\text{\ss}'\mathbf{x}) \tag{7.3}$$

The binomial Logit approach is enriched by using an independent multiple choice approach, a multinomial logistic regression. It is known in short as multinomial Logit (M-Logit) and has the following general form [De Maris 1992, Greene 1993: 666]:

$$P (Y=k) = (e^{\text{\ss}'\mathbf{x}})/(\Sigma^k e^{\text{\ss}'\mathbf{x}}) = \Lambda_K (\text{\ss}'\mathbf{x}) \tag{7.4}$$

where $k = 0, 1, ..., K$ stands for the different choices available. The dependent variable *MODE* is defined to capture different forms of business with CEE:

$MODE = 0$ if the business relationship involves only trade
$\quad\quad\quad = 1$ if the business relationship involves contracts, but no DFI (7.5)
$\quad\quad\quad = 2$ if the business relationship involves DFI.

The present model can thus be expressed as:

$$P (MODE=k) = \Lambda_K \{\text{\ss}' (IC, AS, u, d, e)\} \tag{7.6}$$

An important assumption in the M-Logit is that the choices are independent, that is the odds ratios of the model do not change with the introduction of additional choices. This property is known as 'independence from irrelevant alternatives' (IIA) [Cramer 1991: 47, Greene 1993: 671]. In other words, the M-Logit is indifferent to any similarities, dissimilarities or causal relationships between the k choices.

For $k=0$, the ßs are normalized such that the M-Logit returns ß estimates for each of the remaining K-1 alternative choices. Independent variables are the same as in equation (7.5). The models were estimated using the maximum likelihood procedure provided by LIMDEP. The regression coefficients ß estimate the change in the log odds ratio between any pair of two alternatives. The Logit regression routine provided by LIMDEP (or other software) provides ßs for the base case choice *vis-à-vis* each other alternative. The effects of independent variables on the choice between other alternatives can be calculated by using the differences between the coefficients. Calculating the corresponding standard errors requires a more complex procedure because the full covariance matrix needs to be taken into account [Cramer 1991: 64].[2]

The hypotheses have been set-up for the internalization decision, thus the coefficients for the choice of DFI *vis-à-vis* both exports and contracts are of prime interest. The theoretical predictions on the choice between contracts and trade are less clear. If contracts were an intermediate form between markets and hierarchies, as argued in some of the literature, then the signs should be the same for trade *vis-à-vis* contracts as contracts *vis-à-vis* DFI.

THE DATA-SET

The theoretical model considers the choice of organizational form for a *given* transaction. An empirical test of the model thus has to focus on transactions of similar character to isolate the internalization decision. To control for other influences, two methods are used: firstly reduction of the data-set to include only one type of transaction, secondly, introduction of control variables.

The data-set obtained with the questionnaire survey contains 576 observations of active business relationships which can be used for the analysis. Of these, 411 business relationships are downstream, that is supplying local markets, 17 are upstream, that is importing local produce from the region, and 148 are both up- and downstream (Table 7.2). To separate the types, these definitions have been adopted: downstream businesses have either:
- DFI, motivated by markets (question 8 in the survey), or
- exports, except intermediate goods in connection with subcontracting (question 1), or
- contractual forms of business other than subcontracting (question 1),

but *not* imports, subcontracting (question 1), or DFI motivated by factor costs (question 9). Upstream businesses have the opposite characteristics. Observations with both kinds of business fall in the third category.

Table 7.2 Types of business, by number of observations

	Downstream	Upstream	Both	Full sample
Export & Import	259 (63.0%)	11 (64.7%)	28 (18.9%)	298 (51.7%)
Contracts	53 (12.9%)	4 (23.5%)	27 (18.2%)	84 (14.6%)
DFI	99 (24.1%)	2 (11.8%)	93 (62.8%)	194 (33.7%)
Total	**411** (100%)	17 (100%)	148 (100%)	**576** (100%)

Downstream business, by type of goods transferred

	final goods only	final and other goods	intermediate goods and / or raw mat.	know-how based only	n.a.	Total
Export	192 (70.3%)	13 (38.2%)	38 (76.0%)	-- [a]	16	259
Contracts	27 (9.9%)	4 (11.8%)	14 (28.0%)	7	1	53
DFI [b]	54 (19.8%)	17 (50.0%)	8 (16.0%)	16	4	99
Total	**273** (100%)	34 (100%)	50 (100%)	23	21	**411**

Notes: a = none, by definition, b = DFI includes cases of DFI and contracts, 8 of 54 in the 273 dataset, and 19 of 99 in the 411 data-set. n.a. = firms reporting no information for question 3.

The downstream businesses can be further divided using the information provided in question 3 of the survey. Crucially businesses vary by the extent of local production (Chapter 4). This analysis focuses on businesses without local production, which therefore export final goods for sale in local markets. The Western firm may export by selling to an agent or directly to a customer, it may have a contractual arrangement with a distributor, or it may have invested directly into a local distribution network, or at least a central sales unit. There are 273 such business relationships in the sample. The remaining businesses mostly transfer intermediate goods and raw materials, either exclusively or along with final goods. In 23 cases of contracts or DFI, no exports are reported, which implies that only know-how is transferred. In 21 incidents no information was provided in question 3 although exports were reported.

The tests of theory are primarily based on the sample of downstream businesses which transfer only final goods. This sample is henceforth referred to as 'base' sample (Table 7.3). Since the empirical test of the theoretical model needs to focus on one kind of transaction, it is necessary to use transaction specific criteria. The emphasis here is on testing a theory, thus compromises have to be made with respect to comprehensiveness.

Table 7.3 Definitions of the samples

Samples	Short name	number of observations
Downstream, with only final goods transferred	Base	273
All downstream businesses	Downstream	411
full sample	Full	576
Base, but *not* turnkey and management contracts	excl. turnkey	263
Base, but *not* pharmaceuticals industry	excl. pharma	236

Table 7.4 Some descriptive data on the samples

Industries	Food		Chemicals		Machinery
Base	41 (15.0%)		84 (30.8%)		148 (54.2%)
Downstream	61 (14.8%)		132 (32.1%)		218 (53.0%)
Full	67 (11.6%)		177 (30.7%)		332 (57.6%)

Hosts	Czech	Hungary	Poland	Rumania	Russia
Base	45 (16.5%)	50 (18.3%)	55 (20.1%)	58 (21.2%)	65 (23.8%)
Downstream	76 (18.5%)	78 (19.0%)	90 (21.9%)	80 (19.5%)	87 (21.2%)
Full	125 (21.7%)	116 (20.1%)	130 (22.6%)	88 (15.3%)	117 (20.3%)

Home countries	German	British
Base	147 (53.8%)	126 (46.2%)
Downstream	209 (50.9%)	202 (49.1%)
Full	329 (57.1%)	247 (42.9%)

Experience	International [a]	Less international [a]
Base	137 (50.2%)	136 (49.8%)
Downstream	227 (55.2%)	184 (44.8%)
Full	329 (57.1%)	247 (42.9%)

Notes: a = (Less) international firms: firms with more (less) than 24.2% of turnover abroad. Groups are defined by the median of the base sample, which is thus split 50-50.

By focusing on the downstream businesses without local production, half of all observations are eliminated. This changes the distribution across organizational modes, with the share of DFI falling from 33.7 per cent to 19.8 per cent (Table 7.2). This is because the more business operations a firm has in a country, the more likely they are operated internally. This applies to the joint operation of downstream and upstream business as well as local production for local markets. The pattern gives first support to the common-governance argument.

Table 7.5   Types of contracts

	Base	excl. turnkey	Downstream	Full
Licensing	3	3	12	16
Francising	7	7	12	12
Management contract	--[a]	1	3	6
Turnkey contract	--[a]	6	6	6
Subcontracting	--[a]	--[a]	--[a]	14
Other contract	5	5	11	12
Multiple contracts	2	5	9	18
Total	17	27	53	84

Note: [a] = none, by definition

Table 7.6   Descriptive statistics for independent variables

	Unit of measurement	base sample	Mean & SD downstream	full sample
R&D	percentage	4.85 (4.64)	4.34 (4.31)	4.24 (3.97)
HUMAN_CAP	£ sterling	27,941 (10,947)	27,977 (10,101)	28,385 (9,836)
H_GROW_D	s. appendix 5.3	.822 (.608)	.808 (.586)	.802 (.550)
EMPLOY	10^5	.101 (.153)	.124 (.198)	.147 (.211)
GLOBAL	ratio	.304 (.275)	.339 (.287)	.350 (.284)
CE_EUROPE	ratio	.025 (.024)	.025 (.025)	.026 (.026)

Table 7.4 explores the samples. The base sample includes market oriented businesses transferring final goods alone. In the food industry this appears relatively common, increasing the share of this industry from 11.6 per cent to

15.0 per cent. The machinery industry has more local production and sourcing activities which are deselected from the smaller sample. Similarly, the share of the Visegrad countries in the sample falls from 64.4 per cent to 54.9 per cent as more production is located there than in Russia and Romania. The bias of home countries in the sample is modest as British share increases from 42.9 per cent to 46.2 per cent. In a later stage of the analysis, the sample is divided in subgroups by international experience. According to this criterion, the base sample over-represents less experienced firms.

Table 7.7   Correlations (base sample)

		1	2	3	4	5	6	7	8	9	10	11	12
1	R&D	1.0											
2	HUMAN_CAP	.19	1.0										
3	PHARMA	.56	.02	1.0									
4	NF_CONS	.20	.14	.52	1.0								
5	FOOD	-.23	-.09	-.17	-.25	1							
6	H_GROW_D	-.14	.00	-.23	-.07	.18	1.0						
7	GERMAN	.34	.54	.09	.07	.00	.05	1.0					
8	CZECH	-.02	.02	-.05	.05	-.02	.17	-.06	1.0				
9	HUNGARY	-.01	.14	.01	.00	.01	.11	.02	-.21	1.0			
10	POLAND	-.03	.02	-.01	-.01	-.01	-.15	-.12	-.22	-.24	1.0		
11	RUSSIA	.00	-.04	.00	-.04	.03	-.11	.05	-.25	-.26	-.28	1.0	
12	SIZE	.07	-.06	.05	-.03	-.02	-.08	-.23	-.01	-.01	-.02	0.0	1.0
13	GLOBAL	.14	-.19	.35	.16	-.12	-.14	-.28	.06	-.02	-.03	-.09	.36
14	CE_EUROPE	.11	.19	.08	.01	-.02	.05	.38	-.07	.01	-.10	.05	-.16
15	NONEUR	.01	.13	.01	.05	-.11	.01	-.25	.02	.00	.00	.00	-.07

continued		13	14	15
13	GLOBAL	1.0		
14	CE_EUROPE	-.18	1.0	
15	NONEUR	-.06	-.10	1.0

Note: correlations are significant at 5% level if $r > 0.12$.

So far, the forms of contractual business have not been differentiated. Table 7.5 shows the types of contracts included in the construct 'contracts'. The reduced sample includes most of the franchising and turnkey contracts, plus some other contracts including combinations of several contracts. The small number of observations does not allow a separation of them in the main empirical analysis. Therefore a test is conducted with a reduced data-set, which excludes turnkey projects and management contracts.

Table 7.6 and 7.7 report the descriptive statistics and correlations of the independent variables. The correlations for the other subsamples used in the analysis are similar to those of the base sample.

RESULTS

Tables 7.8a to e report the results of the M-Logit for various sample definitions. The interpretation and hypothesis evaluation focuses on the base sample (Table 7.8a) which fully controls for type of business. The regressions in Tables 7.8b and c take out two groups of observations suspected to distort the result. These are firstly pharmaceutical companies, and secondly turnkey projects and management contracts. Table 7.8d and e report the regressions over the larger samples. Finally the observations excluded in the base sample were analysed, but to economize on space, these regressions are not tabulated. These are firstly businesses with upstream business and, secondly, downstream businesses with local production.

The hypotheses are discussed based on the regression of the base sample. Internalization preferences are reflected in the second and third column which report the coefficients on the odds ratios of DFI versus other available choices. Subsequently the differences observed in other samples are discussed. Note that Tables 7.8b to e omit the trade-versus-contracts column which is not relevant to the research questions.

Information intensity
Exchanges with higher information intensity are subject to potential information asymmetry and thus predicted more likely to be organized internally (H1). The empirical evidence only supports this hypothesis with respect to the choice of DFI *vis-à-vis* trade.

Research intensity (R&D) has the predicted coefficient on DFI versus contracts in the base sample, but it is very insignificant. Human capital intensity (HUMAN_CAP) has a correct sign but appears insignificant throughout. Not even the actual transfer of technology, introduced as control variable T_TECHN, leads to a higher propensity of DFI: firms transferring technology appear, significantly, to prefer contracts over DFI. Note that pharmaceutical companies significantly abstain from DFI. Without this dummy the R&D coefficient would become negative.[3]

Table 7.8a   Multinomial model: base sample

	Trade vs. Contract	Trade vs. DFI	Contract vs. DFI
R&D	.1343 (.075)*	.1413 (.067)**	.0070 (.093)
HUMAN_CAP	.0175 (.042)	.0329 (.027)	.0153 (.047)
PHARMA	-1.6679 (1.20)	-4.4367(1.10)*****	-2.7688 (1.50)*
NF_CONS	- .1992 (.732)	1.3894 (.605)**	1.5886 (.843)*
FOOD	-11.732 (148.1)	.3354 (.760)	11.960 (140.4)
H_GROW_D	.0787 (.455)	-.0600 (.429)	-.1386 (.592)
GERMAN	-1.7466 (.841)**	.4387 (.759)	2.1853 (1.09)**
CZECH	.3027 (.759)	2.2653 (.777)****	1.9727 (.988)**
HUNGARY	.4344 (.733)	1.7292 (.761)**	1.2948 (.980)
POLAND	- .3054 (.757)	2.1688 (.785)***	2.4742 (1.00)**
RUSSIA	- .4173 (.774)	.5753 (.769)	.9927 (1.02)
SIZE	-2.1092 (1.59)	-1.4947 (1.46)	.6144 (1.99)
GLOBAL	.5258 (1.03)	3.7946 (1.03)****	3.2688 (1.312)**
CE_EUROPE	-31.383 (16.4)*	24.536 (9.73)**	55.919 (18.34)****
NONEUR	-1.9888 (.799)**	- 1.2112 (.711)*	.7776 (.961)
T_TECHN	2.4323 (.801)****	- .0265 (.925)	-2.4588 (1.02)**
T_MANAG	.3655 (.629)	3.1375 (.529)*****	2.7720 (.756)****
T_O_FIN	--	--	--
T_FIN_ETAL	--	--	--
T_NONE	--	--	--
UPSTREAM	--	--	--
UP&DOWN	--	--	--
Constant	-1.4320 (1.22)	-7.5949 (1.37)*****	-6.1629 (1.72)****
χ^2	163.840 (34)	log-likelihood	-135.634
correct pred.	82.42%	restricted log-likel.	-217.554
random pred.	54.35%	ρ-statistic	37.66%

Notes: levels of statistical significance: * = 10%, ** = 5%, *** = 1%, **** = 0.5%, ***** = 0.005%.   -- = Variable not included.

Table 7.8b   Multinomial model: base sample, excluding pharmaceuticals

	Trade vs. DFI	Contract vs. DFI
R&D	.1323 (.091)	- .0027 (.123)
HUMAN_CAP	.0391 (.029)	.0402 (.052)
PHARMA	--	--
NF_CONS	.5943 (.691)	1.3768 (.993)
FOOD	.1633 (.833)	11.964 (138.1)
H_GROW_D	- .0733 (.494)	- .2710 (.646)
GERMAN	.8373 (.888)	2.7603 (1.27)**
CZECH	2.8077 (.893)****	2.6594 (1.09)**
HUNGARY	1.9685 (.878)**	1.9567 (1.10)*
POLAND	2.0952 (.908)**	2.6213 (1.11)**
RUSSIA	1.0005 (.853)	1.6500 (1.11)
SIZE	2.1165 (1.70)	.5627 (2.10)
GLOBAL	4.2817 (1.11)****	4.0174 (1.43)****
CE_EUROPE	17.049 (12.5)	65.466 (23.1)****
NONEUR	- .6555 (.806)	1.7067 (1.07)
T_TECHN	- .5323 (.956)	-2.8058 (1.06)***
T_MANAG	3.6369 (.607)*****	2.6238 (.832)****
T_O_FIN	--	--
T_FIN_ETAL	--	--
T_NONE	--	--
UPSTREAM	--	--
UP&DOWN	--	--
Constant	-8.2565 (1.65)*****	-7.6680 (2.00)****

χ^2	163.105 (32)	log-likelihood	-110.105
correct pred.	83.47%	restricted log-l.	-191.657
random pred.	53.38%	ρ-statistic	42.55%

Notes: levels of statistical significance: * = 10%, ** = 5%, *** = 1%, **** = 0.5%, ***** = 0.005%. -- = Variable not included.

Table 7.8c Multinomial model: base sample, excluding turnkey and management contracts

	Trade vs. DFI	Contract vs. DFI
R&D	.1399 (.067)**	- .0697 (.112)
HUMAN_CAP	.0314 (.027)	.0430 (.069)
PHARMA	-4.6522(1.12)*****	-3.1762 (1.61)**
NF_CONS	1.4747 (.630)**	1.2977 (.938)
FOOD	.3306 (.772)	11.012 (138.4)
H_GROW_D	-.1465 (.445)	.0014 (.834)
GERMAN	.5513 (.768)	2.2663 (1.32)*
CZECH	2.1470 (.806)***	.5788 (1.40)
HUNGARY	1.8169 (.784)**	.27818 (1.37)
POLAND	2.0919 (.832)**	1.5568 (1.45)
RUSSIA	.3785 (.808)	- .5289 (1.44)
SIZE	-1.4995 (1.64)	3.0455 (3.39)
GLOBAL	3.9208 (1.08)****	2.8431 (1.59)*
CE_EUROPE	24.752 (9.84)**	60.210 (21.63)***
NONEUR	- 1.2234 (.733)*	- .5436 (1.06)
T_TECHN	- .2486 (.968)	-2.4024 (1.25)*
T_MANAG	3.2558 (.548)*****	3.9376 (.988)****
T_O_FIN	--	--
T_FIN_ETAL	--	--
T_NONE	--	--
UPSTREAM	--	--
UP&DOWN	--	--
Constant	-7.5542 (1.38)*****	-5.1071 (2.16)**

χ^2	157.065 (34)	log-likelihood	-113.935
correct pred.	84.41%	restricted log-l.	-192.468
random pred.	57.93%	ρ-statistic	40.80%

Notes: levels of statistical significance: * = 10%, ** = 5%, *** = 1%, **** = 0.5%, ***** = 0.005%. -- = Variable not included.

Table 7.8d Multinomial model: downstream sample

	Trade vs. DFI	Contract vs. DFI
R&D	.0875 (.053)*	- .1161 (.066)*
HUMAN_CAP	.0324 (.023)	.0371 (.033)
PHARMA	-3.6405(.828)*****	-1.5763 (1.07)
NF_CONS	1.3717 (.532)***	1.2039 (.701)*
FOOD	- .1464 (.596)	.1332 (.713)
H_GROW_D	- .0247 (.315)	-.3006 (.366)
GERMAN	1.3703 (.601)**	2.9767 (.699)*****
CZECH	1.9317 (.667)****	1.6368 (.765)**
HUNGARY	1.9075 (.646)****	1.4587 (.763)*
POLAND	2.0054 (.648)****	1.5887 (.748)**
RUSSIA	.7932 (.648)	1.1347 (.773)
SIZE	.7744 (1.05)	1.9267 (1.19)
GLOBAL	3.2803 (.824)****	2.2063 (.936)**
CE_EUROPE	9.5717 (7.90)	21.118 (11.89)*
NONEUR	- .9850 (.605)	1.0976 (.736)
T_TECHN	1.1462 (.587)*	- .6564 (.585)
T_MANAG	3.2637 (.440)*****	1.8646 (.522)****
T_O_FIN	.1329 (.544)	.3439 (.625)
T_FIN_ETAL	.7947 (.728)	.6778 (.861)
T_NONE	15.225 (170.6)	.9478 (.792)
UPSTREAM	--	--
UP&DOWN	--	--
Constant	-7.9564 (1.24)*****	-5.5529 (1.44)****

χ^2	306.999 (40)	log-likelihood	-215.581
correct pred.	80.05%	restricted log-l.	-369.081
random pred.	45.51%	ρ-statistic	41.59%

Notes: levels of statistical significance: * = 10%, ** = 5%, *** = 1%, **** = 0.5%, ***** = 0.005%. -- = Variable not included.

Table 7.8e   Multinomial model: full sample

	Trade vs. DFI	Contract vs. DFI
R&D	.1152 (.046)**	- .0474 (.051)
HUMAN_CAP	.0261 (.018)	.0011 (.022)
PHARMA	-2.9977(.677)*****	-1.1662 (.766)
NF_CONS	1.0967 (.442)**	.4050 (.482)
FOOD	.0596 (.540)	.2057 (.647)
H_GROW_D	- .0790 (.288)	-.3818 (.317)
GERMAN	.7056 (.476)	2.8194 (.500)*****
CZECH	1.5840 (.572)***	1.2240 (.632)*
HUNGARY	1.9893 (.574)****	1.4465 (.643)**
POLAND	1.5794 (.563)***	1.1368 (.626)*
RUSSIA	.5559 (.575)	.6149 (.645)
SIZE	1.2334 (.833)	2.2505 (.871)***
GLOBAL	2.0780 (.636)****	1.4163 (.666)**
CE_EUROPE	6.4358 (5.73)	2.8468 (6.69)
NONEUR	- .7889 (.498)	1.1174 (.573)*
T_TECHN	1.8359 (.477)****	.0271 (.417)
T_MANAG	3.3070 (.366)*****	2.2353 (.378)*****
T_O_FIN	- .5601 (.225)**	- .3735 (.234)
T_FIN_ETAL	.5605 (.225)**	.3657 (.234)
T_NONE	2.8024 (.726)****	1.1895 (.631)*
UPSTREAM	-1.9140 (1.05)*	-1.4688 (1.13)
UP&DOWN	4.1679 (1.10)****	1.2781 (1.15)
Constant	-6.5218 (.905)*****	-3.5478 (.997)****
χ^2	470.744 (44)	log-likelihood	-333.859
correct pred.	76.22%	restricted log-l.	-569.231
random pred.	40.24%	ρ-statistic	41.35%

Notes: levels of statistical significance: * = 10%, ** = 5%, *** = 1%, **** = 0.5%, ***** = 0.005%. -- = Variable not included.

Support for the hypothesis emerges with the marketing know-how and goodwill effects predicted for consumer goods. Non-food consumer good manufacturers (NF_CONS) prefer DFI over both trade and contracts in all samples. The food industry dummy (FOOD) has insignificant coefficients. Thus, the former firms appear more likely to internalize their local sales operations than exporting to independent agents. Yet, except for this case of non-food consumer goods, no evidence is found of knowledge-based firms preferring DFI over contracts.

The pattern is further examined by excluding pharmaceutical companies, because the PHARMA dummy is correlated with NF_CONS in this sample (Table 7.8b). As a result, not only does the NF_CONS dummy become insignificant, but the positive effect of R&D intensity on the DFI versus trade choice disappears. Thus none of the information variables receives statistical support. A possible source of the insignificance is the different internalization in, for example, franchising and turnkey contracts. Therefore turnkey projects and management contracts have been excluded in model 3. Yet the results of the information variables remain insignificant. Note that the R&D coefficient is negative in all but the base sample.

In the larger samples (Tables 7.8d and e), the pattern of the information proxies hardly changes over the base case. The analysis of market seeking investment with local production (no table) shows a significant positive association of both R&D and HUMAN_CAP with the choice of DFI over trade. This reflects the more sensitive nature of the interface when production is located abroad. Businesses with upstream components (no table) show negative coefficients for the information proxies, other than food. The effect is significant, and surprising, in the case of HUMAN_CAP. The consumer goods argument would not apply to this sample since these business activities focus not only on marketing. Also these models do not show the surprising negative sign for T_TECHN.

Thus, despite extensive examination of the data-set, no positive association can be established between research[4] and human capital intensity and the preference for DFI *vis-à-vis* contracts. However, information intensity of the firm is shown to favour DFI over trade as the market serving mode.

Uncertainty

The empirical results give no support to hypothesis 2 on the impact of uncertainty. The coefficients on H_GROW_D almost all have signs contrary to predictions (except Table 7.8c) and are insignificant. Thus no relationship between the industry uncertainty and internalization can be established in any of the equations. The explanation for this failure could lie in other influences related to industry growth affecting mode choice. Further research may employ alternative proxies to explain the proposition.

Distance

The pattern of country dummies in the base sample suggests that psychic distance reduces internalization. German firms have a higher preference for DFI over both trade and contracts than their British counterparts. Business in the Visegrad countries is more likely to be internalized than business in either Russia or Romania. The Russia dummy does not fit the pattern since Russia is more distant from both Germany and Britain than is Romania. The positive, yet insignificant, effect may be caused by increased internalization to cope with higher opportunism in Russia. It could also be a reaction to market size. The country pattern is fairly consistent across all models.

Theory could not give a clear prediction on the direction of the distance effect. However, the empirical result is fairly clear despite the relatively unsophisticated measures applied. The results imply that psychic proximity reduces the costs of internal organization more than it reduces the costs of market transactions. In terms of the curves in Figure 4.3, the $TC(i)$ curve turns down more than the $TC(e)$ curve does, shifting the critical value to the left and thus enlarging the range where internalization is preferred.

Experience and common governance

Firms with extensive business worldwide, and in the region itself, prefer DFI over both trade and contracts. The coefficients on CE_EUROPE and GLOBAL have the predicted signs and are highly significant.[5] This supports the hypothesis that experience and common governance effects reduce the costs of internal organization of the new operation, and thus favour internalization. However, for firm size (SIZE), the coefficients are insignificant and the alternative hypothesis of no impact cannot be rejected (Table 7.8a). Large firms appear to prefer trade to DFI which in turn is preferred to contracts to serve local markets. In the full sample, the predicted positive effect in favour of DFI over contracting is observed and highly significant (Table 7.8e). However, in that sample the type of local activity in which the firm is engaged is not well controlled for, such that the results need to be considered carefully. A possibility is that the common governance of large firms is very important for production operations, but not for sales operations. This may have caused the insignificant effect of SIZE in the base sample, as size is measured by general employment rather than by a more marketing related proxy such as sales force.

Control variables

The NONEUR control variable indicates that firms with non-European parents prefer DFI to contracts and contracts to trade. This pattern is partly significant, and is presumably a result of the scale of their worldwide operations, which is not appropriately represented in the accounting data for the British or German affiliate in the sample.

The activity dummies should be positive whenever they indicate more interactions between the parent firm and the country. This includes all but the T_O_FIN and the UPSTREAM dummy. The pattern holds with the exception of the T_TECHN dummy. In Tables 7.8a and e, businesses with both up- *and* downstream components are more likely to be internalized, while firms which are only sourcing from the region show a relative preference for imports rather than DFI.

General observations and summary
Apart from the hypothesis tests, two further interesting observations emerge in Table 7.8. First, trade and contracts are preferred by different kinds of businesses, although they are both market transactions. The regression results suggest that contracts are preferred by British and industrial goods manufacturers, as well as by firms with little exposure to the region (CE_EUROPE). Thus, firms use contracts for their peripheral business, if their capabilities are suitable for contractual transfer but not for trade.

Second, some differences can be observed between the alternative samples. Most remarkable is the insignificance of the size variable (SIZE) in the base sample along with the insignificance of GLOBAL in residual samples. Apparently different kinds of common governance and experience are relevant for different types of business. The detailed sample reduction was thus necessary as such differences can be crucial for the evaluation of hypotheses.

To sum up, strong support emerges for the positive impact of psychic distance, and of experience and governance effects, on the propensity of internalization. The positive impact of asset specificity and information variables on the choice of DFI over trade recieves some support. Yet, despite extensive cross-examination of the data-set, no statistical support can be found for a positive relationship between research and human capital intensity and the choice of DFI over contracts.

TESTING INTERACTION EFFECTS

Proposition and Method of Analysis

The theoretical model in Chapter 4 suggests positive interaction effects between product sensitivity and the characteristics of the firm and the environment. Three such effects are illustrated in Figure 7.1. The slope of the $TC(e)$ and $TC(i)$ curves are affected by changes in uncertainty (u), distance (d) and experiences (e). These variables thus influence the position of the critical value s_1 and the gap between the two TC curves. The larger the estimated difference $\{TC(e) - TC(i)\}$, the more likely firms are to choose an internal organizational mode.[6]

Hence, in an environment of high industry uncertainty, the TC(e) curve is steeper. This implies that decisions concerning internalization are more influenced by product sensitivity, that is asset specificity or information asymmetry. Thus,

H6: *the impact of information asymmetry is greater for industries characterized by high uncertainty.*

On the other hand, the costs of internal organization are subject to, among other factors, experience and psychic distance. Hence two more hypotheses on interaction effects can be suggested:

H7: *the impact of information asymmetry is greater for firms with more international experience.*

H8: *the impact of information asymmetry is lesser for business across high psychic distance.*

The eighth hypothesis takes into account the results of the previous section, which showed that distance has a greater effect on internal than on external TC.

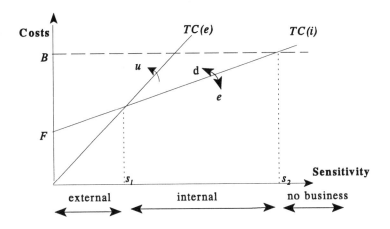

Based on figure 4.3

Figure 7.1   Interaction effects

Regression Analysis

Following a method similar to Walker and Weber [1987], the sample is split into subsamples by different criteria. The effects of distance are tested by separating the observations firstly by the home country of the Western firm, and secondly according to the host country. As only a limited number of observations are available, the separation categories have been divided into Visegrad countries on the one hand, and Russia and Romania on the other. The latter two countries are very different, but both are more distant from the two home countries in the sample. The experience effects are tested by splitting the sample in two almost equal halves defined by the international employment (GLOBAL) of the firms.

The interaction effects of industry uncertainty were tested using two alternative definitions, based on the output growth in the industry, and on the variation of industry growth from the economic average.[7] The results did not show effects significant enough to support H6. They differed between the two concepts of uncertainty, and are therefore not tabulated.

Results

The results of the M-Logit for sub-samples are tabulated in Tables 7.9 to 7.11. The variable H_GROW_D was taken out because of its insignificance throughout. This simplifies the model, and helps to avoid problems of insufficient degrees of freedom. In some cases, country dummies also become redundant. Comparing the preferences for DFI versus trade and DFI versus contracts, pairwise between subsample regressions, inferences can be made on the relative importance of determinants under different conditions.

The main observation is that no consistent evidence emerges to support any of the proposed interaction effects. Only a few coefficients in each table show distinctly different patterns of impact between the two subsamples. In part, this is because of the small sample sizes. However, a similar analysis of the 576 sample did not yield substantially different results. The latter may be biased by interaction with locational decisions and is not reported.

Differences across subsamples can be observed, firstly, for non-food consumer goods (NF_CONS). They are more internalized by British firms (Table 7.9), in the Visegrad countries (table 7.10), and by less internationalized firms (Table 7.11). Apart from the results for the British firms, this is in direct oppposition to the prediction. These goods are even *less* likely to be internalized among German firms which suggests a difference in management and marketing culture. Second, GERMAN firms are more likely to internalize in high uncertainty industries, in the Visegrad countries, and among internationally experienced firms. Third, firm size (SIZE) is, in contrast to the aggregate positively related to internalization for German firms and internationally

Table 7.9 Subsamples: home countries

| | German | | British | |
	Trade vs. DFI	Contract vs. DFI	Trade vs. DFI	Contract vs. DFI
R&D	- .0049 (.103)	- .0811 (.198)	.3757 (.334)	- .0853 (.368)
HUMAN_CAP	.0784 (.039)**	- .0041 (.094)	.2169 (.135)	.1725 (.167)
PHARMA	-2.8392 (1.74)	-2.1541 (2.65)	-13.701(6.64)**	2.2609 (367.4)
NF_CONS	1.0945 (.916)	-4.2395 (2.40)*	6.9579 (3.47)**	9.4840 (3.55)***
FOOD	1.0121 (1.02)	10.678 (275.8)	-7.0507 (347.3)	6.9573 (496.1)
GERMAN	--	--	--	--
CZECH	3.4777 (1.15)****	13.890 (278.9)	2.7100 (1.96)	1.9933 (2.07)
HUNGARY	3.1000 (1.05)****	.7462 (1.58)	1.1939 (1.99)	1.1941 (2.20)
POLAND	2.7617 (1.15)**	13.526 (274.3)	3.3114 (1.92)*	3.5983 (2.06)*
RUSSIA	.2523 (1.01)	- .1619 (1.53)	2.6224 (1.92)	3.0151 (2.15)
SIZE	13.091 (5.89)**	1.0755 (128.0)	- 8.0135 (4.71)*	-4.8327 (4.85)
GLOBAL	4.6174 (1.96)**	9.0560 (4.71)*	10.481 (4.56)**	11.464 (4.83)**
CE_EUROPE	24.536 (14.0)*	34.850 (34.91)	154.3 (62.5)**	248.5 (75.1)****
NONEUR	- 4.3602 (2.15)**	11.035 (269.1)	.5898 (1.75)	4.0520 (2.10)*
T_TECHN	-13.211 (857.9)	-21.806 (857.9)	- .1336 (1.83)	-3.1608 (2.00)
T_MANAG	3.2808(.781)*****	6.1640 (2.36)***	5.0535 (2.03)**	4.2662 (2.10)**
Constant	-9.8053 (2.43)****	-1.7575 (4.79)	-20.746 (7.57)***	-19.510 (7.73)**
χ^2	116.682 (30)		103.800 (30)	
correct pred.	87.76%		84.92%	
random pred.	55.66%		54.23%	
observations	147		126	

Notes: levels of statistical significance: * = 10%, ** = 5%, *** = 1%, **** = 0.5%, ***** = 0.005%. -- = Variable not included.

experienced firms. Fourthly, international experience (GLOBAL) appears more important for firms with extensive experience, than among less experienced firms. This suggests a U-shaped relationship between experience and propensity for internalization. Fifthly, region specific experience and exposure (CE_EUROPE) increases the propensity for internalization among British firms, but not among German firms.

Although there are explanations for each of these observations, they do not correspond to the initially proposed interaction effects For the two variables of

Table 7.10   Subsamples: host countries

	Czech R./Hungary / Poland		Russia / Romania	
	Trade vs. DFI	Contract vs. DFI	Trade vs. DFI	Contract vs. DFI
R&D	.1913 (.088)**	.0060 (.120)	.1083 (.130)	- .0447 (.174)
HUMAN_CAP	.0229 (.038)	.0132 (.068)	.0421 (.042)	.0161 (.081)
PHARMA	-5.6392 (1.59)****	-2.8853 (2.17)	- 3.8004 (1.95)*	-2.2437 (2.49)
NF_CONS	2.2972 (.942)**	2.1955 (1.20)*	.4800 (.969)	.1919 (1.43)
FOOD	- .2551 (1.09)	11.388 (192.2)	.8616 (1.31)	11.895 (204.5)
GERMAN	.8348 (.997)	2.9588 (1.54)*	- .3435 (1.29)	.9454 (1.80)
CZECH	--	--	--	--
HUNGARY	- .7173 (.754)	- .8942 (.964)	--	--
POLAND	- .7539 (.677)	.5437 (.891)	--	--
RUSSIA	--	--	.4327 (.791)	.8841 (1.15)
SIZE	-1.7005 (2.01)	- .4375 (2.445)	- 1.8292 (2.67)*	4.9422 (5.22)
GLOBAL	3.9897 (1.42)***	3.6881 (1.77)**	3.6856 (1.70)**	2.0367(2.30)**
CE_EUROPE	27.583 (13.1)**	70.643 (27.43)**	29.471 (18.3)	66.388 (32.89)**
NONEUR	- 1.7397 (1.01)*	.7362 (1.29)	.4282 (1.12)	1.2940 (1.67)*
T_TECHN	.4819 (1.22)	-1.0213 (1.32)	- .7364 (1.62)	-4.3533 (1.88)**
T_MANAG	3.1403 (.707)*****	1.7440 (.993)*	3.713 (1.08)****	4.5784 (1.56)****
Constant	-5.5824 (1.36)*****	-4.5985 (1.86)**	-7.546 (2.13)****	- 5.7066 (1.43)**
χ^2	110.112 (28)		56.645 (26)	
correct pred.	82.00%		87.80%	
random pred.	46.84%		66.08%	
observations	150		123	

Notes: levels of statistical significance: * = 10%, ** = 5%, *** = 1%, **** = 0.5%, ***** = 0.005%. -- = Variable not included.

most interest, the proxies for research and human capital intensity (R&D, HUMAN_CAP), no statistically significant variation can be found in any case. Thus, the alternative hypothesis of no interaction effects cannot be rejected.

Table 7.11 Subsamples: international experience

	less international firms		more international firms	
	Trade vs. DFI	Contract vs. DFI	Trade vs. DFI	Contract vs. DFI
R&D	.3278 (.180)*	- .0163 (.278)	.4296 (.156)***	.1698 (.350)
HUMAN_CAP	.1433 (.062)**	.3811 (.144)	- .1616 (.082)**	- .2840 (.164)*
PHARMA	-12.361 (1746)	2.4369 (2470)	-6.644 (1.93)****	-3.6915 (4.24)
NF_CONS	.4114 (1.40)	4.6716 (2.41)*	.4085 (.910)	- .3859 (1.32)
FOOD	-.8876 (1.72)	10.090 (300.2)	.0037 (1.21)	8.6019 (294.2)
GERMAN	-3.5223 (1.85)*	-2.6029 (2.70)	2.9688 (1.16)**	4.4032 (2.94)
CZECH	16.434 (270.1)	14.316 (270.1)	1.1209 (1.01)	.5052 (1.59)
HUNGARY	14.560 (270.1)	14.957 (270.1)	1.6123 (.939)*	- .2805 (1.47)
POLAND	15.246 (270.1)	16.389 (270.1)	2.0179 (1.06)*	2.6166 (1.67)
RUSSIA	13.610 (270.1)	16.038 (270.1)	-1.2272 (.877)	-1.1404 (1.42)
SIZE	-4.6064 (3.51)	-10.023 (4.55)**	- 1.0789 (2.73)	31.644 (13.9)**
GLOBAL	-4.9912 (8.16)	-8.0185 (11.1)	10.48 (3.00)****	8.2250 (5.31)
CE_EUROPE	39.153 (19.4)**	120.44 (54.8)**	26.979 (13.8)*	89.646 (45.7)*
NONEUR	-4.897 (2.24)**	3.4680 (3.05)	-4.446 (1.64)****	9.7783 (295.9)
T_TECHN	-9.6977 (452.9)	-15.956 (452.9)	2.7772 (1.64)*	3.5297 (2.57)
T_MANAG	5.760 (1.68)***	4.7858 (2.43)**	3.449(.844)*****	2.5919 (1.56)*
Constant	-22.372 (270.1)	-25.261 (270.1)	-8.193 (2.40)****	- 4.3961 (3.51)**
χ^2	127.094 (32)		115.131(32)	
correct pred.	89.78%		81.62%	
random pred.	59.70%		49.99%	
observations	137		136	

Notes: levels of statistical significance: * = 10%, ** = 5%, *** = 1%, **** = 0.5%, ***** = 0.005%. -- = Variable not included.

TESTING FOR AN ORDINAL RELATIONSHIP

Proposition and Method of Analysis

Williamson [1991], Hennart [1993] and others describe contracts as an intermediate organizational form between the two polar cases of markets and hierarchies (Chapter 4). Contracts combine elements of prices and arbitration as coordination mechanisms. Following this interpretation, MODE should be an ordinal scale for the degree of internalization:

H9:   *Contracts are an intermediate form along an ordinal scale from*
             markets to hierarchies.

Exports are considered as a market mode, DFI as an hierarchical mode, and
contracts as intermediate forms. Correspondingly, the internalization should be
tested using an ordered categorical data model instead of the M-Logit. In this
section, an ordered Logit (O-Logit) is used to estimate the impact of proposed
variables on internalization. The performance of the ordered model is compared
with that of the multinomial model (Tables 7.8a and c). In particular, the results
of the M-Logit regression are discussed with respect to their consistency with the
assumption of an ordinal relationship.

The M-Logit is the more general model as the assumption of an ordinal
relationship is a restriction. It should be adopted if reasonable doubts persist
about the restrictions of the more parsimonious ordered model. No formal test
for categorical dependent variables can prove the ordinal nature of the scale, nor
does a satisfactory measure of fit, comparable to the R^2 in ordinary regression
analysis exist. The χ^2-test statistic commonly reported is a global test of the
predictor set, an analogue to the global F-test used in linear least-squares
regressions. However it is not suitable for a comparison between different
models, because the multinomial model has almost twice as many degrees of
freedom as the O-Logit.

To control for this, De Maris [1992], based on Hosmer and Lemeshow
[1989], suggests a R^2-type measure of fit for logistic regression. Although it is
not a measure of the variance of the model, as is the R^2 for linear regression, it
can be used to compare different models.[8] This ratio is calculated as

$$\rho = (-2\log L_0 - (-2 \log L_1)) / (-2\log L_0) \qquad (7.8)$$

where L_0 stands for the restricted log likelihood for slopes $= 0$, and L_1 for
the log likelihood of the model.

Second, the predictive ability of the model can be compared using the
'correct predictions' of the model. This is not a precise measure but gives some
indication of the fit. A third criterion is the consistency of the coefficients in the
M-Logit with the hypothesis that the dependent variable is ordinal. If contracts
are of a higher order than trade, and DFI of a higher order than contracts along
the same ordinal scale, then the signs of coefficients for the choices between
trade and contracts, and contracts and DFI, should be in the same direction.
Fourth, the assumption of independence of irrelevant alternatives (IIA)
underlying the M-Logit is tested.

Table 7.12 Ordered model

	Base sample	Downstream sample	Full sample
R&D	.0784 (.035)**	.0492 (.024)**	.0491 (.021)**
HUMAN_CAP	.0147 (.014)	.1114 (.011)	.0095 (.009)
PHARMA	-2.0016(.572)****	-1.7577 (.381)*****	-1.1878 (.326)****
NF_CONS	.6732 (.322)**	.7547 (.257)****	.5267 (.203)***
FOOD	- .1674 (.463)	- .1152 (.338)	- .0064 (.301)
H_GROW_D	- .0425 (.194)	- .0478 (.154)	- .0545 (.144)
GERMAN	- .1236 (.327)	.3665 (.229)	.1211 (.177)
CZECH	.8686 (.302)****	.7514 (.252)****	.6007 (.219)***
HUNGARY	.6827 (.294)**	.7431 (.246)****	.7819 (.219)****
POLAND	.7560 (.314)**	.7559 (.238)****	.5928 (.213)***
RUSSIA	.2089 (.311)	.2295 (.248)	.1508 (.220)
SIZE	-1.0574 (.766)	.3010 (.458)	.5503 (.399)
GLOBAL	1.3987 (.474)****	1.2384 (.345)****	.7830 (.277)****
CE_EUROPE	7.7631 (4.37)*	3.1652 (3.26)	2.9982 (2.62)
NONEUR	- .7350 (.319)**	- .5384 (.266)**	.5503 (.399)
T_TECHNOL	.4240 (.353)	.5196 (.235)**	.7830 (.277)****
T_MANAGM	1.3430 (.228)*****	1.4484 (.176)*****	2.9982 (2.62)
T_only_final	--	.0227 (.229)	- .2284 (.108)**
T_final et al.	--	.2722 (.353)	.2285 (.108)**
T_none	--	1.6336 (.455)****	1.0711 (.285)****
UPSTREAM	--	--	- .5425 (.335)
UP&DOWN	--	--	1.5338 (.350)*****
Constant	-2.6091 (.498)*****	-2.7128 (.446)*****	-2.1724 (.341)*****
μ_1	.4793 (.100)*****	.6385 (.089)*****	.6797 (.071)*****
χ^2	114.638 (17)	238.998 (20)	396.886 (22)
log-likelihood	-160.235	-249.582	-370.788
restr. log likel.	-217.554	-369.081	-569.231
ρ	26.35%	32.38%	34.96%
correct pred.	79.90%	78.10%	74.65%

Notes: levels of statistical significance: * = 10%, ** = 5%, *** = 1%, **** = 0.5%, ***** = 0.005%. -- = Variable not included.

Table 7.13 Comparative statistics of M- and O-Logit

	base sample	downstream sample	full sample
ρ-statistic			
M-Logit	37.66%	41.59%	41.35%
O-Logit	26.35%	32.38%	34.96%
correct predictions M-Logit	82.41%	80.05%	76.72%
O-Logit	79.90%	78.10%	74.65%
χ^2-test of IIA	1.3824 (36)	1.4451 (42)	6.3851 (46)

Results

The results of the ordered model are reported in Table 7.12 for all three samples. With an assumed ordinal relationship between trade, contracts and DFI, only one coefficient is estimated for each variable; and the model has only half as many coefficients, plus one: the parameter μ_1. The overall contribution of the models is highly significant, as indicated by high χ^2-statistics. More coefficients are signed as hypothesized, and are significant, than in the multinomial model. This includes two of the product sensitivity proxies, R&D and NON_FOOD. Apparently, the model gives strong support to hypotheses H1, H3 and H4. However, does this more parsimonious model give a sensible depiction of the underlying organizational choices?

Table 7.13 compares the ρ-statistics and the correct predictions for the O- and M-Logit models. The ρ-statistic is substantially higher for the multinomial models, indicating a better explanation of the underlying variation. This evidence is clearest in the base sample, with ρ at 38 per cent for the M-Logit, but only 26 per cent for the O-Logit. The proportion of correct predictions is high in all cases, and slightly better for the M-Logit. The aggregate figures, however, disguise the fact that the ordered models do not correctly predict a single incident of a contract. They merely separate the endpoints of the scale, trade and DFI effectively. The M-Logit predicts 8 out of a total of 27 contracts correctly in the base sample. The proportion for the other samples is similarly high. These two criteria thus favour the M-Logit over the O-Logit.

The choice between the models should, furthermore, take into account the consistency of the pattern of coefficients in the multinomial model with the premises of the ordered model. If the latter was correct, then the coefficient estimates in Tables 7.8a to e should have the same sign for choices of trade versus contracts, and of contracts versus DFI. However, Table 7.12 shows that this is not so: in only 7 of 17 variables in the base sample do contracts appear in the middle position, and the number is not much greater in the larger samples, apart from additional control variables. On a positive note, they include, though insignificantly, R&D and HUMAN_CAP. Thus the consistent-coefficient criterion does not lend support to the ordered model either.

Table 7.14 Implied preference of M-Logit models

	base sample	downstream sample	full sample
R&D	**D > C >> T**	C >> D >> T	C > D >> T
HUMAN_CAP	**D > C > T**	D > T > C	**D > C > T**
PHARMA	**T > C >> D**	**T >> C >> D**	**T > C > D**
NF_CONS	D >>T > C	**D >> C > T**	**D > C > T**
FOOD	D > T > C	T > D > C	D > T > C
H_GROW_D	C > T > D	C > T > D	C > T > D
GERMAN	D > T >> C	D >> T >> C	D > T >> C
CZECH	**D >> C > T**	**D >> C > T**	**D >> C > T**
HUNGARY	**D > C > T**	**D >> C > T**	**D >> C > T**
POLAND	D > T >> C	**D >> C > T**	**D >> C > T**
RUSSIA	D > T > C	D > T > C	D > T > C
SIZE	T > D > C	D > T > C	D > T > C
GLOBAL	**D >> C > T**	**D >> C > T**	**D > C > T**
CE_EUROPE	D >> T >> C	D > T > C	**D > C > T**
NONEUR	T >> D > C	T > D > C	T > D >> C
T_TECHNOL	C >> T > D	T > D >> C	**D > C >> T**
T_MANAGM	**D >> C > T**	**D > C > T**	**D >> C >> T**
T_only_final	--	D > T > C	**T > C > D**
T_final et al.	--	**D > C > T**	**D > C > T**
T_none	--	**D > C > T**	**D >> C >> T**
UPSTREAM	--	--	**T > C > D**
UP&DOWN	--	--	**D > C > T**
correct order	7 of 17 variables	9 of 20 variables	15 of 22 variables

Notes: > = preferred over; >> = significantly preferred over. **Bold** indicates coefficients in line with the 'intermediate form' proposition. Correct order refers to the count of preferences marked in bold.

In the base sample, contracts are preferred to both other modes for business relationships that are *not* NON_FOOD, FOOD, GERMAN, NONEUR, POLAND or RUSSIA, that have low EMPLOY or CE_EUROPE, but transfer technology (T_TECHN). The patterns are mostly confirmed in the larger samples, although interactions with other decisions affect the priorities. Omitting turnkey and management contracts (Table 7.8c), the pattern is not confirmed for NON_FOOD and POLAND, but firms with high R&D and HUMAN_CAP show a first priority for contracts.

Finally, a test of the underlying assumption of independence of irrelevant alternatives (IIA) verifies the suitability of the M-Logit. Appendix 7.1 shows the calculation of a test statistic for the null hypothesis of independence. The resulting χ^2-statistic is very low for all samples (Table 7.13) giving no evidence to justify a rejection of the assumption.

In conclusion, all four criteria - consistency of the coefficients, predictive ability, ρ-ratio, and IIA-test - suggest rejecting the O-Logit in favour of the M-Logit. Thus the assumption that the categorical variable MODE has an ordinal scale is rejected! This in turn implies that the simple markets to hierarchies scale in Williamson [1991] and Hennart [1993] should be rejected. Contractual businesses are thus unsatisfactorily described as an intermediate form on a scale of market to hierarchy. The multinomial model is upheld as best suited to analyse entry mode choice.

Using the ordered model can in fact lead to inappropriate inferences. The R&D coefficient is significant in the ordered model. Yet the multinomial model reveals that this significance is based mainly on the difference between trade and the other two modes. Thus, R&D-intensive firms have higher propensity for technology transfer, but not necessarily for its internalization. On the other hand, the German preference for DFI over contracts is disguised by the ordered model.

INTERPRETATION

The propensity to internalize a business relationship is shown to depend on firm- and country-specific variables. The hypothesis on experience and common governance (H4) receives strong support. Psychic distance also decreases the propensity for internalization, despite a theoretically ambiguous effect (H3). It appears to increase internal TC more than TC of the market. However, little support is found for uncertainty (H2) and information variables (H1). In relation to the latter, the dummy for non-food consumer good manufacturers has a positive effect on the choice between DFI and contracts, but only so in the case of British firms. Whether specific variables are found significant depends upon the type of business analysed. Yet the general evidence is consistent for all samples: positive effects of experience/common governance and of distance, but weak or no support for product sensitivity and uncertainty effects.[9]

Two further analyses have been tested on propositions derived from TC economics. First, interaction effects between product sensitivity and other variables are not in accordance with the hypothesized pattern. However, some interesting variations emerge across home and host countries. Second, the proposition that trade-contracts-DFI should be treated as an ordinal scale receives no statistical support.

Interpreting these results, three interesting inferences can be made:

1. Firms' capabilities to manage and integrate additional operations are more important than their sensitivity to market failure as determinants of DFI.
2. Contracts, international trade and DFI are distinct modes of serving a local market that are insufficiently described by the markets and hierarchies approach.
3. The policies followed by the three Visegrad countries, and their reported DFI capital inflows, do not seem to have a major impact on foreign businesses' entry strategies. Entry modes vary, however, between Visegrad and less advanced transition countries.

Managerial Capabilities versus Market Failure

Internalization decisions are based on the trade-off between the costs of market transactions and those of internal organization. TCE often focuses on potential market failure. Products sensitive to market failure are transferred internally by establishing a DFI to replace market transactions. Less attention is paid to the costs of internal organization, and their variation across firms.

However, firm-specific variables for information-related market failures receive only weak, if any, empirical support in this study. Research and human capital intensity appear of secondary importance both as O-advantage (Chapter 6) and as I-incentive (Chapter 7), although they do influence the preference for greenfield investment over acquisition in Chapter 8. Neither do interaction effects with uncertainty recieve any support. The analysis does not reject TCE empirically. In fact, some statistically significant effects have been shown. However, statistical significance does not translate into economic significance if the effect is small relative to other influences. The reviewed research (Chapter 4) may have placed too much emphasis on statistical significance rather than importance relative to other variables.

On the other hand, experience and proximity are important. The decision to internalize a business relationship depends primarily on the firm's marginal costs of setting up the new affiliate. Corporations with experience in managing international operations, and firms in psychic proximity to the partner country, are best qualified to organize their business internally. They can also take advantage of economies of common governance, and internalize activities that inexperienced and distant competitors organize via markets. Thus, aspects of management capabilities appear more important than characteristics of the transaction.

The relevant economies of common governance vary, however, for different kinds of business activity. The empirical results suggest that international and region-specific experience are important for the internalization of marketing operations, whereas firm size, in terms of employment, favours internalization of production. In a similar way, experiences in the use of contracts would reduce the costs of subsequent contracts of a similar kind.

This result, the importance of experience and common governance effect compared with information and asset specificity aspects, may in part be specific to the transition economies. Firms' capabilities to cope with this environment are relatively important. On the other hand, the local demand may not be sufficiently sophisticated so as to demand the latest technology, but may primarily require affordable products. High-tech firms may thus transfer products at advanced stages of their product cycle, so that internalization is not required.

Contracts as a Distinct Mode of Market Transaction

The determinants of contractual relationships differ from those of both trade and DFI in several cases. Under certain conditions, contractual arrangements appear superior to both trade and DFI. Thus, contracts are not just an intermediate form along a continuum, as implied by Williamson [1991] and Hennart [1993]. Trade, contracts and DFI differ by more than the relative importance of price and hierarchical coordination. Rather, the availability of different modes of market transaction allow adaptation to the specific requirements of a business and a suitable contractual arrangement can substitute for internalization.

The empirical analysis suggests that contracts are preferred by firms transferring technology and thus presumed to be sensitive to market failure. The pattern of coefficients in Table 7.12 gives some indications as to the conditions under which contracts become the primary choice. Contracts are significantly preferred to trade in the case of peripheral business (low CE_EUROPE), by the food industry and R&D-intensive firms. A preference for contracts over both other forms of business is, in the base sample, observed for industrial goods manufacturers, British firms, firms engaged in business with Poland and Russia, and firms with little exposure to the region. If turnkey and management contracts are omitted, research and human capital intensive firms join this list.

The TC model can be applied to explain these preferences: contracts are used when the nature of the product makes exporting prohibitively expensive, but TC(i) of DFI are high relative to the TC(e) of the contract. Yet, what determines the choice between trade and contracts, and how does the choice of DFI differ *vis-à-vis* trade and contracts?

First, the pattern suggests that fixed internal TC are more important as cause of the internalization of contracts than in the case of trade. High fixed costs (F) of setting up an affiliate discourage DFI. Fixed costs per internal transaction are high if the parent firm is small (low EMPLOY) or has only minor sales in the region (low CE_EUROPE). Fixed costs also increase with the investment risk of the project as well as with the psychic distance between host and home countries. Thus, investment in RUSSIA and by UK firms is less likely. Investment goods are generally capital intensive and the capital outlays of a DFI-project are high. This encourages non-equity business activities such as turnkey projects and build-operate-transfer contracts. The fixed TC of internal organization are particularly relevant in the CEE region because of the high investment risk and the high costs of setting up operations in an environment without established local industry and infrastructure. This adds to the costs of setting up business abroad *per se.*

Secondly, contracts enable firms to transfer their marketable capabilities even if their final goods are not tradeable. The location of production of their final good has to be close to the market as in the food industry or for high-technology firms producing bulky good such as industrial machinery. If the final good is not tradeable, the international interface affects an intermediate stage of the production chain. This is more sensitive to information asymmetry and thus to market failure. Thus, tradeability of the final good and sensitivity of the interface are positively related, and the TC of exporting increase with higher transportation costs, while the TC of contracts and direct investment rise only little.

However, contracts are used primarily for technology transfer that is peripheral to the core markets served by the firm. For this reason, firms with little exposure to the region are more likely to use contracts. For their core markets, firms prefer DFI to control the operations. The internalization threshold depends on TC(i) which in turn are determined by corporate capabilities such as experience (e) and common governance (cg). Since contracts are more sensitive to market failure than most exports, the threshold is lower for non-tradeable goods manufacturers and service firms.

The more important the market is, or the closer the transaction is to the core markets of the firm, the more the TC of all three modes increase. However, the TC curves differ by their fixed cost element and their slope. In the case of no transportation costs, exports require few fixed TC but increase steeply. TC of DFI involve substantial fixed TC but rise little in the case of core business. Compared with DFI, contracts have lower fixed costs, but a steeper slope. Summing up the arguments, trade is preferred for tradeable goods, contracts for peripheral business in non-tradeable goods, and DFI for core business.

These observations are interpreted in Figure 7.2. Three different cost planes are drawn for the three modes of business. The TC of the cost-minimizing mode are indicated by shading that part of the plane. As can be seen, DFI is preferred for important markets, contracts for goods with high transportation costs, and exports for low to medium important markets and tradeable goods. Note that this figure has been developed from the empirically observed pattern (inductive) rather than from theory (deductive). Thus, further theoretical work is encouraged.

However, this graph shows why contracts can be perceived as an intermediate form, although they are 'in the middle' (Chapter 4) only in a specific sense. A diagonal line from point 0 to point B, may approximate the concept of sensitivity, as used in chapter four. The pattern of lowest TC over this line suggests that contracts would indeed emerge as the lowest cost option in an intermediate range. Whether or not this case exists is however dependent on the precise shape of the planes, about which ad hoc assumptions have been made for this graph.

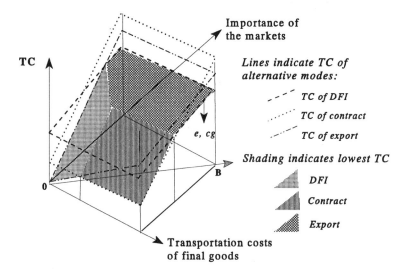

Figure 7.2   A three-dimensional view of TC

The point I wish to emphasize, is that the results suggest that a three-dimensional view of TC would be more insightful than the intermediate form interpretation by for example Hennart and Williamson. However, it is not clear which axes are the best suited for the TC curves to be drawn over. Importance of the market and tradeability emerged as possible determinants from the empirical analysis. Further theoretical modelling of the issues is thus highly desirable, for example considering the asset specificity or information content on an axis in place of market importance.

Economic Policies in the Host Countries

This analysis found few differences among the three Visegrad countries, but significant differences between these and Russia and Romania. This is surprising since the three countries have adopted very diverse policies towards DFI, especially in the privatization process. They also report different volumes of DFI inflow in the years until 1994. Nevertheless, their country dummies are very similar in most equations, except in the residual samples. Thus, the special Hungarian DFI policy had no observable effect on market serving businesses. Yet, it may have increased internalization of local production in DFI.

The lesser extent of internalization in Russia and Romania can be attributed to several complementary factors: regulatory constraints, high investment risk, and psychic distance from countries of origin. The latter aspect is also indicated by the pattern of the German dummy in the host country subsamples: it is significant only for the Visegrad countries. Also, non-food consumer goods are internationalized in the Visegrad countries, but not in Russia and Romania. As predicted, their sensitivity does not interact positively with uncertainty but with proximity and firms' capabilities to manage the operation internally.

NOTES

1. Caves and Mehra [1986], and Hennart and Park [1993] use a similar proxy
2. A computationally easier method is to run the same model again, redefining the dependent variable with a different choice as base case.
3. A number of regressions have been run without this dummy and these frequently resulted in significant negative coefficients of the R&D variable. This effect can be explained by the behaviour of pharmaceutical companies.
4. If a proxy is insignificant throughout, it always includes the possibility of poor quality data. However, the R&D data do show some pattern that would be expected, for instance correlations with PHARMA, and significant impact on greenfield entry in Chapter 8. Measurement differences between German and British accounting systems are controlled for by the GERMAN dummy, and in the subsample regressions by home country which show no significant differences of the coefficients (Table 7.9).
5. In the residual subsamples of observations not in the base sample, GLOBAL was correctly signed but was insignificant. It thus appears less relevant for production operations than for market operations.
6. The graphical model shows a clear cut-off point, s_l. In the empirical analysis, many components are not precisely measurable. Therefore the probability of a given observation fulfilling the conditions for internalization is positively related to the measured, or estimated, difference between TC(e) and TC(i).

7. The subsamples for uncertainty are defined as follows: The sample has been split in two, based on industry-level data from the CEE countries. Since they are subject to high measurement errors, two alternative concepts are used.

   Definition 1 is based on output growth in the period of 1989 to 1991, when a very deep transition recession hit the region. A large fall in output would suggest a major need for industrial restructuring and thus high uncertainty. Definition 2 is based on output growth in the period of 1992 to 1994, when the economies, at least in Poland, the Czech Republic and Hungary, started to recover. Industries with very rapid recovery or continued depression are considered high risk. Average growth rates relative to their country's performance would indicate low uncertainty industries.

   The two dummies for uncertainty are almost orthogonal with a correlation of $r=-0.01$. This is by default but nonetheless a welcome observation: if hypotheses were confirmed for two unrelated concepts of uncertainty, the results would have carried substantial weight, despite the arguably weak measures.

8. Chu and Anderson [1992, p. 157] propose a similar measure, the Akaike-Likelihood-Ratio Index, which uses the log likelihood of the equal probabilities model rather than the restricted log likelihood as a base.

9. This test differs from earlier research, which may account for the differences: (a) some studies do not distinguish between technology intensity as O-advantage and as I-incentive. This applies to Horst [1972], Grubaugh [1987] and Denekamp [1995]. (b) this study surveyed German and British firms, and investment in Eastern Europe. Most prior research focuses on investment in the US or by US firms. It is therefore possible that American culture has dominated empirical research. Davidson and McFetridge [1985], Gatignon and Anderson [1988] and Gomes-Casseres [1989] all used the same 'Harvard MNE project database' of US outward DFI. Interestingly, Hennart [1991a] found no support for the same hypothesis analysing Japanese DFI. Note that this study finds more favourable evidence for TC among the British sample (Table 7.12), which is culturally closer to the US.

   Furthermore, (c) this study uses a broader base population than most studies surveying a random sample of companies and all projects in five selected countries. Earlier studies draw on lists of known projects, which may imply a bias towards large projects; (d) The studies by Gatignon and Anderson [1988], Gomes-Casseres [1989] and Hennart [1991a] analysed JV versus WOS choices. Although many determinants suggested by theoretical work are the same, some additional influences have to be considered (see Chapter 8).

APPENDIX 7.1: TEST FOR INDEPENDENCE OF IRRELEVANT ALTERNATIVES

The M-Logit model assumes that the alternative choices are independent, a property known as 'independence of irrelevant alternatives' (IIA). Under IIA, the coefficients β_m estimated using an M-Logit, should not be more efficiently estimated in the presence of a third alternative. If IIA was *in*appropriate, then without the third alternative the vector of coefficients β_b, obtained with the binomial Logit, should be *in*consistent. Thus, the test has to compare the consistent M-Logit estimator with the efficient estimates of a binomial Logit. If IAA holds, then the binomial Logit should also be consistent. Greene [1993: 671] recommends a test of the IIA assumption based on a test statistic by Hausman and McFadden [1984] of the following form:

$$(\beta_b - \beta_m)' \, [V_b - V_m]^{-1} \, (\beta_b - \beta_m) = \chi^2 \qquad (7A.1)$$

where β_b is estimated without the alternative presumed to be independent, and β_m is an estimate of the coefficients obtained with the unrestricted model, that is the M-Logit. V_b and V_m are the respective estimates of the asymptotic variance-covariance matrices. If the null hypothesis of IIA cannot be rejected, using the M-Logit would be permissible.

Greene discusses this test for a conditional Logit. In a conditional Logit, the variables refer to properties of the choices and not, as in the M-Logit, to properties of the individuals making the choice. For each variable, one coefficient is estimated, whereas for the M-Logit one coefficient for each variable per odds ratio is estimated.

Applying this test to a multinomial model has an additional complication since the M-Logit returns estimates of the coefficients for each odds ratio. Thus, (c-1)n values are estimated, where c is the number of choices and n the number of variables. Excluding the alternative assumed to be irrelevant reduces the number of coefficient estimates to (c-2)n. In the present case of three choices, the reduced model is a binomial Logit. This does not permit the calculation of the above test-statistic because the matrices have unequal dimensions: in the present case, with eighteen variables plus an intercept (n=19): β_b is [19x1], β_m is [38x1], V_b is [19x19] and V_m is [38x38].

Thus, the coefficients obtained with the M-Logit should be compared with those obtained with two binomial Logit regressions. The values needed for the covariance matrices and the vector of coefficients in equation (1) are obtained in the following way:

$$\mathbf{V}_b = \begin{bmatrix} \mathbf{V}_{ct} & \mathbf{0} \\ \mathbf{0} & \mathbf{V}_{dt} \end{bmatrix}, \text{ and } \quad \mathbf{\beta}_b = \begin{bmatrix} \mathbf{\beta}_{ct} \\ \mathbf{\beta}_{dt} \end{bmatrix} \qquad (7A.2)$$

where the indices ct refer to the contacts versus trade Logit, and dt to the DFI versus trade Logit. Using two Logit models to estimate the relationships implies no interaction between the upper and lower parts of the vectors, such that the off-diagonal matrices of the joint covariance matrix $\mathbf{V}_b$ are zero. Under the IIA assumption, these would also be zero in $\mathbf{V}_m$. The χ^2-test tests whether or not this is true. The degrees of freedom are given by the rank of the matrix of variance-covariance differences, usually identical with the number of parameters. For the M-Logit in Table 7.9b, the resulting χ^2-test statistic for IIA-test is 1.3824 with 36 degrees of freedom, which is not significant at any relevant level of error.

8. Form of Ownership and Mode of Entry

This research has so far focused on the determinants of DFI, both in the theoretical models (Chapters 3 and 4) and in the empirical analysis (Chapters 6 and 7). This chapter takes the analysis one step further by investigating investment characteristics. Every investor has to make decisions regarding equity ownership and mode of entry.

In the this chapter these choices are analysed based on the recent International Business literature. It has three related objectives. First, propositions from recent advances in theoretical and empirical research on determinants of joint-ventures (JVs) and of modes of entry are tested. This includes theories of transaction costs economics, the internationalization process model and strategic management. If theories are indeed valid as general theories, they should be applicable to the specific conditions of CEE as well. Second, the determinants specific to the region or individual countries are explored within and beyond the theoretical bases. Special features are expected because of the transition process of the economic environment. Finally, the privatization process in the transition economies attracts substantial amounts of investment. From the investors' perspective, it is a form of acquisition and should thus be driven by the same determinants. Comparing the determinants of acquisition and those of privatization-related acquisitions, provides insights as to how privatization influences the pattern of DFI inflow.

Understanding the forces determining investment characteristics improves both managers' understanding of the transition environment, and governments' understanding of inward DFI. Greenfield projects are set up with resources and technology from the parent company, thus establishing new production facilities and employment. Greenfield investors import more intermediate goods and machinery than investors taking over local firms. Acquisitions are typically less integrated into the investors' multinational network, but more integrated into the local economy. This implies major variations in the ways in which DFI projects interact with the host economy, and thus in the way in which they contribute to economic development and the transformation of the economy. Understanding the determinants of alternative entry modes would be an important step towards assessing the impact of DFI on economic transition and development.

The chapter is structured as follows: first the alternative modes of business and their distribution in the dataset are introduced. Then previous work in the International Business literature is reviewed to establish hypotheses for testing. Since the research questions go beyond the determinants of DFI discussed in chapters three and four, this is a more extensive discussion of the theoretical argument, with particular focus on the role of experience and proximity. Following this discussion, the method of empirical analysis is introduced and finally the results are presented and interpreted.

THE DATA-SET

The study distinguishes four modes of entry and three types of ownership. In addition, acquirers were asked whether or not they participated in the privatization process. In the questionnaire, separate questions were used to address these issues. In question 1, the following options for the type of activity were offered: minority joint-venture (JV), majority JV and wholly owned subsidiary (WOS). For mode of entry, the options were greenfield, acquisition, JV-entry and JV-acquisition (question 3). JV-acquisitions refer to projects where the local partner contributes part of the existing business to the JV, whereas JV-entry refers to newly established businesses. Those who indicated acquisition or JV-acquisition above were furthermore asked whether or not they participated in the privatzation process.

Differences in the concepts of 'JV' in both questions arise from changes over time. The ownership question refers to the organization at the time of the survey, and the mode of entry to the initial organizational form. For instance, a JV may have been taken over by the foreign partner. Statistical differences between these conceptually distinct forms are small and the empirical analysis must show whether or not the distinction is crucial. Both the ownership and mode of entry questions allowed respondents to indicate multiple responses if they had several projects in one country. Many respondents took advantage of this option. For instance, 216 projects were reported, including 81 JVs and 146 WOSs. This sums up to 227, that is 11 incidents with both kinds of affiliate. Similar overlaps emerge for entry modes.

The data set has been introduced in Chapter 5. Two modifications are, however, necessary since 16 observations had to be excluded due to missing values in independent variables, while 17 observations have been added from the write-in section of the questionnaire. The data set, therefore, covers eight Central and East European countries: the Czech Republic, Hungary, Poland, Russia, Romania, Slovenia, Slovakia and Bulgaria.[1]

Since this sample has been drawn from a representative sample of selected German and British manufacturing industries, it is not necessarily representative of a base population of all DFI projects in CEE. The selection bias from this source should be limited since the sample has been stratified by size such that the proportion of firms contacted in each size class was proportional to the share of the size class in a list of firms known to be active. Missing values, however, reduce the proportion of small investor firms, which results in a lower number of JVs and more greenfield entries in Table 8.1 compared to Table 5.9. Also, the chemical industry commands a larger share of this sample than of the sample presented in Table 5.9. These biases should not influence the validity of the empirical results. Write-in countries have been included to make best use of the available data, while retaining sufficient degrees of freedom and limiting sample selection biases. Despite this multitude of potential biases, I believe that the causal relationships do not suffer major distortions. However, some variables need to be interpreted with caution, notably the effects of the country dummies for Slovakia and Slovenia.

Table 8.1 shows the pattern of the dependent variables across home and host countries as well as across industries. The patterns are similar to those in Table 5.9, suggesting that sample selection biases are at acceptable levels. This includes the results of the χ^2-tests for independence of the variables. This categorical test rejects the null hypothesis of independence for several sections of the table.[2] Host country variation is significant for entry modes of ownership, mainly because of a diverging pattern for Russia, but surprisingly not for privatization. Home country variation is significant for ownership and privatization whereas industry variation emerges significantly only for mode of entry and only at a 10 per cent level of significance.

THEORETICAL FOUNDATIONS

Ownership and entry mode are analysed in different streams of the international business literature. The JV research mainly draws on the TC literature or on a firm-government bargaining model. The main arguments of TCE concerns the hybrid organizational structure of JVs. They are partly coordinated by prices and by hierarchy mechanisms. The TC literature, reviewed in Chapter 4, emphasizes the effects of the incomplete internalization and sensitivity to market failure.

The mode of entry literature draws on a variety of sources: Hennart and Park [1993] use TCE, mergers-and-acquisition theory, growth-of-the-firm theory and capital market imperfections. Caves and Mehra [1986] consider organizational costs of integration, the markets for corporate control, and the competitive conditions. Kogut and Singh [1988] focus on the impact of cultural distance on entry mode choice. Other studies in this tradition have been carried out by Zejan [1990], Andersson and Svensson [1994], Svensson [1996] and Hennart,

Table 8.1 Characteristics of DFI projects

Category	British	German	Food	Chem	Mach	Total
Minority JV	20%	11%	15%	12%	16%	14%
Majority JV	15%	31%	26%	19%	30%	25%
Wholly owned S	76%	80%	70%	85%	76%	78%
observations	75	141	27	81	108	216
Greenfield	64%	53%	41%	71%	51%	58%
Acquisition	22%	33%	37%	31%	25%	29%
JV-Entry	13%	24%	19%	13%	28%	21%
JV-Acquisition	15%	17%	19%	15%	18%	17%
observations	73	137	27	80	103	210
Privatization: yes	11%	23%	22%	25%	15%	19%
observations	71	141	27	77	108	212
Category	CR	HU	PL	R	RO	SLN	SVK
Minority JV	8%	6%	12%	41%	33%	40%	-
Majority JV	28%	22%	23%	34%	25%	20%	14%
Wholly owned S	83%	88%	83%	59%	50%	60%	86%
observations	54	50	52	29	12	5	14
Greenfield	60%	55%	62%	43%	45%	60%	79%
Acquisition	34%	34%	35%	11%	27%	40%	7%
JV-Entry	13%	19%	17%	50%	27%	none	14%
JV-Acquisition	15%	17%	12%	32%	18%	40%	7%
observations	53	47	52	28	11	5	14
Privatization: yes	23%	20%	22%	7%	17%	40%	14%
observations	53	49	51	28	12	5	14

χ^2-tests for independence of the variables (with df)

Categories	Mode of Entry	Ownership	Privatization
Host countries	29.833**(18)	30.072***(12)	4,891 (6)
Home countries	4.545 (3)	7.280** (2)	4,459** (1)
Industries	11.109* (6)	3.356 (4)	2,967 (2)

Notes: SVK includes Slovakia and Bulgaria. χ^2-tests refer to the sections of the table market with a dotted line. Significance levels: * = 10%, ** = 5%, *** = 1%.

Larimo and Chen [1995].[3] In CEE, specific issues arise due to the process of systemic transition, especially the rapid opening of the economies and the privatization of state-owned firms [Dunning and Rojec 1993, Estrin, Hughes and Todd 1996].

Ownership and mode of entry are intrinsically related as any entry decision has to be taken in view of the long-term objectives for ownership. Any investor considers first the aspired form of ownership for the affiliate, and then the optimal way to achieve it. Thus, arguments in favour of JV ownership also favour a JV entry, and arguments in favour of acquisition or greenfield also favour WOS. However, a JV may be chosen as the entry mode although ultimately WOS is aspired. Since the decisions are generally made simultaneously, regressing a model on the mode of entry is not sensible with ownership or privatization as independent variables.[4] Also, the size of the local operation is, at least initially, a corollary of the mode of entry and thus not independent.[5]

Table 8.2: Summary of the theoretical arguments

	Ownership	Mode of entry
Proximity and experience	JVs help inexperienced or distant firms to learn, but they would face higher coordination costs.	Post-acquisition costs of restructuring are higher for distant or inexperienced investors, but they need access to local know how.
Transaction cost economics	Firms sensitive to market failure avoid JV, while those in need of complementary inputs favour JV.	Firms core competencies and the managerial tasks required for the project determine the choice of entry mode.
Strategic competition	n.a.	JVs and acquisitions are means to achieve strategic objectives such as quick market entry.
Transition and restructuring	Legal constraints and economic risks inhibit full ownership	Hazards of restructuring post-socialist enterprises discourage acquisitions.

Entry through participation in the privatization process is one possible avenue for acquisitions. By definition then, privatization-entry is a subset of acquisition and JV-acquisition entries. In a reasonably perfect market for privatized firms, participation in the privatization process would be driven by the same forces as acquisition entry. Foreign investors would acquire firms from the privatization agencies if the value of the local assets was attractive. This implies that arguments for acquisition would also apply to privatization entry. Therefore, the analysis starts from the basic premise that coefficients in the privatization model resembles those in the acquisition model.

The nature of the data collected with multiple response questions has implications for the empirical method used: as the different options considered are not exclusive, using a multinomial Logit is not possible. Therefore, every option for ownership and mode of entry is considered separately. A binomial Logit is regressed independently for each, and the comparison of the results across equations will enable an analysis of the consistency of the empirical results. Binomial Logit has been the dominant method of empirical analysis in the field, the only exceptions are Kogut and Singh [1988] and Gatignon and Anderson [1988]. Though less technically sophisticated, it gives results that can be interpreted straightforwardly and it covers all options.

The discussion of the variable influencing mode choice is structured around four themes: experience and proximity, transaction cost economics (TCE), strategic management motives, and economics of transition. The basic premises with respect to ownership and mode of entry are listed in abbreviated form in Table 8.2.

Psychic Proximity and International Experience

Organizing business in an unfamiliar environment involves many additional obstacles, higher costs and higher perceived risk. This includes problems in negotiating with local institutions, cultural differences between business partners as well as communication and travel costs. Costs rise with cultural, language and religious differences, lack of personal contacts and also geographic distance. Perceived risks of various types increase, if investors have less understanding of the local environment. These aspects are combined in the concept of 'psychic distance' (see Chapter 3). In the present context, a major psychic distance evolved due to 40 years of different economic systems and education. Foreign businesses in the region reported problems because of the attitude towards work and leadership, lack of understanding of market processes as well as lack of managerial and financial skills as major obstacles. Psychic distance can be overcome by multinational firms with the relevant experience. Through similar activities in other countries, or establishment of business contacts in the same country, firms develop the human resources necessary for managing local operations.

Thus, psychic proximity and relevant experiences should be major determinants for modes of entry and ownership. However, the direction of the effect is not clear since various costs, associated with either mode of business, increase with distance and lack of experience. The theoretical arguments in the literature usually apply to both psychic proximity and experience, though few authors discuss them jointly. Four effects have been discussed which would have contradicting effects on entry modes (Table 8.3).

Table 8.3: The implications of distance and lack of experience

Proposition	Implied preference
1 Need for mode that facilitates learning & Higher perceived risk	JV > Greenfield and Acquisition
2 Post-acquisition integration costs	Greenfield > Acquisition
3 Need for complementary inputs	Acquisition and JV > Greenfield
4 Coordination problems between JV parents & Problems finding a suitable partner	Greenfield and Acquisition > JV

Firms without international experience choose an organizational form that provides opportunities to learn about the local environment while at the same time serves to minimize their risk exposure. A mode suitable for both objectives is a JV, be it as a temporary or unlimited arrangement. Capital investment risk is shared with a local partner, while profit sharing ensures incentives for both partners to contribute to the success of the venture. International experience would lead to better capabilities to manage and integrate an acquired company. In their 'internationalization process', firms would make incrementally stronger commitments along various dimensions (Chapter 3). Firms with little experience in international business or in CEE would be expected to choose a JV entry. The same applies to firms from distant origins because they have fewer external sources of learning and a higher risk perception.[6]

Proposition 1:   *Inexperienced firms and those from distant origins prefer a mode that facilitates their learning about the local environment and thus prefer JV.*

Second, distant investors would incur larger post-acquisition cost of integrating an existing firm into their global corporation. Psychic distance inhibits the 'organizational fit' of the firms and thus increases the post-acquisition costs of matching the administrative, cultural and personal characteristic of the joint organization [Jemison and Sitkin 1986, Kogut and Singh 1988]. These costs can be avoided with a greenfield entry, or a JV with a local partner. Furthermore, firms in proximity have personal contacts and may find it easier to find a suitable partner with whom to form a successful JV in CEE [OECD 1994].

With international and country experience, investors build the capabilities necessary to restructure and integrate acquired firms. These are particularly important in CEE because acquirers become involved in the restructuring of formerly state-owned enterprises which require major changes of their organizational structures. Foreign investors are reported to avoid costs and conflicts of such organizational changes by establishing greenfield operations where they can introduce their Western business practice [Möllering et al. 1994, OECD 1994]. Firms with long standing business contacts with the region should be more capable of integrating acquired firms. Thus, Proposition 2 arises complementary to Proposition 1. Together they are equivalent to the proposition by Kogut and Singh [1988].

Proposition 2:   *Inexperienced firms and those from distant origins would incur higher costs of restructuring a local firm and therefore prefer greenfield or JV entry over acquisition.*

Third, inexperienced and distant investors need complementary inputs which are obtainable in a more speedy way via an acquisition [Dubin 1975, Casson 1995] or by forming a JV with a local partner [Hennart 1988a, 1991a]. Typically, the local partner's contribution to JVs primarily includes their general knowledge of the local economy, cultural and social environment, labour relations, an so on [for CEE: OECD 1994]. The foreign partner supplies production technology, management know-how and/or intermediate inputs. These are intangible and/or tacit knowledge that cannot be transferred via markets. The local partner's knowledge and capital contribution reduce the risk associated with entering a new market. The more an investor knows the local environment, the less he needs the tacit knowledge of a partner or an acquired firm. This suggests that first-time foreign investors are more likely to expand by acquisition than established MNEs [Casson 1995]. Caves [1982] concludes similarly, arguing that large and experienced firms can better cope with the higher risk of greenfield entry [Svensson 1996]. Gomes-Casseres [1989] proposes that in distant countries JVs are preferred because they provide a source for information needed by entrants not familiar with the local environment. Acquisition and JV are alternative ways to acquire local knowledge, albeit with different consequences for management.

Proposition 3:   *Inexperienced firms and those from distant origins choose a mode of entry that gives them access to complementary inputs and therefore prefer acquisitions or JV over greenfield projects.*

Fourth, JVs are more difficult to manage by distant or inexperienced investors [Contractor 1990]. They find it more difficult to identify a suitable local partner because informal contacts and prior trading relationships are the usual ways of establishing successful partnerships. Culturally distant and inexperienced investors find it more difficult to establish mutual trust which is an imperfect success factor of international JVs. Conflict of corporate and national cultures are reported to be a major source of conflict in joint ventures in Russia [Puffer et al. 1996, Michailova 1997]. They experience more conflicts over objectives and management style of the JV.

Proposition 4:   *Inexperienced firms and those from distant origins would incur more frictions with their local partner in managing a jointly owned firm and therefore prefer full acquisitions and greenfield to JVs.*

Empirically, Proposition 1 receives some but not unanimous support with respect to proximity. Gomes-Casseres [1989] uses a familiarity index and found WOS to be preferred, significantly, in countries familiar to the US investors. Gatignon and Anderson [1988] find investors outside the 'Anglo Saxon' culture to be more likely to invest in JV in the US. Kogut and Singh [1988] use a Hofstede index as measure of psychic distance and find that firms from distant origins have a significant preference for JV as opposed to greenfield or acquisitions as mode of entry into the US. A replication study by Arnott, Gray and Yadav [1995] for DFI in the UK finds, however, a priority of greenfield to acquisition, which in turn is preferred to JV (the first difference is significant). This would support Propositions 2 and 4. Evidence in favour of Proposition 4 is also provided by Hu and Chen [1993] who found DFI in China to be more likely to take the form of JV if it came from Hong Kong. Last, but not least, in Chapter 7, this study found that firms prefer internalization in nearby countries when faced with the choice between DFI and contracts or trade.

Two kinds of experience are considered in prior research: general experience in international business, and experience specific to the country. Country specific experience is analysed in four studies. Proposition 1 is supported by Kogut and Singh [1988], Andersson and Svensson [1994] and Svensson [1996] who find significant signs for a dummy indicating existence of another, older affiliate in same country favouring acquisition. Davidson [1980] finds a positive correlation between experience and WOS entry. On the other hand, the number of years of experience insignificantly favours greenfield in Hennart and Park [1993], weakly supporting Proposition 3.

International experience effects mostly support Propositions 1 and 2. A high share of exports in sales favours acquisitions by small- and medium-size firms in Nordström [1991]. The 'number of countries in which the parent has subsidiaries' has a significant effect in favour of acquisition in Caves and Mehra [1986]. It is however insignificant in Kogut and Singh [1988]. The number of foreign affiliates significantly favours acquisition in Andersson and Svensson [1994] and WOS in Gatignon and Anderson [1988] and Gomes-Casseres [1989, 1991]. Agarwal and Ramaswani [1992] constructed a factor that included various measures of multinationality and was significant in favour of WOS versus JV. In contrast, the 'number of years since first international investment' (logarithmic function) is significant in favour of greenfield in Zejan [1990] which would support Proposition 3.

In this research, lack of international experience is proxied by a dummy showing whether or not the business with CEE is the first major international business operation and accounts for more than half of international sales. This applies to several German firms who take the value of 1 in the variable FIRST.[7] Experience specific to the country is measured by the time since the establishment of first business contacts (EXPERI). The dummy ONLY_PROJ indicates whether or not the investor has multiple DFI projects in the region. If all kinds of experience were positively influencing a choice, EXPERI would have a positive coefficient, and the two dummies have a negative coefficient.

The proximity effects can only be captured with host and home country dummies, where UK firms and investment in the Czech Republic are chosen as base cases. In addition, a control dummy is included for ownership of the parent firm. NONEUR describes firms affiliated to an MNE located outside Europe, mostly in the USA.[8] If psychic proximity had a positive impact on an option, then the dummy GERMAN should have a positive coefficient and NONEUR negative. The host country dummies should show a ranking of coefficients with Hungary and Poland close to zero (the Czech Republic), Slovakia negative, and Russia and Romania even more negative.

Transaction Costs Economics

A JV is an intermediary form between a contractual relationship and a wholly owned affiliate that is particularly common in international business [Parkhe 1993]. JVs have equity contributions by multiple owners sharing control. They operate under a regime of dispute settlement by arbitration that is partly internalized. Market failures are resolved by 'voice' rather than 'exit', that is agents work with each other to remove the market failure. This however comes at a cost as incentives change without giving full control over the operation. This partial internalization of markets cannot fully resolve the problems of market failure. Therefore, the arguments laid out in chapter four in favour of internalization also favour the choice of a WOS over a JV. In particular, businesses subject to asset specificity or information market failure are more likely to seek full control. Industries that are information intensive and thus sensitive to market failure are high-tech firms and marketing oriented consumer goods manufacturers.[9] Both would thus prefer full ownership of their operations in CEE:

H1:   Consumer goods manufacturers and technology intensive firms prefer WOS.

For consumer goods, two dummies are used separating the food and beverage industry (FOOD) and non-food consumer goods manufacturers (NON_FOOD). Technology intensity is proxied by the ratio of R&D expenditures over sales turnover. Results of previous research confirm the preference of human capital intensive investors for WOS [Gatignon and Anderson 1988, Gomes-Casseres 1989, 1990]. Contrary evidence is shown by Kogut and Singh [1987, 1988] as R&D intensive inward investors in the US prefer JV to acquisition. They explain this by the investors' objectives to acquire US technology.

However, some specific situations and objectives may make JVs a preferred form of business. Two arguments are derived from the transaction cost approach by Hennart [1988a]: scale economies at one production stage, and complementary intangible inputs. First, 'scale joint-venture projects' have the same function for all participating investors, for instance investment in a backward integrating production stage by two firms operating at the same stage of the value chain. Such JVs are motivated by the desire to achieve efficient economies of scale at that production stage, but internalize the market for the intermediate products. This type of JV exists in industries where processing facilities are specific to the sources of raw materials such as aluminium smelting and oil refineries. Such JVs are part of a larger cooperation between multinational firms such as 'strategic alliances' [Ohmae 1989, Dunning 1995] or joint research. In the transition economies, JVs are mostly of the second type such that this case would not apply to the present sample.[10]

Second, investors would prefer to internalize the project in a 'link-JV' if it requires complementary contributions that face some kind of market failure from two or more partners [Hennart 1988a, 1991]. This is often due to multiple contributions of technology. Also, small firms may use such a JV if they lack managerial resources or access to capital markets to manage and finance the scale of operations that would fully utilize its competencies. However, the complementary assets motive will overcome the disadvantages of joint ownership only if three conditions apply [Hennart 1988a]:[11]

• The assets acquired have to be firm specific, and
• The assets are quasi public goods, that is they cannot be dissociated from the partner firm and they can be shared at low marginal costs.
• The assets used by the JV are a subset of the assets of the partners, such that

purchasing the whole partner firm would force the acquirer into unrelated fields or suddenly to expand the firm's size. In other words, if the project is small, relative to the size of the partners, internalizing both enterprises is not feasible [Hennart 1989, Kay 1991].[12]

A need for complementary local assets would apply to firms processing natural resources or aspirating local market access. Many chemical industry firms (CHEM), are processing inputs at the source of their raw materials. They probably cannot acquire state-controlled firms with access to natural resources. Also, the food and beverage industry (FOOD) depends on local inputs since transportation costs for agricultural products are high and international trade is inhibited by trade barriers. Even to supply the local markets, they need access to local raw materials. A resource industry dummy was highly significant in favour of JV in Gomes-Casseres [1989, 1990] and Hennart [1991a]. Thus,

H2:   The chemicals and food and beverage industries are more likely to form JVs than the machinery industry.

In consumer goods industries, market access is very important. Market entrants would be interested in obtaining access to distribution channels and in acquiring a local brand name to avoid the costs of building their own brand. Acquisition of a local brand name has been shown empirically to motivate acquisition entry in the US [Anand and Delios 1996, Chen and Zeng 1996]. Reports from CEE also suggest that 'buying a market share' and acquiring distribution channels were major reasons for selecting an entry via privatization-acquisition [Gatling 1993, Dunning and Rojec 1993]. On the other hand, the value of local brand names was low at the very early stages of economic opening, because customers valued Western imports and brand names very highly. After the first wave of Western products, customers returned to local brands if they offered acceptable quality at an affordable price. Case evidence suggests that Western investors even reintroduced local brand names after initially having discarded them [Estrin, Hughes and Todd 1997]. Even without valuable brand names, a local partner can ease market access in various ways. Thus, need for complementary inputs would favour a JV. However, as Hennart's third condition would not apply to many small local firms, acquisition is also an attractive alternative.

H3:   Consumer goods manufacturers are more likely to enter via a JV or an acquisition.

The need for complementary inputs (H3) conflicts with the transfer of know how from the parent (H1). The former favours JVs, the latter WOS, with a theoretically ambiguous net effect. Hennart and Park [1993] use advertising and media expenditures of the parent to test a similar hypothesis. They found no significant effect in their aggregate model, but a 10 per cent significance effect in favour of acquisition in high/low growth industries.

The concepts of TCE can be extended to the choice between greenfield and acquisitions [Hennart and Park 1993]. A major difference between the two modes of entry is that in a greenfield the investor can establish an organization *de novo* and smoothly integrate it into its existing corporate organization and philosophy. Yet an acquisition restructuring of an existing organization. A JV-acquisition needs to be restructured without full control over the operation, increasing the impediments to successful integration. Depending on the nature of the core competences of the investor, the relative costs of these different strategies vary. Companies with superior organizational skills have comparative advantages in integrating new affiliates. Large and diversified firms have a management cadre capable of running acquired firms, which could otherwise be a constraint to firm growth [Penrose 1959/1995]. If they wish to acquire complementary local assets, they can acquire a whole firm. So,

H4:   Large and diversified firms are relatively more likely to enter by acquisition or JV-acquisition.

Greenfield investment would, on the other hand, be suitable for investors with a distinctive, valuable corporate culture. Neither imposing the culture on the acquired firm nor assimilating into the existing culture would achieve optimal deployment of the investors' core competences [Casson 1995: 33]. Expansions with the purpose of creating new outlets for existing resources, would thus favour a greenfield operation *if* the resources are technological or organizational capabilities and costly to implement in an existing organization. Greenfield investment gives, in contrast to partial or full acquisition, an opportunity to design and control the local operations. Firms with technological core competences are most likely to have such a distinctive corporate culture [Andersson and Svensson 1994]. They may also find compatibility problems with the production technology of existing local firms [Fölster and Nyberg 1994]. They would be characterized by high R&D intensity. Thus,

H5:   R&D intensive firms are more likely to enter by greenfield than by any other mode.

Similar firm-specific variables have frequently been used in previous research. The parent size variable has a significant sign for acquisition in Caves and Mehra [1986] and in one model specification by Andersson and Svensson [1994]. Opposing results are reported for Dubin [1975] and Wilson [1980]. A diversification ratio is not significant in Hennart and Park [1993], except in their producer goods subsample, and for very fast or very slow growing industries. A similar index is highly significant in favour of acquisition in Zejan [1990] as is the number of industries of activity in Caves and Mehra [1986]. The positive relation of acquisition and size is also confirmed by Agarwal and Ramaswani [1992], Wilson [1980] and Dubin [1975]. Kogut and Singh [1988] find a non-significant sign of diversification in favour of greenfield. In Hennart and Park [1993], R&D expenditures favour greenfield at 1 per cent level of significance in most specifications, but less in very high or very low growth industries where strategic considerations dominate. Andersson and Svensson [1994] and Svensson [1996] find a similar effect. Kogut and Singh [1988] find a significant effect in favour of JV but not between acquisitions and greenfield.

In this research, firm characteristics are measured by employment and its square for size (SIZE, SIZE_SQ), number of USSIC plus UKSIC codes in the Amadeus database, adjusted for sales turnover for diversification (DIVERS), and as above R&D expenditures.

Strategic Competition

JVs and acquisitions can be important means to improve a firms competitive position *vis-à-vis* its main rivals. In particular, they are a means to acquire complementary inputs needed for a speedy market entry. Delay of entry may be costly, for instance in emerging markets opening to international oligopolistic competition, such as CEE.

The speed of entry is particularly important in industries where first mover advantages can have a special value. A speedy entry and access to the local market can be achieved by forming a JV with, or acquiring, a local firm with local brand names and a local distribution network [Stopford and Wells 1972]. In the transition countries, first mover advantages were perceived to be particularly important because markets were yet untouched by Western consumer goods [Lankes and Venebles 1996, Estrin and Meyer 1997]. Both JVs and acquisitions are reported as means to gain quick market access in CEE [Gatling 1993, OECD 1994, Duvvuri et al. 1995]. First mover advantages are most important in consumer goods industries where brand names dominate. This lends additional support to hypothesis H3.

Second, speed of entry is important in industries that are fast growing in the host economy because of short-term profit opportunities and participation in a growing market [Hennart 1991a]. The standardized variable (H_GROWTH) measures the growth of the industry relative to the average in the host country.

H6:   Entry into fast growing industries is more likely to be in form of a JV or an acquisition.

In prior research, industry growth is partly positive and significant in Zejan [1990], but insignificant in Andersson and Svensson [1994] and Svensson [1996]. Caves and Mehra [1986] and Hennart and Park [1993] use a proxy for deviation from average growth. They argue that slow growing industries would also attract acquisition entry because capacity expansion by greenfield would lead to industry overcapacities [also see Casson 1995]. In CEE, however, existing capacity uses often outdated technology and may be more a burden than an asset for the acquirer. Therefore, the afore mentioned counter argument would not apply here.

In the questionnaire, firms indicated their investment motivation as factor-cost oriented and/or market oriented. For firms suggesting factor costs as their motivation (FACTOR), the speed of entry would be less urgent. They could establish local production gradually as needs for additional capacity arises. As the opening of CEE coincided with a recession in Western Europe, few urgent needs for additional capacity arose at the time.

H7:   *Investors motivated by the low factor-costs are more likely to choose greenfield entry.*

Transition and Restructuring

The process of economic transition from centrally-planned to market economies creates unique conditions in the CEE countries that affect modes of entry. First, the rapid opening induces strategic moves into virgin markets, as discussed above. Second, until recently, the full range of entry modes was not available due to legal constraints. Third, the potential acquisition targets are limited in number, and have to undergo major restructuring in both their managerial organization and their physical asset base.

JVs are popular with governmental institutions because of expected externalities in the economic development. They are also the rationale for subsidies, tax holidays or credit lines available only to international JVs. The actual foreign share in a given venture in a developing country may thus, be a function of the relative bargaining power of the host government *vis-à-vis* the investor as well as performance criteria the host government may impose [Kobrin 1987, Stopford and Strange 1991, Gomes-Casseres 1991].

When CEE countries first permitted DFI, investment was constrained by many regulations, including constraints on foreign equity ownership. For many early investors, a JV was the only feasible mode of establishing a local operation. Since then, the regulations have been eased in many small steps. By 1992, DFI was fairly unregulated in Hungary, Poland and Czechoslovakia, and in most other countries soon afterwards. In Russia many regulations were, however, still in place by the time of the survey in 1994/95 (section 2.2.3).

Consequently, the share of WOS among recent investment projects would be higher. JVs established earlier may or may not have been converted into wholly-owned affiliates. Institutional hysteresis would suggest that organizational forms, once established, are changed only gradually. Thus older projects, especially before 1992, and those in the as yet less liberalized Russia, are more likely to have been set up as JVs:

H8:   *Older investment projects are more likely to be in form of a JV.*

H9:   *Projects in Russia are more likely to operate as JVs.*

Table 8.4 Summary of variables

Variable	level	theory	hypothesis	prediction
FIRST	firm	EP		see Table 8.3
ONLY_PROJ	transaction	EP		see Table 8.3
EXPERI	transaction	EP		see Table 8.3
		TR	H8	JV
GERMAN	firm	EP		see Table 8.3
NONEUR	firm	EP		control
RUSSIA,	host country	EP		see Table 8.3
ROMANIA		TR	H9	JV
SLOVAKIA	host country	EP		see Table 8.3
R&D	firm	TC	H1, H5	WOS, greenfield
NON_FOOD	firm	TC	H1	WOS
		TC	H3	JV, acquisition
FOOD	firm	TC	H1, H2	JV, acquisition
CHEM	firm	TC	H2	JV
		TR	H11	greenfield, JV
SIZE	firm	TC	H4	WOS
DIVERS	firm	TC	H4	acquisition
FACTOR_C	transaction	SC	H7	greenfield
H_GROWTH	host industry	SC	H6	JV, acquisition
LABOUR	firm	TR	H10	green

Notes: HUNGARY, POLAND and SLOVENIA are predicted to have minor differences in comparison to the base case of the Czech Republic. EP = Experience and Proximity, TC = Transaction Cost, SC = Strategic Competition, TR = Transition and Restructuring, transaction = specific to the relationship of the firm with the country.

Post-socialist economies are experiencing a major industrial restructuring process (Chapter 2). This increases the post-acquisition costs for foreign investors. Increasing productivity often requires a lay off of a large number of employees. This is costly to organize and can severely damage the investors' local reputation. Therefore, Dunning and Rojec [1993] suggest that the higher the labour intensity of an industry, the higher the post-acquisition costs due to the overemployment problem. Capital intensive industries would on the other hand raise the cost and entry delay of greenfield ventures compared with acquisition. Labour intensity is measured by the investors' employment over turnover ratio (LABOUR).

H10:   Labour intensive firms prefer greenfield entry.

A particular restructuring cost arises in industries where past production was polluting the environment since environmental standards were far below West European standards. Potential investors refrain from acquisitions because of uncertain environmental liabilities associated with the firms or their property. As these problems are particular severe in the chemical industry (CHEM), less acquisition should be seen in this industry.

H11:   Entry in the chemical industry is more likely to be in form of greenfield or JV but not by acquisition or JV-acquisition.

Table 8.5 Descriptive statistics for independent variables

Independent variable	Unit of measurement	Mean	Standard deviation	Median
R&D	percentage	4.05	3.54	3.15
SIZE	10^5	0.20120	0.07809	0.26523
DIVERS	see appendix 5.3	25.9	6.9	81.7
LABOUR	ratio	9.88	7.19	9.63
EXPERI	years	17.8	21.0	6.0
H_GROWTH	see appendix 5.3	-0.052	0.905	-0.274

Note: The median for GERMAN is one and for all other dummies zero. Differences to Tables 6.4 and 7.3 emerge because this sample only contains firms with DFI projects.

All hypotheses are summarized in Table 8.4 with the relevant variables, their respective level of analysis and predictions. As several models are tested, the predictions are not plus or minus signs, but modes that would be favoured. Most variables are specific to the firm of the Western investor. Three variables,

FACTOR_C, ONLY_PROJ and EXPERI are specific to the relationship of the firm with the host country. H_GROWTH is specific to the industry in the Eastern economy, and six dummies are used for the Eastern Countries. Table 8.5 shows the descriptive statistics and Table 8.6 the correlations of the independent variables. Two rather high correlations between dummy variables arise by their definition: CHEM and NON_FOOD and NONEUR and GERMAN. These interactions need to be considered in the interpretation of the results. The correlation of the size variable, SIZE, with EXPERI and GERMAN is high but acceptable.

Table 8.6 Correlations of the independent variables

Variable	1	2	3	4	5	6	7	8	9	10	11	12
1 SIZE	1.0											
2 SIZE_SQ	.94	1.0										
3 R&D	.06	-.04	1.0									
4 LABOUR	.01	-.11	.03	1.0								
5 DIVERS	-.21	-.13	-.02	.14	1.0							
6 NON_FOOD	.10	.13	.33	-.20	-.06	1.0						
7 FOOD	-.16	-.12	-.19	-.12	-.07	-.25	1.0					
8 CHEM	.07	.12	.30	-.30	-.12	.64	-.29	1.0				
9 GERMAN	-.34	-.36	.26	-.06	-.01	.11	.10	.02	1.0			
10 NONEUR	.09	.09	-.07	-.20	-.06	.05	-.14	.11	-.49	1.0		
11 H_GROWTH	.04	.04	-.01	-.10	-.07	.10	-.00	.06	-.00	.04	1.0	
12 FIRST	-.20	-.13	-.15	-.22	.01	.12	.19	-.03	.22	.03	.16	1.0
13 FACTOR_C	.16	.11	-.01	.09	.14	-.15	-.06	-.21	.09	-.04	-.07	-.09
14 EXPERI	.36	.27	.20	-.06	-.14	.13	-.15	.02	-.05	-.04	.02	-.22
15 ONLY_PROJ	-.06	-.05	-.02	.07	.12	-.15	.08	-.16	-.31	-.06	-.09	-.06

continued			13	14	15
13	FACTOR_C		1.0		
14	EXPERI		.05	1.0	
15	ONLY_PROJ		.08	-.04	1.0

Note: Correlations are significant at 5% level for $r > 0.13$. The only significant correlations of host country dummy are RUSSIA with GERMAN (-0.14) and SLOVENIA with FACTOR_C (0.17).

EMPIRICAL ANALYSIS

The empirical analysis is based on a binary Logit model, that is the dependent variable takes the value of one if the firm chooses the named entry mode or ownership, and zero otherwise. The regression equations for different dependent variables are independent. Any firm may have more than one operation and therefore several modes of entry. The results for opposite modes of entry should be negatively correlated, yet not exact mirror images.

Tables 8.7 to 8.9 report the regression results. All equations have very high predictive power with between 76 per cent and 89 per cent correctly predicted observations. Very high shares of correct predictions arise in unbalanced samples with few ones for the dependent variable. The tables report the correct prediction of a random draw along the correct predictions of the model. They are calculated as $a^2 + (1-a)^2$ where a stands for the proportion of ones in the dependent variable. The model improves the proportion of correct predictions by more than seventeen percentage points in all but one equation: the minority-JV model. χ^2-statistics are also quite high, indicating a significance of the model as a whole. The critical value for 24 degrees of freedom at 1 per cent margin of error is 42.98. Many significant effects are consistent across models. These are overall very satisfactory results.

The regression contains a linear expression for employment. In the relevant range between zero and 120,000 employees the linear element always dominates, that is the marginal effect is positive where SIZE has a positive sign, and negative where SIZE has a negative sign. However, the effect may be smaller for very large firms because the peak or low of the expression is within 15 per cent of the range of SIZE in most cases.

RESULTS AND HYPOTHESIS TESTS

Psychic Proximity and Experience

The psychic distance between the home and the host as well as the investor's international and region specific experiences have theoretically ambiguous effects. Of the four alternative lines of arguments, the empirical analysis gives most support to Proposition 1, focusing on JV as a mode of learning, but also supports other propositions for some variables. Institutional constraints can explain some counter-intuitive results.

Firms with little experience prefer a JV ownership, including entry by JV-acquisition, and avoid full ownership and greenfield projects. This pattern emerges for both international experience at large (proxied by FIRST) and regional experience (ONLY_PROJ) in Tables 8.7 and 8.9. It supports the

Table 8.7 Logit models: form of ownership

	WOS	Minority JV	Majority JV
FIRST	-2.2878 (.784)****	.5995 (1.09)	2.1324 (.760)****
ONLY_PROJ	-1.9344 (.670)****	1.2387 (.963)	.9206 (.656)
EXPERI	- .0115 (.013)	.0276 (.014)**	.0096 (.011)
GERMAN	- .0372 (.648)	- .1184 (.769)	1.3660 (.661)**
NONEUR	1.4242 (.782)*	- .4318 (.840)	- .1422 (.688)
HUNGARY	.3904 (.639)	- .2824 (.829)	- .2792 (.539)
POLAND	.1661 (.608)	.3459 (.719)	- .5605 (.545)
ROMANIA	-2.6792 (.866)****	2.3764 (.892)***	.1052 (.943)
RUSSIA	-1.1832 (.653)*	2.1158 (.719)****	.3718 (.643)
SLOVENIA	-1.4885 (1.21)	2.5293 (1.21)**	-1.1377 (1.32)
SLOVAK_BG	- .0148 (1.02)	-6.0155 (25.8)	-1.0832 (.930)
R&D	.2739 (.100)***	- .2954 (.116)**	- .1995 (.086)**
NON_FOOD	.5812 (.678)	-1.3314 (.737)*	-1.2236 (.588)**
FOOD	-.0997 (.670)	.2785 (.807)	- .2868 (.644)
CHEM	- .9679 (.680)	1.6997 (.752)**	.7999 (.569)
SIZE	-1.6430 (2.97)	6.1293 (3.26)**	12.4603 (3.64)****
SIZE_SQ	2.4603 (2.99)	-6.5076 (3.30)**	-14.4045 (4.71)****
DIVERS	- .0027 (.003)	.0041 (.003)	.0048 (.003)*
FACTOR_C	- .7066 (.488)	.1794 (.553)	1.5481 (.425)****
H_GROWTH	.3809 (.244)	- .0041 (.258)	- .2815 (.225)
LABOUR	- .0287 (.031)	- .0020 (.033)	- .0174 (.033)
Constant	2.1844 (.900)**	-1.9615 (.963)**	-2.2434 (.858)***
observations	215	215	215
variables	20	20	20
χ^2-statistic	65.467	50.522	65.859
correct pred.	84.65%	88.37%	80.00%
random pred.	66.36%	75.32%	62.38%
ones/zeros	169/46	31/184	54/161

Significance levels: * = 10%, ** = 5%, *** = 1%, **** = 0.5%, ***** = 0.005%.

Table 8.8 Logit models: mode of entry

	Greenfield	JV-Entry
FIRST	-1.8396 (.733)**	.4802 (.741)
ONLY_PROJ	-1.4794 (.604)**	.7053 (.712)
EXPERI	- .0210 (.011)*	.0310 (.012)**
GERMAN	- .6982 (.542)	1.3573 (.682)**
NONEUR	1.2976 (.581)**	.0119 (.710)
HUNGARY	- .2037 (.467)	.5370 (.606)
POLAND	.1447 (.475)	.5154 (.590)
ROMANIA	-1.4503 (.838)*	1.4440 (.928)
RUSSIA	- .7272 (.584)	2.6060 (.665)****
SLOVENIA	- .1400 (1.11)	4.6899 (15.7)
SLOVAK_BG	.9747 (.844)	.7665 (.951)
R&D	.1890 (.068)***	- .2159 (.089)**
NON_FOOD	.9927 (.501)**	- .4854 (.631)
FOOD	- .1950 (.535)	-1.2070 (.699)*
CHEM	- .1930 (.490)	- .6184 (.624)
SIZE	-7.8643 (2.54)****	-1.8908 (2.97)
SIZE_SQ	7.9829 (2.63)****	.6129 (2.95)
DIVERS	- .0048 (.025)*	- .0038 (.003)
FACTOR_C	- .0238 (.406)	.2577 (.463)
H_GROWTH	.3980 (.195)**	.2104 (.220)
LABOUR	.0449 (.030)	- .0091 (.036)
Constant	- .5978 (.770)	-1.4711 (.915)
observations	212	210
variables	20	20
χ^2-statistic	70.202	48.808
correct pred.	75.94%	82.38%
random pred.	51.00%	66.88%
ones/zeros	121/91	44/166

Significance levels: * = 10%, ** = 5%, *** = 1%, **** = 0.5%, ***** = 0.005%.

Table 8.9 Logit models: mode of entry

	Acquisition	JV-Acquisition	Privatization
FIRST	.2278 (.760)	2.4324 (1.05)**	-1.5858 (.959)*
ONLY_PROJ	- .6462 (.714)	.9343 (.834)	.0762 (.901)
EXPERI	- .0109 (.012)	.0273 (.014)*	.0012 (.013)
GERMAN	.6091 (.592)	- .9087 (.816)	1.5586 (.781)**
NONEUR	- .1692 (.602)	-2.3985 (1.06)**	- .4781 (.823)
HUNGARY	- .0109 (.486)	.1549 (.695)	- .0391 (.596)
POLAND	- .0409 (.462)	- .6459 (.710)	- .1726 (.568)
ROMANIA	- .7232 (.855)	- .5538 (1.12)	- .4615 (.994)
RUSSIA	-1.8696 (.768)**	.8958 (.726)	-1.7803 (.948)*
SLOVENIA	- .4474 (1.06)	.9808 (1.42)	.3279 (1.16)
SLOVAK_BG	-2.1888 (1.15)*	- .9040 (1.34)	- .4421 (.988)
R&D	- .0917 (.068)	- .0197 (.082)	- .3980 (.110)****
NON_FOOD	-1.2852 (.542)**	- .2442 (.739)	-1.1427 (.679)*
FOOD	.8112 (.576)	.9211 (.800)	.9285 (.688)
CHEM	1.4688 (.547)***	.5399 (.862)	2.4955 (.713)****
SIZE	5.6322 (2.50)**	14.5236 (3.55)*****	7.3680 (3.06)**
SIZE_SQ	-4.3385 (2.42)*	-12.6465 (3.53)****	-5.7685 (2.98)*
DIVERS	- .0002 (.003)	.0078 (.002)****	.0045 (.003)*
FACTOR_C	1.2102 (.418)****	1.0836 (.540)**	1.7814 (.503)****
H_GROWTH	- .4087 (.207)**	- .3125 (.279)	- .3351 (.252)
LABOUR	- .0609 (.049)	- .0794 (.063)	- .0917 (.062)
Constant	-2.2661 (1.00)**	-2.7433 (1.18)**	-2.3549 (1.19)
observations	211	210	212
variables	20	20	20
χ^2-statistic	52.643	70.689	29.815
correct pred.	77.73%	89.05%	86.57%
random pred.	58.90%	71.59%	68.80%
ones/zeros	61/150	36/174	41/171

Significance levels: * = 10%, ** = 5%, *** = 1%, **** = 0.5%, ***** = 0.005%.

Table 8.10 Country patterns: residuals and their standard deviations

a. Wholly-owned affiliate			b. Majority JV		
1. Hungary	0		1. Russia	0	
2. Poland	-0.224	0.645	2. Romania	-0.267	1.02
3. Slovak/BG	-0.376	1.04	3. Czech	-0.372	0.643
4. Czech	-0.390	0.639	4. Hungary	-0.651	0.664
5. Russia	-1.574	0.687**	5. Poland	-0.932	0.673
6. Slovenia	-1.879	1.23	6. Slovenia	-1.509	1.38
7. Romania	-3.070	0.888****	7. Slovak/BG	-1.455	1.02
c. Minority JV			d. Privatization		
1. Slovenia	+0.414	1.16	1. Slovenia	+.3279	1.16
2. Romania	+0.261	0.824	2. Czech	0	
3. Russia	0		3. Hungary	-0.0391	0.596
4. Poland	-1.770	0.668***	4. Poland	-0.1726	0.568
5. Czech	-2.116	0.719****	5. Slovak/BG	-0.4421	0.988
6. Hungary	-2.398	0.774****	6. Romania	-0.4615	0.994
7. Slovak/BG	-8.131	25.8	7. Russia	-1.7803	0.948*
e. Greenfield			f. Acquisition		
1. Slovak/BG	0		1. Czech	0	
2. Poland	-0.830	0.851	2. Hungary	-0.011	0.486
3. Czech	-0.975	0.839	3. Poland	-0.041	0.462
4. Slovenia	-1.115	1.27	4. Slovenia	-0.447	1.06
5. Hungary	-1.178	0.848	5. Romania	-0.723	0.855
6. Russia	-1.702	0.902**	6. Russia	-1.870	0.768**
7. Romania	-2.425	1.09**	7. Slovak/BG	-2.188	1.15*
g. JV-entry			h. JV-acquisition		
1. Russia	0		1. Slovenia	+0.085	1.44
2. Romania	-1.162	0.934	2. Russia	0	
3. Slovak/BG	-1.840	0.971*	3. Hungary	-0.741	0.748
4. Hungary	-2.069	0.649****	4. Czech	-0.896	0.726
5. Poland	-2.091	0.630****	6. Romania	-1.450	1.17
6. Czech	-2.606	0.664****	5. Poland	-1.542	0.765**
7. Slovenia	-7.296	15.7	7. Slovak/BG	-1.800	1.39

Significance levels: * = 10%, ** = 5%, *** = 1%, **** = 0.5%

learning argument in Proposition 1, and is also consistent with the complementary inputs argument in Proposition 3. Thus, firms which lack international or regional experience choose a mode of entry that provides means of learning and complementary inputs. However, acquisition of firms in the privatization process does not offer these learning opportunities. Firms with no prior international experience (FIRST) abstain from these opportunities presumably because of the complexity of the negotiations and the enterprise restructuring. With respect to privatization, post-aquisition costs (Proposition 2) are of major concern. Experienced firms are more likely to establish greenfield projects with full ownership, but also more likely to participate in the privatization process.

The country-specific experience variable, EXPERI, shows positive significant signs on minority JV and JV-entry: firms which for a long time have had business contacts in the region are more likely to have JVs. This pattern is, surprisingly, in line with Proposition 4. This has not been suggested in the literature with respect to experience, but only with respect to proximity. It would suggest that inexperienced firms abstain from JVs because of potential coordination problems between the parents. It is more likely a different effect, arising from legal constraints, that dominates over the experience effect. Older projects were set up under a different legal framework (H8). The changing pattern of entry modes over times has also been reported in a number of earlier studies, including Hood and Young [1994], Möllering et al. [1994], Duvvuri et al. [1995] and Sharma [1995].

Because of institutional hysteresis this also affects the present ownership of operations: JVs, especially minority JVs, were established during the time of legal constraints and continue operating as JVs, even with foreign minority shares. Up until the time of the survey, in winter 1994/95, only some of them had been either discontinued or had been taken over by either partner. Thus, a temporary regulation had a lasting effect. New projects are established predominantly by acquisition or greenfield investment and with full foreign ownership, while old projects are still in a form of JV.

Proximity effects have been analysed using dummies for both home and host countries. No unanimous results emerge. German firms prefer majority JVs, JV-entry and acquisition (including privatization) to JV-acquisition and greenfield. Firms affiliated to non-European, mainly American, parents have a higher preference for WOS and greenfield. This pattern supports Proposition 2 (post-acquisition costs) and Proposition 4 (coordination costs). The advantage of proximity appears particularly relevant for participation in the privatization process. The results should however be considered carefully because the home country dummies would also capture differences unrelated to proximity.

The results for the host country dummies are consistently supporting Proposition 1. This evidence is in line with the results presented in Chapter 7 where proximity favoured DFI over contracts and trade. Table 8.10 illustrates the pattern across the seven host countries. The priorities have been tabulated separately based on regressions using the most preferred country as a base case.[13] Mode of entry and ownership vary substantially: the ranking of countries changes for each option.

Major differences emerge in the ownership pattern, especially between the three Central European countries on the one hand, and Russia and Romania on the other: minority JVs are most common in Romania and Russia, significantly more so than in the Czech Republic, Poland and Hungary (Table 8.10.c). Investors in Slovakia have the lowest preference for minority JVs but with a large margin of error. Interestingly, no significant differences emerge across countries with respect to the preference for majority JVs (Table 8.10.b). WOSs are significantly more common in the Visegrad countries than in Russia and Romania (Table 8.10.a), which is the mirror image of the preferences for JVs.

Entry modes differ along similar lines. Greenfield and acquisition projects are more common in the three Central European countries, whereas JVs are preferred in the two more distant countries. The pattern of JV-acquisitions does not seem to follow a proximity pattern (Table 8.10.h). Here the specific modalities of the privatization process may explain the variation: apparently investors were frequently asked to take only partial ownership in state-owned enterprises in Russia. In Slovakia and Poland, privatization agencies did not favour JV-acquisition.

Slovakia takes the predicted intermediate position for JVs but, at the expense of acquisition, greenfields are more common. This may be due to a lack of attractive takeover targets. Slovakia was industrialized during socialist rule with strong emphasis on military and heavy industry while light and machinery industries were based in the Czech part of Czechoslovakia.

This host country pattern is as predicted by Proposition 1. However, the credit for the effect must be shared with the transition argument with respect to the legal environment (H9), because of a positive correlation between the distance from the West and the extent of legal restrictions. These are even more restrictive in Russia and Romania, and would be sufficient explaination as to why minority JVs are more likely there. The fact that the effect is significant for minority JVs, but not majority JVs, may support H9.

In conclusion, the institutional framework interacts with the proposed experience and proximity variables so that their contribution is diluted. For first time investors and one project investors, proposition 1 is confirmed: they prefer JVs as a means to learn about the environment and acquire complementary assets. Specific conditions in the transition countries, especially the liberalization over the five years prior to data collection, make it impossible to detect the gradually developing involvement by investors over time. Therefore, older projects are more likely to be in the form of a JV. Differences across host countries are in line with Proposition 1, which suggested that in distant locations JVs would be preferred. It could however also be a result of legal constraints.

The pattern for both country experience and host country differences is most significant for minority JVs. Psychic distance appears to encourage minority-JVs (and contracts) as a mode involving low exposure and capital commitment, as well as discouraging participation in the privatization process.

Transaction Cost Economics

TCE arguments centred around the issues of market failure, complementary inputs and core competences. All three aspects receive strong support.

As predicted in H1, R&D has a positive and highly significant sign for WOS and greenfield and a negative significant effect on all concepts related to JV.[14] This strongly supports the argument that research-intensive firms are eager to maintain full control over their operation and are unlikely to share control with JV partners. This is even more remarkable when considering that the R&D proxy performed poorly in Chapter 7. The result also supports H5, which suggested that R&D-intensive firms face more obstacles with the integration of acquired firms using a different organizational or managerial approach.

Technology-intensive firms avoid the privatization process even more vehemently. Such firms would find it very difficult to adapt and integrate an existing firm with a post-Soviet organizational culture and structure into the parent firms' corporation. Therefore, post-acquisition restructuring costs particularly affect privatized, former state-owned firms.

Non-food consumer goods manufacturers (NON_FOOD) have the same priority of preferences as R&D-intensive firms. In particular, they prefer greenfield projects to acquisitions and privatization. Thus, their concerns about the transfer of marketing knowledge and brand names (H1) and integrating local operations, outweigh their need for complementary local inputs from a JV partner or acquired firm (H3). The suggestion that these firms would enter the region by acquiring local firms and use them only as a distribution network [Dunning and Rojec 1993, Sereghyová 1995] is not confirmed by this analysis.

Firms in the two broadly-defined resource-based industries, FOOD and CHEM, prefer acquisitions, especially those in the privatization process, and JV-acquisitions rather than establishing a new JV. The CHEM industry also has a significant preference for JV ownership, while the effects of FOOD are insignificant. In these industries the need for complementary inputs appears to be a dominating over considerations concerning post-acquisition costs of restructuring and integrating the acquired firm. Note the opposite priorities suggested by the results for the food and non-food consumer goods industries.

Hypothesis H4 considered the relationship between firms' core competences and the best mode to utilize them in a foreign environment. Large and diversified firms were hypothesized to be best equipped to manage acquired operations. The size effect receives strong support. Large firms have a relative preference for acquisitions, JV-acquisitions and privatization. They also appear better equipped to manage JVs than are small firms. Small firms prefer greenfield operations that give them the possibility of starting an operation at a small scale in accordance with their financial and managerial resources. Diversified firms were expected to prefer acquisition entry as their competences are in managing firms with a variety of activities. The effect emerges only (but highly significantly) for JV-acquisition, presumably the mode of entry most difficult to manage, and acquisitions in the privatization process. Otherwise, the variable is insignificant but consistent with the hypothesis.

In conclusion, the analysis shows strong support for arguments developed in the transaction cost section: firms sensitive to market failure avoid JVs, and the nature of the core competences of the firm determines the preferred mode of entry. Firms capable of restructuring and integrating another firm choose acquisition entry and participate in the privatization process.

Strategic Competition

Three factors affecting the impact of strategic competition on the mode of entry have been suggested. All three were motivated by the presumed urgency of entry in some industries, but they are clearly rejected in the analysis.

The NON_FOOD and FOOD dummies were predicted to indicate a preference for JV and acquisition entry because consumer goods manufacturers are especially concerned about speedy access to local markets. NON_FOOD, however, fails to support this proposition, as it did for the proposition H3 that derived the same prediction from the need for complementary local inputs. The rejection of both hypotheses shows that consumer goods industries in CEE differ from similar industries in other markets. Apparently, the local industry is of little interest to potential buyers, although it possesses knowledge on the local environment, local brand names and access to distribution channels. Privatization appears to be more of an obstacle than an opportunity in these industries. Thus, the positive effect of internalization incentives in favour of WOS (H1) dominates.

Entry in fast-growing industries is also in the form of greenfield with wholly owned operations, but not via acquisition. Possible explanations are: (a) the growth of the industry could be a result, rather than a cause, of foreign investment. For instance, if one firm acquired a leading and growing firm, the following firm may not find a suitable local target firm; (b) growing industries can accommodate more entrants without frictions between competitors; (c) the highest growth may occur in sectors neglected during the socialist regime. Their growth could be caused primarily by foreign investors or newly established local firms. In any case, the transition-specific pattern of industrial growth seems to create conditions of competition different from the pattern found in other markets.

The third proposition suggested that investors using factor-cost differentials to supply worldwide markets would be less inclined to use acquisitions because they have less urgency in implementing their projects. This, too, is rejected since factor-cost oriented investors prefer JVs and acquisitions, including privatized firms. This suggests that existing production facilities are more suitable for supplying low-cost products for exports than for supplying the local market. It may be an outcome of an industrial policy by privatization agencies who give preference to investors who intend to export at least some of their products.

Transition Environment

No support is given to either of the two hypotheses on the specific post-acquisition costs of restructuring a local firm. The chemical industry dummy has a positive significant sign on acquisition and JV-acquisition, and thus seems undeterred by potential environmental liabilities, as proposed by H11. According to H10, labour-intensive firms would prefer a greenfield entry. Yet the labour intensity dummy is correctly signed but insignificant in all models.

In conclusion, the competitive nature of transition economies seems different from that in mature market economies. The expected strategic motivations for mode of entry decisions do not apply under these conditions. In particular, acquisition is not preferred where speed of entry was presumed to be important. Yet factor-cost oriented investors choose acquisition, although they are presumed to have less urgency of entry. Specific effects suggested for the transition environment did not materialize either.

CONCLUSIONS

Three objectives have been stated for this chapter: testing DFI theory on ownership and entry mode, exploring the pattern of privatization-related DFI, and exploring the special features of CEE and cross-country differences.

On the International Business Literature

The experience and proximity propositions and TCE received support for similar lines of argument. In fact, the former could be integrated into the latter, although the theoretically ambiguous effects would be more difficult to illustrate within one common framework. The arguments which receive empirical support are:

- JVs are used as an opportunity to learn;
- firms sensitive to market failure prefer wholly owned operations;
- firms with unique core competences prefer greenfield operations;
- legal constraints influence ownership patterns;
- firms with capabilities to restructure and integrate an acquired firm are more

likely to choose acquisition and JV-acquisition, and participate in the privatization process.

On the other hand, some arguments that are common in the international business literature receive little or no support in this analysis:

- Psychic distance does not inhibit JVs although coordination between the partners becomes more difficult.
- Firms presumed to demand a speedy entry into new markets do not choose acquisitions or JVs. This refers to consumer goods manufacturers, high growth industries, and investors seeking local markets (rather than low factor costs).
- Firms presumed to require complementary inputs are rarely shown to choose JV or acquisition as entry mode. Only resource-based industries prefer acquisitions, though not JV ownership. Inexperienced firms, and projects in distant host countries, choose JV and JV-acquisition, but not acquisitions. Firms from distant home countries and non-food consumer goods manufacturers choose neither.

These results lend support to the TC approach, more so than those presented in the previous chapter. The market failure motivation for internalizing business transactions is more important for the choice between JV and WOS than it is for the markets and hierarchies decision between trade or contracts and DFI. In particular, technology and marketing-intensive firms (R&D, NON_FOOD) avoid both JVs and acquisitions in order to protect their know-how as well as to secure an implementation of their own organizational structure in the new affiliate.

Apparently JVs are more sensitive to transaction costs than contracts. Although the literature discusses the contracts versus DFI choice along the same lines as the JV versus WOS choice, there are inherent differences. A contractual arrangement can more clearly stipulate the responsibilities of each partner and limit the risks. A joint venture, on the other hand, is more dependent on post-signature behaviour of both partners and thus more subject to opportunism or uncertainty concerning the partners' capabilities and objectives. Therefore, JVs are more sensitive to information asymmetry than are contracts.

With respect to experience and psychic proximity, the theoretical discussion developed opposing propositions. With this theoretical ambiguity, the empirical results suggest that for experience, propositions 1 (learning) and 3 (complementary inputs) dominate over propositions 2 and 4. Firms which are unfamiliar with the local environment prefer JVs or trade, or contracts, see chapter seven. These modes enable them to reduce investment risk. In addition, JVs enhance learning and provide access to complementary inputs.

Transition-Specific Effects

Relative to the emphasis in the international business literature, the nature of investors' capabilities emerges as a very important determinant in this study. Investors face restructuring of obsolete organizational and technological structures in formerly state-owned enterprises. The post-acquisition restructuring costs may exceed costs of acquisition especially for acquisitions of formerly state-owned firms. This reduces the number of entries by acquisition, except for firms with the managerial resources to cope with the economic restructuring. The low attraction of the physical capital stock is also the cause of a new phenomenon in CEE, called 'brownfield' [Estrin, Hughes and Todd 1997]. Investors acquire a local firm, or form a JV, but establish completely new production facilities akin to the old factory. The acquired firm serves as a reservoir of skilled employees and facilitates relationships with local networks and government agencies.

The acquisition of firms in the privatization process is driven by similar forces as acquisitions overall. In Meyer and Estrin [1997] this is shown in greater detail. First, firms which combine advantages of proximity and international experience are most likely to participate. This provides one explanation as to why neighbouring countries, such as Germany and Austria, have had a dominant role in foreign investment early in the systemic transition. Second, privatization policy was successful in attracting projects that use factor costs and export at least part of their output. This is in spite of the fact that labour-intensive Western firms are less likely to be involved in the process.

Third, firms with the managerial capabilities needed to restructure a firm, are more likely to participate, while technology-intensive firms prefer to set up new operations. Firms offered in the privatization process face more problems of organizational restructuring than those that could be acquired through other means. Therefore, firms well-equipped to manage firms in CEE are more likely to invest: these are large, diversified and internationally experienced firms. On the other hand, firms with core competences in proprietary technology avoid the privatization process.

Fourth, and contrary to expectations, firms do not acquire privatized firms in order to fulfill the strategic objectives of acquiring complementary assets or of achieving a speedy entry to the market. It appears that the procedures of the privatization process do not permit speedy entry. Negotiations concerning a privatization-acquisition may be lengthy as the process involves many parties, including multiple government agencies and firm management and workers' councils which may have quite contrasting objectives [Rojec and Jermakowicz 1995, Antal 1995, Brouthers and Bamossy 1997]. Therefore, the prime motive for acquisitions, from a perspective of strategic competition, does not apply.

Host Countries

With respect to the countries in CEE, the evidence shows major differences that can be related to the local environment, in particular the prior industrial structure and the progress in economic transition.

- No significant differences emerge between the Czech Republic, Hungary and Poland in any of the options analysed for mode of entry or ownership, even though the estimates for these countries have the lowest standard errors, giving the test a high power. Given the different policies followed towards DFI in these countries, this is a surprising result.
- Slovakia followed the other three Visegrad countries with respect to the ownership pattern but has distinct patterns of mode of entry: the highest preference for greenfield, a higher preference for JV-entry, and a significantly lower preference for acquisitions. The low attractiveness of acquisitions in Slovakia is however, *not* due to less activity in the privatization process. Rather it may be due to the initial conditions and the less attractive industrial structure.
- Russia has less WOS, greenfields and acquisitions but a higher share of minority JVs, JV-entry and JV-acquisition than the four Visegrad countries. This suggests that the Russian environment favours JVs over other modes of entry or ownership. Both legal restrictions and greater psychic distance to the countries of origin contribute to this effect. Also, investors are less likely to participate in the privatization process, which indeed offers fewer opportunities for foreign investors.
- Romania has a pattern very similar to Russia's except that JV-acquisitions are not particularly common, and no differences in privatization participation were detected. The number of DFI projects in the sample is, however, small.
- Slovenia is difficult to assess, based on the present data set, since the small number of observations results in large standard errors. The indications are that the investment environment in Slovenia is different from that of other transition economies.

NOTES

1. Slovenia includes one project in Croatia. Slovakia (11 projects) and Bulgaria (3) have been grouped together. These countries are taken from the write-in section of the questionnaire. The information was of the same quality as that from the core countries the Czech Republic, Hungary, Poland, Romania and Russia, such that no major sample self selection would impede the analysis.

2. Also, χ^2-test for equality among proportions were made, which compare the proportions in each cell to the proportions in the total sample. They found significant differences only for Russia, with respect to both mode of entry and ownership. Notably, the hypothesis of equal proportions cannot be rejected for the write-in countries. If they had been significant, a sample self-selection could have been suspected which would require omission of these observations.

3. A related stream of research analyses differences in performance of DFI projects as a function of entry modes, including recently Li and Guisinger [1991], Woodcock, Beamish and Makino [1994], Nitsch, Beamish and Makino [1996], Barkema, Bell and Pennings [1996]. Related are also the empirical studies on expansion [Yip 1982] and entry [Chatterjee 1990] in a domestic US environment.

4. Caves and Mehra [1986], Hennart and Park [1993] and Padmanabhan and Cho [1996] distinguish only between greenfield and acquisition, but include a variable for share in ownership (that is JVs).

5. Any greenfield project starts small, whereas the size of an acquisition is mainly determined by the available targets, which may even be larger than the ultimately desired size, at least in terms of employment. Nevertheless, prior research included size as an independent variable. The size of the subsidiary relative to the parent was significant in Caves and Mehra [1986], Kogut and Singh [1988] and Hennart and Park [1993]. In Caves and Mehra [1986], it was, however, *not* significant for the subsamples of firms with low R&D, high advertising, and non-durable goods.

6. For instance, US firms are said to prefer JV in CEE because they have a higher perception of the risk [van Dam et al. 1996].

7. I also tested the influence of international experience directly with the variable 'share of turnover outside the home market'. This variable was frequently significant but correlated to several other variables.

8. The effect of NONEUR is, however, also subject to other influences as this is not a representative sample of US firms. For instance, they have considerable international experience which works against the effect predicted above. It was not sensible to introduce a similar European parent dummy because there were only 7 such observations in the sample, of which 5 were accounted for by one particular MNE whose core business activity may well be centred in the host country rather than the nominal home country.

9. On the performance of different arrangements of control in JVs see Beamish and Banks [1987], Geringer and Hebert [1991] and sources cited therein. Lyles and Baird [1994] address these issues in the case of Hungary and Fey [1995] for Russia.

10. It would apply if two Western firms had invested in one jointly-owned project in CEE. In the questionnaire, no such projects were reported.

11. As a static theory, TCE analyses JV as an equilibrium ownership form. JV as a temporary form is not considered, and the distinction between entry mode and the form of ownership is meaningless.

12. The third condition is not in accordance with Dunning [1993, p. 238] who argued that complementary assets would motivate JVs 'where resource commitments are substantial and where the outcome of the venture is highly uncertain'.

13. The standard deviations are naturally larger for countries with only few observations in the sample. Therefore, smaller standard deviations are obtained for the three Visegrad countries than for any other country. The selection of base country has been adjusted accordingly in some cases.

14. Given the results of Chapter 7, a dummy for the pharmaceutical industry was added in a separate experiment. This was never significant and did not alter the results for the R&D variable, though in some incidents the collinearity reduced the level of significance.

PART FOUR

Conclusions

9. Conclusions

This study presents an analysis of direct foreign investment (DFI) in the transition economies in Central and Eastern Europe (CEE). Chapter 2 evaluated the accumulated available statistical and qualitative evidence in order to assess research questions specific to the region. In Chapters 2 and 3, the theoretical literature on DFI in economics and management was reviewed and extended with an analytical framework for international internalization decisions. On this basis, a questionnaire instrument was developed covering business relationships with five countries in CEE. Using a postal survey, data were collected for 269 German and British companies.

The empirical part examined the decision process of firms entering the region. Hypotheses derived from general economic theory were tested under the special conditions of economic transition. Methods of empirical analysis were innovative for the research on entry decisions, in that multiple decisions were analysed in the same broad data-set of potential investors, and integrated with a three-step decision model. At the first stage, the propensity of firms to be active was examined. The second stage investigated their choice between trade, contracts and DFI. The third analysis tested hypotheses concerning the entry mode and ownership preferences of actual investors. Most theoretical propositions were confirmed, with several notable exceptions, however. This concluding chapter interprets the research results and discusses the implications for both the international business literature and for research and policy in the economics of transition.

THE INTERNATIONAL BUSINESS LITERATURE

Research Findings and Implications
In the OLI paradigm, Dunning [1993] considers two types of ownership advantages: first, property rights and/or intangible asset advantages, and second, advantages of common governance. In Chapter 4, a general framework showed how the trade-off between internal and external transaction costs determines internalization decisions, and thus the choice of DFI over market-based forms of international business. The two components of the OLI paradigm are related, as intangible assets affect transaction costs and common governance affects

management costs.

The empirical results suggest that the capabilites of firms to manage a business are more important than the market characteristics, both for the decision to become active, and for the choice of organizational form and entry mode. The most important ownership advantages arise from common governance related to size, international and regional experience, diversification, growth and the country of origin. Hardly any DFI is induced by the advantages of intangible assets. For the internalization decision, proximity, size and experience are at least as important as sensitivity to market failure. Thus, *the capability of a firm to manage a business appears more important than the characteristics of the market.*

Of the components of the TC framework, *some support is found for information content* while evidence for asset specificity and for interaction effects with uncertainty is weak. This result is in line with the reviewed empirical literature (Chapter 4) which is more supportive of the impact of information than of any other variable. The results confirm the explicit treatment of internal and external TC in the theoretical model, as well as the conceptual distinction between asset specificity and information asymmetry. The underlying causes of market failure differ, and knowledge-related issues may be more important internationally than in a national context.

Third, *psychic proximity not only encourages the emergence of international business, but also its internalization.* The country pattern found in Chapters 7 and 8 suggests that business in proximity is more likely in the form of DFI than contracts; likewise full ownership, acquisition and participation in the privatization process are more likely than joint ventures or greenfield projects. Thus, proximity appears to affect internal TC and costs of integration of an acquired firm more than it affects TC of market transactions.

A fourth interesting result is the inferior performance of the markets versus hierarchies approach in Chapter 7. A scale from markets based on price-mechanisms to hierarchically organized firms appears insufficient to account for the variety of international business. The superiority of the M-Logit *vis-à-vis* the O-Logit suggests that *contracts are a distinct form of business rather than an intermediate between markets and hierarchies.* In fact, contracts are chosen by many firms which were expected to favour internalization because they are subject to information intensity. Contracts appear to be sufficient to protect their interests, especially for business outside their core markets. Figure 7.2 offered a graphical illustration and an interpretation of this result.

Together, the results suggest that the capabilities of a firm to manage a new operation are the major determinants of internalization. The causality in the decision process may be as follows: firms take strategic decisions on the type of activity they would like to undertake in a country, that is which parts of the production chain to locate there. This decision defines the interface between the business units in the two countries. The capabilities of the firm to manage the new venture, together with the nature of the interface, determine the organizational form. The relative advantages of available organizational forms for an interface can additionally create feedback effects such that decisions are interdependent.

Similar arguments concerning firm's capabilities and influences specific to transactions determine the choice of entry mode. *Firms with unique competences embedded in their organizational or technological structure abstain from modes that require the sharing of control or that impede the implementation of an organizational design.* They prefer either contracts or greenfield investment. Both modes avoid sharing control over uncodifyable or difficult-to-value knowledge. Contracts may be used to transfer clearly defined technology or stages of the production chain. Greenfield projects allow the recreation of major units based entirely on the parent's organization and technological concepts. On the other hand, in an acquired firm, implementation of organization or technology may be impeded by the inherited structures that are resistant to change. A JV could face problems due to both the inherited structures of the partner, and the diffusion of sensitive knowledge.

As a corollary of this, *companies with capabilities for managing a variety of activities are more prone to invest directly, particularly by acquiring, restructuring and integrating local firms.* Large and internationally active diversified firms are less concerned about technological spillovers than about putting their management capabilities to work. Global MNEs are also more capable of managing a wholly owned affiliate. Firms with less experience in international management prefer to form a JV with a local partner with the objective to acquire know-how on the local environment, despite the higher cost of managing a JV. This learning effect dominates among opposing theoretical effects of experience and psychic proximity in the empirical analysis.

One explanation for the shift towards common governance and management capabilities as explanatory variables is the globalization of business. Most firms in the sample, especially the large firms that are most active in CEE, have developed into multinational enterprises which have acquired competences throughout a multi-country or global network. They are increasingly independent of the specific competitive advantages they obtained in their country of origin [Narula 1995]. At this stage of development, organizational or managerial competences become more important for corporate strategy than the nature of the technological expertise. These competences in turn depend on experiences and economies of common governance.

These results expose fundamental weaknesses in the TCE approach:

- By focusing on market failure, TCE analysts may overlook important aspects of internalization decisions, especially the capabilities of firms to

manage operations.
- By focusing on markets and hierarchies as the fundamental modes of organization, TCE analysts often do not consider the diversity of organizational arrangements.
- By focusing on given transactions, TCE analysts may overlook the dynamic interaction between organizations and transactions and the way in which established organizations can develop new additional transactions.

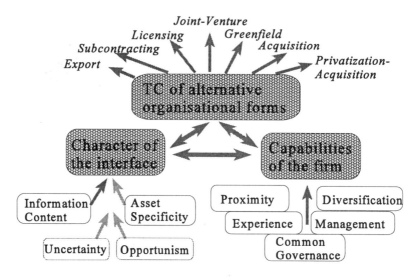

Figure 9.1   Choice of transaction modes: an interpretation

Conceptual work on TC can bridge most of these weaknesses. However, *limitations arise with the operationalization for empirical research questions.* Thus, TCE is unsatisfactory for the empirical explanation of internalization decisions in firm-level analysis. However, it helps to identify factors influencing these decisions. The comprehensive model in Chapter 4 incorporates many aspects, explicitly showing the eclectic character of TCE, and emphasizing the trade-off between internal and external TC. The actual determinants are even more complex. Each organizational mode has different TC, which vary with growing output, over time and in relation to other dynamic influences. Formally, the choice should be expressed as:

$$MODE = j \text{ if } TC_j = \text{Min } (TC_1, \ TC_2, \ ..., \ TC_j, \ ..., \ TC_n) \qquad (9.1)$$

where $TC_{1,2,...}$ are functions of the character of the interface and the capabilities of the firm. Figure 9.1 offers a conceptual interpretation which additionally considers a possible interaction between the capabilities of a firm and the interfaces it creates.

Evaluation of the Methodology

Limitations are unavoidable for a study with broad objectives in a previously unexplored territory. The data-set was subject to a compromise between the objectives of understanding DFI in CEE and testing propositions of general theory. The challenge was to make the best use possible of the available data, requiring a careful interpretation of the evidence.

For issues in transition economics, the data-set would ideally comprise all potential investors and all manufacturing investment in the region. This would allow macro-level predictions and policy advice. Such a base population is, however, impossible to construct. The base population covers the three most important manufacturing industries in two very distinct countries of origin. Results thus apply to these industries in Germany and the UK. To a considerable extent, results may be generalized since these are major industries in contrasting home countries. However, additional effects are likely for specific industries and home countries.

Research in the field of International Business can often rely on more sophisticated databases than has been the case in this study. The focus on CEE makes it difficult to obtain data of the quality and sample size used in empirical tests of general theories using US or UK data. Data availability severely constrained the selection of independent variables, especially for industry level data in the host country, for instance industry concentration. In addition, a questionnaire may focus on a small number of industries that are of specific interest from a theoretical perspective at the expense of being able to generalize to a broader base. Relatively unsophisticated proxies or dummies have been used for some of the theoretical concepts. More sophisticated measures would yield more robust results, but were not obtainable without complicating the questionnaire and thus reducing the return rate.

The return rate of questionnaires was high and did not suggest sample selection biases, although a modest selection bias against German SME's emerged due to missing values for some firm-specific variables. A selection issue also arises for the sample used in Chapter 8. It is not a representative sample of all DFI projects, but representative of the activities of the selected and stratified base population of Western firms. This is implicit in the analytical approach, using the same base population for each stage of the analysis.

The decision model itself may be challenged (Figure 5.1). It is based on the assumption that decisions are taken sequentially and are not interdependent. Although more complex empirical models are available, this thesis gives preference to the model because it generates straight forward interpretable coefficients and is superior to prior research that has analysed only selected decisions within the decision-making process.

As with most questionnaire surveys, the information provided is based on retrospective memory that may not be objective. Since most questions requested factual information and few evaluative or perceptional variables are used in the analysis, this should not cause a major bias in this study. Finally, empirical data-analysis can reject hypotheses but cannot prove a causal relationship between variables. Thus, the inferences in the previous section are an interpretation of patterns detected empirically in the data.

Further Research

The empirical tests may be *refined using more complex econometric techniques*, such as a nested Logit model for the decisions regarding activity and organizational form (Chapters 6 and 7) or by including contracts and DFI in the base population, thereby replicating the test by Chu and Anderson [1992]. This would allow a test of specific theoretical propositions, such as the determinants of contracts versus DFI and the interdependence of various alternative choices. However, with the given data-set such aggregations would result in degrees of freedom problems unless some interesting independent variables with missing values were omitted. Future research on these issues should explore alternative data-sets, as indicated in the discussion on methodology.

Theoretical work may consider *alternative approaches to the reigning TCE paradigm*. This study is 'normal science', in that it applies existing theories and paradigms [Kuhn 1962]. The TCE approach is applied and although it is not rejected, the author believes that developing alternative approaches to these issues is worthwhile. In other words, a shift in the dominant conceptual approaches to these issues may be forthcoming. Where should one search for new paradigms? Contemporary research is based on three current approaches: transaction cost economics, industrial organization and game theory, and the resource-based view. Harold Demsetz [1988: 161] suggests that the TC paradigm still has potential, although not in the established way of applying it:

> our thinking may be too constrained by our past successes. Some important problems are amenable to solution by application of the logic of both transaction cost theory and agency theory, but other problems, equally important, are not. Coase's work is best honoured by using it as the foundation to build a still richer set of tools.

Based on the experience of conducting this study, the present author suggests three lines of inquiry: dynamic models of DFI, alternative modes of organizing transactions, and the activity of management.

First, a major weakness of TCE is its static nature. *Dynamic alternatives* should be developed further since experience, strategic interaction and changing environments are important determinants of multinational business activity. These include internationalization process models, strategic investment, new international trade models and the developmental model (Chapter 3). The latter needs to be refined as one of its key propositions is not supported in the empirical analysis: the competitive push in the home country does not lead to DFI seeking low factor-costs in CEE, but to market-oriented investment.

Second, *organizational forms for transactions should be mapped with concepts other than markets and hierarchies*. One suggestion is to map organizational forms along multiple scales in terms of characteristics (adjustment mechanisms, time horizons, control, risk) and determinants (technological and environmental volatility, management capabilities, psychic distance). Trade, contracts and wholly-owned affiliates may be positioned in different corners of such a matrix, with JVs in an intermediate position. Figures 4.7 and 4.8 illustrate such approaches based on Root [1987] and Buckley and Casson [1996]. Figure 7.2 shows the TC of alternative modes of business as a function of the tradeability final goods and the relative importance of the target market. The choice depends on firm and environmental characteristics, as analysed in this study and information exchanges across the interface of a transaction. Further analysis needs to explain why many firms in this sample appear to consider contracts to be sufficient to overcome imperfect markets.

Third, the dissatisfaction with the basic premises of TCE and agency theory for that matter led to new research in management and economics that could be called '*the search for the new theory of the firm*'. Scholars are experimenting with new concepts. A common starting point is the view that firms do things that markets do not or cannot do. Many discussions surround the issues of knowledge and innovation. Firms are social organizations that follow an evolutionary pattern of accumulation of knowledge [Kogut and Zander 1992, 1995]. They organize teamwork [Alchian and Demsetz 1972], innovate [Teece 1995, Ghoshal and Moran 1996], focus on 'value creation' [Ghoshal and Moran 1996a] and 'dynamic capabilities' [Teece and Pisaro 1994]. Firms provide a role for entrepreneurial judgement and decision making [Casson 1991 - also Knight 1929]. They differ in their ability to manage knowledge [Demsetz 1988] and in their corporate culture, and thus the level of trust within and between firms [Casson 1991, 1995].

This study supports the shift of attention away from market failure towards firms as organizations. Common governance, experience and managerial capabilities are empirically supported in the analysis. How do these firm characteristics influence the ability to manage knowledge accumulation, evaluation and diffusion, and thus the choice of modes of business? Figures 7.2 and 9.1 may stimulate new theoretical modelling.

Multinational businesses entering CEE may employ novel corporate strategies, especially in greenfield ventures. They do not have to deal with inherited organizational structures that inhibit social change. In fact, DFI in CEE provides opportunities for experimentation with new management ideas and corporate governance systems [Kogut 1996]. In turn, this offers opportunities for academic inquiry: researchers looking for a new theory of the firm or analysing any particular aspect of strategic management could *analyse new features of international business as they emerge in business with CEE.* Consequently, this implies that the results of this study are relevant beyond the region of CEE.

THE LITERATURE IN ECONOMICS OF TRANSITION

Research Findings

Besides the scientific results for the Economics of the Multinational Enterprise, this study yields interesting insights specific to the CEE region. Research in the field of Transition Economics is more exploratory and policy-oriented, and so are these conclusions. The main result is that *determinants of multinational business activity in CEE are largely consistent with those suggested by the literature* and the observed patterns in other parts of the world. Only a few specific environmental conditions of CEE are shown to affect the pattern of inward DFI.

First, *the variation of DFI projects among the Visegrad countries is surprisingly small* given the variation of aggregate inflows of DFI capital. Hungary is among the most successful recipients of DFI capital in emerging markets in per capita terms, receiving almost twice as much DFI as Poland or the Czech Republic. Nevertheless, no statistically significant differences emerged for any of the business activities analysed in the empirical part of this study. Secondary variations include British and consumer goods manufacturers favouring the larger Polish market. Business with the Czech Republic has a slightly larger component of factor-cost oriented activity, including subcontracting and DFI. Local production in Hungary may be more likely to be internalized. However, in general, manufacturing MNEs follow very similar strategies in relation to the three countries. In contrast, data on capital flows are dominated by a few large projects, especially due to the privatization of utilities and other large corporations.

The main differences within the region are between the Visegrad countries and the other two countries of the study, Russia and Romania. Romania is lagging with a substantial margin by most measures of activity. British companies have rarely integrated Romania into their CEE expansion. This lag is more apparent in DFI, but to a smaller extent in the trade pattern. At the time of data collection in 1994, Romanian businesses were not yet considered attractive business partners.

Russia is a potentially attractive market with businesses waiting *ante portas*. They are interested, but are not yet willing to risk fully-fledged involvement. The survey shows that Russia has almost as many business contacts as Central Europe but a different structure of underlying business. *Most businesses follow a risk-averse strategy with a focus on the potential long-term benefits of an early market entry.* They prefer trading relations without DFI, that is contractual arrangements and investment in JVs, to investing in wholly owned affiliates. Correspondingly, JVs and JV-acquisitions are the most common modes of entry and few investors participate in the privatization process. This could be a result of the higher risk of a less developed economic and institutional environment, but could also result from a larger psychic distance where entrants follow low-risk learning strategies.

Second, German firms are more active in the region than their British counterparts. This fact is now well-established for the volume of DFI capital flows, and this study established it at the level of firms. By various measures, Germans are more deeply involved and more likely to use differentials in factor costs. The region accounts for a larger share of their overall business. Small German firms in particular are more active than their British counterparts.

These *differences may be attributed to the geographic, historical and cultural proximity and to more extensive contacts to the region before 1989.* Hypotheses of proximity favouring internalization received empirical support in Chapters 7 and 8. In addition, this study discussed the impact of differences in the economic environment. *The developmental model illustrates how push factors in the home environment induce DFI.* German firms face more pressures on their competitiveness due to high labour costs, currency appreciation, and the deep recession following German unification. These push factors induce firms to seek new opportunities in the East, particularly those that have reached barriers to growth with their present strategy. The negative effect of firm growth also supports this argument, suggesting that slow-growing firms are more active in CEE. This is remarkable as these firms typically have fewer managerial and financial resources. According to the growth theory of the firm [Penrose 1959/1996], their limited resources would inhibit expansion.

The different reactions of the German and British business communities to the opening of the East have feedback effects on the economic restructuring of Western Europe. German industry is adapting to the changing environment, with entry to major new markets, the internationalization of medium-size firms, and the relocation of production. British industry is only remotely affected as some enterprises expand their global markets. This development will probably affect the process of structural change within the European Union. Germany is experiencing the upgrading and expansion of advanced industries and a loss of competitiveness in low-tech industries. Thus, the two economies may be moving further apart from each other rather than converging.

Third, no evidence suggests that the search for low labour costs has been a major motive for firms investing in CEE. The survey finds only five firms indicating factor costs as their only motivation. Most investors reporting factor-cost motivation also report the market motive. This implies that *only jointly with attractive markets do lower factor costs attract inward DFI*. Furthermore, the importance of factor costs is an industry-specific phenomenon. Low labour costs have in part motivated 41 per cent of DFI in the machinery industry, but only 19 per cent of the projects in the chemicals industry. Note that this study does not cover the textile and clothing industries in which low factor costs are likely to be more important. Consequently, the proposition of the developmental model that investment would primarily seek factor costs is not supported. Competitive pressures and the recession seem to induce firms to seek new markets at least as much as lower labour costs. Since the study covers the largest sectors of the manufacturing industry, and labour costs are less relevant in services or primary industries, this conclusion may be generalized: with possible industry-specific exceptions, low labour costs are not the dominant motive for DFI in CEE.

Why is this so? Whether or not factor costs play an important role in a firm's locational decision depends on its labour intensity, minimum efficient economies of scale and transportation costs. These vary substantially between industries and between the two home countries. Low labour cost operations are not sensible, for instance in the capital-intensive chemicals industries, or the food industries where transportation is cost-intensive. For German firms, transportation costs are less of a deterrent as a matter of geography. In addition, labour cost considerations are more important due to the higher West-East wage differential. The survey also showed a substantial number of subcontracting arrangements by German firms. These use factor-cost differences without capital commitment and may be the first steps to a relocation of production. Since the survey was conducted shortly after the opening of CEE, it contains few projects that require long implementation lags. This would affect factor-cost oriented projects more than market entry strategies.

However, the general trend in Western Europe is towards capital-intensive production and manufacturing close to the customer. Thus there are few firms left in, say, Germany who would have their competitive advantages in managing labour-intensive operations. At their advanced stages of internationalization, firms are increasingly competing on the basis of organizational rather than technological capabilities. They undertake market and strategic asset-seeking DFI rather than factor-cost minimizing strategies.

Fourth, *changes in local environments lead only gradually to changes in multinational investment activity*, due to decision and implementation lags as well as hysteresis effects. In this study, two implications of such lags were observed: (i) investment from distant origins took longer to materialize. With less access to information and contacts, British and American DFI was small compared with German and Austrian DFI in the first years of transition. It surged only in 1995. (ii) legal constraints on ownership have been removed in most countries, but existing operations are still maintained as JVs although new projects now are predominantly fully foreign-owned.

Fifth, *firms do not enter the region through acquisitions of local firms with the strategic objective of acquiring local know-how and obtaining speedy market access*. These arguments in the International Business literature are not confirmed in this study (apart from the food industry dummy). Transition-specific influences lead to surprising effects. Investors prefer greenfield entry even when complementary inputs are predicted to be valuable, such as with consumer goods industries, or when speed of entry is important, such as for fast growing industries. The trend towards greenfield entry implies that these objectives are becoming even less important. The cause of this trend may be a lack of attractive targets or discouraging features of the privatization process.

Privatization accounts for half the acquisitions and JV-acquisitions in the sample. It attracts large volumes of direct investment capital, but it does not affect the number of firms investing in the country in the industries studied here. *The incidence of DFI by MNEs in a country seems unaffected by opportunities related to privatization*, but invested capital is affected. However, privatization attracts an over-proportional number of investors from Germany. Their historical, cultural and geographic proximity to the region eases both participation in the process and the integration of acquired firms into their global operations. As expected, technology-intensive firms abstain from acquisitions and, especially, from the privatization process. Privatization agencies seem to favour factor-cost seeking investors, presumably as a result of industrial policy by privatization agencies.

What accounts for these patterns? The lack of attractive target firms and the costs of restructuring reduce the attraction of acquisitions *vis-à-vis* greenfield operations. The negotiation process needed to acquire a firm involves multiple stakeholders and is time consuming. The post-acquisition costs of acquiring formerly state-owned firms are an additional deterrent to acquisitions. Foreign investors are expected to induce enterprise restructuring, thereby creating a competitive local manufacturing base. This conflicts with many objectives that investors may have, such as a local market focus, a small and efficient workforce, and adaptation to the parent firm's organization, technology and brand names. Primarily firms with financial and managerial resources are able to engage in industrial restructuring and thus participate in the privatization process.

The pattern indicates that sales to foreign investors may contribute to the restructuring of existing enterprises through the introduction of modern market-oriented management and organizational restructuring. However, it fails to attract firms bringing specialist technology which is an over-optimistic expectation. Furthermore, acquiring a firm in the privatization process may not offer opportunities for quick market access. The tedious process of negotiating privatization-acquisitions appears to delay sales and thus reduces the value of the assets. In addition, it may strengthen the dominance of investors from neighbouring countries.

Finally, how does this study answer the research question that originally motivated this project: 'why is there so little DFI?' It has to be noted that 'little investment' refers to the volume of capital flows which are the most frequently cited statistics. They were small in most CEE countries compared to other emerging markets until 1994, but has since risen substantially. The low levels of capital inflows are, as the data in this study show, not related to a lack of business activity, but rather to a lack of large projects with substantial capital flows.

First, this may be attributed to time lags that are involved in the decision processes of large investment projects. This is especially the case if there is no time pressure, for instance because of opportunities in the privatization process. Second, the number of attractive acqution targets is limited such that investors increasingly prefer greenfield projects. This requires less initial capital outlays than an acquisition. Third, the high economic risk in the region, especially in Russia leads to risk-reducing entry strategies, encouraging for instance joint-ventures and contractual alternatives to DFI. Fourth, demand is not as sophisticated as in the industrialized countries. Therefore, local demand did not justify the capital investment needed for many capital-intensive production processes. Finally, labour cost-seeking investment is not emerging on a large scale and, if it is, it is not capital intensive. In fact, the actual capital flows, not only in CEE countries, may probably be better explained by a small number of major privatization projects than by the number of manufacturing firms setting up operations in the country.

Policy Implications

The Visegrad countries have received considerable DFI inflows and most firms in the sample are active. The countries still have a long way to go to establish all the structures and routines of a market economy. However, they have established core processes fostering a productive evolution of the required socio-economic structures [Murrell 1996]. The general expectation is that these processes continues and will guarantee political stability and that economic growth suffices to attract DFI. Investors acknowledge the progress of the economic transition process in these countries.

The prime policy objective in these countries is *to sustain and make the best of international business activity and DFI inflows.* The small number of firms in CEE indicating an orientation towards factor costs in CEE suggests that host countries are not taking full advantage of their comparative advantages. Low labour costs, even productivity-adjusted, are insufficient to attract investment as this advantage is shared with many other regions in the world. They are rarely the sole motive for investment, but usually combine with market-oriented objectives. More investors will produce locally only if local markets are also attractive. Investors may develop the export potential from the region once they have saturated the local market. Privatization is the most important means of industrial policy, and the empirical results suggest that it is used to encourage export-oriented ventures.

A different contribution of foreign investment is the transfer of technology. The potential contribution of investment in the special conditions of economic transition has been discussed recently by McMillan [1993], Kogut [1996], Estrin Hughes and Todd [1997] and Meyer [1997]. This study has emphasized that contractual arrangements may substitute DFI for many operations. Host governments need to consider whether they can achieve objectives such as inward technology transfer and market access through contractual arrangements. In this case, policy and economic analysis should focus less on DFI than on broader concepts of international business.

The shift over time from JVs and acquisitions towards greenfield entry changes the contributions of foreign investors. *They are contributing less to the restructuring of formerly state-owned enterprises, but more to the development of a new private sector.* Greenfield projects affect employment creation, technology transfer and productivity. The emphasis of foreign investors on greenfield projects finds its parallel in the domestic economy. The recent growth of CEE economies, especially Poland, is attributed primarily to the growth of a new private sector, and not to the reformed and privatized formerly state-owned enterprises. [Johnson and Loveman 1995, Richter and Schaffer 1996]. This study strengthens the expectation that the new private sector, domestic or foreign owned, may flourish in the next years as economic transition progresses.

Industrial policy may foster growth by encouraging the new private sector. However, promoting the new businesses and greenfield investment does not contribute to solving a principal transition problem: restructuring state-owned enterprises. Without a Western partner, but with a greenfield competitor, they may find it harder to survive and their eventual restructuring or dissolution could become even more costly for the host economy. If policy intends to encourage either entry mode, it needs to consider these trade-offs and different investors' relative preferences for each mode.

In Russia and Romania, the main concern is still the low level of foreign investment. By 1994, many firms are present in Russia but without a major capital commitment, while Romania seems to have a low priority in most firms' regional strategies. Here, the policy priority should be on reforming the local environment so as to improve conditions for both domestic and multinational businesses. The secondary attraction for foreign investors is an indicator of a slow transition process as investors react sensitively to 'weak' local environments. The current lag in attracting DFI also indicates that the economy benefits less from externalities attributed to DFI. It is beyond the scope of this study to determine whether or not the impact of such externalities is economically significant.

The differences between the Visegrad countries and the other two countries suggest that DFI inflows depend on the economic conditions in the host country. This includes the presence of local entrepreneurs as partners and quality suppliers, education profiles, the structure of domestic demand and income, the institutional framework and infrastructure. By these criteria, Russia and Romania lag behind the Visegrad countries. This has an implication of wider relevance: *DFI is not a 'kick-starter' to economic development.* A minimum level of economic development is certainly a precondition for attracting major DFI inflows. Once development has taken off, inward DFI may accelerate the development process and, in CEE, the economic transition. This indicates that governments should create a domestic environment conducive to market-led business development to foster both local and foreign businesses.

Directions for Further Research

Research on DFI in CEE began with country surveys and has recently moved on to the analysis of more specific issues. The demand for descriptive summary papers on Central Europe has been well-satisfied. As the pattern of DFI has been established in broad terms, the focus of this study has been on determinants and characteristics of investment. Numerous suggestions could be made on specific issues that future research should address.

From this study, the most interesting research questions appear to be the effects of country of origin, strategic investment motivations, the comparative analysis of emerging markets, the impact of DFI on economic transition and development, and government policy. For thorough analysis, the collection of better data would be very helpful, considering not only capital flows but business operations by number, size, performance and so on.

This study analysed differences between two countries of origin. With only two countries in the study, relating differences in activities to the underlying determinants specific to the country of origin has been difficult. Thus, a wider range of home countries should be analysed, considering for instance the USA which is a major investor in the region, as well as other Western European countries. Among other things, this would permit a test of the push factors proposed by the developmental model.

Strategic behaviour of foreign investors was hypothesized but could not be shown in the empirical analysis due to a high level of aggregation of the data. In Chapter 8, the standard propositions on strategic motives for acquisition entry were not supported. An interesting line of inquiry would explore the specific features of entry strategies in the transition context: what are the strategic motives of foreign investors in virgin markets, and the interaction between potential investors, local institutions, and local businesses?

The developmental model was a first attempt to use the experience of other emerging markets to analyse and predict patterns of DFI in the region. An interesting analysis would test the propositions of the model systematically in a wider context comparing the emerging markets of Eastern Europe, East Asia and Latin America. This research should integrate the development economics literature on DFI [for instance Enos 1989, Lall 1996] with the emerging literature in CEE.

From the host country perspective, the main issue is the impact of DFI on the economic transition and development in the region. No study has yet analysed the 'impact' on the CEE economies comprehensively. The interesting questions are, at this stage: how and how much does DFI contribute to economic transition and development? Understanding why firms invest in the region is a first step towards understanding their interaction with the local environment. This interaction may generate externalities of foreign investment. Future research could draw on related work on DFI in developing countries. It also has to consider the special conditions of economic transition, and the role of technology transfer that has become so important in recent years. Implications of DFI for the balance of trade and balance of payments may be secondary.

An interesting aspect is the relationship between project characteristics and impact variables. The ultimate interest of impact analysis would be the value added in the host economy as a source of employment, tax revenues and private income. Of importance are channels of impact related to human capital:

* the transfer of technological and managerial expertise to the local affiliates,
* the introduction of new value systems and business culture [Casson 1994],
* the diffusion of know-how beyond the foreign-owned affiliate
* the industrial restructuring of the economies and the evolution of new systems of corporate governance [Kogut 1996], and
* the restructuring of acquired former state- owned enterprises, who benefit from access to investors' resources, but may be constraint by their global strategy.[1]

If such externalities to the local economy were shown, a case could be made for an active industrial policy to encourage DFI. This relates to another under-researched issue, the effectiveness of government policy towards inward DFI. The evidence from other countries seems to suggest that specific policies, such as incentives or tax holidays, have little impact on the volume of DFI. However, they may affect location within a country and DFI performance, for example export propensity [Guisinger et al. 1985, Safarian 1993]. This line of inquiry needs to be extended to the CEE region, considering the special conditions of transition as well as the motives of DFI observed in this study.

NOTE

1. My own research interest develops, after completing the current book, towards the impact of DFI on enterprise level, see Meyer [1998, 1998a] and Meyer and Bjerg Møller [1998]. Also Myant [1997], and Zemplinerova [1997] do interesting work on this topic, focusing on industry level analysis.

Bibliography

Abel, István and John P. Bonin (1992): Debt Service, Foreign Direct Investment and Transformation to Market: A simple model, CEPR discussion paper, no. 625.

Acocella, Nicola (1995): Theoretical Aspects of Mutual Relations between Foreign Direct Investment and Foreign Trade with Special Reference to Integration Theory, in R. Schiattarella (ed.): *New Challenges for European and International Business,* Rome: Confindustria.

Aczel, Amir D. (1993): *Complete Business Statistics*, Homewood, Boston: Irwin.

Adyubei, Yuri (1993): Foreign Investment in the Commonwealth of Independent States: Growth, Operations and Problems, in P. Artisien, M. Rojec and M. Svetlicic, (eds.): *Foreign Investment in Central and Eastern Europe*, London: St. Martin's Press, pp. 85-108.

Agarwal, Jamuna P. (1980): Determinants of Foreign Direct Investment: A Survey, *Weltwirtschaftliches Archiv* 116, 739-73.

Agarwal, Jamuna P., Rolf J. Langhammer, Matthias Lücke and Peter Nunnenkamp (1995): Export Expansion and Diversification in Central and Eastern Europe: What can be Learnt from East and Southeast Asia? Kiel Discussion Papers no. 261, Institut für Weltwirtschaft, Kiel, November.

Agarwal, Sanjeev and Sridhar N. Ramaswani (1992): Choice of Foreign Market Entry Mode: Impact of Ownership, Location and Internalisation Factors, *Journal of International Business Studies* 23, 1-27.

Aghion, Philippe and Wendy Carlin (1997): Restructuring Outcomes and the Evolution of Ownership Patterns in Central and Eastern Europe, in Salvatore Zecchini (ed.): *Lessons from the Economic Transition*, Dordrecht: Kluwer, pp. 241-62.

Agmon, Tamir and Donald R. Lessard (1977): Investor Recognition of Corporate International Diversification, *Journal of Finance* 32, 1049-55.

Aharoni, Yair (1966): *The Foreign Investment Decision Process*, Boston: Harvard Business School.

Aizenman, Joshua (1992): Exchange Rate Flexibility, Volatility and Domestic and Foreign Direct Investment, *IMF Staff Papers*, 890-922.

Akerlof, K (1970): The market for 'lemons': Qualitative Uncertainty and the Market Mechanism, in *Quarterly Journal of Economics* 74, 448-500.

Alchian, Armen A. and Harold Demsetz (1972): Production, Information Costs, and Economic Organisation, *American Economic Review* **62**, 777-95.

Ali, Shaukat and Hafiz Mirza (1996): Entry Mode and Performance in Hungary and Poland: The Case of British Firms, Academy of International Business, UK chapter conference at Aston University, 29-30. March, Proceedings pp. 1-23.

Aliber, Robert Z. (1970): A Theory of Foreign Direct Investment, in C.P. Kindleberger (ed.): *The International Corporation*, Cambridge, MA: MIT Press.

Anand, Jaideep and Andrew Delios (1996): Greenfield vs. Acquisition: The Role of Distribution and Advertising in Foreign Entry in the US, AIB Conference, Banff, September.

Anderson, Erin M. and Hubert Gatignon (1986): Modes of Foreign Entry: A Transaction Costs Analysis and Propositions, *Journal of International Business Studies*, Fall, 1-26.

Anderson, Erin M. and David C. Schmittlein (1984): Integration of the Sales Force: An Empirical Examination, *Rand Journal of Economics* **145**, 385-95.

Andersson, Otto (1993): On the Internationalisation Process of the Firm: A Critical Analysis, *Journal of International Business Studies* **24**, no. 2, 209-31.

Andersson, Thomas and Roger Svensson (1994): Entry Modes for Direct Investment Determined by the Composition of Firm-Specific Skills, *Scandinavian Journal of Economics* **96**, 551-60.

Andreff, Madeleine and Wladimir Andreff (1998): Foreign Direct Investment in Russia and C.I.S. Countries: Employment and Attractiveness, in: W. Andreff and X. Richet (eds): *Foreign Direct Investment in Transforming Economies*, forthcoming.

Antal, Zoltan (1995): *Privatisation and Firm Behaviour in National Transformation: The Case of Hungary*, Unpublished PhD Thesis, London Business School, University of London.

Arnott, David, Sid Gray and Sanjay Yadav (1995): National Cultures and Market Entry Strategies: Some Evidence from Inward Investment in the UK, paper presented at the AIB conference, Seoul, November.

Arrow, Kenneth J. (1971): *Essays in the Theory of Risk Bearing*, Chicago.

Arva, Lázló (1994): Direct Foreign Investment: Some Theoretical and Practical Issues, Magyar Nemzeti Bank (National Bank of Hungary), NBH Workshop Studies no. 1, July.

Aswicahyona, H.H. and Hal Hill (1995): Determinants of Foreign Ownership in LDC Manufacturing: An Indonesian Case Study, *Journal of International Business Studies*, **26**, 139-58.

Aydalot, P. (1986): *Milieux innovateurs en Europe*, Paris: GREMI.

Bajo-Rubio, Oscar (1991): Determinantes Macroeconomicos y Sectorales de la Inversion Extranjers Directa en España, *Información Commercial Española*, Agosto-Septiembre, 53-74.

Bajo-Rubio, Oscar and Simon Sosvilla-Rivero (1994): An Econometric Analysis of Foreign Direct Investment in Spain 1964-89, *Southern Economic Journal* **61**, 104-20.

Bakal, Mart (1992): Foreign Investment and Privatization projects, working paper, CERGE, Prague, April.

Barkema, Harry G., John H.J. Bell and Johannes M. Pennings (1996): Foreign Entry, Cultural Barriers, and Learning, *Strategic Management Journal* **17**, 151-66.

Baldwin, Richard (1994): *Pan-European Trade Arrangements beyond the Year 2000*, London: CEPR.

Baldwin, Richard E., Joseph F. Francois and Richard Portes (1997): The Costs and Benefits of Eastern Enlargement: The Impact on the EU and Central Europe, *Economic Policy* **24**, 125-76.

Baldwin, Richard and Paul R. Krugman (1989): Persistent Trade Effects of Large Exchange Rate Shocks, *Quarterly Journal of Economics* **104**, 635-54.

Barrel, Ray and Nigel Pain (1991): An Econometric Analysis of US Foreign Direct Investment, European Meeting of the Econometric Society, Cambridge.

Bartlett, Christopher and Sumantra Ghoshal (1989): *Managing across Borders: The Transnational Solution*, Boston: HBS Press.

Basu, Swati, Saul Estrin and Jan Svejnar (1997): Employment and Wage Behaviour of Industrial Enterprises in Transition Economies: The Cases of Poland and Czechoslovakia, *Economics of Transition* **5**, 271-288.

Batra, Raveendra N. und Josef Hadar (1979): Theory of the Multinational Firm: Fixed versus flexible Exchange Rates, *Oxford Economic Papers* **31**, 258-69.

Beamish, Paul W. (1985): The Characteristics of Joint-Ventures in Developing and Developed Countries, *Columbia Journal of World Business* **20**, 13-20.

Beamish, Paul W. and John C. Banks (1987): Equity Joint Ventures and the Theory of the Multinational Enterprise, *Journal of International Business Strategy* **18**, 1-15.

Beckermann, W. (1956): Distance and the Pattern of Intra-European Trade, *Review of Economics and Statistics* **28**, 31-40.

Bellak, Christian (1997): Austrian Manufacturing MNEs: Long-Term Perspectives, *Business History* **39**, 47-71.

Benito, Gabriel R.G. and Geir Gripsrud (1992): The Expansion of Foreign Direct Investments: Discrete Rational Locational Choices or a Cultural Learning Process? *Journal of International Business Studies* **23**, 461-76.

Benito, Gabriel R. G. and Lawrence S. Welch (1994): Norwegian Companies in Eastern Europe: Past Involvements and Recent Changes, in P.J. Buckley and

P.N. Ghauri (eds): *The Economics of Change in East and Central Europe: Its Impact on International Business*, London: Academic Press, pp. 235-48.

Bhagwati, Jagdish (1985): *Dependence and Interdependence*, Oxford.

Bilkey, W.J. and G. Tesar (1977): The Export Behaviour of Smaller Sized Wisconsin Manufacturing Firms, *Journal of International Business Studies*, Spring/Summer, 93-8.

Blomström, Magnus and Ari Kokko (1995): Foreign Direct Investment and Politics: The Swedish Model, CEPR Discussion Paper no. 1266, London, November.

Bobeva, Daniela and Alexander Bozhkov (1996): Foreign Investments in the Bulgarian Economy, in: Iliana Zloch-Christy (ed.): *Bulgaria in a Time of Change, Economic and Political Dimensions*, Adershot: Avebury.

Bochniarz, Zbigniew and Wladyslaw Jermakowicz (1993): Foreign Direct Investment in Poland: 1986-90, in P. Artisien, M. Rojec and M. Svetlicic (eds): *Foreign Investment in Central and Eastern Europe*, London: St. Martin's Press, pp. 85-108.

Böckenhoff, Gerd and Kristian Möller (1993): Foreign Direct Investment into Hungarian Food Industries: Explaining Differences by Industry-Specific Characteristics, VII EAAE Congress, Stresa, Italy, 7-10 September, Proceedings Vol. F, 147-60.

Bolton, Patrick and Gerard Roland (1992): The Economics of Mass Privatisation, CEPR Discussion Paper.

Booth, Simon and Shane Record (1995): Foreign Direct Investment in Eastern and Central Europe: Problems of Institutional and Economic Misconduct in the Transition, University of Reading, Department of Economics, Discussion Paper no. 309, April.

Borensztein, Eduardo and Manmohan S. Kumar (1991): Proposals for Privatisation in Eastern Europe, *IMF Staff Papers* **38**, 300-26.

Borish, Michael and Michel Noël (1996): Private Sector Development During Transition - The Visegrad Countries, World Bank Discussion Paper no. 318.

Borsos, Julianna (1995): *Domestic Employment Effects of Finnish FDIs in Eastern Europe*, ETLA - The Research Institute of the Finnish Economy, Series B, no. 111, Helsinki: Taloustieto.

Borsos, Julianna and Mika Erkkilä (1995): Regional Integration in the Baltic Rim - FDI and Trade-based Interaction of Finland, Estonia and St. Petersburg, ETLA - The Research Institute of the Finnish Economy, Discussion Paper no. 539, September.

Boudier-Bensebaa, Fabienne (1998): German Relocations to Poland and Hungary, in: W. Andreff and X. Richet (eds): *Foreign Direct Investment in Transforming Economies*, forthcoming.

Boyko, Maxim, Andrei Shleifer and Robert Vishny (1995): *Privatizing Russia*, Cambridge, MA: MIT Press.

Brabant, Jozef M. van (1993): *Industrial Policy in Eastern Europe: Governing the Transition,* Dordrecht: Kluwer.

Brada, Josef C. (1981): Technology Transfer by Means of Industrial Cooperation: A Theoretical Appraisal, in Paul Marer and E. Tabaczynski (eds): *Polish-U.S. Industrial Cooperation in the 1980's,* Bloomington: Indiana University Press.

Brada, Josef C. (1996): Privatisation Is Transition - Or Is It? *Journal of Economic Perspectives* 10, no. 2, 67-86.

Brada, Josef C., Inderjit Singh and Adam Török (1994): *Firms Afloat and Firms adrift: Hungarian Industry in the Transition,* Armonk, NY: Sharpe.

Bradshaw, Michael J. (1995): *Regional patterns of Foreign Investment in Russia,* London: Royal Institute of International Affairs.

Brainard, S. Lael (1993): A Simple Theory of Multinational Corporations and Trade with a Trade-off between Proximity and Concentration, National Bureau of Economic Research, Working Paper no. 4269, February.

Brewer, Thomas L. (1993): Government Policies, Market Imperfections, and Foreign Direct Investment, *Journal of International Business Studies* 24, no. 1, 101-20.

Brewer, Thomas L. (1994): Indicators of Foreign Direct Investment in the Countries of Central and Eastern Europe: A Comparison of Data Sources, *Transnational Corporations* 3, no. 2, 115-26.

Brezinski, Horst (1994): Die Rolle der ausländischen Direktinvestitionen im Rahmen des Transformationsprozesses in Polen, Freiberg Working Papers no. 94/3, Technical University Bergakademie Freiberg, Faculty of Economics and Business.

Bridgewater, Sue, Peter McKiernan and Robin Wensley (1995): Strategic Investment Decisions by Western Firms in Ukraine: The Role of Relationships in Home and Host Market Networks, in P. Chadraba (ed.): *The Central and Eastern European Markets: Guideline for New Business Ventures,* New York: Haworth.

Brouthers, Keith D. (1995): The Influence of International Risk on Entry Mode Strategy in the Computer Software Industry, *Management International Review* 35, 1995/1.

Brouthers, Keith D. and Gary J. Bamossy (1997): The Role of Key Stakeholders in International Joint-Venture Negotiations: Case Studies from Eastern Europe, *Journal of International Business Studies* 28, 285-308.

Brunetti, Aymo and Beatrice Weder (1997): Investment and Institutional Uncertainty, Technical Paper no. 4, Washington: International Finance Corporation.

Buckley, Peter J. (1985): New Forms of International Industrial Co-operation, in P.J. Buckley and M.C. Casson : *The Economic Theory of the Multinational Enterprise,* London: MacMillan, pp. 39-59.

Buckley, Peter J. (1988): The Limits of Explanation: Testing the Internalisation Theory of the Multinational Enterprise, *Journal of International Business Studies* 19, 181-93.

Buckley, Peter J. (1990): Problems and Developments in the Core Theory of International Business, *Journal of International Business Studies* 21, 657-65.

Buckley, Peter J. and Mark Casson (1976): *The Future of the Multinational Enterprise*, London 1976.

Buckley, Peter J. and Mark Casson (1985): *The Economic Theory of the Multinational Enterprise*, London: MacMillan.

Buckley, Peter J. and Mark Casson (1996): An Economic Model of International Joint Venture Strategy, *Journal of International Business Studies* 27, 849-76.

Buckley, Peter J. and Malcolm Chapman (1995): The Perception and Measurement of Transaction Costs, paper presented at the Academy of International Business, Seoul, November.

Buckley, Peter J. and H. Davis (1981): Foreign Licensing in Overseas Operations: Theory and Evidence from the UK, in R. Hawkins and A.T. Prasad (eds): *Research in International Business and Finance*, Greenwich, Conn.

Buckley, Peter J., G.D. Newbold and J. Thurwell (1979): Going International - The Foreign Direct Investment Behaviour of Smaller UK Firms, in L.G. Mattson and F. Wiedersheim-Paul (eds): *Recent Research on the Internationalisation of Business*, Stockholm: Almquist and Wicksell.

Calderón-Rossel, Jorge R. (1985): Towards the Theory of Foreign Direct Investment, *Oxford Economic Papers* 37, 282-291.

Calvo, Guillermo A. and Fabrizio Corricelli (1993): Output Collapse in Eastern Europe, *IMF Staff Papers* 40, 32-52.

Calvo, Guillermo A., Ratna Sahay and Carlos A. Vegh (1995): Capital Flows in Central and Eastern Europe: Evidence and Policy Options: IMF Working Paper no. 95/57, May.

Canning, Anna and Paul Hare (1996): Political Economy of Privatisation in Hungary: A Progress report, paper presented at the conference 'The Institutional Framework of Privatisation and Competition Policy in Economies in Transition', London Business School, September.

Cantwell, John A. (1989): *Technological Innovation and Multinational Corporations*, Oxford: Basil Blackwell.

Cantwell, John A. (1991): A Survey of Theories of International Production, in: Christos N. Pitelis and Roger Sugden (eds): *The Nature of the Transnational Firm*, London: Routledge, pp. 16-63.

Cantwell, John A. (1993): The Internationailization of Business and the Economic Development of Poland and Eastern Europe, Discussion Paper no. 180, Department of Economics, University of Reading, September.

Casson, Mark (1982): Transaction Costs and the Theory of the Multinational Enterprise, in Alan M. Rugman (ed.): *New Perspectives in International Business*, London: Croom Helm.

Casson, Mark (1987): *The Firm and the Market*, Oxford: Basil Blackwell.

Casson, Mark (1991): Modelling the Multinational Enterprise: A Research Agenda, *Millennium Journal of International Studies* 20, 271-86.

Casson, Mark (1994): Enterprise Culture and Institutional Change in Eastern Europe, in P.J. Buckley and P.N. Ghauri (eds): *The Economics of Change in East and Central Europe*, London: Academic Press.

Casson, Mark (1995): *The Organisation of International Business*, Studies in the Economics of Trust Volume Two, Aldershot: Elgar.

Casson, Mark (1997): *Information and Organization: A New Perspective on the Theory of the Firm*, Oxford: Clarendon Press.

Caves, Richard E. (1971): International Corporations: The Industrial Economics of Foreign Investment, *Economica* 38, 1-27.

Caves, Richard E. (1974): Causes of Direct Investment: Foreign Firm's Share in Canadian and United Kingdom Manufacturing Industries, *Economica* 38, 1-27.

Caves, Richard E. (1982): *Multinational Enterprise and Economic Analysis*, Cambridge: Cambridge University Press.

Caves, Richard E. and Sanjeev Mehra (1986): Entry of Foreign Multinationals into U.S. Manufacturing Industries, in Michael Porter (ed.): *Competition in Global Industries*, Harvard Business School Press, Boston.

Cavusgil, S.T. (1980): On the Internationalization Process of Firms, *European Research* 8, November,273-81.

Cavusgil, S.T. and J.R. Nevin (1981): Internal Determinants of Export Marketing Behaviour: An Empirical Investigation, *Journal of Marketing Research* 18, February, 114-19.

Chan, C.L. Chang and Y.M. Zhang (1995): The Role of Foreign Direct Investment in China post 1978 Economic Development, *World Development* 23, p.691-703.

Chang, Sea Jin (1995): International Expansion Strategy of Japanese Firms: Capability Building through Sequential Entry, *Academy of Management Journal* 38, 383-407.

Charman, Ken (1996): Joint-Ventures in Kazakhstan: The View from the Foreign Partners, Discussion paper no. 41, CISME Centre, London Business School, October.

Charman, Ken (1996a): Joint-Ventures in Kazakhstan: The View from the Local Partners, Discussion paper no. 42, CISME Centre, London Business School, October.

Chase, C.D., J.L. Kuhle and C.H. Walther (1988): The Relevance of Political Risk in Direct Foreign Investment, *Management International Review* 18, no. 3, 31-9.

Chatterjee, Sayan (1990): Excess Resources, Utilization Costs, and Mode of Entry, *Academy of Management Journal* **33**, 780-800.

Chen, Shih-Fen and Ming Zeng (1996): Reputation Barriers, Marketing Capabilities, and Japanese Investors' Choice of Entry Strategy into the US, Working Paper no. 97-27, Graduate School of Management, University of California at Riverside, November.

Chiles, Todd H. and John F. McMackin (1996): Integrating Variable Risk Preferences, Trust, and Transaction Cost Economics, *Academy of Management Review* **21**, 73-99.

Chu, Wujin and Erin M. Anderson (1992): Capturing Ordinal Propositions of Categorical Dependent Variables: A Review with Application to Modes of Foreign Entry, *International Journal of Research in Marketing* **9**, 149-60.

Clague, Christopher and Gordon C. Rausser, (eds) (1992): *The Emergence of Market Economies in Eastern Europe*, Cambridge, MA: Blackwell.

Clegg, Jeremy (1990): The Determinants of Aggregate International Licensing Behaviour: Evidence from Five Countries, *Management International Review* 30, p. 231-251.

Clegg, Jeremy (1995): The Determinants if United States Foreign Direct Investment in the European Community: A Critical Reappraisal, in: Roberto Schiattarella (ed.): New Challenges for European and International Business, EIBA conference proceedings, p. 465-484.

Clemons, Eric K., Sashidhar P. Reddi, and Michael C. Row (1993): The Impact of Information Technology on the Organisation of Economic Activity: The Move to the Middle Hypothesis, *Journal of Management Information Systems* **10**, no. 2, 9-35.

Coase, Ronald H. (1937): The Nature of the Firm, *Economica* **4**, 386-405.

Coffee, J.C. Jnr (1996): Institutional Investors in Transitional Economies: Lessons from the Czech Experience, in R. Frydman, C.W. Gray and A. Rapazynski (eds): *Corporate Governance in Central Europe and Russia*, vol. 1, London and Budapest: Central European University Press.

Collins, Susan and Dani Rodrik (1991): *Eastern Europe and the Soviet Union in the World Economy*, Institute for International Economics.

Commander, Simon, Quimao Fan and Mark E. Schaffer,(eds) (1996): *Enterprise Restructuring and Ecomomic Policy in Russia*, Washington, DC: World Bank.

Comisso, Ellen (1997): *'Implicit' Development Strategies and Cross-National Production Networks,* paper presented at workshop 'Will there be a Unified European Economy', Kreisky Forum and BRIE, Vienna, June.

Conner, Kathleen R. (1991): A Historical Comparison of Resources-Based Theory and Five Schools of Thought Within Industrial Economics: Do we have a new Theory of the Firm? *Journal of Management* **17**, 121-54.

Contractor, Farok J. (1981): The Role of Licensing in International Strategy, *Columbia Journal of World Business* **16**, 73-83.

Contractor, Farok J. (1984): Choosing between Direct Investment and Licensing: Theoretical Considerations and Empirical Tests, *Journal of International Business Studies* **15**, no. 3, 167-88.

Contractor, Farok J. (1990): Ownership Patterns of US Joint-Ventures Abroad and the Liberalisation of Foreign Government Regulation in the 1980's: Evidence from the Benchmark Surveys, *Journal of International Business Studies* **21**, 55-73.

Contractor, Farok J. and Sumit K. Kundu (1996): The Determinants of Modal Choice: Analyzing the Organisational Forms in the International Hotel Industry, AIB Conference, Banff, September.

Corbo, Vittorio, Fabrizio Corricelli and Jan Bossak (eds) (1991): *Reforming Central and Eastern European Economies: Initial Results and Challenges*, Washington, DC: World Bank.

Cowling, Keith and Roger Sugden (1987): *Transnational Monopoly Capitalism*, Brighton: Wheatsheaf.

Cramer, J.S. (1991): *The Logit Model: An Introduction for Economists*, London: Arnold.

Csaba, Lázló (1995): *The Capitalist Revolution in Eastern Europe*, Aldershot: Elgar.

Csáki, György (1993): East-West Corporate Joint-Ventures: Promises and Disappointments, *Eastern European Economics* **31**, no. 4, 51-81.

Cukierman, A., Sebastian Edwards and Guido Tabellini (1992): Seignorage and Political Instability, *American Economic Review* **82**.

Culem, C.G. (1988): The Locational Determinants of Direct Investments among Industrialised Countries, *European Economic Review* **32**, 885-904.

Cushman, David O. (1985): Real Exchange-Rate Risk, Expectations and the Level of Direct Investment, *Review of Economics and Statistics* **67**, 297-308.

Cushman, David O. (1988): Exchange-Rate Uncertainty and Foreign Direct Investment in the United States, *Weltwirtschaftliches Archiv* **124**, 322-36.

Cyert, R.D. and James R. March (1963): *A Behavioural Theory of the Firm*, Englewood Cliff, NJ: Prentice-Hall.

Dam, Q. van, Keith D. Brouthers, Lance E. Brouthers and George Nakos (1996): Investments in Central and Eastern Europe: A Comparison of Dutch and U.S. Firm Activities, Academy of International Business, UK chapter conference at Aston University, 29-30. March, Proceedings pp. 162-82.

Davidson, William H. (1980): The Location for Foreign Direct Investment Activity: Country Characteristics and Experience Effects, *Journal of International Business Studies* **11**, no. 2, 9-22.

Davidson, William H. (1982): *Global Strategic Management*, New York: Wiley.

Davidson, William H. and Donald G. McFetridge (1984): International Technology Transactions and the Theory of the Firm, *Journal of Industrial Economics* **32**, 253-64.

Davidson, William H. and Donald G. McFetridge (1985): Key Characteristics in the Choice of International Technology Transfer Mode, *Journal of International Business Studies* 16, no. 2, 5-21.

De Castro, Julio O. and Klaus Uhlenbruck (1997): Characteristics of Privatization: Evidence from Developed, Less-Developed and Former Communist Countries, *Journal of International Business Studies* 28, 123-45.

De Maris, Alfred (1992): *Logit Modelling: Practical Applications*, Sage University Papers, Newbury Park: Sage.

De Melo, Martha and Alan Gelb (1997): Transition to Date: A Comparative Overview, in S. Zecchini (ed.): *Lessons from the Economic Transition: Central and Eastern Europe in the 1990s*, Dordrecht: Kluwer, pp. 59-78.

De Menil, Georges (1997): Trade Policies in Transition Economies: A Comparison of European and Asian Experiences, in W.T. Woo, S. Parker and J.D. Sachs (eds): *Economies in Transition: Comparing Asia and Europe*, Cambridge: MIT Press, pp. 257-297.

Demsetz, Harold (1988): The Theory of the Firm Revisited, *Journal of Law Economics and Organisation* 4, 141-61.

Demsetz, Harold (1995): *The Economics of the Business Firm*, Cambridge: Cambridge University Press.

Denekamp, Johannes G. (1995): Intangible Assets, Internalization and Foreign Direct Investment, *Journal of International Business Studies* 26, 493-504.

Desai, Padma (ed.) (1997): *Going Global: Transition from Plan to Market in the World Economy*, Cambridge, MA: MIT Press.

Devreux, John and Bryan Roberts (1997): Direct Foreign Investment and Welfare in Transforming Economies: The Case of Central Asia, *Journal of Comparative Economics* 24, 297-312.

Dixit, Avinash (1980): The Role of Investment in Entry Deterrence, *Economic Journal* 90, 95-106.

Dixit, Avinash (1990): Investment and Hysteresis, *Journal of Economic Perspectives* 6, 107-32.

Dodsworth, John R., Erich Spitäller, Michael Braulke, Keon Hyok Lee, Kenneth Miranda, Christian Mulder, Hisanobu Shishido and Krishna Srinavasan (1996): Vietnam: Transition to a Market Economy, IMF Occasional Paper no. 135, Washington, DC.

Döhrn, Roland (1996): EU Enlargement and Transformation in Eastern Europe: Consequences for Foreign Direct Investment, *Konjunkturpolitik* 42, 113-32.

Drábek, Zdenek (1993): Foreign Investment in Czechoslovakia: Proposals for Fine-Tuning Measures of Policy Reform, *Eastern European Economics* 31, no. 4, 6-18.

Dubin, Michael (1975): *Foreign Acquisitions and the Spread of the Multinational firm*, D.B.A. thesis, Graduate School of Business Administration, Harvard University.

Dunning, John H. (1977): Trade Location of Economic Activity, and the Multinational Firm. A search for an Eclectic Approach, in B. Ohlin, P.O. Hesselberger and P.M. Wijkman (eds): *The International Allocation of Economic Activity*, London.

Dunning, John H. (1980): The Location of Foreign Direct Investment Activity, Country Characteristics and Experience Effects, *Journal of International Business Studies*, pp. 9-22.

Dunning, John H. (1981): *International Production and Multinational Enterprise*, London: Allen and Unwin.

Dunning, John H. (1981a): Explaining the International Direct Investment Position of Countries: Towards a Dynamic or Developmental Approach, *Weltwirtschaftliches Archiv* 119, 30-64.

Dunning, John H. (1986): The Investment-Development Cycle and Third World Multinationals, in: Khushi M. Khan (ed.): *Multinationals of the South. New Actors in the International Economy*, London: Croom Helm.

Dunning, John H. (1988): *Explaining International Production*, London: Allen and Unwin.

Dunning, John H. (1991): The Prospects for Foreign Direct Investment in Eastern Europe, *Development and International Cooperation* 7, June, p. 21-40.

Dunning, John H. (1993): *Multinational Enterprises and the Global Economy*, Wokingham: Addison-Wesley.

Dunning, John H. (1995): Reappraising the Eclectic Paradigm in an Age of Alliance Capitalism, *Journal of International Business Studies* 26, p. 461-492.

Dunning, John H. and Matija Rojec (1993): *Foreign Privatisation in Central and Eastern Europe*, CEEPN Technical Paper Series no. 2, Central and Eastern European Privatisation Network, Ljubljana.

Duvvuri, Stefan, Andreas Gyenis, Marcel Kanz and Stephan Szakal (1995): *Direktinvestitionen in Ungarn, Eine Umfrage zu Motiven, Erfahrungen und Zukunftsperspektiven deutscher Investoren in Ungarn*, 2nd edition, editor: German-Hungarian Chamber of Commerce, Bielefeld: Bertelsmann.

Dyker, David (1996): FDI, Subcontracting and Strategic Alliances: Do they help the Transition Economies Raise Productivity? *EIU Country Forecast: Economies in Transition*, 3/96, p. 16-24.

Earle, John and Saul Estrin (1996): Employee Ownership in Transition, in R. Frydman, C.W. Gray and A. Rapazynski (eds): *Corporate Governance in Central Europe and Russia*, vol. 2, London and Budapest: Central European University Press, pp. 1-61.

Earle, John, Saul Estrin and Larissa Leshchenko (1996): Ownership Structures, Pattern of Control, and Enterprise Behavior in Russia, in S. Commander, Q. Fan and M.E. Schaffer (eds): *Enterprise Restructuring and Economic Policy in Russia*, Washington, DC: World Bank, pp. 205-52.

Eatwell, John, Michael Ellman, Mats Karlsson, Mario Nuti and Judith Shapiro (1996): *Transformation and Integration: Shaping the future of Central and Eastern Europe*, London: IPPR.

Eccles, Robert G. and Harrison C. White (1988): Price and Authority in Inter-Profit Center Transactions, *American Journal of Sociology* **94**, S17-S51 (supplement).

Economist Intelligence Unit (1996): Country Forecast: Economics in Transition, Regional overview, 1st quarter 1996.

Edwards, Sebastian (1990): Capital Flows, Foreign Direct Investment, and Debt-Equity Swaps in Developing Countries, NBER working paper no. 3497.

Ellman, Michael (1989): *Socialist Planning*, 2nd ed, Cambridge: CUP.

Engelhard, Johann and Stefan Eckert (1994): Abschlußbericht zum Forschungsprojekt Markteintrittsverhalten deutscher Unternehmen in osteuropäischen Ländern, Bamberger Betriebswirtschaftliche Beiträge nr. 98/1994.

Enos, J.L. (1989): Transfer of Technology, *Asian Pacific Economic Literature* **3**, 3-37.

Ernst, Maurice, Michael Alexeev and Paul Marer (1996): *Transforming the Core: Restructuring Industrial Enterprises in Russia and Central Europe*, Boulder: Westview Press.

Erramilli, M. Krishna (1996): Nationality and Subsidiary Ownership Pattern in Multinational Corporations, *Journal of International Business Studies* **27**, 225-48.

Erramilli, M. Krisha and C.P. Rao (1990): Choice of Foreign Market Entry Modes by Service Firms: Role of Market Knowledge, *Management International Review* **30**, 135-50.

Errunza, Vihang R. and Lemma W. Senbet (1984): International Corporate Diversification, Market Valuation and Size-Adjusted Evidence, *Journal of Finance* 19, p. 727-43.

Estrin, Saul (ed.) (1994): *Privatisation in Central and Eastern Europe*, Harlow: Longman.

Estrin, Saul (1994a): Economic Transition and Privatisation: The Issues, in Saul Estrin (ed.): *Privatisation in Central and Eastern Europe*, Harlow: Longman.

Estrin, Saul, Josef C. Brada, Alan Gelb and Inderjit Singh (eds) (1995): *Restructuring and Privatisation in Central and Eastern Europe: Case Studies of Firms in Transition*, London: Sharpe.

Estrin, Saul and Martin Cave, eds (1993): *Competition and Competition Policy in Eastern Europe*, London: Pinter.

Estrin, Saul and John S. Earle (1995): Employee Ownership in Transition, London Business School, CIS-Middle Europe Centre, Discussion Paper no. 18, February.

Estrin, Saul, Alan Gelb and Inderjit Singh (1995): Shock and Adjustment by Firms in Transition: A Comparative Study, *Journal of Comparative Economics* **21**, 131-54.

Estrin, Saul, Kirsty Hughes and Sarah Todd (1997): *Foreign Direct Investment in Central and Eastern Europe: Multinationals in Transition*, London: Pinter.

Estrin, Saul and Klaus Meyer (1998): The East European Business Environment: Opportunities and Tripwires for Foreign Investors, *Thunderbird International Business Review*, May/June, forthcoming.

Estrin, Saul and Xavier Richet (1998): A Comparison of Foreign Investments in Bulgaria, the Czech Republic and Slovenia, in W. Andreff and X. Richet, (eds): *Foreign Direct Investment in Transforming Economies*, forthcoming.

Estrin, Saul and Robert Stone (1996): A Taxonomy of Mass Privatization, *Transition* (World Bank) 7, 8-9.

Ethier, William J. (1986): The Multinational Firms, *Quarterly Journal of Economics* **101**, 806-33.

Ethier, William J. and James Markusen (1996): Multinational Firms, Technology Diffusion and Trade, *Journal of International Economics* **41**, 1-28.

European Bank for Reconstruction and Development, EBRD (1994): *Transition Report,* London: EBRD.

European Bank for Reconstruction and Development, EBRD (1995): *Transition Report 1995, Investment and Enterprise Development*, London: EBRD.

European Bank for Reconstruction and Development, EBRD (1996): *Transition Report 1996: Infrastructure and Savings*, London: EBRD.

European Bank for Reconstruction and Development (1997): *Transition Report: Enterprise Performance and Growth*, London: EBRD.

Fagre, Nathan and Louis T. Wells, Jr. (1982): Bargaining Power of Multinationals and Host Governments, *Journal of international Business Studies* **13**, no. 3, 33-50.

Fan, Quimiao and Mark E. Schaffer (1994): Government Financial Transfers and Enterprise Adjustments in Russia, with Comparisons to Central and Eastern Europe, London School of Economics, Centre for Economic Performance, Discussion Paper no. 191, February.

Fey, Carl (1995): Important Design Characteristics for Russian-Foreign Joint-Ventures, *European Management Journal* **13**, 405-415.

Fey, Carl (1996): Key Success Factors for Russian-Foreign Joint-Ventures, *International Executive*, May.

Fingleton, John, Eleanor Fox, Damien Neven and Paul Seabright (1996): *Competition Policy and the Transformation of Central Europe*, London: CEPR.

Fischer, Stanley and Alan Gelb (1991): Issues in the Reform of Socialist Economies, in V. Corbo, F. Coricelli and J. Bossak (eds): *Reforming Central and Eastern European Economies: Initial Results and Challenges*, Washington, CD: World Bank, pp. 65-82.

Fischer, Stanley, Ratna Sahay and Carlos A. Végh (1996): Stabilization and Growth in Transition Economies: The Early Experience, *Journal of Economic Perspectives* **10**, 45-66.

Flowers, E. B. (1976): Oligopolistic Reaction in European and Canadian Direct Investment in the United States, *Journal of International Business Studies* **7**, 43-55.

Fölster, S. and S. Nyberg (1994): Entry and the Choice between Greenfield and Takeover: The Neglected Technological Determinants, IUI Working Paper no. 389, Stockholm: IUI.

Forsgren, M. (1989): Foreign Acquisitions: Internalization or Network Interdependency, in L. Hallén and J. Johanson (eds): *Networks of Relationships in International Industrial Marketing*, Greenwich: JAI Press.

Freeman, Nick L. (1994): Vietnam and China: Foreign Direct Investment Parallels, *Communist Economies and Economic Transformation* **6**, 75-98.

Froot, Kenneth A. and Jeremy C. Stein (1991): Exchange Rates and Foreign Direct Investment: An Imperfect Capital Markets Approach, *Quarterly Journal of Economics* **106**, 1191-217.

Frydman, Roman and Andrzej Rapaczynski (1993): *Privatisation in Eastern Europe: Is the State Withering Away*? Budapest and London: Central European University Press.

Frydman, Roman and Andrzej Rapaczynski (1997): Corporate Governance and the Political Effects of Privatisation, in S. Zecchini (ed).: *Lessons from the Economic Transition: Central and Eastern Europe in the 1990s*, Dordrecht: Kluwer.

Frye, Timothy and Andrei Shleifer (1997): The Invisible Hand and the Grabbing Hand, *American Economic Review* **87**, Papers and Proceedings, 354-8.

Gál, Peter (1993): Lage und Analyse der ausländischen Direktinvestitionen in Ungarn und die Folgen für den Technologie-Transfer, in J. Engelhard (ed.): *Ungarn im neuen Europa: Integration, Transformation, Markteintritts-strategien*, Wiesbaden: Gabler.

Gatignon, Hubert and Erin Anderson (1988): The Mulitinational Corporation Degree of Control over Subsidiaries: An Empirical Test of a Transaction Cost Explanation, *Journal of Law, Economics and Organisation* **4**, 305-66.

Gatling, Rene (1993): *Foreign Investment in Eastern Europe: Corporate Strategies and Experience*, Research Report written in association with Creditanstalt Bankverein, London: Economist Intelligence Unit.

Genco, Pietro, Siria Taurelli and Claudio Viezzoli (1993): Private investment in Central and Eastern Europe: Survey Results, Working Paper no. 7, European Bank for Reconstruction and Development, London.

Geringer, J. Michael and Louis Hebert (1991): Measuring Performance of International Joint Ventures, *Journal of International Business Studies* **22**, 249-63.

Ghoshal, Sumantra and Peter Moran (1996): Bad for Practice: A Critique of the Transaction Cost Theory, *Academy of Management Review* **21**, 13-47.

Ghoshal, Sumantra and Peter Moran (1996a): Value Creation by Firms, London Business School, Strategic Leadership Research Program, Working Paper no. 11.

Goldsbrough, David J. (1979): The Role of Foreign Direct Investment in the External Adjustment Process, *IMF Staff Papers* **26**, 725-55.

Gomes-Casseres, Benjamin (1989): Ownership Structures of Foreign Subsidiaries. Theory and Evidence, *Journal of Economic Behaviour and Organisation* **11**, 1-25.

Gomes-Casseres, Benjamin (1991): Firm Ownership Preferences and Host Government Restrictions. An Integral Approach, *Journal of International Business Studies* **21**, 1-22.

Graham, Edward M. (1975): *Oligopolistic Imitation and European Direct Investment in the United States*, DBA Dissertation, Harvard University.

Graham, Edward M. (1978): Transatlantic Investment by Multinational Firms: A Rivalistic Phenomenon, *Journal of Post Keynesian Economics* **1**, 82-99.

Graham, Edward M. (1985): Intra-Industry Direct Investment, Market Structure, Firm Rivalry, and Technological Performance, in A. Erdilek (ed.): *Multinationals as Mutual Invaders, Intra-Industry Direct Foreign Investment*, London: Croom-Helm.

Granovetter, Mark (1985): Economic Actions and Social Structure: The Problem of Embeddedness, *American Journal of Sociology* **91**, 481-510.

Gray, Cheryl and William Jarocz (1993): Foreign Investment Law in Central and Eastern Europe, Policy Research Working Paper no. 1111, The World Bank, Washington, DC, March.

Graziani, Giovanni (1998): Central-Eastern Europe in the Web of International Relocations: The Case of Italian Textile and Clothing Industry, in W. Andreff and X. Richet (eds): *Foreign Direct Investment in Transforming Economies*, forthcoming.

Greene, William H. (1993): *Econometric Analysis*, 2nd ed, New York: MacMillan.

Gregory, P. and P. Stuart (1988): *Soviet Economic Structure and Development*, New York: Harper and Row.

Grosse, R. and J. Behrman (1992): Theory in International Business, *Transnational Corporations* **1**, 93-116.

Grubaugh, Stephen G. (1987): Determinants of Direct Foreign Investment, *Review of Economics and Statistics* **69**, 149-52.

Grubert, Harry and Jack Mutti (1991): Taxes, Tariffs and Transfer Pricing in Multinational Corporation Decision Making, *Review of Economics and Statistics* **73**, 285-93.

Guerrieri, Paolo (1995): Technology, Structural Change and Trade Pattern of Eastern Europe in the Transition Period, EAEPE conference 'Transforming Economies and Societies: Towards and Institutional Theory of Economic Change' Krakow, Poland, 19-21 October.

Guisinger, Stephen E. et al. (1985): *Investment Incentives and Performance Requirements, Pattern of International Trade, Production and Investment*, New York: Praeger.

Gutman, Patrick (1992): The Opening of the USSR to Foreign Capital: from Concession during NEP to Joint Ventures under Perestroika, in M. Lavigne (ed.): *The Soviet Union and Eastern Europe in the Global Economy*, Cambridge: Cambridge University Press.

Gutman, Patrick (1993): Joint-Ventures in Eastern Europe and the Dynamics of Reciprocal Flows in East-West Direct Investments: Some New Perspectives, in P. Artisien, M. Rojec and M. Svetlicic (eds): *Foreign Investment in Central and Eastern Europe*, London: St. Martin's Press, pp. 54-81.

Haapanranta, Pertii (1996): Competition for Foreign Direct Investments, *Journal of Public Economics* **63**, 141-53.

Haiss, Peter and Gerhard Fink (1995): Western Strategies in Central Europe, in Petr Chadraba (ed.): *The Central and Eastern European Markets: Guideline for New Business Ventures*, New York: Haworth, pp. 37-46.

Hallwood, Paul (1990): *Transaction Costs and Trade between Multinational Corporations: A Study of Offshore Oil Production*, London: Unwin-Hyman.

Hamar, Judit (1994): Foreign Direct Investment and Privatisation in Hungary, *Acta Oeconomica* **16**, 183-212.

Hartman, D.G. (1979): Foreign Investment and Finance with Risk, *Quarterly Journal of Economics* **93**.

Harwitt, Eric (1993): Japanese Management Methods and Western Investment in Eastern Europe, *Columbia Journal of World Business*, Fall, 46-61.

Hausman, J. and D. McFadden (1984): Specification Tests for the Multinomial Logit Model, *Econometrica* **52**, 1219-40.

He, X. and Stephen E. Guisinger (1992): Does Tax Neutrality Matter? Fresh Funds Investment versus Reinvested Earnings, Academy of International Business, USA Northeast Chapter, Annual Proceedings, Baltimore.

Hedlund, Gunnar (1980): The Role of Foreign Subsidiaries in Strategic Decision Making in Swedish Multinational Corporations, *Strategic Management Journal* **1**, 23-26.

Helpman, Elhanan (1984): A Simple Theory of International Trade with Multinational Corporations, *Journal of Political Economy* **92**, 451-71.

Helpman, Elhanan (1985): Multinational Corporations and Trade Structure, *Review of Economic Studies* **52**, 443-57.

Helpman, Elhanan and Paul Krugman (1985): *Market Structure and Foreign Trade*, Cambridge: MIT Press.

Hennart, Jean-François (1982): *A Theory of Multinational Enterprise*: Ann Arbor, MI: University of Michigan Press.

Hennart, Jean-François (1988): Upstream Vertical Integration in the Aluminium and Tin Industries, A Comparative Study of the Choice between Market and Intrafirm Coordination, *Journal of Economic Behaviour and Organisation* **9**, 281-99.

Hennart, Jean-François (1988a): A Transaction Costs Theory of Equity Joint Ventures, *Strategic Management Journal* **9**, 361-74.

Hennart, Jean-François (1989): Can the 'New Forms of Investment' substitute for the 'Old Forms': A Transaction Cost Perspective, *Journal of International Business Studies* **20**, 211-34.

Hennart, Jean-François (1991): The Transaction Cost Theory of the Multinational Enterprise, in C.N. Pitelis and R. Sugden (eds): *The Nature of the Transnational Firm*, London: Routledge, pp. 81-116.

Hennart, Jean-François (1991a): The Transaction Cost Theory of Joint-Ventures: an Empirical Study of Japanese Subsidiaries in the United States, *Management Science* **37**, 483-97.

Hennart, Jean-François (1993): Explaining the Swollen Middle: Why most Transactions are a mix of 'Market' and 'Hierarchy', *Organization Science* **4**, 529-47.

Hennart, Jean-François (1995): Transaction Cost Theory and the Free-Standing Firm, in Roberto Schiatarella (ed.): *New Challenges for European and International Business* (proceedings, 22nd EIBA conference), Urbino, pp. 21-38.

Hennart, Jean-Francois, Jorma Larimo and Shih-Fen Chen (1995): *Does National Origin Affect the Propensity of Foreign Investors to Enter the United States through Acquisitions?*, Discussion Paper no. 189, Proceedings of the University of Vaasa.

Hennart, Jean-François and Jorma Larimo (1996): The Impact of Culture on the Strategy of Multinational Enterprises, Proceedings of the University of Vaasa, Discussion paper no. 185.

Hennart, Jean-François and Young-Ryeoul Park (1993): Greenfield vs. Acquisition: The Strategy of Japanese Investors in the United States, *Management Science* **39**, 1054-70.

Hennart, Jean-François and Young-Ryeoul Park (1994): Location, Governance and Strategic Determinants of Japanese Manufacturing Investment in the United States, *Strategic Management Journal* **15**, 419-36.

Hill, Charles W. (1995): National Institutional Structures, Transaction Cost Economizing and Competitive Advantage: The Case of Japan, *Organization Science* **6**, 118-31.

Hill, Hal (1990): Foreign Investment and East Asian Economic Development, *Asian Pacific Economic Literature* **4**, no. 2, 21-58.

Hirsch, Seev (1976): An International Trade and Investment Theory of the Firm, *Oxford Economic Papers* **28**, 258-70.

Hitt, Michael A., Robert E. Hoskisson and R. Duane Ireland (1994): A Mid-Range Theory of Interactive effects of International and Product Diversification on Innovation and Performance, *Journal of Management* **20**, 297-326.

Hoesch, Donata and Hartmut Lehmann (1994): Ostöffnung und Reformpolitik in den ostmitteleuropäischen Staaten: Auswirkungen auf die Wirtschaft Bayerns, *Ifo Schnelldienst* no. 30/94, 14-23.

Hofstede, Geert (1980): *Cultures Consequences: International Differences in Work-Related Values* Beverly Hills, CA: Sage.

Hood, Neil and Stephen Young (1983): *Multinational Investment Strategies in the British Isles: A Study of MNE's in the Assisted Areas and the Republic of Ireland,* London: HSMO.

Hood, Neil and Stephen Young (1994): The internationalisation of business and the challenge of East European Development, in P.J. Buckley and P.N. Ghauri (eds): *The Economics of Change in East and Central Europe,* London: Academic Press.

Hooley, Graham, Tony Cox, David Shipley, John Fahy, Jozef Beracs and Kristina Kolos (1996): Foreign Direct Investment in Hungary: Resource Acquisition and Domestic CompetitiveAdvantage, *Journal of International Business Studies* **27**, 683-709.

Horst, Thomas (1972): Firm and Industry Determinants of the Decision to Invest Abroad: An Empirical Study, *Review of Economics and Statistics* **54**, 258-66.

Horstmann, Ignatius and James R. Markusen (1987a): Strategic Investments and the Development of Multinationals, *International Economic Review* **28**, 109-21.

Horstmann, Ignatius and James R. Markusen (1987b): Licensing versus Direct Investment: A Model of Internalization by the Multinational Enterprise, *Canadian Journal of Economics* **20**, 464-81.

Horstmann, Ignatius and James R. Markusen (1992): Endogenous Market Structures in International Trade: Natura Facit Saltum, *Journal of International Economics* **32**, 109-29.

Horstmann, Ignatius and James R. Markusen (1996): Exploring New Markets: Direct Investment, Contractual Relationships, and the Multinational Enterprise, *International Economic Review* **37**, 1-19.

Hosková, Adela (1992): Foreign Capital in the CSFR, *Prague Economic Papers* **3**, 253-62.

Hosmer, D.W. and S. Lemeshow (1989): *Applied Logistic Regression,* New York: Wiley.

Hu, Michael Y. and Haiyang Chen (1993): Foreign Ownership in Chinese Joint-Ventures: A Transaction Cost Analysis, *Journal of Business Research* **26**, 149-60.

Hughes, Gordon and Paul Hare (1992): Industrial Restructuring in Eastern Europe: Policies and Prospects, *European Economic Review* **36**, 670-76.

Hughes, Kirsty (1995): European Enlargement, Competitiveness and Integration, Discussion paper no. 17, CIS-Middle Europe Centre, London Business School, February.

Hultman, Charles W. and Randolph L. McGee (1988): Factors Influencing Foreign Investment in the US, 1970-1986, *Revista Internazionale di Scienzi Economiche e Commerciali* **35**, 1061-66.

Hunya, Gabor (1992): Foreign Direct Investment and Privatisation in Central and Eastern Europe, *Communist Economics and Economic Transformation* **4**, 501-11.

Hunya, Gabor (1996): Foreign Direct Investment in Hungary: A Key Element of Economic Modernization, Research Report no. 226, Vienna Institute for Comparative Economic Studies (WIIW), February.

Hymer, Stephen H. (1976): *The International Operations of National Firms: A Study of Direct Foreign Investment* (PhD-theses 1960), published Cambridge, Mass.

IMF, World Bank, OECD and EBRD (1991): *A Study of the Soviet Economy*, Paris: OECD.

Itagaki, Takao (1981): The Theory of the Multinational Firm und Exchange Rate Uncertainty, *Canadian Journal of Economics* **14**, 276-97.

Ito, Kiyohiko and Vladimir Pucik (1993): R&D Spending, Domestic Competition and Export Performance of Japanese Manufacturing Firms, *Strategic Management Journal* **14**, 61-75.

Jacquemin, A. (1989): International and Multinational Strategic Behaviour, *Kyklos* **42**, 495-514.

Jemison, David B. and Sim B. Sitkin (1986): Corporate Acquisitions: A Process Perspective, *Academy of Management Review* **11**, 145-63.

Jansson, Hans (1993): *Transnational Corporations in Southeast Asia*, Aldershot: Elgar.

Johanson, Jan and Jan-Erik Vahlne (1977): The Internationalization Process of the Firm, A Model of Knowledge Development and Increasing Foreign Market Commitment, *Journal of International Business Studies,* Spring/Summer.

Johanson, Jan and Jan-Erik Vahlne (1990): The Mechanism of Internationalisation, *International Marketing Review* **7**, no. 4, 11-24.

Johanson, Jan and Finn Wiedersheim-Paul (1975): The Internationalization of the Firm - Four Swedish Cases, *Journal of Management Studies* **12**, 305-22.

Johnson, Simon and Gary W. Loveman (1995): *Starting Over in Eastern Europe*, Cambridge: Harvard Business School Press.

Kaminski, Bartlomiej, Zhen Kun Wang and L. Alan Winters (1996): *Foreign Trade in Transition: The International Environment and Domestic Policy*, Studies of Economics in Transformation no. 20, Washington, DC: World Bank.

Kateseli, Louka T. (1991): Foreign Direct Investment and Trade Interlinkages in the 1990: Experience and Prospects of Developing Countries, CEPR Discussion paper, no. 687, London: CEPR.

Kay, Neil M. (1991): Multinational Enterprise as Strategic Choice: Some Transaction Cost Perspectives, in C.N. Pitelis and R. Sugden (eds): *The Nature of the Transnational Firms*, Routledge, pp. 137-54.

Kay, Neil M. (1992): Markets, False Hierarchies and the Evolution of the Modern Corporation, *Journal of Economic Behaviour and Organisation* **17**, p. 315-33.

Kekič, Laza (1996): Assessing and Measuring Progress in the Transition, *EIU CountryForecast: Economies in Transition*, 2nd quarter 1996.

Kim, W. Chan and Peter Hwang (1992): Global Strategy and Multinationals' Entry Mode Choice, *Journal of International Business Studies*, **23**, 29-53.

Kindleberger, Charles P. (1969): *American Business Abroad*, New Haven: Yale University Press.

Kindleberger, Charles P. (1984): *Multinational Excursions*, Cambridge, MA: MIT Press.

Kiss, Judit (1995): Privatisation and Foreign Capital in the Hungarian Food Industry, *Eastern European Economics* **4**, 24-37.

Klavens, Jonathan and Anthony Zamparutti (1995): *Foreign Direct Investments and Environment in Central and Eastern Europe*, Washinton, DC: The World Bank.

Klein, Benjamin, Robert G. Crawford and Armen Alchian (1978): Vertical Integration, Appropriable Rents and the Competitive Contracting Process, *Journal of Law and Economics* **21**, 297-336.

Klein, Michael W. and Eric Rosengren (1994): The Real Exchange Rate and Foreign Direct Investment in the United States: Relative Wealth vs. Relative Wage Effects, *Journal of International Economics* **36**, no. 3-4 (May), 373-89.

Knickerbocker, F.T. (1973): *Oligopolistic Reaction and Multinational Enterprise*, Boston.

Knight, Ben K.G. and David Webb (1997): Investing in Poland and the Czech Republic: The Experience So Far, *European Management Journal* **15**, no. 3, June.

Knight, Frank (1929): *Risk, Uncertainty and Profit*, Boston.

Kobrin, Stephen J. (1982): *Managing Political Risk: Strategic Response to Environmental Change*, Berkeley: University of California Press.

Kobrin, Stephen J. (1987): Testing the Bargaining Hypothesis in the Manufacturing Sector in Developing Countries, *International Organisation*, 609-38.

Kogut, Bruce (1983): Foreign Direct Investment as a Sequential Process, in C.P. Kindleberger and D. Audretsch (eds): *The Multinational Corporation in the 1980's*, Cambridge, MA: MIT Press.

Kogut, Bruce (1988): Joint-Ventures: Theoretical and Empirical Perspectives, *Strategic Management Journal* 9, 3-322.

Kogut, Bruce (1996): Direct Investment, Experimentation, and Corporate Governance in Transition Economies, in: R. Frydman, C.W. Gray and A. Rapazynski (eds): *Corporate Governance in Central Europe and Russia*, vol. 1, London and Budapest: Central European University Press, pp. 293-332.

Kogut, Bruce and Sea Jin Chang (1996): Platform Investments and Volatile Exchange Rates: Direct Investment in the US by Japanese Electronic Companies, *Review of Economics and Statistics*, November.

Kogut, Bruce and Nalin Kulatilaka (1996): Direct Investment, Hysteresis, and Real Exchange Rate Volatility, *Journal of Japanese and Internatioanl Economics* 10, 12-36.

Kogut, Bruce and Harbir Singh (1987): Entering the United States by Joint-Venture: Industry Structure and Competitive Rivalry, in F. Contractor and P. Lorange (eds): *Cooperative Strategies in International Business*, Lexington, MA: Lexington Press.

Kogut, Bruce and Harbir Singh (1988): The Effect of National Culture on the Choice of Entry Mode, *Journal of International Business Studies* 19, no. 3, 411-32.

Kogut, Bruce and Udo Zander (1992): Knowledge of teh Firm, Compinative Capabilities, and the Replication of Technology, *Organization Science* 3, 381-97.

Kogut, Bruce and Udo Zander (1993): Knowledge of the Firm and the Evolutionary Theory of the Multinational Corporation, *Journal of International Business Studies*, 625-45.

Kogut, Bruce and Udo Zander (1995): Knowledge, Market Failure and the Multinational Enterprise: A Reply, *Journal of International Business Studies* 26, 417-26.

Kohlhagen, Steven W. (1977): Exchange Rate Changes, Profitability, and Direct Foreign Investment, *Southern Economic Journal* 44, 43-52.

Kojima, Kiyoshi (1978): *Direct Foreign Investment*, London: Croom Helm.

Kojima, Kiyoshi and Terutomo Ozawa (1984): Micro- and Macro-Economic Models of Direct Foreign Investment: Towards a Synthesis, *Hitotsubashi Journal of Economics* 25, 1-20.

Konings, Jozef (1996): Foreign Direct Investment in Transition Economies, Leuven Institute for Central and East European Studies, Working Paper 56/1996.

Kornai, Janos (1986): The Hungarian Reform Process: Visions, Hopes and Reality, *Journal of Economic Literature* **24**, 1687-737.

Kravis, Irving B. and Robert P. Lipsey (1982): The Location of Overseas Production and Production for Export by US Multinational Firms, *Journal of International Economics* **12**, 201-23.

Krugman, Paul (1983): The 'New Theories' of International Trade and the Multinational Enterprise, in: D.B.A. Audretsch and C.P. Kindleberger, eds.: *The Multinational Corporation in the 1980's*, Cambrigde, MA: MIT Press.

Krugman, Paul (1991): *Geography and Trade*, Cambridge, MA: MIT Press.

Krugman, Paul (1992): A Dynamic Spatial Model, National Bureau of Economic Research, Working Paper no. 4219.

Krugman, Paul and Anthony Venebles (eds) (1994): *The Location of Economic Activity: New Theories and New Evidence*, London: Center for Economic Policy Research.

Kubista, Vaclav (1995): Foreign Capital in Industrial Enterprises in the Czech Republic, in *Joint Ventures in Transformation Countries in the Context of Overall Investment Strategies of their Partners*, ACE Research project, Barcelona: Grup d'Anàlisi de las Transició Econòmica, pp. 225-68.

Kuhn, Thomas S. (1962): *The Structure of Scientific Revolutions*, University of Chicago Press.

Kumar, N. (1987): Intangible Assets, Internalization and Foreign Production, Direct Investment and Licensing in India, *Weltwirtschaftliches Archiv* **123**, 325-45.

Kumar, N. (1990): *Multinational Enterprises in India*, London: Routledge.

Kurz, Constance and Volker Wittke (1997): *From 'Supply Base Driven' to 'Market Driven' Integration: Patterns of Integrating Central-Estern European Economies by using their Industrial Capacities,* paper presented at workshop 'Will there be a Unified European Economy', Kreisky Forum and BRIE, Vienna, June.

Lall, Senyaja (1991): Direct Foreign Investment in South East Asia by NIEs: Trends and Prospects, *Banca Nazionale del Lavorno Quarterly Review* **179**, 463-80.

Lall, Senyaja (1996): *Learning from the Asian Tigers: Studies in Technology and Industrial Policy*, London: MacMillan.

Lane, Sarah J. (1994): The Pattern of Foreign Direct Investment and Joint Ventures in Hungary, *Communist Economies and Economic Transformation* **6**, 341-65.

Lane, Sarah J. (1995): Capitalising on Capitalism: US Investment in Transition Economies, Working Paper no. 95-16, School of Management, Boston University, April.

Langlois, Richard N. (1992): Transaction-Cost Economics in Real Time, *Industrial and Corporate Change* **1**, 99-127.

Langlois, Richard N. (1995): Transaction Costs, Production Costs, and the Passage of Time, paper presented at the 22nd EARIE Conference in Juan-les-Pins, September.

Lankes, Hans-Peter and Anthony Venebles (1996): Foreign Direct Investment in Economic Transition: The Changing Pattern of Investments, *Economics of Transition* **4**, 331-47.

Lankes, Hans-Peter and Anthony J. Venebles (1996a): Foreign Direct Investment in Eastern Europe and the Former Soviet Union: Results from a Survey of Investors, Working Paper, EBRD.

Larimo, Jorma (1985): The Foreign Direct Investment Behaviour of Finnish Companies, paper presented at the 11th EIBA conference, Glasgow, December.

Laurila, Juhani and Inkeri Hirvensalo (1996): Direct Investment from Finland to Eastern Europe, Results of the 1995 Bank of Finland Survey, *Review of Economies in Transition* no. 5, 5-25.

Lecraw, Donald J. (1984): Bargaining Power, Ownership and the Profitability of Transnational Corporations, *Journal of International Business Studies* **15**, 27-43.

Lecraw, Donald J. and A.J. Morrison (1991): Transnational Corporation - Host Country Relations: A Framework for Analysis, South Carolina Essays in International Business, no. 9.

Lee, Chung H. (1990): Direct Foreign Investment, Structural Adjustment, and International Division of Labor: A 'Dynamic Macroeconomic theory of Direct Foreign Investment', *Hitotsubashi Journal of Economics* **31**, no. 2, 61-72.

Lemoine, Francoise (1997): Integrating Central and Eastern Europe in the European Trade and Production Network, paper presented at the Kreisky Forum for International Dialog, Workshop on'Will There be a Unified European Economy', Vienna, June.

Li, Jiatao and Stephen Guisinger (1991): Comparative Business Failures of Foreign-controlled Firms in the United States, *Journal of International Business Studies* **22**, 209-44.

Li, Jiatao and Stephen Guisinger (1992): The Globalization of Service Multinationals in the Triad Nations: Japan, Europe and North America, *Journal of International Business Studies* **23**.

Lim, D. (1983): Fiscal Incentives and Direct Foreign Investment in Less Developed Countries, *Journal of Development Studies* **19**, 207-12.

Lipton, David and Jeffrey Sachs (1991): Privatization in Eastern Europe: The Case of Poland, in Vittorio Corbo, Fabrizio Coricelli and Jan Bossak: *Reforming Central and Eastern European Economies: Initial Results and Challenges*, Washington, DC: World Bank.

Lizondo, J. Saúl (1991): Foreign Direct Investment, in: *Determinants and Systemic Consequences of international capital flows*, IMF Occasional Paper no. 77, Washington, DC: IMF, 68-82.

Logue, Dennis E. and Thomas D. Willet (1977): The Effects of Exchange Rate Adjustments on International Investment, in P.B. Clark, D.E. Logue and R.E. Sweeny (eds): *The Effects of Exchange Rate Adjustment*, Washington, DC, pp. 137-150.

Loree, David W. and Stephen E. Guisinger (1995): Policy and Non-Policy Determinants of US Equity Foreign Direct Investment, *Journal of International Business Studies* **26**, 281-300.

Love, David L. (1995): Knowledge, Market Failure and the Multinational Enterprise: A Theoretical Note, *Journal of International Business Studies* **26**, 399-408.

Luostarinen, Reijo (1979): *Internationalization of the Firm: An Empirical Study of the Internationalization of Firms with Small and Open Domestic Markets with special Emphasis on Lateral Rigidity as a Behavioural Characteristic in Strategic Decision Making* Helsinki: Helsinki School of Economics, 3rd ed 1989.

Lyles, Marjorie A. (1993): An Evaluation of the Private Sector in Hungary: A Study of Small/Medium Joint Ventures and Enterprises, mimeo, Indiana University Business School.

Lyles, Marjorie A. and Inga S. Baird (1994): Performance of Joint-Ventures in Two Eastern European Countries: The Case of Hungary and Poland, *Management International Review* 34, p. 313-329.

Lyles, Marjorie A., Nancy M. Carter and Inga S. Baird (1996): New Ventures in Hungary: The Impact of US Partners, *Management International Review* **36**, 355-70.

Lyles, Marjorie A. and Jane E. Salk (1995): Knowledge Acquisition from Foreign Parents in International Joint Ventures: An Empirical Examination in the Hungarian Context, *Journal of International Business Studies* **27**, 877-903.

McCulloch, Rachel (1988): International Competition in Services, in M. Feldstein (ed.): *The United States in the World Economy*, Chicago: University of Chicago Press.

McFetridge, Donald G. (1995): Knowledge, Market Failure and the Multinational Enterprise: A Comment, *Journal of International Business Studies* **26**, 409-16.

McManus, J.C. (1972): The Theory of the Multinational Firm, in G. Pacquet (ed.): *The Multinational Firm and the Nation State*, Toronto: Collier, MacMillan.

McMillan, Carl H. (1991): *Canada-USSR Joint-Ventures: A Survey and Analytical Review*, Toronto: Canada-USSR Business Council.

McMillan, Carl H. (1992): Foreign Direct Investment Flow to the Soviet Union and Eastern Europe: Nature, Magnitude and International Implications, *Journal of Development Planning* **23**, 305-25.

McMillan, Carl H. (1993): The Role of Foreign Direct Investment in the Transition from Planned to Market Economies, *Transnational Corporations* 2, p. 97-119.

McMillan, Carl H. (1993b): Foreign Direct Investment in the Soviet Union, 1987-91: Legacies for the Successor States, in P. Artisien and Y. Adjubei (eds): *Foreign Investment in Russia and other Soviet Successor States*, London: MacMillan Press.

McMillan, Carl H. (1994): Foreign Investment in Russia: Soviet Legacies and Post-Soviet Prospects, Occasional Paper no. 5, Centre for Research on Canadian-Russian Relations at Carleton University, Ottawa.

Maddala G.S. (1983): *Limited Dependent and Qualitative Variables in Econometrics*, Cambridge: Cambridge University Press.

Malecki, E.J. (1991): The R&D Location Decision of the Firm and 'Creative' Regions - A Survey, *Technovation* **6**, 205-22.

Malmberg, Anders, Örjan Sölvell and Ivo Zander (1996): Spatial Clustering, Local accumulation of Knowledge and Firm Competitiveness, *Geografiska Annalen* (Sweden).

Mansfield, Edwin, Anthony Romeo and Samuel Wagner (1979): Foreign Trade and US Research and Development, *Review of Economics and Statistics*, February, 49-57.

Marinov, Marin A. and Svetla T. Marinova (1997): Privatisation and Foreign Direct Investment in Bulgaria: Present Characteristics and Future Trends, *Communist Economies and Economic Transformation* **9**, no. 1.

Markusen, James R. (1984): Multinationals, Multi-plant Economies and the Gain from Trade, *Journal of International Economics* **16**, 205-16.

Markusen, James R. (1991): The Theory of Multinational Enterprise: A Common Analytical Framework, in Eric D. Ramstatter (ed.): *Direct Foreign Investment in Asia's Developing Economies and Structural Change in the Asia-Pacific Region*, Boulder, CO: Westview Press.

Markusen, James R. (1995): The Boundaries of Multinational Enterprises and the Theory of International Trade, *Journal of Economic Perspectives* **9**, no. 2, 169-89.

Markusen, James R. (1997): Trade versus Investment Liberalization, mimeo, Universitat Pompeu Fabra (Spain), March.

Markusen, James R. and Anthony J. Venebles (1995): The Increased Importance of Multinationals in North American Economic Relationships: A Convergence Hypothesis, in W.J. Ethier and V. Grilli (eds): *The New Transatlantic Economy*, London: Cambridge University Press.

Markusen, James R., Anthony J. Venebles, Denise Eby Konan and Kevin H. Zhang (1996): A Unified Treatment of Horizontal Direct Investment, Vertical Direct Investment, and the Pattern of Trade in Goods and Services, NBER working paper.

Marshall, Alfred (1890/1916): *Principles of Economics: An Introductory Volume*, 7th ed, London: MacMillan.

Marton, Katherin (1993) Foreign Direct Investment in Hungary, *Transnational Corporations* 2, 111-34.

Mascarenhaas, Briance (1986): International Strategies of Non-Dominant Firms, *Journal of International Business Studies* 17, no. 1, 1-25.

Masten, Scott, James Meehan and Edward Snyder (1991): The Costs of Organisation, *Journal of Law, Economics and Organisation* 7, 1-25.

Merton, Robert K. (1968): *Social Theory and Social Structure*, New York: Free Press.

Meschi, Xavier (1995): Structure and Organisational Performance of International Joint-Ventures Based in Hungary, in Roberto Schiattarella (ed.): *New Challenges for European and International Business*, Proceeding of the 21 EIBA Conference, Urbino, vol. 1, pp. 109-130.

Meyer, Klaus E. (1994): Direct Foreign Investment in Central and Eastern Europe: Understanding the Statistical Evidence, London Business School, CIS-Middle Europe Centre Discussion Paper no. 12, June.

Meyer, Klaus E. (1995): Foreign Direct Investment in the Early Years of Economic Transition, A Survey, *Economics of Transition* 3, 301-20.

Meyer, Klaus E. (1995a): Direct Foreign Investment in Eastern Europe: The Role of Labour Costs, *Comparative Economic Studies* 37, 69-88.

Meyer, Klaus E. (1995b): Business Operations of British and German Companies with the Economies in Transition: First Results of a Questionnaire Survey, London Business School, CIS-Middle Europe Centre, Discussion Paper no. 19, July.

Meyer, Klaus E. (1996): Direct Foreign Investment in East Asia and in Eastern Europe: A Comparative Analysis, Discussion Paper no. 34, CISME-Centre, London Business School; forthcoming in P. Artisien-Maksimenko and M. Rojec (eds.): *Foreign Investment and Privatisation in Eastern Europe*, MacMillan.

Meyer, Klaus E. (1997): Research on Foreign Direct Investment in Central and Eastern Europe: What have we got and where do we go? in Jorma Larimo and Tuija Mainela (eds): *Choice and Management of Entry Strategies in International Business*, Vaasa: Vaasan Yliopisto.

Meyer, Klaus E. (1998): Enterprise Transformation and Foreign Investment in Eastern Europe, *Journal of East-West Business*, forthcoming: May/June.

Meyer, Klaus E. (1998a): On the Impact of FDI on Economic Transition and Development, in: Jorma Larimo (eds.): title t.b.a., Vaasa: Vaasan Yliopisto, forthcoming.

Meyer, Klaus E., Tim Ambler and Chris Styles (1994): Study on Outward Direct Investment: Survey of the Literature, report prepared for the UK Department of Trade and Industry, London Business School.

Meyer, Klaus E. and Saul Estrin (1997): Privatization Acquisition and Direct Foreign Investment: Who Buys State-owned Enterprises? *MOST-MOCT Economic Policy in Transitional Economies* 7, 159-72.

Meyer, Klaus E. and Inger Bjerg Møller (1998): Manging Deep Restructuring: Danish Experiences in Eastern Germany, Working Paper no. 10, Center for East European Studies, Copenhagen Business School, February.

Meyer, Klaus E. and Peter Rühmann (1993): Direktinvestitionen im Ausland, *Das Wirtschaftsstudium* 22, 62-7.

Michailova, Snejina (1997): Interface between Western and Russian Management Attitudes: Implications for Organizational Change, Working Paper no. 8, Center for East European Studies, Copenhagen Business School, June.

Miles, R.E. and C. Snow (1978): *Organizational Strategy, Structure and Process*, New York: McGraw-Hill.

Miller, Kent D. (1992): A Framework for Integrated Risk Management in International Business, *Journal of International Business Studies* 23, 311-31.

Millner, Chris and Eric J. Pentecost (1992): Locational Advantage and US Foreign Investment in UK Manufacturing, mimeo, Loughborough University.

Mirow, Michael (1996): Kooperations- und Akquisitionsstrategien in Osteuropa am Beispiel der Elektroindustrie, *Zeitschrift für betriebswirtschaftliche Forschung* 48, 934-46.

Möller, Kristian (1996): *Investieren in die Ernährungswirtschaft Osteuropas: Ein Beurteilungsrahmen zur Risikoanalyse*, Köln: Verlag DHI (Diss., University of Kiel).

Möllering, Jürgen, Radovan Rádl and Jörg-Mark Zimmermann (1994): *Deutsche Direktinvestitionen in der Tschechischen Republik: Motive, Erfahrungen, Perspektiven, Ergebnisse einer Umfrage*; editor: German-Czech Chamber of Commerce, Bielefeld: Bertelsmann.

Møllgaard, H. Peter (1997): Danfoss Compressors' Investment in Slovenia: Motives and Obstacles: Working paper no. 7-97, Institut for Nationaløkonomi, Copenhagen Business School.

Monteverdi, Kirk and David J. Teece (1982): Supplier Switching Costs and Vertical Integration in the Automobile Industry, *Rand Journal of Economics*, 206-13.

Motta, Massimo (1992): Multinational Firms and the Tariff-Jumping Argument: A Game Theoretic Analysis with some Unconventional Conclusions, *European Economic Review* 36, 1557-71.

Motta, Massimo (1994): International Trade and Investments in a Vertically Differentiated Industry, *International Journal of Industrial Organisation* 12, 179-96.

Motta, Massimo and George Norman (1996): Does Economic Integration Cause Foreign Direct Investment, *International Economic Review* **37**, 757-84.

Mundell, Robert A. (1957): International Trade and Factor Mobility, *American Economic Review* **47**, 321-35.

Murrell, Peter (1992): The Evolution in Economic and the Economic Reform of the Centrally Planned Economies, in C.C. Clague and G. Rausser (eds): *The Emergence of Market Economies in Eastern Europe*, Cambridge, MA: Blackwell, pp. 35-53.

Murrell, Peter (1992a): Comment: Multinational Corporations in the East European Transformation, in: M.W. Klein and P.J.J. Welfens: *Multinationals in the new Europe and Global Trade*, Berlin: Springer, pp. 153-161.

Murrell, Peter (1996): How Far has the Transition Progressed? *Journal of Economic Perspectives* **10**, no. 2, 25-44.

Mutinelli, Marco (1994): Italian Industrial Foreign Direct Investment in Central and Eastern Europe, 20th EIBA conference, Warsaw 11-13 December.

Myant, Martin (1997): Foreign Direct Investment and Industrial Restructuring in the Czech Republic, paper presented at the workshop 'Central and Eastern Europe: Institutional Change and Industrial Development, Aalborg University, Tannishus, November.

Mygind, Niels (1994): *Societies in Transition*, Copenhagen Business School: Institute of Economics.

Mygind, Niels (1997): The Economic Performance of Employee-owned Enterprises in the Baltic Countries, working paper no. 6, Center for East European Studies, Copenhagen Business School, May.

Mygind, Niels (1997a): The Internationalization of the Baltic Economies, paper presented at the workshop 'Will there be a Unified European Economy?', Kreisky Forum and BRIE, Vienna, June.

Narula, Rajneesh (1995): *Multinational Investment and Economic Structure: Globalisation and Competitiveness*, London: Routledge.

National Economic Research Associates, NERA (1991): Foreign Direct Investment to the Countries of Central and Eastern Europe, mimeo.

Naujoks, Petra and Klaus-Dieter Schmidt (1994): Outward Processing in Central and East European Transition Countries: Issues and Results from German Statistics, Kiel Working Papers no. 631, Kiel Institute of World Economics.

Newfarmer, Richard S., ed. (1985): *Profits, Progress and Poverty*, Notre Dame: University Notre Dame Press.

Nigh, Douglas (1985): The Effect of Political Events on United States Direct Foreign Investment: A Pooled Time-series Cross-Sectional Analysis. *Journal of International Business Studies* **16**, no. 1, 1-14.

Nigh, Douglas (1986): Political Events and Foreign Direct Investments: An Empirical Examination, *Managerial and Decision Economics* **7**, 99-106.

Nitsch, Detlev, Paul Beamish and Shige Makino (1996): Entry Mode and Performance of Japanese FDI in Western Europe, *Management International Review* **36**, 27-43.

Nordström, Kjell (1991): *The Internationalization Process of the Firm - Searching for New Patterns and Explanations*, Stockholm: Institute of International Business.

Nuti, D. Mario (1994): Mass Privatisation: Costs and Benefits of Instant Capitalism, Discussion Paper nr. 9, CIS-Middle Europe Centre, London Business School, May.

Nuti, D. Mario (1995): Inflation, Interest and Exchange Rates in Transition, London Business School, CIS-Middle Europe Centre, Discussion Paper no. 22, December.

Nuti, D. Mario and Richard Portes (1993): Central Europe: The Way Forward, in Richard Portes (ed.): *Economic Transformation in Central Europe* London: CEPR.

Organisation for Economic Cooperation and Development, OECD (1993): *Establishing a Reporting System for Direct Foreign Investment Statistics*, Proceedings of a Technical Meeting, Paris: OECD, Centre for Co-operation with European Economies in Transition.

Organisation for Economic Cooperation and Development, OECD (1993a): *DFI relations between OECD and the Dynamic Asian Economies*, Paris: OECD.

Organisation for Economic Cooperation and Development, OECD (1994): *Assessing Investment Opportunities in Economies in Transition*, Paris: OECD.

Organisation for Economic Cooperation and Development, OECD (1995): *Direct Foreign Investment Handbook 1995*, Paris: OECD.

Ohmae, Keiichi (1989): The Global Logic of Strategic Alliances, *Harvard Business Review*, March, 143-55.

O'Sullivan, Patrick (1993): An Assessment of Ireland's Export-Led Growth Strategy via Foreign Direct Investment: 1960-1980, *Weltwirtschaftliches Archiv* **129**, 140-58.

Ouchi, William G. (1980): Markets, Bureaucracies, and Clans, *Administrative Science Quarterly* **25**, 129-42.

Ozawa, Terutomo (1979a): *Multinationalism, Japanese Style*, Princeton, N.J.

Ozawa, Terutomo (1979b): International Investment and Industrial Structure: New Theoretical Implications from the Japanese Experience, *Oxford Economic Papers* **31**, 72-92.

Ozawa, Terutomo (1992): Foreign Direct Investment and Economic Development, *Transnational Corporations* **1**, 27-54.

Padmanabhan, Prasad and Kang Rae Cho (1996): Ownership Strategy for a Foreign Affiliate: An Empirical Investigation of Japanese Firms, *Management International Review* **36**, 45-65.

Padmanabhan, Prasad and Kang Rae Cho (1996a): What Role does Decision Specific Experience Play in Foreign Ownership and Eastablishment Mode Strategies of Multinational Firms? An Empirical Investigation of Japanese Firms, AIB conference, Banff, September.

Pain, Nigel (1993): An Econometric Analysis of Foreign Direct Investment in the United Kingdom, *Scottish Journal of Political Economy* **40**, 1-23.

Pain, Nigel (1996): Continental drift: European Integration and the Location of UK Foreign Direct Investment, National Institute of Economic and Social Research, Discussion paper No. 107, November.

Papánek, Gábor (1995): A Comparison of Basic Data on the Performance of Enterprises with and without Foreign Equity Capital Participation, in: Joint Ventures in Transformation Countries in the Context of Overall Investment Strategies of their Partners, ACE Research project, Barcelona: Grup d'Anàlisi de las Transició Econòmica, pp. 269-88.

Parker, Stephen, Gavin Tritt and Wing Thye Woo (1997): Some Lessons Learned from the Comparison of Transition in Asia and Eastern Europe, in W.T. Woo, S. Parker and J.D. Sachs (eds): *Economies in Transition: Comparing Asia and Europe*, Cambridge: MIT Press, pp. 3-16.

Parkhe, Arvind (1993): 'Messy' Research, Methodological Predispositions, and Theory Development in International Joint Ventures, *Academy of Management Review* **18**, 227-58.

Pavitt, Keith (1985): Technology Transfer Among the Industrially Advanced Countries: An Overview, in N. Rosenberg and C. Frischtak (eds): *International Technology Transfer: Concepts, Measures, and Comparisons*, New York: Praeger.

Pavitt, Keith (1987): International Patterns of Technological Accumulation, in N. Hood and J.-E. Vahlne (eds): *Strategies in Global Competition*, London.

Pellegrin, Julie (1997): *Outward Processing Traffic between the EU and the CEECs*, paper presented at workshop 'Will there be a Unified European Economy', Kreisky Forum and BRIE, Vienna, June.

Penrose, Edith (1959): *The Theory of the Growth of the Firm*, 3rd edition with new preface, London: Oxford University Press, 1995.

Pfeffer, Jeffrey and G.R. Salancik (1978): *The External Control of Organizations*, New York: Harper & Row.

Pfohl, Hans-Christian, Ferenc Trenton, Stephan L.K. Freichel, Melinda Hegedüs and Volker Schultz (1992): Joint Ventures in Ungarn, *Die Betriebswirtschaft* **52**, 655-73.

Pindyck, Robert S. (1991): Irreversibility, Uncertainty and Investment, *Journal of Economic Literature* **26**, 1110-48.

Pinto, Brian, Marek Belka and Stefan Krajewski (1993): Transforming State Enterprises in Poland: Microeconomic Evidence in Adjustment, *Brookings Papers of Economic Activity*, 213-70.

Pinto, Brian and Sweder van Wijnbergen (1994): Ownership Structure and Corporate Control in Poland: The Myth of the Failing State Sector, mimeo, London School of Economics, February.

Pitelis, Christos N. and Roger Sugden (eds) (1991): *The Nature of the Transnational Firms,* London: Routledge.

Pohl, Gerhard, Robert E. Andersen, Stijn Claessens and Simeon Djankov (1997): Privatization and Restructuring in Central and Eastern Europe, World Bank Technical Paper no. 368, Washington, DC: World Bank..

Polanyi, M. (1958): *Personal Knowledge: Towards a Post-critical Philosophy,* Chicago: University of Chicago Press.

Portes, Richard (1994): Transformation Traps, *Economic Journal* **104**, 1178-89.

Porter, Michael E. (1990), *The Competitive Advantage of Nations*, London: MacMillan.

Prahalad, C.K. and Gary Hamel (1990): The Core Competence and the Corporation, *Harvard Business Review*, May, 71-91.

Puffer, Sheila et al (1996): *Business and Management in Russia*, Cheltenham, UK and Lyme, US: Elgar.

Puffer, Sheila M. and Daniel J. McCarthy (1995): Finding the Common Ground in Russian and American Business Ethics, *California Management Review* **37**, no. 2, 29-46.

Pugel, Thomas A. (1981): The Determinants of Foreign Direct Investment: An Analysis of US Manufacturing Industries, *Managerial and Decision Economics* **2**, 220-28.

Pye, Robert B.K. (1997): Foreign Direct Investment in Central Europe (The Czech Republic, Hungary, Poland, Romania and Slovakia): Results from a Survey of Major Western Investors, City University Business School, Finance Working Paper: A.97/1, London, April.

Quaisser, Wolfgang (1995): Ausländische Direktinvestitionen im polnischen Transformationsprozeß, Working Paper no. 184, Osteuropa-Institut München, October.

Radice, Hugo (1995): Organizing Markets in Central and Eastern Europe: Competition, Governance and the Role of Foreign Capital, in E.J. Dittrich, G. Schmidt and R. Whitley (eds): *Industrial Transformation in Europe,* London et al.: Sage Publications.

Radice, Hugo (1995a): The Role of Foreign Direct Investment in the Transformation of Eastern Europe, in H.J. Chang and P. Nolan (eds): *The Transformation of Communist Economies*, MacMillan.

Radulescu, Marian (1996): Foreign Direct Investment in Romania, mimeo, Romanian Forecasting Institute and Heriot-Watt University, Edinburgh.

Ramstatter, Erik (ed.) (1991): *DFI in Asia's Developing Economies and Structural Change in the Asia Pacific Region*, Boulder, CO: Dartmouth.

Reid, S. D. (1981): The Decision Maker and Export Entry and Expansion, *Journal of International Business Studies* **12**, no. 4, 101-12.

Richter, Andrea and Mark E. Schaffer (1996): The Performance of De Novo
    private Firms in Russian Manufacturing, in S. Commander, Q. Fan and M.E.
    Schaffer (eds): *Enterprise Restructuring and Economic Policy in Russia*,
    Washington, DC: World Bank, pp. 253-274.
Rojec, Matija, Bozo Jasovic and Igor Kusar (1994): Privatisation Through
    Foreign Investment in Slovenia: Concepts, Experiences and Policy Options,
    Centre for International Cooperation and Development - CICD, Ljubljana,
    May.
Rojec, Matija and Wladyslaw W. Jermakowicz (1995): Management versus
    State in Foreign Privatisations in Central European Countries in Transition,
    in R. Schiattarella (ed.): *New Challenges for European and International
    Business*, Proceedings of the 21. EIBA conference, Urbino, vol. 1, 353-380.
Rojec, Matija and Marjan Svetlicic (1993): Foreign Direct Investment in
    Slovenia, *Transnational Corporations* **2**, 135-51. (also: *Communist
    Economics and Economic Transformation* **5**, 103-14.)
Rolfe, Robert J. and Timothy S. Doupnik (1996): Going East: Western
    Companies invest in East/Central Europe, *Multinational Business Review*,
    Fall, 1-12.
Rollo, Jim and Alasdair Smith (1993): The Political Economy of Eastern Europe
    Trade with the European Community: Why so sensitive? *Economic Policy*
    16, 139-81.
Root, Franklin J. (1983): *Foreign Market Entry Strategies*, New York: Amacon.
Root, Franklin R. (1987): *Entry Strategies for International Markets*, Lexington,
    MA: Lexington Books.
Root, Franklin R. and A.A. Ahmad (1978): The Influence of Policy Instruments
    on Manufacturing Direct Foreign Investment in Developing Countries,
    Journal of International Business Studies **9**, no. 3, 81-93.
Root, Franklin R. and A.A. Ahmad (1979): Empirical Determinants of
    Manufacturing Direct Foreign Investment in Developing Countries,
    Economic Development and Cultural Change **27**.
Rugman, Alan M. (1981): *Inside the Multinationals: The Economics of Internal
    Markets,* London: Croom Helm.
Rugman, Alan M. (1985): Internalization is Still a General Theory of Foreign
    Direct Investment, *Weltwirtschaftliches Archiv*.
Safarian, A.E. (1993): *Multinational Enterprise and Public Policy: A Study of
    the Industrial Countries*, Aldershot: Elgar.
Saggi, Kamal (1996): Entry into a Foreign Market: Foreign Direct Investment
    versus Licensing, *Review of International Economics* **4**, 99-104.
Samonis, Valdas (1992): Earning or Learning? Western Direct Investment
    Strategies in Post-Soviet Economies, *MOCT/MOST,* no. 3, 101-12.
Sander, Birgit (1995): Siemens - A Multinational's Strategy to Investment in the
    Central-East European Transformation Countries, Kiel Working paper no.
    709, Institute of World Economic, Kiel, October.

Sanna-Randaccio, Francesca (1996): New Protectionism and Multinational Companies, *Journal of International Economics* **41**, 29-52.

Savary, Julien (1992): The International Strategies of French Firms and Eastern Europe: The Case of Poland, *MOCT/MOST* no.3, 69-95.

Scaperlanda, Anthony and Laurence J. Maurer (1969): The Determinants of US Direct Investment in the EEC, *American Economic Review* **59**, 558-68.

Scharfstein, David and Jeremy Stein (1990): Herd Behaviour and Investment, *American Economic Review* **80**, 465-79.

Schneider, Friedrich and Bruno S. Frey (1985): Economic and Political Determinants of Foreign Direct Investment, *World Development* **13**, no. 2, 161-75.

Scott, Norman (1992): The Implications of the Transition for Foreign Trade and Investment, *Oxford Review of Economic Policy* **8**, no. 1, 44-57.

Selowsky, Marcelo and Ricardo Martin (1997): Policy Performance and Output Growth in the Transition Economies, *American Economic Review 87, Papers and Proceedings*, 349-53.

Sels, Annabel (1996): Strategic Foreign Direct Investment in Central and Eastern Europe: An Overview of Statistical Evidence, Preliminary Empirical Work and the Idiosyncrasies of Theoretical Research on FDI in Central and Eastern Europe, mimeo (PhD interim report), Katholieke Universiteit Leuven, January.

Sereghyová, Jana (1995): Dichotomy Between Expectations Causing Enterprises in Central European Countries in Transition to Seek Foreign Capital Participations, in: *Joint Ventures in Transformation Countries in the Context of Overall Investment Strategies of their Partners*, ACE Research project, Barcelona: Grup d'Anàlisi de las Transició Econòmica, pp. 49-98.

Sereghyová, Jana (1995a): New Patterns of Capital Participation of Transnationals in Central European Countries in Transition seen from the local 'Stake-Holders' point of view, in Joint Ventures in Transformation Countries in the Context of Overall Investment Strategies of their Partners, ACE Research project, Barcelona: Grup d'Anàlisi de las Transició Econòmica, pp. 179-224.

Shane, Scott (1994): The Effect of National Culture on the Choice between Licensing and Direct Investment, *Strategic Management Journal* **15**, 627-42.

Sharma, Avraham (1995): Entry Strategies of US Firms to the Newly Independent States, Baltic States and East European Countries, *California Management Review* **37**, no. 3. 90-109.

Shelanski, Howard A. and Peter G. Klein (1995): Empirical Research in Transaction Cost Economics: A Review and Assessment, *Journal of Law, Economics and Organisation* **11**, 335-61.

Simon, Hermann (1996): *Hidden Champions*, Cambridge, MA: Harvard Business School Press.

Singer, Miroslav and Jan Svejnar (1994): Using Vouchers to Privatise the Economy, The Czech and Slovak Case, *Economics of Transition* **2**, 17-32.

Sinn, Hans-Werner and Alfons J. Weichenrieder (1997): Foreign Direct Investment, Political Resentment and the Privatisation process in Eastern Europe, *Economic Policy* **24**, 179-98.

Smith, Alasdair (1987): Strategic Investment, Multinational Corporations and Trade Policy, *European Economic Review* **31**, 98-96.

Smith, Stephen C., Beom-Cheol Con and Milan Vodopivec (1997): Privatization Incidence, Ownership forms, and Firm Performance: Evidence from Slovenia, *Journal of Comparative Economics* **25**, 158-179.

Sölvell, Örjan (1987): *Entry Barriers and Foreign Penetration. Emerging Pattern of International Competition in two Electrical Industries*, Institute of International Business, Stockholm: Stockholm Institute of Economics.

Sölvell, Örjan, Ivo Zander and Michael E. Porter (1991): *Advantage Sweden*, Stockholm: Norstedts.

Stehn, Jürgen (1992): *Ausländische Direktinvestitionen in Industrieländern: theoretische Erklärungsansätze und empirische Studien*, Kieler Studien no. 245, Tübingen: Mohr (Siebeck).

Stevens, Guy G.C. (1993): Exchange Rates and Foreign Direct Investment: A Not *International Finance Discussion Papers*, no. 444, Board of Governors of the Federal Reserve System, Washington, DC.

Stopford, John (1976): Changing Perspectives on Investment of British Manufacturing Multinationals, *Journal of International Business Studies* **7**.

Stopford, John and Susan Strange (1991): *Rival States, Rival Firms: Competition for World Market Share*, Cambridge: CUP.

Stopford, John and Louis D. Wells Jr. (1972): *Managing the Multinational Enterprise: Organisation of the Firms and Ownership of the Subsidiaries*, London: Longman.

Sugden, Roger and Rachel Thomas (1994): Inward Investment in Eastern Europe: Objectives, mimeo, Research Centre for Industrial Strategy, Department of Commerce Birmingham, November.

Svensson, Roger (1996): *Foreign Activities of Swedish Multinational Corporations*, Economic Studies 25, Department of Economics, Uppsala University.

Svetlicic, Marjan (1994): Foreign Direct Investment and the Transformation of Central European Economies, mimeo, University of Reading and University of Ljubljana.

Swedenborg, B. (1979): *The Multinational Operations of Swedish Firms: An Analysis of Determinants and Effects*, Stockholm: Industriens Utredningsinstitut.

Szymanski, Stefan (1996): Policy Implications Comparing Joint Venture Responses in Kazachstan and Samara, Discussion Paper no. 43, CISME-Centre, London Business School, October.

Teece, David (1977): Technology Transfer by Multinational Firms: The Resource Costs of Transferring Technological Know-how, *Economic Journal* **87**, 442-91.

Teece, David (1986): Transaction Cost Economics and the Multinational Enterprise, *Journal of Economic Behaviour and Organisation* **1**, 21-45.

Teece, David J. (1995): Firm Organization, Industrial Structure, and Technological Innovation, mimeo, Walter A. Haas School of Business, University of California at Berkeley, October.

Teece, David and Gary Pisaro (1994): The Dynamic Capabilities of Firms: An Introduction, *Industrial and Corporate Change* 3, 537-56.

Terpstra, Vern and Chwo-Ming Yu (1988): Determinants of Foreign Investment of US Advertising Agencies, *Journal of International Business Studies* **19**, no. 1, 33-46.

Thiran, Jean-Marc and Hideki Yamawaki (1995): Regional and Country Determinants of Locational Decisions: Japanese Multinationals in European Manufacturing, paper presented at the 22nd EARIE conference, Juan-les-Pins, September.

Thornton, Judith (1997): Strategies of Foreign and Foreign-Assisted Firms in Russia, ACES conference paper, New Orleans, January.

Tolentino, Paz Estrello E. (1987): *The Global Shift in International Production and the Growth of Multinational Enterprises from Developing Countries: the Philippines*, PhD thesis, University of Reading.

Tolentino, Paz Estrello E. (1993): *Technological Innovation and Third World Multinationals*, London: Routledge.

Török, Adám (1994): Industrial Policy and Foreign Direct Investment in Hungary, Reprint 17/1994, Leuven Institute for Central and East European Studies.

Tulder, Rob van and Winfried Ruigrok (1997): *European Cross National Production Networks in The Auto Industry: How Eastern Europe is Becoming the Low End of European Car Complexes,* paper presented at workshop 'Will there be a Unified European Economy', Kreisky Forum and BRIE, Vienna, June.

United Nations, UN (1992): *World Investment Directory, Vol.2, Central and Eastern Europe*, New York: United Nations.

United Nations, UN (1994): *World Investment Report 1994: Transnational Corporations, Employment and the Workforce*, New York: United Nations.

United Nations, UN (1995): *World Investment Report 1995: Transnational Corporations and Competitiveness*, New York: United Nations.

United Nations, UN (1996): *World Investment Report 1996: Investment, Trade and International Policy Arrangement*, New York: United Nations.

United Nations Economic Commission for Europe, UNECE (1996): *East-West Investment News*, no. 1, spring 1996.

United Nations Economic Commission for Europe, UNECE (1996a): *Economic Report for Europe*, Geneva: UN.

Urban, Waltraut (1992): Economic Lessons for the East European Countries from Two Newly Industrializing Countries in the Far East? Wiener Institut für International Wirtschaftsvergleiche, Forschungsberichte no. 182.

Vannini, Stefano (1995): Essays on the Strategic Behaviour of Multinational enterprises, CIACO, PhD thesis, Nouvelle série no. 252, Louvain-la-Neuve.

Veuglers, R. (1991): Locational Determinants and Ranking of Host Countries: An Empirical Assessment, *Kyklos* **44**, 3463-82.

Veuglers, R. (1995): Strategic Incentives for Multinational Operations, *Managerial and Decisions Science* **16**, 47-57.

Vernon, Raymond (1966): International Investment and International Trade in the Product Cycle, *Quarterly Journal of Economics* **80**, 190-207.

Vernon, Raymond (1979): The Product Cycle Hypothesis in a New International Environment, *Oxford Bulletin of Economics and Statistics* **41**, 255-79.

Vernon, Raymond (1994): Research on Transnational Corporations: Shedding Old Paradigms. A Review of the United Nations Library on Transnational Corporations, *Transnational Corporations* **3**, 137-56.

Vissi, Ferenc (1995): Foreign Direct Investment and Competition, *Russian and East European Finance and Trade* **31**, no. 3, 58-73.

Wagner, Joachim and Claus Schnabel (1994): Determinants of German Foreign Direct Investment: Evidence from Micro Data, *Zeitschrift für Wirtschafts- und Sozial-wissenschaften* **114,** 185-91.

Walker, Gordon and David Weber (1987): Supplier Competition, Uncertainty and Make-or-Buy Decisions, *Academy of Management Journal* **30**, 589-96.

Wang, Zhen Quan (1993): Foreign Direct Investment in Hungary: A Survey of Experience and Prospects, *Communist Economies and Economic Transformation* **5**, 245-53.

Welfens, Paul J.J. and Piotr Jasinski (1994): *Privatisation and Foreign Direct Investment in Transforming Economies*, Aldershot: Dartmouth.

Wells, Louis T. (1986): Investment Incentives: An Unnecessary Debate, *CTC Debate,* Autumn, 58-60.

Wells, Louis T. (1993): Mobile Exporters: New Foreign Investors in East Asia, in: K.A. Froot (ed.): *Direct Foreign Investment Today*, NBER, London: Routledge, pp. 173-96.

Wernerfelt, Birger (1984): A Resource-Based view of the Firm, *Strategic Management Journal* **5**, 171-80.

Whitmore, Katherine, Senjaya Lall and Jung-Taik Hyun (1989): Foreign Direct Investment from the Newly Industrialized Economies, World Bank, Industry and Energy Department working paper, Industry Series Paper no. 22.

Williamson, Oliver E. (1975): *Markets and Hierarchies: Analysis and Antitrust Implications*, New York: Free Press.

Williamson, Oliver E. (1981): The Modern Corporation: Origins, Evolution, Attributes, *Journal of Economic Literature* **19**, 1537-68.

Williamson, Oliver E. (1985): *The Economic Institutions of Capitalism*, New York: Free Press.

Williamson, Oliver E. (1991): Comparative Economic Organisation: The Analysis of Discrete Structural Alternatives, *Administrative Science Quarterly* **36**, 269-96.

Williamson, Oliver E. (1995): Economic Organisation: The Case for Candor, *Academy of Management Review* **21**, 48-57.

Wilson, Brent (1980): The Propensity of Multinational Companies to Expand through Acquisitions, *Journal of International Business Studies* **12**, no. 2, 59-65.

Wimmer, Frank and Markus Wesnitzer (1993): Die Perspektive der Konsumgüterindustrie, in J. Engelhard (ed.): *Ungarn im neuen Europa: Integration, Transformation, Markteintrittsstrategien*, Wiesbaden: Gabler.

Woo, Wing The (1997): Improving the Performance of Enterprises in Transition Economies, in W.T. Woo, Stephen Parker and Jeffrey Sachs (eds): *Economies in Transition: Comparing Asia and Europe*, Cambridge: MIT Press.

Woodcock, Charles P., Paul Beamish and Shige Makino (1994): Ownership-based Entry Mode Strategies and International Performance, *Journal of International Business Studies* **25**, 253-73.

Woodward, Douglas and Robert J. Rolfe (1993): The Location of Export-Oriented Foreign Direct Investment in the Caribbean Basin, *Journal of International Business Studies* **24**, no. 1, 121-44.

Woodward, Douglas, Frank Hefner, Jeffrey Arpan, James Kuhlman and William R. Folks Jr. (1995): The Impact of FDI on Transitional Economies: The Case of Coca-Cola in Poland and Romania, Working Paper, Centre for International Business Education and Research, College of Business Administration, University of South Carolina, November.

World Bank (1992): *Foreign Direct Investment in the States of the Former USSR*, Studies of Economies in Transformation no. 5, Washington, DC: World Bank.

World Bank (1996): *World Development Report: From Plan to Market*, Washington, DC: World Bank.

Yamawaki, Hideki (1993): Location Decisions of Japanese Multinational Firms in European Manufacturing Industries, in K. Hughes (ed.): *European Competitiveness*, Cambridge: Cambridge University Press, pp. 11-28.

Yamin, Mohammad (1991): A Reassessment of Hymer's contribution to the Theory of the Transnational Corporation, in Christos N. Pitelis and Roger Sugden: *The Nature of the Transnational Firm*, London: Routledge.

Yip, George (1982): Diversification Entry: Internal Development versus Acquisition, *Strategic Management Journal* **3**, 331-45.

Young, Stephen, James Hamill, Colin Wheeler and J. Richard Davies (1989): *International Market Entry and Development*, Hemel Hempstead: Harvester Wheatsheaf.

Yu, Chwo-Ming and Kiyotaki Ito (1988): Oligopolistic Reaction and Foreign Direct Investment: The Case of the US Tire and Textiles Industries, *Journal of International Business Studies* **19**, 449-60.

Zander, Udo and Bruce Kogut (1995): Knowledge and the Speed of Transfer and Imitation of Organizational Capabilities: An Empirical Test, *Organization Science* **6**, 76-92.

Zecchini, Salvatore (ed.) (1997)*: Lessons from the Economic Transition: Central and Eastern Europe in the 1990's*, Dordrecht: Kluwer.

Zejan, Mario C. (1990): New Ventures or Acquisitions. The Choice of Swedish Multinational Enterprises, *Journal of Industrial Economics* **38**, 349-55.

Zemplinerova, Alena (1997): The Role of Foreign Enterprises in the Privatization and Restructuring of the Czech Economy, Research Report no. 238, Vienna Institute for Comparative Economic Studies (WIIW), June.

Zhan, Xiaoning James (1993): The Role of Foreign Direct Investment in Market-oriented Reforms and Economic Development: The Case of China, *Transnational Corporations* **2**, 121-47.

Zouweren, Linda van, Marco Grillo, Keith D. Brouthers and Gary L. Bamossy (1996): A Framework for Negotiations between Multinational Companies and State Owned Companies, Academy of International Business, UK chapter conference at Aston University, 29-30 March, Proceedings pp. 183-203.

Index